CROSS-CULTURAL RESEARCH METHODS IN PSYCHOLOGY

Cross-cultural research is now an undeniable part of mainstream psychology and has had a major impact on conceptual models of human behavior. Although it is true that the basic principles of social psychological methodology and data analysis are applicable to cross-cultural research, a number of issues are distinct to it, including managing incongruities of language and quantifying cultural response sets in the use of scales. *Cross-Cultural Research Methods in Psychology* provides state-of-the-art knowledge about the methodological problems that need to be addressed if a researcher is to conduct valid and reliable cross-cultural research. It also offers practical advice and examples of solutions to those problems and is a must-read for any student of culture.

David Matsumoto is an internationally acclaimed author and psychologist. He received his BA from the University of Michigan in 1981 with high honors in psychology and Japanese. He subsequently earned his MA (1983) and PhD (1986) in psychology from the University of California at Berkeley. He is currently Professor of Psychology and Director of the Culture and Emotion Research Laboratory at San Francisco State University, where he has been since 1989. Matsumoto has studied culture, emotion, social interaction, and communication for more than 25 years. His books include well-known titles such as *Culture and Psychology* and *The Cambridge Dictionary of Psychology*. He is the recipient of many awards and honors in the field of psychology, including being named a G. Stanley Hall lecturer by the American Psychological Association. He is the series editor for Cambridge University Press's Culture and Psychology series. He is also editor for the *Journal of Cross-Cultural Psychology*.

Fons J. R. van de Vijver earned his PhD in psychology from Tilburg University in the Netherlands in 1991. He has published more than 300 articles, chapters, and books, mainly in the domain of cross-cultural psychology. The most important themes in his work on psychological acculturation and multiculturalism are the domain dependence of acculturation strategies and behaviors, the assessment of acculturation, cultural distance, antecedents and consequences of multiculturalism, and the stability of multiculturalism. He holds a chair in cross-cultural psychology at Tilburg University and is Extraordinary Professor at North-West University, South Africa. Van de Vijver is one of the most frequently cited cross-cultural psychologists in Europe. He is the current vice dean for research and former vice dean for education of his faculty and vice director of Babylon, the interdisciplinary research center for studies of multicultural societies at Tilburg University. He was President of Division 2, Assessment and Evaluation, of the International Association of Applied Psychology and is now President-Elect of the European Association of Psychological Assessment.

CULTURE AND PSYCHOLOGY

Series Editor

David Matsumoto, *San Francisco State University*

As an increasing number of social scientists come to recognize the pervasive influence of culture on individual human behavior, it has become imperative for culture to be included as an important variable in all aspects of psychological research, theory, and practice. Culture and Psychology is an evolving series of works that brings the study of culture and psychology into a single, unified concept.

Ute Schönpflug, *Cultural Transmission: Psychological, Developmental, Social, and Methodological Aspects*

Evert van de Vliert, *Climate, Affluence, and Culture*

Cross-Cultural Research Methods in Psychology

Edited by

David Matsumoto
San Francisco State University

Fons J. R. van de Vijver
Tilburg University

CAMBRIDGE UNIVERSITY PRESS
Cambridge, New York, Melbourne, Madrid, Cape Town, Singapore,
São Paulo, Delhi, Dubai, Tokyo, Mexico City

Cambridge University Press
32 Avenue of the Americas, New York, NY 10013-2473, USA

www.cambridge.org
Information on this title: www.cambridge.org/9780521758420

First published 2011

Printed in the United States of America

A catalog record for this publication is available from the British Library.

Library of Congress Cataloging in Publication data

Cross-cultural research methods in psychology / edited by David Matsumoto,
Fons J. R. van de Vijver.
p. cm. – (Culture and psychology)
Includes bibliographical references and index.
ISBN 978-0-521-76525-1 (hardback) – ISBN 978-0-521-75842-0 (pbk.)
1. Psychology – Research – Cross-cultural studies. I. Matsumoto, David Ricky. II. Vijver, Fons
J. R. van de. III. Title. IV. Series.
BF76.5.C76 2010
150.72 – dc22 2010012760

ISBN 978-0-521-76525-1 Hardback
ISBN 978-0-521-75842-0 Paperback

CONTENTS

PART II. DATA ANALYSIS AND INTERPRETATION

CONTRIBUTORS

KLAUS BOEHNKE
Jacobs University Bremen

MICHAEL HARRIS BOND
The Chinese University of Hong Kong

DALE L. DINNEL
Western Washington University

RONALD FISCHER
Victoria University of Wellington

JOHNNY R. J. FONTAINE
Ghent University

ROBERT J. GRISSOM
San Francisco State University

RONALD K. HAMBLETON
University of Massachusetts

ALLYSON L. HOLBROOK
University of Illinois at Chicago

TIMOTHY P. JOHNSON
University of Illinois at Chicago

JOHN J. KIM
San Francisco State University

KWOK LEUNG
City University of Hong Kong

PETRA LIETZ
Australian Council for Educational Research

DAVID MATSUMOTO
San Francisco State University

JOHN B. NEZLEK
College of William & Mary

MARGRIT SCHREIER
Jacobs University Bremen

SHARON SHAVITT
University of Illinois at Chicago

STEPHEN G. SIRECI
University of Massachusetts

FONS J. R. VAN DE VIJVER
Tilburg University

DIANNE A. VAN HEMERT
University of Amsterdam

ADALBERT WILHELM
Jacobs University Bremen

APRIL L. ZENISKY
University of Massachusetts

Cross-Cultural Research Methods in Psychology

1

Introduction to the Methodological Issues Associated With Cross-Cultural Research

FONS J. R. VAN DE VIJVER AND DAVID MATSUMOTO

Although once considered to be at the margins of psychological science, the study of culture has blossomed into one of the most important areas of research today. Studies involving cultural variables appear more frequently than ever before in mainstream journals in developmental, clinical, personality, and social psychology, as well as in specialty journals such as the *Journal of Cross-Cultural Psychology*, *Culture and Psychology*, *International Journal of Intercultural Relations*, and the *Journal of Cross Cultural Management* (van de Vijver, 2006). Theorists are also increasingly incorporating culture as an important variable into their theories and models of psychological processes.

The methodological backbone spurring the blossoming of cultural science in psychology is cross-cultural research, in which two or more cultural groups are compared on psychological variables of interest. This is true regardless of the theoretical approach or perspective one adopts in understanding cultural influences on mind and behavior. For instance, methodological differences used to exist between those who called themselves cross-cultural psychologists versus those who called themselves cultural psychologists, with the former basing most of their work on cross-cultural comparison and the latter arguing that such comparisons were unwarranted, unjustified, and unnecessary (Greenfield, 1997; Shweder, 1999). Today, however, even those who call themselves cultural psychologists clearly use cross-cultural research methods as the method of choice in conducting research (e.g., Heine et al., 2001; Kitayama, Mesquita, & Karasawa, 2006; Markus, Uchida, Omoregie, Townsend, & Kitayama, 2006).

Indeed, there are many potentials and advantages that cross-cultural comparisons afford. They test the boundaries of knowledge and stretch the

We would like to thank Rinus Verkooijen for his editorial assistance.

methodological parameters under which such knowledge is created and vetted in psychology. They highlight important similarities and differences across cultures. They bring researchers in disparate and divergent cultures together for a common cause. Their findings promote international and intercultural exchange, understanding, and cooperation. They contribute to a broader and deeper understanding of human behavior and the mind. Finally, cross-cultural theories can provide frameworks that accommodate both individual and cultural sources of variation (Berry, Poortinga, Segall, & Dasen, 2002).

However, with the potentials and advantages come some risks and liabilities, the foremost of which is the production of cultural knowledge that is incorrect because of flawed methodological procedures. Cross-cultural research brings with it a whole host of methodological issues that go much beyond monocultural studies, from issues concerning translation, measurement equivalence, sampling, data analytic techniques, and data reporting. To be sure, good cultural science is first and foremost good science, and many concepts that ensure the methodological rigor of any quality scientific enterprise is applicable to cross-cultural research as well. Thus, it is important for any cross-cultural researcher to have excellent baseline methodological skills.

Cross-cultural research also brings with it a host of issues and problems that are unique to cross-cultural studies, and it is important to be knowledgeable about and address these as well. The risk of producing cultural knowledge that is incorrect or not replicable is too great if these methodological pitfalls are not understood and addressed. Given the importance of cross-cultural research in producing a global psychology that truly has the potential for helping to create a better world, it is incumbent on cultural scientists to be fully aware of these issues and their solutions. Many of the risks associated with cross-cultural research are enhanced when it is conducted without the full awareness and sensitivity of the various issues associated specifically with it.

The purpose of this book is to introduce researchers to those risks and describe recent methodologies to minimize them, so that cross-cultural research can reach its potential.

CULTURAL DISTANCE AND RIVAL HYPOTHESES

Cross-cultural studies often involve quasi-experimental designs, in which samples are not randomly selected from a population or assigned to conditions (researchers cannot randomly assign an individual to a culture).

This can result in the incomplete matching of samples, which has various ramifications in cross-cultural studies, but one is critical. Interpreting findings about similarities and differences is much more difficult in cross-cultural studies than in experimental studies that are based on random assignment of participants. The interpretation of cross-cultural differences is often threatened by bias and the lack of equivalence (topics that deserve their own chapter and are covered in Chapter 2 by van de Vijver and Leung), which give rise to many rival explanations for the cross-cultural differences observed. For example, do cross-cultural differences in test scores of reading reflect "real" differences in reading skill across the countries involved in a study, or do the differences reflect curriculum differences across the countries? Were the children in the cultures involved not entirely comparable in terms of relevant background characteristics such as socioeconomic status, or was the test differentially appropriate for all the countries involved?

Various procedures have been proposed to deal with rival explanations for cross-cultural findings, such as the inclusion of additional variables in a research design to confirm or disconfirm specific interpretations. An example is the "unpackaging" of cross-cultural differences (see Chapter 4 by Bond and van de Vijver in this volume). The choice of variables to deal with rival explanations is mainly based on theoretical considerations; yet methodological considerations also play a role. The number of rival explanations depends on the *cultural distance* of the groups involved in a study. More dissimilar groups may show more differences in target variables, but it is also more likely that they differ in background variables. Suppose that extroversion has been measured in the United States, Canada, and Japan. Cultural differences between the American and Canadian samples will be easier to interpret than the collective North Americans' differences from the Japanese sample. For example, differences in response styles, such as acquiescence and an extremity response pattern, are more likely to affect the comparisons between Japan and the two North American groups. Cultural distance creates a paradox in cross-cultural measurement: The larger the cross-cultural distance between groups, the more likely cross-cultural differences will be observed, but the more likely these differences may be influenced by uncontrolled variables. In other words, the easier it is to find significant cross-cultural differences, the more difficult it is to interpret them.

Cultural distance can be measured as a psychological variable by asking respondents from a country how much difference they feel toward a set of other countries; similarly, immigrants from different ethnicities can be asked how much difference they feel toward the dominant culture.

A second prevailing view on cultural distance focuses on country-level variables such as social indicators, values, and religions. Examples have been proposed by Hofstede (2001), Schwartz (1992), Inglehart (1997), Georgas and Berry (1995), the Chinese Culture Connection (1987), and House, Hanges, Javidan, Dorfman, and Gupta (2004), to mention a few. The most frequently quoted of these models, that of Hofstede, views cross-cultural differences in work-related values as four-dimensional (power distance, masculinity, uncertainty avoidance, and individualism); long-term orientation was added in a later version. Both "subjective" and "objective" measures of cultural distance have been found to predict cross-cultural differences in psychological variables (e.g., Galchenko & van de Vijver, 2007; Hofstede, 2001). Regardless of the method of measurement, one of the basic issues researchers may become aware of is the relationship among cultural distance, the probability of generating differences, and rival hypotheses that account for such differences.

A Taxonomy of Cross-Cultural Studies

The number of rival explanations to be accounted for in cross-cultural studies also depends on the *type of research question.* Three dimensions are proposed here to classify the research questions raised in cross-cultural research (and hence, cross-cultural studies; van de Vijver, 2009). The first dimension refers to the presence or absence of *contextual factors* in a research design. Contextual factors may involve characteristics of the participants (such as socioeconomic status, education, and age) or their cultures (such as economic development and religious institutions). From a methodological perspective, contextual factors involve any variable that can explain, partly or fully, observed cross-cultural differences (Poortinga & van de Vijver, 1987). Including such factors in a study will enhance its validity and help rule out the influence of biases and inequivalence because an evaluation of their influence can help to (dis)confirm their role in accounting for the cultural differences observed. For example, administering a measure of response styles can help to evaluate the extent to which cross-cultural differences on extroversion are influenced by these styles.

The second dimension involves the distinction between *exploratory* and *hypothesis-testing* studies. Exploratory studies attempt to increase our understanding of cross-cultural differences by documenting similarities and differences. Researchers tend to stay "close to the data" in exploratory studies, whereas hypothesis-testing studies make larger inferential jumps by testing theories of cross-cultural similarities and differences. Unfortunately, the validity of these inferential jumps is often threatened by cross-cultural biases and inequivalence. The methodological strengths and weaknesses of exploratory and hypothesis-testing studies mirror each other. The main strength of exploratory studies is their broad scope for identifying cross-cultural similarities and differences, which is particularly important in underresearched domains of cross-cultural psychology. The main weakness of such studies is their limited capability to address the causes of the observed differences. The focused search for similarities and differences in hypothesis-testing studies leads to more substantial contributions to theory development and explicit attempts to deal with rival explanations but is less likely to discover interesting differences outside of the realm of the tested theory.

What is compared across cultures is addressed in the third dimension. A distinction is made between *structure-* and *level-oriented studies.* The former involve comparisons of constructs (e.g., is depression conceptualized in the same way across cultures?), their structures (can depression be assessed by the same constituent elements in different cultures?), or their relationships with other constructs (do depression and anxiety have the same relationship in all countries?). The latter involve the comparisons of scores (do individuals from different cultures show the same level of depression?). Structure-oriented studies focus on relationships among variables and attempt to identify similarities and differences in these relations across cultures.

Brouwers, van Hemert, Breugelmans, and van de Vijver (2004) found in a content analysis of articles published in the *Journal of Cross-Cultural Psychology* that the number of level-oriented studies is about twice the number of structure-oriented studies. From a methodological perspective, structure-oriented studies are much simpler than level-oriented studies, which are usually more open to alternative interpretations. For example, suppose that a neuroticism questionnaire has been administered in two countries and that the two countries differ in extremity scoring. If all the items are phrased in the same direction (which is often the case in personality measurement), cross-cultural differences in extremity scoring will be confounded with valid differences in neuroticism. As a consequence, cross-cultural differences in means are difficult to interpret. However, as long as extremity scoring only affects the item means and leaves item correlations and covariances unchanged, the factor structure, which is often examined in structure-oriented studies, will not be affected.

In summary, studies with cultural groups that have a large cultural distance from each other are likely to be more threatened by biases and inequivalence. Studies that do not include contextual factors, that are designed to evaluate hypotheses and advance a theory, and that target level-oriented cultural differences are also more threatened by biases and inequivalence.

Cross-Cultural Research Designs

By far the most important part of any cross-cultural study, and in our opinion for any study in general, is knowing which research questions to ask in the first place. The purpose of conducting research is to contribute to a body of knowledge that is institutionalized in what is known as the research literature. Indeed, the research literature is any field's institutional memory of the cumulative knowledge gathered over the years, and it is to this memory and body of knowledge that any study should contribute. Thus, any consideration of research designs starts first with a comprehensive and functional knowledge of that research literature – the institutional memory – so that one understands what gaps in the knowledge exist, and thus which research questions should be addressed and how the field can be advanced. An appreciation of the knowledge gaps should be combined with adequate methodological knowledge. It is only in the combination of theory and method that real contributions can be made by exploiting the strengths of both. It happens all too often that researchers exclusively focus on substantive issues of a study, thereby neglecting bias issues or the additional power of good design and analysis. Similarly, it also happens too often that sophisticated statistical techniques and elegant research designs have to "salvage" studies that are neither novel nor insightful.

Understanding why any study is to be conducted in the first place leads to questions about how to conduct it, which is a discussion in the realm of research methodology. Questions related to the taxonomy described earlier apply here. Is the study exploratory in nature or hypothesis testing? Does it or should it include contextual variables? Is it structure oriented or level oriented? Of course, no one study can do everything, and in our opinion, it is better to do something of a limited scope very well than to try to conduct a study that addresses too much not so well.

Still, it is important for today's researchers to keep some things in mind. The field has gone much beyond the need merely to document differences between two or more cultures on any psychological variable. Indeed, because of cultural distance, it is fairly easy to document differences on something, provided the cultures being compared are disparate enough. Instead, one of the major challenges that faces cross-cultural researchers today concerns how to isolate the source of such differences and identify the active cultural (vs. noncultural) ingredients that produced those differences. Indeed, it is the empirical documentation of those active cultural ingredients to which cross-cultural research designs must pay close attention.

In doing so, researchers must consider a number of theoretical issues (discussed more thoroughly in Matsumoto & Yoo, 2006). For example, is the source of the differences to be explained cultural? Examining this question forces researchers to have a definition of what is culture and what is not and to find ways to measure it objectively. Some researchers, for instance, may consider values to be a part of culture, but country-level characteristics such as climate, population density, or social structure are not. Because definitions (and operationalizations) of culture (and not culture) can be as varied as the individual researchers who create or adopt such definitions, our advice is not to be overly ambitious by trying to create definitions with which everyone will agree (especially because experience shows that such definitions become broad, unwieldy, and uninformative for the aspects of culture that are relevant in any specific study) but to be more modest and practical, making one's definitions and thus operations explicit so that others know what they are.

Another issue that researchers face in identifying active cultural ingredients that produce differences concerns a level-of-analysis issue. Cultural variables exist on the group and individual levels. Furthermore, studies themselves can be entirely on the individual or cultural level, or involve a mixture of the two in varying degrees with multiple levels (see Chapter 11 by Nezlek). Different variables at different levels of analysis bring with them different theoretical and methodological implications and require different interpretations back to the research literature.

In the realm of individual-level approaches to culture, other issues that arise concern exactly what those individual-level cultural variables are, how to measure them, and how to distinguish between them and noncultural variables on the individual level. For example, what is the difference between measuring "cultural attitudes" on the individual level and personality? Certainly a variable is not "cultural" just because a researcher says it is; a well-thought-out rationale based in theory and data must support the identification and distinction of such variables.

Another theoretical question that researchers must face in designing studies concerns their theoretical model of how things work. A commonly held view is that culture "produces" differences in a fairly top-down theoretical bias held by many. How do we know this to be true, however, and more important, how does one demonstrate it empirically? It may very well be that individual-level psychological processes and behaviors produce culture in a bottom-up fashion, or that both top-down and bottom-up processes occur simultaneously. Regardless of how one believes things are put together, it behooves researchers to adopt research design strategies that are commensurate with their beliefs and models.

Isolating the active cultural ingredients that produce differences can lead to the use of unpackaging studies (see Chapter 4 by Bond and van de Vijver), experiments, or other methodologies. Each, of course, has its own risks and benefits. After a basic paradigm is adopted, however, researchers need to deal with the nitty-gritty of the science, including sampling, translation, measurement bias and equivalence, data analysis, and the like. These are the nuts and bolts of cultural science on which the remainder of the book focuses.

PREVIEW OF THE BOOK

After this chapter, this book is divided into two parts. Part I deals with conceptual and methodological issues that researchers should be aware of during the design phase of their studies. Part II deals with computational methods and procedures for data analysis after data have been collected. Although the topics covered are not orthogonal to each other by any means, we do have a bias ourselves, which we state explicitly here: No sophisticated or complex data analysis can ever fix a bad design or poorly collected data. Thus, although cultural scientists are often keen to learn about the latest in statistical methodologies, it behooves them to pay close attention to the conceptual issues described in Part I that aid them in designing quality studies in the first place.

Part I

It is easy to approach the study of culture with some biases, the largest of which centers around the constructs of equivalence and bias. As you can read in Chapter 2 by van de Vijver and Leung, bias refers to differences in a measurement instrument that do not have exactly the same meaning within and across cultures (Poortinga, 1989), whereas equivalence refers to the level of comparability of measurement outcomes. These constructs are crucial to good cross-cultural research and underlie almost all of the topics discussed in the remainder of this book, which is why it is the topic of the first chapter. There, van de Vijver and Leung describe several types of bias, such as construct bias, method bias, and item bias, as well as types of equivalence, including construct inequivalence, structural or functional equivalence, metric or measurement unit equivalence, and scalar or full-score equivalence. They provide guidelines and suggestions for dealing with issues concerning equivalence and bias, both before data collection and after. And they discuss procedures by which researchers can optimize adaptations of tests and survey instruments. This important chapter, therefore, serves as a foundational basis for all of the subsequent chapters.

One of the major issues that cross-cultural researchers face concerns how to deal with language, especially in terms of the instruments and procedures of a study. Of all the methodological issues that face cultural scientists, none is more unique to cross-cultural research than the fact that cross-cultural studies often require the collection of data in two or more linguistic groups. As such, issues concerning equivalence between the languages used in the study become of paramount importance. Even if words are translated into different languages, this does not mean that the resulting translations are equivalent to the originals. In Chapter 3, Hambleton and Zenisky describe 25 criteria with which to evaluate the adequacy of translations done for cross-cultural research. The criteria span major topics such as General Translation Questions, Item Format and Appearance, Grammar and Phrasing, Passages and Other Item-Relevant Stimulus Materials, and Cultural Relevance and/or Specificity. The evaluation sheet they offer readers at the end of their chapter is an especially useful tool for researchers to use.

Cross-cultural research is largely based on quasi-experimental designs, and as such, when differences are found, it is impossible to draw conclusions about the source of those differences. Despite that, cross-cultural scientists often do draw those interpretations, with little or no empirical justification, and thereby commit an ecological fallacy (Campbell, 1961). In the realm of cultural science, when researchers attribute the source of observed differences in a quasi-experimental design to culture, this mistaken inference has been termed the *cultural attribution fallacy* (Matsumoto & Yoo, 2006). One way to address this limitation in quasi-experimental designs is to include variables in the data collection that operationalize meaningful dimensions of culture and then empirically test the degree to which those variables account for the differences. Such variables are called context variables, and quasi-experimental designs that include context variables are known as unpackaging studies, which is the topic of Chapter 4 by Bond and van de Vijver.

When doing cross-cultural work, it is impossible to access only participants from the local introductory psychology participant pool. Thus, another way in which issues concerning equivalence and bias affect cross-cultural work is in sampling. Indeed, it is easy for samples across cultures to differ on many demographic characteristics, and these demographics often confound any observed differences. Thus, it may be difficult at times to draw conclusions based on culture versus demographics. In Chapter 5, Boehnke, Lietz, Schreier, and Wilhelm discuss issues concerning sampling on both the individual and cultural levels and provide guidelines for researchers that allow for empirically justified conclusions to be drawn while being sensitive to particular needs and issues associated with samples from different cultures.

Another way in which people of different cultures may vary is in the use of response scales. Whereas early cross-cultural research viewed different cultural biases in the use of scales as nuisance variables that needed to be controlled, theoretical and empirical perspectives today view such biases as potentially important aspects of culture and personality (Smith, 2004). Thus, in Chapter 6, Johnson, Shavitt, and Holbrook discuss these issues, paying close attention to concerns about socially desirable responding, acquiescence, and extreme responding. Like all chapters in the book, they not only describe the issues raised by these constructs but they also provide useful guidelines and suggestions for cultural scientists.

Part II

The chapters in Part II deal with issues concerning data analysis and interpretation. Chapter 7, by Fischer and Fontaine, deals with methods for investigating and establishing structural equivalence. As introduced in Chapter 2, structural equivalence is an important aspect of measurement procedures in cross-cultural research, and Fischer and Fontaine discuss four techniques for testing it – multidimensional scaling, principal component analysis, exploratory factor analysis, and confirmatory factor analysis. For each, they describe a step-by-step approach to the analysis, alternative procedures, and its strengths and weaknesses.

Whereas Chapter 7 deals with structure-oriented techniques, Chapter 8 by Sireci describes level-oriented statistical techniques to analyze the functioning, efficiency, and equivalence of items. He differentiates between item bias, item impact, and differential item functioning (DIF) and describes five methods for evaluating DIF – delta plot, standardization, Mantel–Haenszel, item response theory (IRT) likelihood ratio, and logistic regression. As Sireci explains, these five methods provide a wide variety of options for evaluating DIF, and the choice of method will depend on several factors including sample sizes, type of test item (dichotomous or polytomous), and concerns regarding types of DIF.

One of the biases in the thinking of cross-cultural psychologists is the focus on finding differences and the primacy of significance testing. Of course there is nothing wrong with documenting differences, but an exclusive or even primary focus on differences can easily blur a balanced treatment of both cross-cultural differences and similarities, and cultural scientists should be interested in both. Furthermore, it is easy to obtain "statistically significant" results in cross-cultural research today because of the relative ease obtaining larger sample sizes and because statistical significance is directly proportional to sample size. Statistical significance, however, does not necessarily reflect practical importance in the real world; two or more cultures' means may be statistically different from each other but may not really reflect important differences among the individuals of those cultures. To aid in the determination of more empirically justified interpretations of data, the field has developed a number of measures of effect size. In Chapter 9, Matsumoto, Kim, Grissom, and Dinnel describe the limitations of traditional null hypothesis significance testing (NHST), and describe a number of statistical procedures that go beyond NHST to aid in the tempered interpretation of data.

The past decade or two have seen an explosion of cross-cultural psychological research involving many cultures, much of it aided by technological improvements in communication and transportation technologies. This has resulted in changes in the nature of data, allowing researchers to investigate structural relationships among psychological phenomena not only at the individual level, which is the traditional approach, but also at the cultural level. Consequently, it has become clear over the past few years that relationships among variables on the individual level may or may not be the same on the cultural level. In Chapter 10, Fontaine and Fischer introduce methods of testing structural relationships on the individual and cultural levels. As in Chapter 8, they discuss four techniques for testing structural relations at multiple levels – multidimensional scaling, principal component analysis, exploratory factor analysis, and confirmatory factor analysis; for each, they describe a step-by-step approach to the analysis, offer alternative procedures, and discuss its strengths and weaknesses.

Cross-cultural data are often inherently nested data, with data from individuals with specific personalities collected in specific situations, within specific cultures located in specific ecologies. These kinds of multilevel data allow for the possibility of analyzing the relationship between data at different levels, allowing researchers to document empirically the associations among ecological, cultural, individual, and situational variables and individual-level means or relationships among variables. In Chapter 11, Nezlek describes multilevel random coefficient models (MRCM) for handling such nested data. He contrasts MRCM with traditional statistical techniques based on ordinary least squares analyses and walks readers through a step-by-step description of how and why MRCM can be used to analyze cross-cultural data.

Finally, Chapter 12 discusses an increasingly relevant topic. Over the years, an impressive number of cross-cultural studies have been conducted. Procedures to synthesize research findings are known as meta-analysis. Such procedures hold important promise for cross-cultural psychology. Van Hemert describes the main issues of cross-cultural meta-analyses. The chapter describes the similarities and differences between regular meta-analyses and cross-cultural meta-analyses. Cross-cultural meta-analyses enable the systematic study of country differences and similarities in psychological functioning, based on secondary data, as well as associations of these differences with other psychological and nonpsychological country differences.

CONCLUSION

The chapters presented in this book introduce readers to the potential methodological problems and pitfalls of conducting cross-cultural research and provide practical, real-world recommendations for solutions, with many concrete examples. The ultimate goal of this book is to aid the ever-increasing number of scientists interested in conducting cross-cultural research to produce a better cultural science, to promote the production of valid and reliable findings in the field, and to encourage better theory construction and models for incorporating culture that lend themselves to practical, real-world applications. The ultimate end of science is the construction of knowledge toward a better world, and it is our hope that this volume can aid researchers in producing a better cultural science for a better intercultural world.

REFERENCES

Berry, J. W., Poortinga, Y. H., Segall, M. H., & Dasen, P. R. (2002). *Cross-cultural psychology: Research and applications.* Cambridge, England: Cambridge University Press.

Brouwers, S. A., Van Hemert, D. A., Breugelmans, S. M., & Van de Vijver, F. J. R. (2004). A historical analysis of empirical studies published in the *Journal of Cross-Cultural Psychology. Journal of Cross-Cultural Psychology, 35*, 251–262.

Campbell, D. T. (1961). The mutual methodological relevance of anthropology and psychology. In F. L. Hsu (Ed.), *Psychological anthropology* (pp. 333–352). Homewood, IL: Dorsey.

Chinese Culture Connection. (1987). Chinese values and the search for culture-free dimensions of culture. *Journal of Cross-Cultural Psychology, 18*, 143–164

Galchenko, I., & Van de Vijver, F. J. R. (2007). The role of perceived cultural distance in the acculturation of exchange students in Russia. *International Journal of Intercultural Relations, 31*, 181–197.

Georgas, J., & Berry, J. W. (1995). An ecocultural taxonomy for cross-cultural psychology. *Cross-Cultural Research, 29*, 121–157.

Greenfield, P. M. (1997). Culture as process: Empirical methods for cultural psychology. In J. W. Berry, Y. H. Poortinga, & J. Pandey (Eds.), *Handbook of cross-cultural psychology*: Vol. 1. *Theory and method* (pp. 301–346). New York: Allyn and Bacon.

Heine, S. J., Kitayama, S., Lehman, D. R., Takata, T., Ide, E., Leung, C., et al. (2001). Divergent consequences of success and failure in Japan and North America: An investigation of self-improving motivations and malleable selves. *Journal of Personality and Social Psychology, 81*, 599–615.

Hofstede, G. (2001). *Culture's consequences: Comparing values, behaviors, institutions, and organizations across nations* (2nd ed.). Thousand Oaks, CA: Sage.

House, R. J., Hanges, P. J., Javidan, M., Dorfman, P., & Gupta, V. (Eds.) (2004). *GLOBE, cultures, leadership, and organizations: GLOBE study of 62 societies.* Newbury Park, CA: Sage.

Inglehart, R. (1997). *Modernization and postmodernization: Cultural, economic, and political change in 43 societies.* Princeton, NJ: Princeton University Press.

Kitayama, S., & Cohen, D. (Eds.). (2007). *Handbook of cultural psychology.* New York: Guilford Press.

Kitayama, S., Mesquita, B., & Karasawa, M. (2006). Cultural affordances and emotional experience: Socially engaging and disengaging emotions in Japan and the United States. *Journal of Personality and Social Psychology, 91*, 890–903.

Markus, H. R., Uchida, Y., Omoregie, H., Townsend, S. S. M., & Kitayama, S. (2006). Going for the gold: Models of agency in Japanese and American contexts. *Psychological Science, 17*, 103–112.

Matsumoto, D., & Yoo, S. H. (2006). Toward a new generation of cross-cultural research. *Perspectives on Psychological Science, 1*, 234–250.

Poortinga, Y. H. (1989). Equivalence of cross cultural data: An overview of basic issues. *International Journal of Psychology, 24*, 737–756.

Poortinga, Y. H., & Van de Vijver, F. J. R. (1987). Explaining cross-cultural differences: Bias analysis and beyond. *Journal of Cross-Cultural Psychology, 18*, 259–282.

Shweder, R. A. (1999). Why cultural psychology? *Ethos, 27*, 62–73.

Schwartz, S. H. (1992). Universals in the content and structure of values: Theoretical advances and empirical tests in 20 countries. In M. Zanna (Ed.), *Advances in experimental social psychology* (Vol. 25, pp. 1–65). Orlando, FL: Academic Press.

Smith, P. B. (2004). Acquiescent response bias as an aspect of cultural communication style. *Journal of Cross-Cultural Psychology, 35*, 50–61.

Van de Vijver, F. J. R. (2006). Culture and psychology: A SWOT analysis of cross-cultural psychology. In Q. Jing, H. Zhang, & K. Zhang (Eds.), *Psychological science around the world* (Vol. 2, pp. 279–298). London: Psychology Press.

Van de Vijver, F. J. R. (2009). Types of cross-cultural studies in cross-cultural psychology. In *Online readings in psychology and culture* (Unit 3, Chapter 7). International Association for Cross-Cultural Psychology. Retrieved from http://orpc.iaccp.org/index.php?option=com_content&view=article&id=11%3Avandevijver&catid=3%3Achapter&Itemid=4 on April 1, 2010.

PART I

CONCEPTUAL ISSUES AND DESIGN

2

Equivalence and Bias: A Review of Concepts, Models, and Data Analytic Procedures

FONS J. R. VAN DE VIJVER AND KWOK LEUNG

INTRODUCTION

This chapter addresses the methodological issues associated with equivalence and bias in cross-cultural research. These issues are a consequence of the nonexperimental nature of the research designs of cross-cultural studies. True experiments are based on the random assignment of participants to different experimental conditions, which presumably ensures that confounding variables are equated across experimental conditions. However, participants cannot be randomly assigned to cultures, and groups that are compared in cross-cultural studies can hardly ever be seen as matched on all background variables that are relevant for the constructs of interest. Cross-cultural psychology is not unique in the impossibility of matching groups; many studies in clinical and educational psychology involve situations in which intact groups are studied, and the assumption of the similarity of background characteristics across groups is unrealistic. The inability to conduct true experiments to address essential questions in cross-cultural psychology implies that we have to be careful in conducting our studies, being cognizant of relevant methodological knowledge and tools. It also implies that cross-cultural studies are always threatened by bias and inequivalence when cultural groups are being compared.

This chapter reviews the extant knowledge of these methodological issues. Our main message is that maximizing the validity of inferences should be the main concern of cross-cultural research and that methodological rigor in terms of establishing cross-cultural equivalence and suppressing bias across cultures plays a crucial role in this endeavor. We first describe a taxonomy of equivalence and bias, how they can be assessed, and the measures that can be taken to increase the validity of cross-cultural inferences. The second part gives an overview of procedures for adapting tests and survey questionnaires across cultures. Conclusions are presented in the final section.

A TAXONOMY OF EQUIVALENCE AND BIAS

Bias and Equivalence: Definitions

Bias and equivalence are key terms in the methodology of cross-cultural studies (van de Vijver, 2003). Bias refers to differences in a measurement instrument that do not have exactly the same meaning within and across cultures (Poortinga, 1989). A cross-cultural study shows bias if differences in measurement outcomes (categorizations or scores) do not correspond to cross-cultural differences in the construct purportedly measured by the instrument. If scores are biased, individual differences within a culture (*within-culture differences*) do not have the same meaning as cultural differences (*between-culture differences*). For example, scores of a coping questionnaire that show bias may be valid measures of coping if they are compared within a single cultural group, whereas cross-cultural differences based on this questionnaire may be influenced by other factors, such as translation issues, item inappropriateness, or differential response styles. Differences due to bias are not random but systematic. A replication of a study with a biased instrument in similar samples will show the same biased results.

Johnson (1998), after reviewing the literature on equivalence, collected a bewildering set of more than 50 definitions of the concept, which he reduced to two types: Interpretive equivalence definitions focus on "equivalence of meaning" (p. 6), and procedural equivalence definitions focus on "measures and procedures used to make cross-cultural comparisons" (p. 7). With a slight reinterpretation, his distinction corresponds to a major divide in the procedures advocated in the equivalence literature. On one hand, there are approaches that focus on *enhancing* equivalence. Examples are adaptations of stimulus materials to ensure the ecological validity of a test (an example of how this can be done in intelligence testing is described in the next section) and *cognitive pretesting* in survey research in which an instrument is administered to participants in a nonstandard manner (Harkness, van de Vijver, & Johnson, 2003). Information is obtained about how questions, response categories, and other assessment aspects are interpreted so that a comparison can be made between intended and actual interpretations. On the other hand, there are procedures that focus on *testing* equivalence. Well-known procedures include the numerous statistical techniques for identifying anomalous items in an instrument (e.g., Holland & Wainer, 1993). A cursory reading of the literature suggests that equivalence enhancing and testing procedures tend to be mutually exclusive in that most applications focus on either aspect even when they address a similar topic. For example, the literature on translation equivalence focuses on how translation as a research procedure can ensure the similarity of stimulus materials presented in the source and target languages, whereas translation–back-translation procedures focus on how to achieve this similarity for given particular stimulus materials. A comprehensive equivalence framework should describe how equivalence is both ensured and assessed.

In the context of this chapter, equivalence refers to the level of comparability of measurement outcomes. For example, do diagnostic categories have the same meaning across cultures (Is obsessive-compulsive disorder identical across the cultures studied)? Do persons from different cultures with the same diagnosis suffer from the same clinical syndrome? Do scores on personality scales have the same meaning within and between cultures? Bias threatens the equivalence of measurement outcomes across cultures, and it is only when instruments are free from bias that measurement outcomes are equivalent and have the same meaning within and across cultures.

Bias and equivalence are two sides of the same coin. Cross-cultural equivalence requires the absence of biases, and the presence of cross-cultural bias always results in some form of inequivalence. Nonetheless, research on cross-cultural bias and equivalence tends to highlight different issues, and a joint consideration of bias and equivalence provides a more comprehensive view of how valid cross-cultural comparisons can be made.

Equivalence

Taxonomies of equivalence of psychological tests often use hierarchical levels of equivalence (e.g., Poortinga, 1989). This tradition is followed here; four hierarchically nested types of equivalence are described in this section: construct, structural or functional, metric or measurement unit, and scalar or full score equivalence.

Construct Inequivalence

Constructs that are inequivalent lack a shared meaning, which precludes any cross-cultural comparison. In the literature, claims of construct inequivalence can be grouped into three broad genres, which differ in the degree of inequivalence (partial or total). The first and strongest claim of inequivalence is found in studies that opt for a strong emic, relativistic viewpoint, which argues that psychological constructs are inextricably tied to their natural context and cannot be studied outside this context. Any cross-cultural comparison is then erroneous because psychological constructs are cross-culturally inequivalent.

The second genre is exemplified by psychological constructs that are associated with specific cultural groups. The best examples are culture-bound syndromes. A good example is Amok, which occurs in Asian countries, such as Indonesia and Malaysia. It is characterized by a brief period of violent aggressive behavior among men. The period is often preceded by an insult, and the patient shows persecutory ideas and automatic behaviors. After this period, the patient is usually exhausted and has no recollection of the event (Azhar & Varma, 2000). Violent aggressive behavior among men is universal, but the combination of triggering events, symptoms, and lack of recollection is culture-specific. Such a combination of universal and culture-specific aspects is characteristic for all culture-bound syndromes. The case of the Japanese Taijin Kyofusho is another example (Suzuki, Takei, Kawai, Minabe, & Mori, 2003; Tanaka-Matsumi & Draguns, 1997). Taijin Kyofusho is characterized by an intense fear that one's body is discomforting or insulting for others by its appearance, smell, or movements. The description of the symptoms suggests a strong form of a social phobia (a universal), which finds culturally unique expressions in a country in which conformity is a widely shared norm. Suzuki et al. (2003) argued that most symptoms of Taijin Kyofusho can be readily classified as social phobia, which (again) illustrates that culture-bound syndromes may involve both universal and culture-specific aspects that do not co-occur in other cultures.

The third genre of inequivalance is empirically based and found in comparative studies in which the data do not show any evidence for comparability of construct; inequivalence is the consequence of a lack of cross-cultural comparability. Van Leest (1997) administered a standard personality questionnaire to mainstream Dutch and Dutch immigrants. The instrument showed various problems, such as the frequent use of colloquialisms. The structure found in the Dutch mainstream group could not be replicated in the immigrant group. It was concluded, therefore, that the constructs measured in both groups were inequivalent.

Structural or Functional Equivalence

An instrument administered in different cultural groups shows structural equivalence if it measures the same construct(s) in all these groups. In operational terms, this condition requires identity of underlying dimensions (factors) in all groups, that is, whether the instrument shows the same factor structure in all groups. Structural equivalence has been examined for various cognitive tests (Jensen, 1980), Eysenck's Personality Questionnaire (Barrett, Petrides, Eysenck, & Eysenck, 1998), and the five-factor model of personality (McCrae & Costa, 1997). Functional equivalence as a specific type of structural equivalence refers to identity of nomological networks. A questionnaire that measures, say, openness to new cultures shows functional equivalence if it measures the same psychological construct in each culture, as manifested in a similar pattern of convergent and divergent validity (i.e., nonzero correlations with presumably related measures and zero correlations with presumably unrelated measures). Tests of structural equivalence are applied more often than tests of functional equivalence. The reason is not statistical–technical. With advances in statistical modeling (notably path analysis as part of structural equation modeling), tests of the cross-cultural similarity of nomological networks are straightforward. However, nomological networks are often based on a combination of psychological scales and background variables, such as socioeconomic status, education, and sex. In the absence of a guiding theoretical framework, the use of psychological scales to validate other psychological scales can easily lead to an endless regression in which each scale used for validation has itself to be validated.

Metric or Measurement Unit Equivalence

Instruments show metric (or measurement unit) equivalence if their measurement scales have the same units of measurement but a different origin (such as the Celsius and Kelvin scales in temperature measurement). This type of equivalence assumes interval- or ratio-level scores (with the same measurement units in each culture). Measurement unit equivalence applies when a source of bias shifts the scores of different cultural groups differentially but does not affect the relative scores of individuals within each cultural group. For example, social desirability and stimulus familiarity influence questionnaire scores more in some cultures than in others, but they may influence individuals within a given cultural group in a similar way. When the relative contribution of both bias sources cannot be estimated, the interpretation of group comparisons of mean scores remains ambiguous.

Scalar or Full Score Equivalence

Only in the case of scalar (or full score) equivalence can direct cross-cultural comparisons be made; this is the only type of equivalence that allows for the conclusion that average scores obtained in two cultures are different or equal. Scalar equivalence assumes both an identical interval or ratio scale and an identical scale origin across cultural groups.

Bias

Bias refers to the presence of nuisance factors (Poortinga, 1989). If scores are biased, their psychological meaning is culture- or group-dependent, and group differences in assessment outcomes need to be accounted for, at least to some extent, by auxiliary psychological constructs or measurement artifacts (see Table 2.1 for an overview). Bias is not an inherent characteristic of an instrument but arises in the application of an instrument in at least two cultural groups. As a consequence, an instrument is not inherently biased but may become so when scores from specific cultural groups are compared.

Construct Bias

This kind of bias leads to construct inequivalence. Construct bias can be caused by incomplete overlap of construct-relevant behaviors. An empirical example can be found in Ho's (1996) work on filial piety (defined as a psychological characteristic associated with being "a good son or daughter"). The Chinese conception, which includes the expectation that children should assume the role of caretaker of elderly parents, is broader than the corresponding Western notion. An inventory of filial piety based on the Chinese conceptualization covers aspects unrelated to the Western notion, whereas a Western-based inventory will leave important Chinese aspects uncovered.

Construct bias can be caused by differential appropriateness of the behaviors associated with the construct in the different cultures. Studies in various non-Western countries (e.g., Azuma & Kashiwagi, 1987; Grigorenko et al., 2001) show that descriptions of an intelligent person go beyond the school-oriented domain and involve social aspects such as obedience; however, the domain covered by Western intelligence tests is usually restricted to scholastic intelligence.

Method Bias

Method bias is used here as a label for all sources of bias due to factors often described in the methods section of empirical papers. Three types of method bias are distinguished here, depending on whether the bias comes from the sample, administration, or instrument. First, sample bias is more likely to jeopardize cross-cultural comparisons when the cultures examined

Table 2.1. *Overview of types of bias and ways to deal with it*

Type and source of bias	Ways to deal with it
Construct bias	
• Only partial overlap in the definitions of the construct across cultures • Differential appropriateness of the behaviors associated with the construct (e.g., skills do not belong to the repertoire of one of the cultural groups) • Poor sampling of all relevant behaviors indicative of a construct (e.g., short instruments) • Incomplete coverage of the relevant aspects/facets of the construct (e.g., not all relevant domains are sampled)	• Decentering (i.e., simultaneously developing the same instrument in several cultures) • Convergence approach (i.e., independent within-culture development of instruments and subsequent cross-cultural administration of all instruments) • Consult informants with expertise in local culture and language[a] • Use samples of bilingual participants[a] • Conduct local pilot studies (e.g., content analyses of free-response questions)[a] • Nonstandard instrument administration (e.g., "thinking aloud")[a]
Method bias	
• Incomparability of samples (e.g., differences in education and motivation)[b] • Differences in administration conditions, physical (e.g., noise) or social (e.g., group size)[c] • Ambiguous instructions for respondents and/or guidelines for research administrators[c] • Differential expertise of administrators[c] • Tester/interviewer/observer effects (e.g., halo effects)[c] • Communication problems between respondent and interviewer (in the widest sense)[c] • Differential familiarity with stimulus materials[c] • Differential familiarity with response procedures[d] • Differential response styles (e.g., social desirability, extremity tendency, and acquiescence)[d]	• Cross-cultural comparison of nomological networks (e.g., convergent/discriminant validity studies, and monotrait-multimethod studies) • Connotation of key phrases (e.g., similarity of meaning of key terms such as *somewhat agree*) • Extensive training of interviewers and administrators • Detailed manual/protocol for administration, scoring, and interpretation • Detailed instructions (e.g., with adequate examples and/or exercises) • Include background and contextual variables (e.g., educational background) • Gather collateral information (e.g., test-taking behavior or test attitudes) • Assessment of response styles • Conduct test–retest, training, and/or intervention studies

(continued)

Table 2.1 *(continued)*

Type and source of bias	Ways to deal with it
Item bias	
• Poor translation and/or ambiguous items • Nuisance factors (e.g., items may invoke additional traits or abilities) • Cultural specifics (e.g., differences in connotative meaning and/or appropriateness of item content)	• Judgmental methods (e.g., linguistic and psychological analysis) • Psychometric methods (e.g., differential item functioning analysis)

[a] Also used for dealing with method bias.
[b] Sample bias.
[c] Administration bias.
[d] Instrument bias.

differ in many respects. A large cultural distance often increases the number of alternative explanations that need to be considered. Fernández and Marcopulos (2008) described how incomparability of norm samples made international comparisons of the Trail Making Test (an instrument to assess attention and cognitive flexibility) impossible. In the personality and social domain, recurrent rival explanations include cross-cultural differences in social desirability and stimulus familiarity (testwiseness). The main problem with both social desirability and testwiseness is their relationship with country affluence; more affluent countries tend to show lower scores on social desirability (van Hemert, van de Vijver, Poortinga, & Georgas, 2002). Participant recruitment procedures are another source of sample bias in cognitive tests. For instance, the motivation to display one's attitudes or abilities may depend on the amount of previous exposure to psychological tests, the freedom to participate or not, and other sources that may show cross-cultural variation.

Second, administration method bias can be caused by differences in the procedures or modes used to administer an instrument. For example, when interviews are held in respondents' homes, physical conditions (e.g., ambient noise, presence of others) are difficult to control. Respondents are more prepared to answer sensitive questions in a self-completion mode than in a face-to-face interview. Examples of social environmental conditions include individual (vs. group) administration, the physical space between respondents (in group testing), and class size (in educational settings). Other sources of research administration that can lead to method bias include ambiguity in the questionnaire instructions or guidelines or a differential application of these instructions (e.g., more instructions are given for open-ended questions in some cultures). The effect of test administrators or interviewers on measurement outcomes has been empirically studied; regrettably, many studies adopted inadequate designs and did not cross the cultures of testers and testees systematically. We still do not know much about how the cultural backgrounds of testers and testees interact in influencing test scores. In cognitive testing, the presence of the tester is usually not very obtrusive (Jensen, 1980). In survey research, there is more evidence for interviewer effects (Groves, 1989; Lyberg et al., 1997). Deference to the interviewer has been reported; participants were more likely to display positive attitudes to an interviewer than in self-administered questionnaires (e.g., Aquilino, 1994). A final source of administration bias is constituted by communication problems between the respondent and the tester or interviewer. For example, interventions by interpreters may influence the measurement outcome. Communication problems are not restricted to working with translators. Language problems are particularly salient when an interview or test is administered in the second or third language of interviewers or respondents.

Third, instrument bias is a common source of bias in cognitive tests. An example can be found in Piswanger's (1975) application of the Viennese Matrices Test (Formann & Piswanger 1979). A Raven-like figural inductive reasoning test was administered to high-school students in Austria, Nigeria, and Togo (educated in Arabic). The most striking findings were the cross-cultural differences in item difficulties related to identifying and applying rules in a horizontal direction (i.e., left to right). This was interpreted as bias in terms of the different directions in writing Latin-based languages as opposed to Arabic.

Item Bias

This type of bias refers to anomalies at the item level and is called *item bias* or *differential item functioning* (Camilli & Shepard, 1994; Holland & Wainer, 1993). According to a definition that is widely used in education and psychology, an item is biased if respondents with the same standing on the underlying construct (e.g., they are equally intelligent) do not have the same mean score on the item because of different cultural origins. Of all bias types, item bias has been the most extensively studied; various psychometric techniques are available to identify item bias (e.g., Camilli & Shepard, 1994; Holland & Wainer, 1993; van de Vijver & Leung, 1997).

Item bias can arise in various ways, such as poor item translation, ambiguities in the original item, low familiarity or appropriateness of the item content in certain cultures, and the influence of culture-specific nuisance factors or connotations associated with the item wording. For instance, if a geography test administered to pupils in Poland and Japan contains the item "What is the capital of Poland?," Polish pupils can be expected to show higher scores on the item than Japanese students, even in pupils from the two countries with the same level of knowledge in geography. The item is biased because it favors one cultural group across all test score levels. Gomez, Burns, and Walsh (2008) examined differential item functioning in behaviors associated with oppositional defiance disorder. Australian, Malaysian Malay, and Malaysian Chinese parents had to rate their children on behaviors such as "is touchy," "argues," and "blames others." Using item response theory, the authors found that the item about being touchy was more prevalent among Malaysian parents. The authors interpret this difference as a consequence of cross-cultural differences in required obedience across the two cultures and the ensuing lower tolerance of deviant behavior by Malaysian parents who are assumed to "have higher standards of childhood behaviours (including compliance with instructions and requests from adults) compared to Australian parents" (p. 18).

Dealing With Bias and Equivalence Threats

The foregoing discussion illustrates that bias can jeopardize the validity of cross-cultural research in various ways. It is, therefore, not surprising that numerous procedures have been developed to deal with bias and to examine equivalence so as to assess the implications of bias on the comparability of test scores. Procedures to deal with bias can be classified depending on whether they affect how a study is conducted (such as study design, adaptation of stimulus materials, and administration procedure) or how data are analyzed. The first type is constituted by a priori procedures, because they affect a study before the actual data collection; the second type, a posteriori procedures, affects data analysis. These two kinds of procedures are complementary and not compensatory. Sophisticated study designs coupled with weak data analysis or, conversely, cross-culturally inadequate measurement instruments that are sophisticatedly analyzed both give rise to poor cross-cultural studies. The validity of the inferences from cross-cultural studies (and hence, the quality of such studies) can be maximized by a combination of a priori and a posteriori procedures.

A Priori Procedures

A priori procedures that have been proposed are distinguished on the basis of the type of bias they address (construct, method, or item bias). The first example of dealing with construct bias is cultural decentering (Werner & Campbell, 1970). The idea behind this approach is to remove cultural particulars from stimuli and to formulate items in such a way that the appropriateness of the item content is maximized for all cultural groups involved. In a modified form, decentering is used in large-scale projects in which researchers from most or all participating countries jointly develop the stimulus materials; examples can be found in the International Social Survey Programme (http://www.issp.org) and the European Social Survey (http://www.europeansocialsurvey.org). In the so-called convergence approach, instruments are independently developed in different cultures, and all instruments are then administered to participants in these cultures (Campbell, 1986).

The cross-cultural comparison of nomological networks constitutes an interesting possibility to examine construct and/or method bias. An advantage of this infrequently employed method is its broad applicability. The method is based on a comparison of the correlations of an instrument with various other instruments across cultures. The adequacy of the instrument in each country is supported if it shows a pattern of positive, zero, and negative correlations that is expected on theoretical grounds in all cultures studied. For example, views toward waste management, when measured with different items across countries, may have positive correlations with concern for the environment and for air pollution and a zero correlation with religiosity. Tanzer and Sim (1991) found that good students in Singapore worry more about their performance during psychological assessment than do weak students, whereas the opposite was found in most test-anxiety research in other cultures. For the other components of test anxiety (i.e., tension, low confidence, and cognitive interference), no cross-cultural differences were found. The authors attributed the inverted worry–achievement relationship to characteristics of the educational system of Singapore, especially the *kiasu* (fear of losing) syndrome, which is deeply entrenched in the Singaporean society, rather then to construct bias in the internal structure of test anxiety.

Various procedures have been developed that mainly address method bias. The more obvious approach involves the extensive training of research administrators and interviewers. Such training and instructions are required to ensure that studies and interviews are administered in the same way across cultural groups. If the cultures of the administrator or interviewer and the interviewee differ, as is common in studies involving multicultural groups, it is important to make the administrator or interviewer aware of the relevant cultural specifics such as taboo topics (e.g., Goodwin & Lee, 1994).

A related approach amounts to the development of a detailed manual and administration protocol. The manual should ideally specify the research or interview procedure and describe contingency plans on how to proceed when problems and difficulties arise (e.g., specifying when and how follow-up questions should be asked in open-ended questions).

The procedures just described attempt to reduce or eliminate unwanted cross-cultural differences in administration conditions to maximize the comparability of the measures obtained. Additional procedures are needed to deal with cross-cultural differences that cannot be controlled by careful selection and wording of questions or response alternatives. Education is a good example. Studies involving widely different cultural groups cannot avoid the substantial difference in the educational background of the participants, which in turn may bias the cross-cultural differences obtained. In some studies, it may be possible to match participants from different groups on education by stratified sampling. However, this approach can have serious limitations; the samples obtained are unlikely to be representative of their countries. This problem is particularly salient when comparing countries with a population with large variation in average educational level. For example, if samples of Canadian and South African adults are chosen that are matched on education, it is likely that at least one of the samples is not representative of its population. Clearly, if one is interested in a country comparison after controlling for education, this poor representativeness does not create a problem. If the two samples are obtained by some random sampling scheme, educational differences are likely to emerge. The question may then arise as to whether the educational differences can account for the observed cultural differences. For example, to what extent could differences in attitudes toward euthanasia be explained by educational differences? If individual-level data on education are available, various statistical techniques, such as covariance and regression analysis (explained in the fourth chapter of this book), can be used to address this question (Poortinga & van de Vijver, 1987). The use of such explanatory variables provides a valuable tool to probe the nature of the observed cross-cultural differences.

A perennial issue in survey research is the prevalence of response effects and styles, especially social desirability, acquiescence, and an extremity response pattern, which are important sources of method bias (Harzing, 2006; van Hemert et al., 2002). There is tentative evidence that individuals from less affluent, more collectivistic countries show more acquiescence and social desirability. When response styles could be expected to influence responses differentially across cultural groups, the administration of a questionnaire to assess such styles provides a valuable tool to interpret cross-cultural differences obtained and to rule out alternative interpretations. In other cases, response styles may be avoided by adapting the instrument. Hui and Triandis (1989) found that Hispanics tended to choose extreme scores on a 5-point rating scale more often than White Americans, but this difference disappeared when a 10-point scale was used.

Evidence on the presence of method bias can also be gathered by conducting test–retest, training, or intervention studies. Patterns of pretest–posttest change that are different across cultures point to the presence of method bias. Van de Vijver, Daal, and van Zonneveld (1986) administered a short training of inductive reasoning to primary-school pupils from the Netherlands, Surinam, and Zambia. The Zambian participants showed larger increments in scores, in both the experimental and an untrained control group, than the other groups. The large increments in the Zambian group may be due to a lack of experience with the test procedure. Because the increase was also observed in the control condition, the increase is more likely to have been due to knowledge of the test and the testing situation than to increments in inductive reasoning. Van de Vijver (2008) administered a set of five computer-assisted reaction time tests of increasing cognitive complexity to 35 secondary school pupils in Zimbabwe and the Netherlands in four consecutive school days to explore the existence and nature of cross-cultural differences in reaction-time tests measuring basic cognitive operations. The simplest tasks were choice reaction-time measures, and the complex tasks involved series of figures that either were identical or comprised pairs of identical figures and an "odd one out" that had to be identified. No cross-cultural differences were observed in the simple tests, but the Dutch pupils were faster than Zimbabwean pupils on the more complex tests. A seemingly straightforward interpretation would be that the Dutch pupils had a better mastery of basic cognitive operations. However, Zimbabwean pupils showed larger performance increments at retesting, which would point to the opposite interpretation. This internally inconsistent pattern can be reconciled by (again) referring to the learning processes of the Zimbabwean pupils after the first exposure to the assessment situation and the tasks at hand, which were not shown by the Dutch pupils. Most of the cross-cultural differences could be statistically accounted for by socioeconomic status, which makes it likely that background-related factors produced the cultural differences at the first testing. Results of the retest also cast doubt on the validity of the first test administration in that cross-cultural differences were apparently influenced by factors other than basic cognitive skills.

Two kinds of procedures are used to assess item bias: judgmental (linguistic or psychological) procedures and psychometric procedures. An example of the former can be found in Grill and Bartel (1977), who examined the Grammatic Closure subtest of the Illinois Test of Psycholinguistic Abilities for bias against speakers of nonstandard forms of English. In the first stage, potentially biased items were identified. Error responses of African American and European American children indicated that more than half the errors on these items were accounted for by responses that are appropriate in nonstandard forms of English. The psychometric procedures are described in the following section.

A Posteriori Procedures

Three commonly applied procedures for testing the cross-cultural equivalence of instruments are described here. The first addresses *structural equivalence* and uses *exploratory factor analysis.* This analysis answers the question of whether an instrument that has been applied in two or more cultures measures the same underlying constructs in each. The procedure starts with conducting a factor analysis for each country separately. There is structural equivalence if the factors identified are similar across the countries. In exploratory factor analysis, factor loadings can be rotated arbitrarily. As a consequence, factor structures found in different countries should be rotated toward each other before their congruence is assessed. Standard procedures for these target rotations are available (e.g., Chan, Ho, Leung, Chan, & Yung, 1999; van de Vijver & Leung, 1997). If the number of cultures involved is not larger than three or four, the factor structures found in each of these cultures are compared in a pairwise manner. If more countries are involved, the number of pairwise comparisons becomes prohibitively large. In such cases, data are usually pooled, and a factor analysis is conducted on these pooled data (e.g., Leung & Bond, 2004). Factor solutions obtained in the separate countries are then compared with this pooled factor structure. In the case of ordinal-level data, multidimensional scaling procedures are applied, followed by generalized Procrustes analysis (Borg & Groenen, 1997; Commandeur, 1991). An example of such a procedure can be found in a study by Fontaine, Poortinga, Delbeke, and Schwartz (2008), in which they compared the structure of human values found in student and teacher samples in 38 countries to the theoretically expected structure that has two dimensions (called protection and growth). They found very good correspondence between the expected and observed structure in all samples; yet, the student data showed a slightly better fit than the teacher data, and higher levels of societal developments in a society were

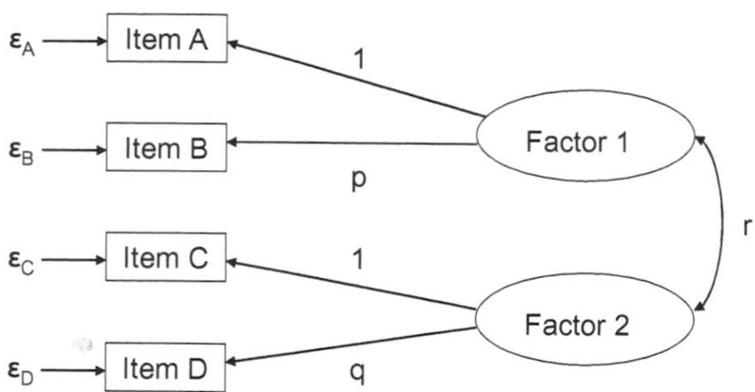

Figure 2.1. Hypothetical confirmatory factor analytic model.

associated with a slightly better contrast between growth and protection values.

Extensive experience with the use of exploratory factor analysis in assessing structural equivalence has shown that the procedure often yields valuable information and is quite sensitive in detecting major cultural differences in a factor structure. Its main shortcoming is its relatively low power to detect minor cultural differences in a factor structure. It has been found repeatedly that relatively long tests with some problematic items often show favorable results, because the procedure does not pick up the problematic items. Additional disadvantages of the procedure are the focus on factor loadings and the absence of any test of identity of other parameters, such as factor correlations and unique variances.

The second procedure is based on *confirmatory factor analysis*. This technique is much more flexible than exploratory factor analysis and can address various levels of equivalence (or invariance in the terminology of structural equation modeling). An illustration is given in Figure 2.1. Suppose that an instrument consisting of four items and measuring two factors has been administered in two cultures. Item A and Item C have a loading of one in both groups to fix the scale metric of the latent factors. The test of *configural invariance* tests whether the same pattern of straight and curved arrows can be used to describe the underlying factor structure in both groups. This is a weaker test of invariance than the structural equivalence test used in exploratory factor analysis in that the latter tests for similarity of factor loadings, which need not be the case in configural invariance. The test of *metric equivalence* addresses the identity of factor loadings of Item B and Item D in both groups (denoted by p and q in Figure 2.1). It is determined in this step whether the regression coefficient that links the item scores to their latent factor is the same for all cultural groups. This test is somewhat stricter than the test of structural equivalence in exploratory factor analysis in that confirmatory factor analysis is based on covariance matrices that contain information about the metric of the original scales, whereas exploratory factor analysis is based on correlations that do not have information about the scale metric. Finally, *scalar invariance* can be tested by examining the slopes that link the items scores to their latent factor.

Given the many parameter values that are estimated in confirmatory factor analysis, but are not yet considered in the previous tests described, it is not surprising that various other tests of cross-cultural invariance have been proposed. It is indeed common now to use a slightly different set of hierarchically nested invariance models than presented in the previous paragraph (an extensive hierarchy is described by Vandenberg & Lance, 2000, and Vandenberg, 2002). The first test is called configural invariance, as just described. The second is called invariance of measurement weights, which is similar to the test of metric equivalence described. The third is called structural covariances, which tests the cross-cultural invariance of the covariances between the latent factors (denoted by *r* in Figure 2.1). If there is only one latent factor in a model, the invariance of the error of this latent factor is examined (called structural residuals). The fourth model, called measurement residuals, tests the cross-cultural identity of the error components of the observed variables (denoted by ε in Figure 2.1). The use of such sequential tests highlights an important, attractive feature of confirmatory factor analysis; the four models that are tested here are hierarchically nested, which means that subsequent models can be created from earlier models by imposing more equality constraints on parameters across cultures. Nested models have so-called incremental fit statistics, which means that the difference in the chi-square statistic of the models with different numbers of constraints also follows a chi distribution with a number of degrees of freedom that is equal to the number of imposed constraints. A good example of the use of confirmatory factor analysis in cross-cultural psychology can be found in Spini (2003). He tested the equivalence of 10 value types from the Schwartz Value Survey, using data from 21 countries. Nested models of invariance were tested for each of the 10 values separately. With the exception of hedonism, configural and metric equivalence was found for all values. Finally, if the number of cultures involved is large, pairwise comparisons are not practical. The equivalence of a factor structure across a large number of cultures can be assessed in a confirmatory manner by meta-analytic structural equating modeling (Cheung, Leung, & Au, 2006), which in essence regards the evaluation of a factor structure across many cultures as a specific form of meta-analysis.

The main strengths of confirmatory factor analysis in testing cross-cultural equivalence are its flexibility in testing various kinds (levels) of equivalence and the possibility of testing hierarchically nested models. Its main weakness is the limited applicability in some conditions. As with other applications of structural equation modeling, the use of confirmatory factor analysis in testing equivalence is hampered by problems with fit statistics. Sensitivity to large sample sizes of the incremental chi-square statistic is one problem; the lack of widely accepted rules for determining a significant and meaningful difference when other statistics flag a nontrivial increase or decrease in fit is another one. Applications of confirmatory factor analysis in testing equivalence in data involving many cultural groups suffer from additional problems. If a poor fit is found, it is often not clear whether the problem is due to misspecifications of the underlying model or to minor cross-cultural differences that are psychologically trivial.

A great variety of statistical techniques have been proposed to deal with *item bias* or *differential item functioning* (Camilli & Shepard, 1994; van de Vijver & Leung, 1997). An illustration based on analysis of variance is used here. Item bias analysis is employed to establish *scalar equivalence.* The instrument that is scrutinized for bias should be unidimensional. Item bias analysis can be used in combination with exploratory factor analysis if the latter is used for addressing structural equivalence. The exploratory factor analysis then identifies equivalent factors, followed by an item bias analysis that examines the appropriateness of items in more detail. An item is biased if persons from different cultural groups with the same position on the underlying trait do not have the same expected score on the item. In operational terms, this definition specifies that apart from random fluctuations, persons from different cultures with the same total test score should have identical means on an item. Hypothetical examples of biased and unbiased items are presented in Figure 2.2. It is assumed that an instrument has been administered in two cultural groups, Culture A and Culture B. Before the analysis, the sample (including all participants from both countries) is split up according to the total score on all the items (of the unifactorial instrument). Five score levels are identified here, ranging from *very low* to *very high.* The number of score levels to be distinguished is somewhat arbitrary. The more scoring levels are distinguished, the more sensitive the analysis will be and the more likely item bias can be identified. However, distinguishing many score levels may yield score groups with few observations. As a rule of thumb, a number of 50 participants in a score level has been proposed (van de Vijver & Leung, 1997). An analysis of variance is then computed for each item separately, with score level and

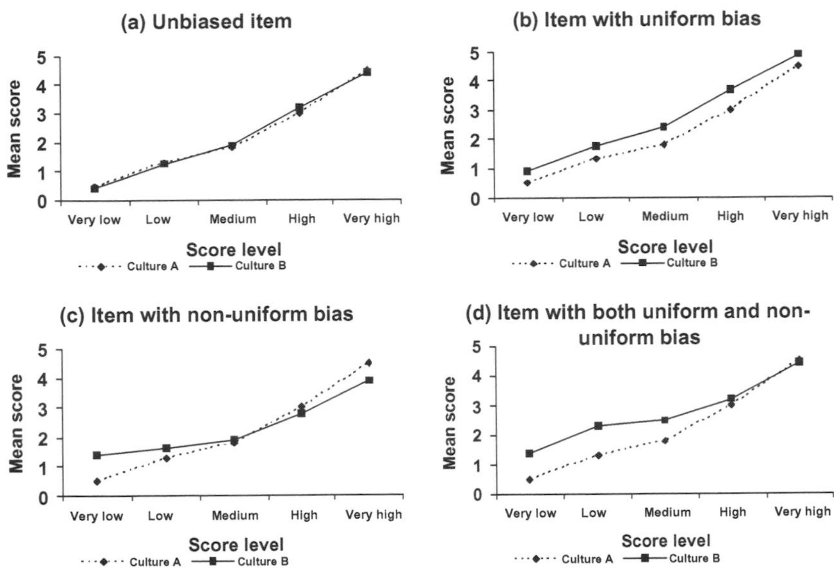

Figure 2.2. Examples of unbiased and biased items.

country as independent variables and the item score as dependent variable. We plot mean scores of participants against their score level for the two cultural groups, and four outcomes can be identified (see Figure 2.2). An item is unbiased if the curves for the two cultural groups are close to each other; the analysis of variance will only show a main effect for score level (Panel a in Figure 2.2). An item shows uniform bias if the main effect of country is significant, which means that the curve of one country is above the curve of the other country (Panel b). The item is then systematically more attractive or easier for members of one culture. An item can also be more discriminating in one culture than in the other culture (Panel c). The analysis of variance will then show a significant score level by country interaction. Panel d displays a situation in which both the main effect of culture and the score level by culture interaction are significant.

The use of analysis of variance in item bias detection is flexible and easy to implement. In addition to analysis of variance, many other statistical techniques have been proposed to deal with item bias. Item response theory is often applied for educational and achievement data in which the item responses are dichotomously scored as right or wrong. The main weakness of analysis of variance in identifying item bias is its sensitivity toward sample size. If the sample size is small or the distributions of scores are very dissimilar across cultures, it may be difficult to find adequate cutoff scores for distinguishing score levels (see studies by Muniz and colleagues who proposed relaxing alpha levels to 0.20 for the detection of item bias in small samples; Fidalgo, Ferreres, & Muniz, 2004; Fidalgo, Hashimoto, Bartram, & Muniz, 2007; Muniz, Hambleton, & Xing, 2001). Large sample sizes and large numbers of countries in a bias analysis also create problems. Experience shows that criteria for statistical significance cannot be used in these situations, because many or even most items are biased by conventional criteria. These problems can be largely avoided by using effect sizes instead of significance criteria. For example, a useful rule of thumb can be based on Cohen's classification of small, medium, and large effects. We find the use of medium effect size a useful rule, which means that an item is biased if the proportion of variance accounted for by the main effect of culture and the interaction of score level and culture is at least 0.06 (van de Vijver, Valchev, & Suanet, 2009).

A strong argument can be made that the analysis of bias and equivalence should always precede substantive analyses of cross-cultural similarities and differences, in much the same way as an analysis of the internal consistency of an instrument is conducted before further analyses. The replicability of findings in cross-cultural research would improve if the issue of bias is dealt with more consistently. However, experience also shows that the application of bias and equivalence analyses is not without problems. Three problems that are shared by all the analyses discussed in this section are mentioned here. It should be emphasized that these are not inherent problems of the techniques but problems with the way these techniques are usually implemented. First, criteria for bias and equivalence are often applied in a mechanical manner. An item with a significance value just above 0.05 in an item bias analysis is retained, whereas an item with a significance value just below 0.05 is eliminated. Clearly, decisions about bias and equivalence should be based on a combination of statistical and substantive considerations. The finding that a latent factor challenges the metric equivalence of a confirmatory factor analytic model in two cultures may provide interesting information about cross-cultural differences. Mechanically removing this factor from the analysis may save the metric equivalence of the remaining factors of the instrument, but it may also mask interesting cross-cultural differences. Second, the techniques seem to favor short instruments, which often show high levels of equivalence and few biased items. The question of whether such short instruments provide an adequate representation of the underlying construct is hardly ever asked, let alone answered. From a substantive point of view, short instruments may not adequately cover the underlying construct because they restrict the assessment to a small set of items with presumably universal applicability. Third, the focus on structural, metric, and scalar equivalence in confirmatory factor analysis may have detracted attention from method bias. Various sources of method bias cannot be identified with these techniques, such as cross-cultural differences in response styles, social desirability, and educational background, and the difficulty in equating administration conditions across cultures (e.g., an interviewer has a higher status in one culture than in another culture).

OPTIMIZING ADAPTATIONS OF TESTS AND SURVEY QUESTIONNAIRES

Many cross-cultural studies involve an existing instrument, which is usually developed in a Western context. The instrument has to be applied in another cultural (and linguistic) context. The question then arises as to how the instrument can be adapted to the new context. Adaptation studies have three stages: design, data collection, and data analysis. Methodological issues of the last two stages have been dealt with in the description of bias. Here, we pay special attention to the design procedures (*a priori procedures* in the terminology of a previous section) that can be used to minimize the various sources of bias described earlier and to maximize the validity of the adaptations.

The traditional method of test adaptations focuses on linguistic issues. The most commonly applied procedure is to use translation–back-translation (Brislin, 1980), in which a forward translation is independently back-translated, and the latter version is compared with the original. The procedure is easy to implement and can help to identify translation problems. However, experience with the procedure has also revealed shortcomings. The translations often produce a stilted language in the translation that compromises the readability and comprehensibility of the original text. Furthermore, it is increasingly appreciated that translating an instrument is not only a linguistic exercise, but that a good translation also retains cultural aspects of the original whenever possible and should modify the content of an item if a literal translation would produce a culturally inequivalent item.

It is not surprising that since the late 1990s, the term *adaptation* is increasingly used as the generic term for translating psychological instruments (e.g., Hambleton, Merenda, & Spielberger, 2005). In the parlance of this chapter, a good translation of an instrument is equivalent to the original. This equivalence can involve conceptual, cultural, linguistic, and measurement features (Harkness & van de Vijver, 2010). Each of these

Table 2.2. *Types of adaptations*

Domain	Type of adaptation	Description and example
Concept	Concept-driven	Adaptation to accommodate differences in indicators of concepts in different cultures (e.g., different public figures are needed in different countries to equate familiarity across cultures)
	Theory-driven	Adaptation based on theory (e.g., tests of short-term memory span should use short stimuli to be sensitive, which may require the use of different stimuli across cultures)
Culture	Terminological/ factual-driven	Adaptation to accommodate specific cultural or country characteristics (e.g., conversion of currency)
	Norm-driven	Adaptation to accommodate cultural differences in norms, values, and practices (e.g., avoidance of loss of face)
Language	Linguistics-driven	Adaptation to accommodate structural differences between languages (e.g., the English word *friend* refers to both a male and a female person, whereas many languages have gender-specific nouns for male and female friends)
	Pragmatics-driven	Adaptation to accommodate conventions in language usage (e.g., level of directness of requests by interviewers)
Measurement	Familiarity/ recognizability-driven	Adaptations to address differential familiarity with assessment procedures for specific stimuli across cultures (e.g., use of differential pictures in a pictorial test)
	Format-driven	Adaptation to minimize cultural differences due to formats of items or responses (e.g., adaptations in response scales to reduce impact of extreme responses)

features can influence the final result (see Table 2.2). Within each type, we distinguish two subtypes, thereby defining eight kinds of adaptations (for related classifications, see Harkness et al., 2003, and Malda et al., 2008).

The first two kinds of adaptation aim at improving the agreement of the concepts in the source and target cultures. A concept-driven adaptation accommodates differences in the indicators of culture-specific concepts, such as knowledge of the name of a well-known person in the country (as an indicator of crystallized intelligence). Selecting the names of persons in a cross-cultural study may not be easy. Some public figures are widely known, such as the U.S. president; still, it would be unrealistic to assume that the name of the president is equally well known to persons from various cultures. However, if culture-specific names are chosen, the item may still measure crystallized intelligence, but the cross-cultural comparability of the scores obtained may be problematic, because it is probably impossible to find an exact match of the original item, and item bias is likely to emerge. Who is equally known in a country like the United Kingdom as the U.S. president is in the United States? The British prime minister is a public figure who is less prominent in the media than the U.S. president, and the British queen may be a better choice. It is always difficult to determine whether cultural differences in the scores obtained are due to cultural differences in crystallized intelligence or differences in the familiarity of the public figures used.

Theory-driven adaptations involve modifications that are based on theoretical considerations. An instrument with items that have a strong theoretical basis may require extensive adaptations to ensure that the items in the adapted version still comply with the theory (to avoid construct bias). An example comes from a study that adapted the Kaufman Assessment Battery for Children, Second Edition, for use among Kannada-speaking children in India (Malda et al., 2008). One of the subtests measures short-term memory. A child is asked to repeat a series of digits in the same sequence as presented by the examiner (the number of digits per series increases from two to nine digits in the test). The digits of the original English version all have one syllable (the number seven is not used). The choice of one-syllable digits is based on Baddeley's phonological loop model (Baddeley, Thomson, & Buchanan, 1975), which states that the number of items that can be stored in working memory depends on the number of syllables and that more items can be recalled if they are shorter. As a consequence, the test is more sensitive when digits with fewer syllables are used. However, all digits from 1 to 10 are bisyllabic in Kannada, except 2 and 9, which have three syllables. The digits for the Kannada version used bisyllabic digits as much as possible. Trisyllabic digits were introduced only late in the test (in series of eight and nine digits).

The two culture-related adaptations refer to the "hard" and "soft" aspects of culture, respectively. Terminological or factual-driven adaptations are modifications that are needed because some items refer to country-specific aspects that are less known or unknown elsewhere. An example is the conversion of currency (e.g., dollars to yen). Although the changes are straightforward in theory, their implementation can create additional problems. For example, a British item about refilling a car with petrol may refer to liters and pounds: "A driver goes to a petrol station to fill his car with 60 liters of petrol that costs 0.90 pound per liter. What does the driver have to pay?" The conversion of the item to American terms (petrol to gas) and measures (liters to gallons and pounds to dollars) seems straightforward, but a direct substitution has low realism in the new cultural context; few cars have gas tanks of 60 gallons, and a price of 90 cents for a gallon is not realistic. Obviously, the item has to be adapted to make it equivalent in the American context.

Norm-driven adaptations accommodate cultural differences in norms, values, and practices, which are the "soft" aspects of a culture. An item about the celebration of birthdays should take into account that cultures differ considerably in the relevance attributed to birthdays. In some cultures, there is a well-developed and widely known cultural script for various components of birthdays (such as giving presents, having a party, and singing specific songs). Items dealing with such scripts need modification when used in countries with different customs.

The distinction between "hard" and "soft" adaptations also applies to linguistic applications. The "hard" adaptations, called *linguistics-driven adaptations*, refer to adaptations for accommodating structural differences between languages. For example, the English word "friend" can indicate both a male and a female person, whereas some languages use gender-specific words for male and female friends, such as German (*Freund* and *Freundin*) and French (*ami* and *amie*). Other examples are language differences in pronominalization. For example, in the English expression "his friend," we know that the person referred to is male (but we do not know the gender of the friend), whereas in the French expression *son ami* the ambiguity is not in the gender of the friend (*ami* refers to a male) but in the gender of possessive pronoun *son*, which could refer to both a male and a female.

The adaptations reflecting how a language is used in a cultural group, which may be regarded as the "softer" side of a language, are called pragmatics-driven adaptations. These refer to modifications for accommodating culture-specific conventions in language usage, such as discourse conventions. The extensive literature on politeness (e.g., Brown & Levinson, 1987) indicates that a close translation of requests often does not convey the same level of directness and politeness in different cultures. The distinction between culture-driven and pragmatics-driven adaptations can be fuzzy. We reserve the latter for adaptations that are more language-related and the former for more culture-related modifications, but we acknowledge that adaptations can contain elements of both. For example, politeness clauses are related to how a language is used (pragmatics-driven), but they are also a reflection of cultural scripts that regulate the interaction between strangers and between persons who have a different standing in society. The hard and soft adaptations are mainly aimed at eliminating item bias.

The two kinds of measurement-related modifications involve different presentational and procedural aspects of instruments. The first type, familiarity- or recognizability-driven adaptations, results from differential familiarity of cultures with assessment procedures for specific stimuli, which can lead to method bias. In a study described earlier, the Kaufman test was adapted for use among Kannada-speaking children in India and involved a test based on the drawing of a burglar (Malda et al., 2008). A pilot study made it clear that Kannada children did not recognize the depicted person as a burglar; the black-and-white horizontally striped shirt and the small mask over the eyes were not associated with a burglar. Adaptations (such as a large bag on the burglar's back) were needed to clarify the picture. In another subtest of the battery, a child has to move a dog toy (called "Rover") to a bone on a checkerboard-like grid that contains obstacles (rocks and weeds) by making as few moves as possible. When the original dog of the test kit was used to indicate the moves, the children tended to start the path to the bone in the direction that the dog was facing. To prevent this, we used a pawn that is similar on all sides so that it does not implicitly suggest a direction.

Finally, format-driven adaptations involve modifications in formats of items or responses to avoid unwanted cross-cultural differences. For example, differences in the extremity tendency in responding, another source of method bias, may be reduced by using more options in Likert-type response scales. Other examples come from the literature on mode effects (e.g., Groves, 1989). Epstein, Barker, and Kroutil (2001) found that Americans were more likely to report mental health problems in a computer-assisted self-administered interview than in an interviewer-administered paper-and-pencil survey.

CONCLUSION

Theoretical and methodological developments and increased experience with both small- and large-scale cross-cultural studies have enlarged our toolkit and deepened the appreciation of the methodological dos and don'ts of cross-cultural studies. Nonetheless, we note that each study has some particulars that are unique to the study and may have to be dealt with on an ad hoc basis. The main methodological issues of a study can usually be mapped out before the commencement of the project. Knowledge of theories, contacts with individuals from the target culture, and appreciation of how equivalence and bias can be tested are important ingredients of good cross-cultural studies. Hofer, Chasiotis, Friedlmeier, Busch, and Campos (2005) illustrated how inferences derived from projective picture stimuli, often regarded as not amenable to the scrutiny of psychometrics, can have a firm methodological grounding by examining the construct, method, and item bias of these stimuli. Two implicit motives (need for power and need for affiliation) were assessed in Cameroon, Costa Rica, and Germany using picture stimuli. Through analyses of bias and equivalence, the authors identified "unbiased culture-independent sets of picture stimuli... that can be used for cross-cultural comparisons of these two implicit motives" (p. 689). Indeed, current development in cross-cultural research methodology has provided solutions to some problems that were deemed to be hard to tackle for a long time.

It has been argued in this chapter that maximizing the validity of inferences should be the main concern of cross-cultural research (Leung & van de Vijver, 2008). The way to achieve this may be complicated and hard to reach, but the recipe is deceptively simple: Combine a strong design with adequate analysis. We need to design our studies and adapt our instruments in ways that take into account cultural, linguistic, and psychometric considerations. The deployment of appropriate data analytic procedures will then show us to what extent we have been successful in eliminating bias and achieving equivalence. We hope that the methodological procedures discussed in this chapter can provide impetus to the further development of cross-cultural research and help researchers arrive at valid, defensible inferences about cross-cultural similarities and differences observed.

REFERENCES

Aquilino, W. S. (1994). Interviewer mode effects in surveys of drug and alcohol use. *Public Opinion Quarterly, 58*, 210–240.

Azhar, M. Z., & Varma, S. L. (2000). Mental illness and its treatment in Malaysia. In I. Al-Issa (Ed.), *Al-Junun: Mental illness in the Islamic world* (pp. 163–185). Madison, CT: International Universities Press.

Azuma, H., & Kashiwagi, K. (1987). Descriptors for an intelligent person: A Japanese study. *Japanese Psychological Research, 29*, 17–26.

Baddeley, A. D., Thomson, N., & Buchanan, M. (1975). Word length and the structure of short-term memory. *Journal of Verbal Learning and Verbal Behavior, 14*, 575–589.

Barrett, P. T., Petrides, K. V., Eysenck, S. B. G., & Eysenck, H. J. (1998). The Eysenck Personality Questionnaire: An examination of the factorial similarity of P, E, N, and L across 34 countries. *Personality and Individual Differences, 25*, 805–819.

Borg, I., & Groenen, P. (1997). *Modern multidimensional scaling: Theory and applications.* New York: Springer.

Brislin, R. W. (1980). Translation and content analysis of oral and written materials. In H. C. Triandis & J. W. Berry (Eds.), *Handbook of cross-cultural psychology* (Vol. 2, pp. 389–444). Boston: Allyn and Bacon.

Brown, P., & Levinson, S. C. (1987). *Politeness: Some universals in language usage.* New York: Cambridge University Press.

Camilli, G., & Shepard, L. A. (1994). *Methods for identifying biased test items.* Thousand Oaks, CA: Sage.

Campbell, D. T. (1986). Science's social system of validity-enhancing collective belief change and the problems of the social sciences. In D. W. Fiske & R. A. Shweder (Eds.), *Metatheory in social science* (pp. 108–135). Chicago: University of Chicago Press.

Chan, W., Ho, R. M., Leung, K., Chan, D. K. S., & Yung, Y. F. (1999). An alternative method for evaluating congruence coefficients with Procrustes rotation: A bootstrap procedure. *Psychological Methods, 4*, 378–402.

Cheung, M. W. L., Leung, K., & Au, K. (2006). Evaluating multilevel models in cross-cultural research: An illustration with social axioms. *Journal of Cross-Cultural Psychology, 37*, 522–541.

Commandeur, J. J. F. (1991). *Matching configurations.* Leiden, the Netherlands: DSWO Press Leiden.

Epstein, J. F., Barker, P. R., & Kroutil, L. A. (2001). Mode effects in self-reported mental health data. *Public Opinion Quarterly, 65*, 529–549.

Fernández, A. L., & Marcopulos, B. A. (2008). A comparison of normative data for the Trail Making Test from several countries: Equivalence of norms and considerations for interpretation. *Scandinavian Journal of Psychology, 49*, 239–246.

Fidalgo, A. M., Ferreres, D., & Muniz, J. (2004). Utility of the Mantel–Haenszel procedure for detecting differential item functioning in small samples. *Educational and Psychological Measurement, 64*, 925–936.

Fidalgo, A. M., Hashimoto, K., Bartram, D., & Muniz, J. (2007). Empirical Bayes versus standard Mantel–Haenszel statistics for detecting differential item functioning under small sample conditions. *Journal of Experimental Education, 75*, 293–314.

Fontaine, J. R. J., Poortinga, Y. H., Delbeke, L., & Schwartz, S. H. (2008). Structural equivalence of the values domain across cultures: Distinguishing sampling fluctuations from meaningful variation. *Journal of Cross-Cultural Psychology, 39*, 345–365.

Formann, A. K., & Piswanger, K. (1979). *Wiener Matrizen-Test. Ein Rasch-skalierter sprachfreier Intelligenztest* [The Viennese Matrices Test. A Rasch-calibrated nonverbal intelligence test]. Weinheim, Germany: Beltz Test.

Gomez, R., Burns, G. L., & Walsh, J. A. (2008). Parent ratings of the oppositional defiant disorder symptoms: Item response theory analyses of cross-national and cross-racial invariance. *Journal of Psychopathology and Behavioral Assessment, 30,* 10–19.

Goodwin, R., & Lee, I. (1994). Taboo topics among Chinese and English friends: A cross-cultural comparison. *Journal of Cross-Cultural Psychology, 25,* 325–338.

Grigorenko, E. L., Geissler, P. W., Prince, R., Okatcha, F., Nokes, C., Kenny, D. A., et al. (2001). The organisation of Luo conceptions of intelligence: A study of implicit theories in a Kenyan village. *International Journal of Behavioral Development, 25,* 367–378.

Grill, J. J., & Bartel, N. R. (1977). Language bias in tests: ITPA Grammatic Closure. *Journal of Learning Disabilities, 10,* 229–235.

Groves, R. M. (1989). *Survey errors and survey costs.* New York: Wiley.

Hambleton, R. K., Merenda, P. F., & Spielberger, C. D. (Eds.) (2005). *Adapting educational and psychological tests for cross-cultural assessment.* Mahwah, NJ: Erlbaum.

Harkness, J. A., & Van de Vijver, F. J. R. (2010). *Developing instruments for cross-cultural research.* Manuscript in preparation.

Harkness, J. A., Van de Vijver, F. J. R., & Johnson, T. P. (2003). Questionnaire design in comparative research. In J. A. Harkness, F. J. R. Van de Vijver, & P. Ph. Mohler (Eds.), *Cross-cultural survey methods* (pp. 19–34). New York: Wiley.

Harzing, A. (2006). Response styles in cross-national survey research: A 26-country study. *Journal of Cross Cultural Management, 6,* 243–266.

Ho, D. Y. F. (1996). Filial piety and its psychological consequences. In M. H. Bond (Ed.), *Handbook of Chinese psychology* (pp. 155–165). Hong Kong: Oxford University Press.

Hofer, J., Chasiotis, A., Friedlmeier, W., Busch, H., & Campos, D. (2005). The measurement of implicit motives in three cultures: Power and affiliation in Cameroon, Costa Rica, and Germany. *Journal of Cross-Cultural Psychology, 36,* 689–716.

Holland, P. W., & Wainer, H. (Eds.) (1993). *Differential item functioning.* Hillsdale, NJ: Erlbaum.

Hui, C., & Triandis, H. C. (1989). Effects of culture and response format on extreme response style. *Journal of Cross-Cultural Psychology, 20,* 296–309.

Jensen, A. R. (1980). *Bias in mental testing.* New York: Free Press.

Johnson, T. (1998). Approaches to equivalence in cross-cultural and cross-national surveys. *ZUMA Nachrichten Spezial No. 3: Cross-cultural survey equivalence,* 1–40.

Leung, K., & Bond, M. H. (2004). Social Axioms: A model for social beliefs in multicultural perspective. *Advances in Experimental Social Psychology, 36,* 119–197.

Leung, K., & Van de Vijver, F. J. R. (2008). Strategies for strengthening causal inferences in cross-cultural research: The consilience approach. *Journal of Cross Cultural Management, 8,* 145–169.

Lyberg, L., Biemer, P., Collins, M., De Leeuw, E., Dippo, C., Schwarz, N., & Trewin, D. (1997). *Survey measurement and process quality.* New York: Wiley.

Malda, M., Van de Vijver, F. J. R., Srinivasan, K., Transler, C., Sukumar, P., & Rao, K. (2008). Adapting a cognitive test for a different culture: An illustration of qualitative procedures. *Psychology Science Quarterly, 50,* 451–468.

McCrae, R. R., & Costa, P. T. (1997). Personality trait structure as human universal. *American Psychologist, 52*, 509–516.

Muniz, J., Hambleton, R. K., & Xing, D. (2001). Small sample studies to detect flaws in item translations. *International Journal of Testing, 1*, 115–135.

Piswanger, K. (1975). *Interkulturelle Vergleiche mit dem Matrizentest von Formann* [Cross-cultural comparisons with Formann's Matrices Test]. Unpublished doctoral dissertation, University of Vienna, Austria.

Poortinga, Y. H. (1989). Equivalence of cross-cultural data: An overview of basic issues. *International Journal of Psychology, 24*, 737–756.

Poortinga, Y. H., & Van de Vijver, F. J. R. (1987). Explaining cross-cultural differences: Bias analysis and beyond. *Journal of Cross-Cultural Psychology, 18*, 259–282.

Spini, D. (2003). Measurement equivalence of 10 value types from the Schwartz Value Survey across 21 countries. *Journal of Cross-Cultural Psychology, 34*, 3–23.

Suzuki, K., Takei, N., Kawai, M., Minabe,Y., & Mori, N. (2003). Is Taijin Kyofusho a culture-bound syndrome? *American Journal of Psychiatry, 160*, 1358.

Tanaka-Matsumi, J., & Draguns, J. G. (1997). Culture and psychotherapy. In J. W. Berry, M. H. Segall, & C. Kagitcibasi (Eds.), *Handbook of cross-cultural psychology* (Vol. 3, pp. 449–491). Needham Heights, MA: Allyn and Bacon.

Tanzer, N. K., & Sim, C. Q. E. (1991). *Test anxiety in primary school students: An empirical study in Singapore* (Research Report 1991/6). Department of Psychology, University of Graz, Graz.

Vandenberg, R. J. (2002). Toward a further understanding of and improvement in measurement invariance methods and procedures. *Organizational Research Methods, 5*, 139–158.

Vandenberg, R. J., & Lance, C. E. (2000). A review and synthesis of the measurement invariance literature: Suggestions, practices, and recommendations for organizational research. *Organizational Research Methods, 2*, 4–69.

Van de Vijver, F. J. R. (2003). Bias and equivalence: Cross-cultural perspectives. In J. A. Harkness, F. J. R. Van de Vijver, & P. Ph. Mohler (Eds.), *Cross-cultural survey methods* (pp. 143–155). New York: Wiley.

Van de Vijver, F. J. R. (2008). On the meaning of cross-cultural differences in simple cognitive measures. *Educational Research and Evaluation, 14*, 215–234.

Van de Vijver, F. J. R., Daal, M., & Van Zonneveld, R. (1986). The trainability of abstract reasoning: A cross-cultural comparison. *International Journal of Psychology, 21*, 589 615.

Van de Vijver, F. J. R., & Leung, K. (1997). *Methods and data analysis for cross-cultural research.* Newbury Park, CA: Sage.

Van de Vijver, F. J. R., Valchev, V., & Suanet, I. (2009). Structural equivalence and differential item functioning in the Social Axioms Survey. In K. Leung & M. H. Bond (Eds.), *Advances in research on social axioms* (pp. 51–80). New York: Springer.

Van Hemert, D. A., Van de Vijver, F. J. R., Poortinga, Y. H., & Georgas, J. (2002). Structural and functional equivalence of the Eysenck Personality Questionnaire within and between countries. *Personality and Individual Differences, 33*, 1229–1249.

Van Leest, P. F. (1997). Bias and equivalence research in the Netherlands. *European Review of Applied Psychology, 47*, 319–329.

Werner, O., & Campbell, D. T. (1970). Translating, working through interpreters, and the problem of decentering. In R. Naroll & R. Cohen (Eds.), *A handbook of cultural anthropology* (pp. 398–419). New York: American Museum of Natural History.

3

Translating and Adapting Tests for Cross-Cultural Assessments

RONALD K. HAMBLETON AND APRIL L. ZENISKY

INTRODUCTION

The number of educational and psychological measures being translated and adapted into multiple languages and cultures is very much on the increase. Cross-cultural research has become important in the fields of education and psychology, and articles addressing translation and adaptation over the past 30 years have increased by 350% (van de Vijver, 2009). Journals such as the *European Journal of Psychological Assessment* and the *International Journal of Testing* (see, e.g., the recent special issue on the topic of advances in test adaptation research, Gregoire & Hambleton, 2009) are full of articles either advancing the methodology for test translation and adaptation or describing initiatives to translate and adapt particular tests, especially popular intelligence, achievement, and personality tests. Interest among policy makers, educators, and the public in international comparative studies such as those sponsored by the Organization for Economic Cooperation and Development (OECD) (see the Programme for International Student Achievement and better known as PISA), and the International Association for the Evaluation of Educational Achievement (IEA) (see Trends in International Mathematics and Science Studies and better known as TIMSS), is also considerable. Because of the policy implications of these large-scale international assessments, governments are willing to spend large sums of money to see that these studies are carried out correctly. This means that state-of-the-art methodology for test translation and adaption is expected to be used. The use of the International Test Commission (ITC) Guidelines for Test Adaptation (see, e.g., Hambleton, 2005; van de Vijver & Hambleton, 1996) has become important to guide as well as to evaluate current initiatives to carry out test translation and adaptation studies.

The ITC Guidelines for Test Adaptation emphasize the importance of both judgmental reviews and the compilation of empirical evidence. For more on the types of empirical evidence, readers are referred to the edited book by Hambleton, Merenda, and Spielberger (2005), or they can read methodological articles such as the one prepared by van de Vijver and Tanzer (2004). Regarding judgmental reviews, what we have observed in practice is that those involved in the test translation and adaptation process are committed to conducting judgmental reviews, but a valid, empirically based judgmental review form to use is not often on hand to help guide this process. The ITC Guidelines highlight the importance of these judgmental reviews but provide only a few examples for how these judgmental reviews should be conducted across educational or psychological contexts. Sometimes review forms are developed in practice, though all too often they may be (a) incomplete (e.g., they may fail to address the issue of culture in producing a valid translation and adaptation of a test or fail to address many other important features), (b) unclear, or (c) inefficient because they include redundant questions or even irrelevant questions.

The purpose of this chapter is to describe our recent efforts to produce a comprehensive, clear, and validated review form to standardize the checking of translated and adapted items on educational and psychological tests. Our goal is to strengthen the judgmental review aspect of the adaptation process to assist researchers and testing agencies in bringing their work into compliance with the ITC Guidelines for Test Adaptation. The questions on the Review Form in the Appendix were developed and chosen for inclusion because they reflected translation–adaptation problems that have often been described in the cross-cultural research literature. Often these problems are detected in what are typically called *translation differential item functioning* studies or *translation DIF* studies (see, e.g., van de Vijver & Tanzer, 2004).

DEVELOPMENT OF THE TRANSLATION AND ADAPTATION REVIEW FORM

Initially, we carried out a comprehensive review of the cross-cultural research literature and searched for translation DIF articles that included descriptions of the sorts of problems that surfaced in the translation and adaptation process, or were identified later during the research as problems. This review involved research on educational tests as well as personality and attitude measures. For example, Hambleton, Yu, and Slater (1999) noted that they had found problems with translating questions involving units of measurement in an English–Chinese comparative study of mathematics achievement (e.g., inches, feet, and yards to centimeters and meters; or Fahrenheit degrees to Centigrade degrees). [This particular empirical finding (and others that were similar) became part of our Item Translation and Adaptation Review Form as Question 23: "Are measurement/current units (distance, etc.) from the source language version of the item in the appropriate convention for the country using the target language version of the item?"]

One of the unique features of the Review Form is that all of the questions on it are associated with problems that have been identified in the field of test translation and adaptation and have been documented in the literature. Presumably, if these problems can be identified during the judgmental review process and later corrected, the subsequent empirical analyses will be more valid. What we are advocating is similar to a traditional item review in the test development process. Test items are developed, but before the potentially expensive process of empirical analysis, they are comprehensively reviewed so that problematic items can be detected and deleted, and many others can be revised before their inclusion in empirical analyses such as item analysis, factor analysis, differential item functioning studies, and reliability studies.

Ultimately, we organized our empirical findings of translation and adaptation problems into 25 questions on the Review Form (see Appendix) around five broad topics: General Translation Questions, Item Format and Appearance, Grammar and Phrasing, Passages and Other Item-Relevant Stimulus Materials (if relevant), and Cultural Relevance or Specificity. Our original Review Form with 42 questions was found to include a number of questions that were redundant, and in addition, the questions were not organized in any particular way. Preliminary reviews of the Review Form convinced us that we would need to organize the questions in a meaningful way to increase efficiency, and we needed to eliminate the redundancy in the questions. The Review Form was reduced and edited, and categories were formed to organize the remaining questions. We carried out a small field test of the Review Form in an English to Spanish translation and adaptation study (see, Elosúa, Hambleton, & Zenisky, 2008). The information gathered about participants' use of the form in that study provided the basis for a final review.

What follows is a discussion of the 25 questions, and a selection of the research we found that led to the 25 questions included on our Review Form.

General Translation Questions

The process of evaluating a test translation or adaptation effort begins with focused reflection on the quality of the overall translation. The four questions in this first group, as described subsequently, offer reviewers of translated or adapted assessment instruments the opportunity to consider the meaning of each test question across the source and target languages of interest and determine the extent to which the versions of the test questions are practically equivalent. In educational testing, *equivalence* entails not only meaning but also the difficulty of the items and related elements such as passages or other stimulus materials, especially in cases in which comparisons across language groups will be made. Other aspects of equivalence that have meaning for surveys or attitude measures include commonality and attractiveness, as well as similarity in connotation.

1. Does the item have the same or highly similar meaning in the two languages?

When translating test items from one language to another, the essence of comparability is, of course, meaning: Does the question ask the same thing of examinees in both the source and target language versions? The literature on translation DIF underscores both more obvious and very fine nuances of meaning as common sources of observed statistical differences in how a question can be understood and answered in different languages. In some cases, observed differences in meaning have also been hypothesized to stem from deficiencies in translation (Ellis, 1989; Elosúa & López-Jaúregui, 2007; Sireci & Allalouf, 2003).

An example of changes introduced through translation was detailed in Binkley and Pignal (1997). In an item involving a recipe for scrambled eggs, the heading for the recipe differed in the different language versions ("Ingredients for 4 people," "*Ingredients pour quatre portions*," and "*Proportions pour 4 personnes*"). The different versions meant slightly different things, and these variations had consequences for translation DIF because the associated items asked about sizing a recipe up or down to feed different numbers of guests. "Ingredients for 4 people," in the context of cooking, is differently explicit from "Ingredients for four portions."

Translators will sometimes produce a literal translation that is quite faithful to the original text in absolute terms but strays from the original item's intended connotation, and this is a particular area of concern in the context of personality and attitude measures. On a translation of an item on the Beck Depression Inventory, Azocar, Areán, Miranda, and Muñoz (2001) described the translation of "I believe" in Spanish as *Yo creo*. In retrospect, these authors noted that these words were not linguistic equivalents because the connotation of the English verb "believe" is stronger than the Spanish verb *creer*, which can indicate some hesitancy.

Also looking at literal translations, Auchter and Stansfield (1997) detailed several items assessing spelling in English that were translated to other languages. The homonyms "their" and "there" are often confused in English and can reasonably be used to assess certain English word skills, although few Spanish speakers would confuse *hay*, *su*, and *allí*. Here, equivalence is not achieved with respect to item difficulty across language versions. Similarly, in assessing the English knowledge of differences between "wood" and "would," in Spanish *madera* is not likely to be mistaken for *hubiera*. Similarly, word pairs that are polar opposites in one language may not be in another. This is the case with the English words "systematic" and "spontaneous." In Chinese, "spontaneous" has additional extended meanings that shade the extent to which this item means the same in Chinese as it was intended to in English (Osterlind, Miao, Sheng, & Chia, 2004).

Allalouf (2003) as well as Allalouf, Hambleton, and Sireci (1999), observed that some of the DIF that was detected in their respective studies could be explained by simple differences in connotation. This finding was echoed in a study by Sireci and Berberoglu (2000) in which two of three flagged items were simply found to mean different things in the two language versions; for example, in an attitudinal survey, the English item "The instructor took individual learning differences into account" was translated in the Turkish version as inquiring about the instructor's awareness of models of learning styles rather than an understanding of individual differences in learning exhibited by students' themselves (the latter being the intended meaning).

2. Is the language of the translated item of comparable difficulty and commonality with respect to the words in the item in the source language version?

Evaluating the quality of an item's translation also focuses on the specifics of the language used in that translation. As Bhushan (1974) pointed out, word choice in translation can significantly affect the accessibility of the items across language groups. Certain words or ideas may be more common in either the source or target languages, and as expressed by Butcher and Garcia (1978), one challenge is "choosing between one expression that is an exact equivalent but is rarely used and a more commonly used but less equivalent one" (p. 473). It is possible to have a translation be "correct" in the absolute sense, but when (a) words of low frequency are used or (b) words are used in a way that is not common in the target language, the items may not be comparable (Solano-Flores, Contreras-Niño, & Backhoff-Escudero, 2005). This appears to be among the most common sources of translation DIF reported in the psychometric literature. Sireci and Allalouf (2003) reported that 16 of 42 items flagged as translation DIF in their analyses were due to differences in word difficulty, as defined by how common various words are in the source language versus in the target language. If the words and tone of the source or target versions are more or less formal, then this can likewise be a source of differences in item difficulty (Binkley & Pignal, 1997).

One illustrative example from Ercikan (1998) involved the French translation of the English sentence, "The animal preyed on other animals." The French version read "The animal fed on other animals," and it was hypothesized that because "fed" is a considerably more common word than "preyed," French examinees could be advantaged by this translation: The use of "fed" in the French version was technically correct but resulted in a change in difficulty from the source language version. Similarly, on the topic of difficulty, Lin and Rogers (2006) related a phrase from an item that was difficult (at best) in English, and even more so in French: the English version read "four fewer $10 bills than $5 bills" compared with the French "*billets de 10$ de moins que da billets de 5$* [four $10 bills less than $5 bills]."

Language differences resulting in difficulty differences can be particularly prevalent in certain question formats; Allalouf (2003) and Allalouf, Hambleton, and Sireci (1999) reported on the challenge of maintaining the relationship intended by analogy items due to word choice in the translation process, where a "hard" word from the item stem in the source version is translated into a relatively trivial word in the target language. Translation DIF in analogy items was also reported by Angoff and Cook (1988) and Gafni and Canaan-Yehoshafat (1993). Clearly, across item formats (and particularly so in educational tests), a challenge for translators is to be cognizant of the difficulty of a word in the source language version and the importance of keeping that difficulty constant (to the extent possible) across language versions.

3. Does the translation introduce changes in the text (omissions, substitutions, or additions) that might influence the difficulty of the item in the two language versions?

Changes in text introduced through translation generally fall into three categories: omissions, substitutions, or additions. Each of these may result in translation DIF, and a number of examples of this are present in the literature. Gierl and Khaliq (2001) reported on an item in which the English version was phrased "this number in standard form is" versus the French version, "*ce nombre est*" ("the number is"). On a question asking about where a bird with webbed feet is likely to live, the translation of "webbed feet" from English to Swedish resulted in "swimming feet," which was found on review to be a bit of a giveaway (Hambleton, 1994). Collapsing sentences was put forth as the likely explanation for translation DIF in that it simplified an item stem considerably in the following example from Solano-Flores et al. (2005): "Danny buys three pencils that cost 14 cents each. How much money does he need?" versus "If Danny buys three pencils that cost 14 cents each, how much money does he need?" Gierl and Khaliq (2001) noted that in one item, a word that appeared in only the stem of the English form was in all four answer choices of the French version, making the latter more stilted.

Other studies have looked into sources of differences in meaning across translated instruments and found that some items seemed to exhibit problems due to the absence of linguistic equivalence (Collazo, 2005; Gierl & Khaliq, 2001). For example, Hilton and Skrutkowski (2002), in looking at a survey about experiences treating patients with cancer, found that no simple equivalent for the word "cope" existed in French.

4. Are there differences between the target and source language versions of the item related to the use of metaphors, idioms, or colloquialisms?

Words that form an expression in one language but not another are considered a source of translation DIF (Allalouf, 2003; Ercikan, 2002, Solano-Flores et al., 2005). Collazo (2005) detailed an item with the idiom "to tell someone off," which did not have a Spanish parallel. Similarly, the French *la chaîne de montage* is a more complex phrasing than the English counterpart "assembly line" (Lin & Rogers, 2006). Gierl and Khaliq (2001) offered a few additional examples, such as "traditional way of life" and "animal power" in English compared with *les traditions* and *à l'aide des animaux* in French. Van Eeden and Mantsha (2007) referenced a translation of the Sixteen Personality Factor Questionnaire, Fifth Edition, in which the English phrase "happy-go-lucky" had no equivalent in the South African language Tshivenda.

Also, it is important to note that idiomatic expressions often have specific connotations in the source language that can be difficult to translate and may result in noticeably longer amounts of text in the target language version of the item to communicate the nuances of meaning that were more natural in the source language version.

Item Format and Appearance

When translating a test, another important consideration in ensuring consistency between source and target language versions is the notion of how items look and are answered in both versions. Evaluating comparability in this context involves reflecting on the types of formats to be used as well as the physical appearance of items on the page (or screen, in the case of computerized tests) and is the focus of the next five questions on the review questionnaire. If respondents in the target language are not as readily prepared to complete a series of multiple-choice or other selected-response item, then this may manifest as translation DIF. Likewise, if items are formatted differently across languages, such as positioned on two pages in one and one page in another, or without the use of text emphasis such as underlining or italicizing, the results may be disparate and not permit the desired cross-lingual comparisons to be made.

5. Is the item format, including physical layout, the same in the two language versions?

Among the issues that arise in translation is the idea that (to the extent possible) an item should look the same or highly similar in all language versions. The research suggests that in preparing translated versions of instruments, items should remain in the same order and page location in all versions (O'Connor & Malak, 2000), and typesetting differences should also be taken into account (Stansfield, 2003). This latter point is illustrated by the particular complexity associated with translating documents between languages with Roman characters (e.g., English, Spanish), and non-Roman characters (e.g., Russian, Arabic, and the various Asian languages). In some cases, the act of changing the characters used may lengthen or shorten the format of an item in a noticeable way, and translators should be aware of this possibility.

Ercikan (1998) described an item that was written as text but was quantitative in nature, and in the French version the actual question of the item was separated from the data contained in the rest of the item stem by a paragraph break. This was not the case in other versions, thereby potentially making the item easier for the French-speaking test takers.

Some format considerations are specific to certain item types as well. Whenever possible, response options for multiple-choice items should remain in the same order (O'Connor & Malak, 2000). Another difficulty that was noted by Allalouf, Hambleton, and Sireci (1999) concerned the use of blanks in sentence completion-type items, in that their research showed that through the translation process some items were changed to have either different numbers of blanks or longer or shorter ones in some translated sentences, thereby affecting the difficulty in the target language version.

6. Is the length of the item stem and, if applicable, answer choices about the same in the two language versions?

Because of differences in how languages may express certain concepts, the length of different components of items may vary greatly between the source and target language versions. Lin and Rogers (2006) described one item that was statistically more difficult in French than in English, and part of the problem was hypothesized to involve the length of the stem (189 words in French compared with 153 in English). Similar differences were also found in comparisons of items between Russian and Hebrew (Allalouf, Hambleton, & Sireci, 1999), Italian and English (Joldersma, 2004), and French versions of items prepared for administration in Switzerland, Canada, and France (Ercikan, 1999). Sireci and Allalouf (2003) found between-language differences in length not only for stems but also for answer choices in the multiple-choice item format. Whenever possible, translators should try to maintain comparable item lengths across item versions because there may be a cumulative fatigue effect due to the use of longer items as a general rule (which may in turn contribute to compromising the validity of comparisons across languages, if one version is considerably longer than another).

7. Will the format of the item and task required of the examinee be equally familiar in the two language versions?

One important aspect of educational or psychological assessment is the question of the familiarity of a question format or task itself across languages and cultures. Hambleton (2001), in referencing the ITC Guidelines for Test Adaptation, noted that some item types are truly novel in different languages and cultures, and care should be taken to ensure that the nature of the task to be used in different language versions is sufficiently common across the cultures (for example, any bias suspected might be addressed with a practice item or two added to the instructions). As noted by van de Vijver and Poortinga (2005), people in different countries may not know or clearly understand the mechanics of how to respond to a particular kind of item, and therefore this differential familiarity with items can show up as translation DIF.

In the United States and many other countries, the multiple-choice item format is quite standard, whereas constructed-response questions may be more common in Europe and elsewhere (Wolf, 1998). Van de Vijver and Hambleton (1996) suggested that the ability to answer multiple-choice items is highly dependent on previous knowledge and experience with a particular education framework, a concern echoed by Tanzer (2005). The true–false format may likewise not translate well across languages and was once described as "the American test" because it was so unfamiliar in other countries and cultures (Butcher, 2004). Tanzer (2005) described a case in which the Viennese Matrices Test was given to Arabic-educated high school students in Nigeria and Togo, and the results were compared to the Austrian calibration sample. The items were found to be considerably harder for the Arabic-educated students, who had trouble identifying and applying rules left to right given the nature of the task (completing matrices), as compared with top-to-bottom.

To be sure, educational testing is not the only domain in which differences in the extent to which test takers are familiar with item formats may cause problems for translated assessments. Drasgow and Probst (2005) described research indicating that people in different cultures use response scales for psychological tests in different ways. These variations often are pronounced with respect to (a) the use (or lack of use) of extreme ratings or (b) tendencies to exhibit acquiescent behaviors.

Ultimately, in selecting item formats for use with instruments that will be translated into multiple languages, Hambleton (2005) recommends the use of a variety of item types (a suggestion also made by McQueen & Mendelovits, 2003) to try and balance out any biases introduced by the choice of item formats in an assessment instrument. When a test is being developed with cross-national comparisons as an original goal (rather than a post hoc adaptation), the decision to provide a balance of item types can be informed by careful consideration of the kinds of item formats commonly used in the different countries in which the measure will be used, and sample items should be offered to test takers at the start of test sessions to allow them to go through the steps required to answer test questions of each type.

8. If a form of word or phrase emphasis (bold, italics, underline, etc.) was used in the source language item, was that emphasis used in the translated item?

Different font styles and typefaces can be a source of translation and adaptation DIF (Gierl & Khaliq, 2001; Solano-Flores et al., 2005). Joldersma

(2004) presented two versions of an item (Italian and English, respectively) in which the Italian version of the item did not bold the accompanying preposition that would be the equivalent to the English "to" (which was bolded). O'Connor and Malak (2000) recommended that if the original form of emphasis was not appropriate for the target version of the item (as might be the case in some languages or cultures), then alternates that are acceptable should be found (e.g., italics instead of capital letters).

9. For educational tests, is there one correct answer in both the source and target language version of the item?

A fundamental tenet of a good selected-response item (such as the multiple-choice format) is that there should be only one correct answer for a given question. Typically, item review or statistical analysis of pretest data will reveal if an item is miskeyed or if more than one plausible answer is present. However, by translating an item from one language version to another, one possible outcome is that the original item is revealed as flawed in some way, such as having more than one correct answer to begin with or for other errors relating to the quality of the answer choices to be introduced (Solano-Flores et al., 2005). O'Connor and Malak (2000) reiterate that translators must be extremely careful in their work to ensure that they do not make changes that alter the likelihood of another possible correct answer for an item.

Grammar and Phrasing

The next topic to be addressed in evaluating translations of educational or psychological measures is grammar and syntax. Languages differ in how they structure words to express ideas, and such variations can at times support or hinder efforts to create parallel versions of items for cross-lingual use. The emphasis in the six questions in this section of the Review Form is on differences in expression that result in either simplifying or making text more complex, resulting in differences in difficulty between the source and target language versions.

10. Is there any modification of the item's structure such as the placement of clauses or other word order changes that might make this item more or less complex in the target language version?

A number of researchers on the topic of test translation have focused efforts to understand translation DIF on how the syntactical structure of a test question can change in the translation process. The grammatical forms and arrangement of clauses found in different languages can be a problem for translation (Allalouf, 2003). A particularly challenging domain to translate may be language arts tests, which require translators to align structures such as subject–verb agreement (Stansfield, 2003). Elosúa and López-Jaúregui (2007) suggested that knowledge of differences in the syntactical ordering of sentence elements (subject, verb, and object) in different languages helps in understanding this source of translation DIF (e.g., Spanish is subject–verb–object, whereas Basque is subject–object–verb).

When a translation is completed in such a way as to be too literal, the resulting syntax may be erroneous or unnatural in its expression in the target language (Solano-Flores et al., 2005). The grammatical structure of translated items may more susceptible to problems when the sentence completion item format is used. This item format often requires considerable effort to ensure the flow of the source version in the target version (Beller, Gafni, & Hanani, 2005).

11. Are there any grammatical clues that might make this item easier or harder in the target language version?

The grammar of translated items can at times offer test takers cues that allow an item to vary in difficulty in translation between the source and target language. Errors such as obvious inconsistencies between the stem and options in multiple-choice items are easily fixed, as are inconsistencies among options in multiple-choice items (Solano-Flores et al., 2005). Sometimes, words from the source language version may be mistakenly retained in the target version ("A *by* 95 $" rather than "A *par* 95 $" in an English to French translation cited by Lin & Rogers, 2005; emphasis added). How adverbs relate to adjectives is another potential source of grammar-based translation DIF (Collazo, 2005), as are verb tenses and the use of singular or plural nouns (Allalouf, 2003) and comparatives (Ellis, 1989). Linguistic experts can be helpful in spotting these types of problems.

12. Are there any grammatical structures in the source language version of the item that do not have parallels in the target language?

Grammatical differences in languages may create problems in translating verb tenses (Butcher & Garcia, 1978) and plurals (Beller, Gafni, & Hanani, 2005), for example. As described by Beller, Gafni, and Hanani (2005), plurals can be expressed as two and also more than two in Arabic. In a report on dual-language assessment work, Solano-Flores, Trumbull, and Nelson-Barber (2002) related the case of the following directions found on a test question: "You can use words, numbers, and/or pictures." In Spanish, the literal equivalent of "and/or" is '*y/o*,' but the authors note that that phrasing is extremely rare in common usage and would not be found in writing appropriate for elementary students (for whom this question was intended).

13. Are there any gender or other references that might make this item be cued in the target language version?

When translating items between languages, some languages define nouns as either masculine or feminine, and if a translation is not done carefully, these references can cue test takers to the correct answer. Joldersma (2004) provided an example of this in which gender and number were reinforced in the item stems. There, the item involved a question about where a toy was to be placed, and in Italian (the target language in this case) the noun *sedia* and the preposition '*della*' together provided clues to the correct answer (the toy's location). Similarly, Sireci and Berberoglu (2000) reported that in translating a test between English and Turkish, a particular gender pronoun did not have a translation equivalent, resulting in an awkward Turkish version. In an English–Welsh translation, the case of translating "a white cat" was a challenge because "cat" is a female noun in Welsh (*cath*). The word "white" in Welsh is *gwyn*, but because "cat" is a feminine noun, the phrase became *cath wen* (Jones, 1998).

Fitzgerald (2005) also noted that problems could arise in translation with the use of the pronoun "you." Many languages, such as Spanish, among others, can express "you" in both the formal and familiar. In translation, the preferred decision for the process is to adopt the common usage of the intended population of test takers. Moreover, the English "you" can refer to a single person or to multiple persons. Many languages do not have this ambiguity.

14. Are there any words in the item that, when translated, change from having one meaning to having more than one common meaning?

One issue that has emerged in the translation literature is the idea of word choice and the reality that some words may have additional shades of meaning in the target language that may affect the quality and connotation of the translation. The different meanings could be culture-specific nuances of the source language meaning or could be more unique to the target language (Allalouf, 2003; Sireci & Allalouf, 1999; also Allalouf, Hambleton, & Sireci, 1999). In reviewing translated items, the persons involved should watch for this as a potential source of confusion.

An example of this involves the case of the word "work" in English. Ercikan (1998) referenced an item that was highly technical and used a number of physics terms such as "energy," "power," and "work." "Work" has a specific meaning in the context of physics but also has a meaning outside of that domain. This turned out to be problematic when directly translating the item into French, because it appeared that no simple physics context meaning was found for the word in that target language. Therefore, the distractor involving that word in French did not function the same as in the English version of the item.

Ellis (1989) described a similar situation with an item in which the task was to identify the word from an array of answer choices that is closest in meaning to a particular word ("pulley"). The closest cognate to "pulley" among the choices in English was "wheel." However, the best translation for "pulley" in German was *flasche*, although the German *flasche* can also mean bottle. Thus, as Ellis pointed out, in this item, the structure offered no context for those intended test takers to choose the "pulley" meaning of *flasche* compared with the "bottle" meaning, and thus the item as written may have been more difficult for German-speaking test takers.

15. Are there any changes in punctuation between the source and target versions of the item that may make the item easier or harder in the translated version?

Often, in the course of translating items, the syntax of the target language results in changes to the structure of a sentence, and this can be a source of translation DIF. Binkley and Pignal (1997) described an item in which examinees were to select a sentence within a passage that illustrated a main idea. In comparing the Canadian and French versions, the Canadian version was considerably shorter relative to the French version, which spanned four lines and was broken midway through with a semicolon. The directions were not clear on whether test takers should select the entire sentence or a portion thereof (was a sentence the entire text from start to finish, or was the portion before or after the semicolon sufficient?).

Passages and Other Item-Relevant Stimulus Materials (If Present)

In many cases, items do not consist of only stem-and-answer choices but rather reference a passage or some form of data/information presentation (a table, chart, or graph). Too often, the focus in translation and adaptation review is on the items and not the stimulus materials. These components of items must receive a similarly careful examination from item reviewers to ensure that they are appropriate for use and are translated properly. The first author recalls chairing the first international review committee for PISA in 1999 and noted that a high percentage of the problems identified in the judgmental review were associated with the passages and not the test items themselves. Passages were challenged because they were judged as unsuitable in many countries (e.g., passages about drugs, religious issues, and criticism of governments), or they were judged to be unfamiliar to students in many countries (e.g., passages about graffiti and suicide). Sometimes the passages were judged as uninteresting, too long, too complex, and so forth. All of these shortcomings could have an impact on motivational levels for examinees that may not be consistent across language and cultural groups, thus introducing a source of bias into the results.

16. When the passage is translated from the source language to the target language, do the words and phrases of the translated version convey similar content and ideas to the source version?

Guidelines from Malak and Trong (2007) that were used to inform translation procedures for the Progress in International Reading Literacy Study (PIRLS, 2006) suggest that (a) care should be taken to ensure that the source and translated versions of passages reflect comparable levels of language complexity and formality and (b) no additions, omissions, or clarifications of text should emerge in the translated versions of passages. At the same time, idioms should be translated to communicate meaning rather than be translated word for word, and the grammar of the translated version should be equivalent in difficulty to that of the source version but appropriate to the target version of the passage. These PIRLS guidelines support flexibility in translation and allow for minor adaptations of passage elements to ensure cultural relevance and correctness. Permissible types of cultural adaptations for passages include vocabulary, expressions, and names of people and places.

17. Does the passage depict any individual or groups in a stereotypic fashion through occupation, emotion, situation, or otherwise?

As is standard in item development, content review for passages and items translated between languages should flag those that are potentially inappropriate for intended test takers. This is especially necessary when cross-cultural depictions of persons are involved. Hambleton (2001) referenced several potentially problematic representations such as gypsies and bullies. The notion of bullies was likewise raised by McQueen and Mendelovits

(2003) in discussing an article from a Japanese newspaper that was considered for inclusion on PISA. This article was seen as reinforcing negative ideas about the Japanese educational system (and, on a point related to the next review question, was also flagged as a problem because of its depiction of suicide).

18. Does the passage involve writing on a controversial or inflammatory topic, or might the passage be perceived as demeaning or offensive to anyone?

Avoiding controversial and inflammatory topics on assessments for which such ideas are not relevant is an important part of limiting construct-irrelevant variance and ensuring that an educational or psychological instrument does not cause undue emotional distress for respondents. Topics that can be controversial in passages (and have been found as problematic in international assessments) include drugs, war, religion, and politics, and persons developing such measures may wish to proceed with caution in using these subjects as the focal point of passages (Hambleton, 2001).

McQueen and Mendelovits (2003) noted that except in the case of stereotypes and other offensive meaning, passages are not typically changed. They described an example in which a change was made to a passage relating to a characterization of people (one country involved in PISA changed "cripple" to "lame man" in one passage). Another example given in the same article involved the Egyptian Sphinx and the difficulties that have been encountered in restoring the ancient monuments (this passage was not used on cultural–political grounds).

19. Does the passage include content or require skills that may be unfamiliar to some students in either of the two language or cultural groups?

Another critical aspect of translating passages and other stimulus materials for items is the possibility that the topic is inappropriate for the target language version because the content of the passage is unfamiliar to people who speak that language or are of that culture (van de Vijver & Poortinga, 2005). In many cases, some ideas may be self-explanatory in one version but not in the target version (Beller, Gafni, & Hanani, 2005). In conducting an English to Chinese translation, Hambleton (2001) mentioned differential familiarity across cultural groups with a number of concepts, such as "hamburgers," "flight schedules," and "graffiti."

A further concern involves passage-based sets, which can be challenging psychometrically in any language because of the statistical dependence that can come about due to answering a set of items based on a common stimulus (Yen, 1984). In the context of a translated and adapted measure, if a topic or main idea word or phrase is unfamiliar to respondents in the target language, this can have implications for performance on an entire set of items rather than on a single item only. This issue of differential familiarity was noted by Lin and Rogers (2006), who referenced a situation in which some French-speaking students were not clear about the meaning of *égout* (sewer), and this had implications for a sequence of several items.

20. Except for necessary translations of text or labels, are graphics, tables, and other item elements the same in the source and target language versions of the item?

As with passages, tables, charts, graphs, and images can be an essential part of a item and necessarily must be dealt with in the course of translating an assessment from one language to another. On some tests, it has happened that graphic components have either been omitted or added to the target version, or tables have been sized differently in different versions of an assessment (Solano-Flores et al., 2005). Binkley and Pignal (1997) illustrated how a map image varied considerably between the French versions produced for Switzerland, Canada, and France, respectively. A busy, overly elaborate dot pattern appeared in the ocean area of the map in the Swiss French version but not in either of the two other language versions. Another item described by Binkley and Pignal (1997) asked test takers to complete a time sheet, but the different language versions included different bolding on the summary lines for one version of the table compared with the other, and this was determined to be a source of problems for comparing performance on the item across languages.

O'Connor and Malak (2000) recommended that whenever possible, translation of elements of graphic components of items be limited to the necessary translation of text or labels. A potential difficulty that may arise in limiting translation to aspects of images was noted by Stansfield (2003), in that spacing and formatting can sometimes be a problem in images, to the extent that images may need to be re-created, further introducing potential sources of incomparability. An additional caution was raised by Tanzer (2005). He noted that the cultural appropriateness of all graphics (and especially images) should be evaluated for use in the target language version of the test item. Examples of this could include review of graphics for Western styles of dress, historical accuracy, and the depiction of racial and ethnic groups.

Cultural Relevance and Specificity

The final topic to be addressed in a review of translation and adaptation incomparability involves culture and the cross-national environment in which an instrument is to be administered. As items are reviewed for use in different language versions, the social context and appropriateness of the content are critical aspects for consideration and review by persons familiar with the intended audiences for those items.

21. Have terms in the item in one language been suitably adapted to the cultural environment of the second language version?

Specific terms that are used in items in one language may not be appropriate for use in the target language, and so part of the process of translating an instrument is reflecting on the concepts and ideas of the source version of an item. This applies to common or everyday contexts, but also to technical terms, whether such terms are inaccurately translated or insertions or omissions are made erroneously (Solano-Flores et al., 2005).

McQueen and Mendelovits (2003) suggested amending various item elements such as names of people, places, organizations, telephone numbers, and the like to assist in "localizing" the target version of a test (e.g., use "Maria" for "Mary," or replace the American "sidewalk" with the British "footpath"). Content changes such as "centre" for "center" and content substitutions such as "sailing" for "skiing," "hot plate" for "Bunsen burner," and "kiwi" for "robin" are also often appropriate (O'Connor & Malak, 2000).

Stansfield (2003) related one example of how elements of a question might need to be changed across languages and cultures in describing an assessment for auto mechanics given across countries; in this case the basics of an internal combustion engine are largely the same, but it may nonetheless be necessary to adapt items to reflect terms and content differences that are present in the different countries (in this case, the United States and France). The same principle holds for many certification and licensure tests in medicine, dentistry, architecture, accounting, and many more subject areas. Questions about television watching should probably not be used where there is little or no electricity or where television is not likely to be a known technology among intended participants (van Haaften & van de Vijver, 2003). Bhushan (1974) cited the following analogy item: "The mayor is to a city as a governor is to a [blank]." The relationship to be illustrated by this analogy item may not work in some places, depending on the structure of government in place and whether the positions of governor and mayor exist in the way referenced in the source version of the item.

22. Are there cultural differences that would have an effect on the likelihood of a response being chosen when the item is presented in the source or target language version?

Certainly, cultural differences exist in how answers are chosen. The expression of emotion across cultures is one such example and can certainly affect how different people respond to different psychological inventories such as the Beck Depression Inventory (Azocar et al., 1991). Another dimension of this course of problems in translation relates to differences in curriculum. Depending on when certain knowledge and skills are taught to test takers, an item may not represent the language and curriculum of the target country and thus may be flagged as DIF because of these cultural factors.

23. Are measurement and currency units (distance, etc.) from the source language version of the item in the appropriate convention for the country using the target language version?

Part of translating an instrument from one language to another involves ensuring that the aspects of an item are appropriate for the intended country. McQueen and Mendelovits (2003) and Wolf (1998) recommended changing the units of measurement, currency, and other quantitative indicators or labels into those used locally for the target language version of a test. A quick inquiry to determine whether a country uses standard or metric measurement, for example, can be a critical part of ensuring that an item is locally suited for the intended country's test takers. This is certainly the experience for companies involved in international credentialing and licensure such as Microsoft (Fitzgerald, 2005) and educational assessments such as TIMSS (O'Connor & Malak, 2000) and other mathematics tests (Hambleton & Kanjee, 1995).

However, translating units of measurement can also have unintended effects on items. Gierl and Khaliq (2001) and Gierl, Rogers, and Klinger (1999) cited the example of how time is expressed in English and French contexts, respectively. The French clock is a 24-hour clock, whereas the English use a 12-hour clock. A question asked how much time was spent on a task starting at 5:20 a.m. when the end time was specified as 8:15 p.m. in the English version and 20:15 in the target (French) version, and in English the distractor based on an erroneously read end time of 8:15 a.m. was considerably more attractive than the comparable distractor (directly translated) in the French language version.

Wolf (1998), Stansfield (2003), O'Connor and Malak (2000), and Solano-Flores et al. (2005) also described another point that translators must present correctly in translating numbers. The use of periods and commas in expressing numbers varies among countries (for example, English- and Spanish-speaking nations): 10,215.64 compared with 10.215,64.

24. Are the concepts covered in the item at about the same level of abstraction in the two language versions?

Abstract ideas present a particular challenge for translation, and ensuring that the content of items is described in similarly abstract ways across language versions is not an easy task for translators. When a word to be translated is an abstract concept, the translation task becomes focused on ideas. For example, because feminism may be unknown or is defined differently in some cultures, a passage with a biography and some lyrics by singer Ani DiFranco was dropped from PISA because the focus on some of the questions were on the Western-style feminist ideas presented in her lyrics (McQueen & Mendelovits, 2003). "Depression," "motives," and other ideas relating to feelings are quite abstract and can be a considerable source of translation difficulty (van Eeden & Mantsha, 2007). Similar challenges have arisen in the process of translating many psychological instruments (Butcher & Garcia, 1978).

25. Does the concept or construct of the item have about the same familiarity and meaning in both the source and target language versions?

Naturally, among the critical aspects involved in judging the quality of a translation is the extent to which a translation appropriately reflects the society and customs of the target language (Hambleton, 2001). Different countries and languages have inherent cultural knowledge and assumptions, and this has implications for translation in the context of assessing knowledge and skills across countries. Sometimes, content interacts with culture and limits the extent to which an item can be used in cross-national assessments (Sireci & Allalouf, 2003), and careful analysis of the cultural representations and customs of the target language or country can be quite helpful in successfully translating an assessment (Elosúa & López-Jaúregui, 2007).

A simple thing, such as how a jar is opened in Germany versus an English-speaking culture, can potentially be a source of translation DIF (Ellis, 1989). Health inspections were found not to be common across countries and therefore were determined unsuitable for use as situational contexts on Microsoft certification exams (Fitzgerald, 2005). The American English term "freedom rider" does not have a Spanish counterpart (Auchter & Stansfield, 1997).

CONCLUSIONS

We hope that the two-page Item Translation and Adaptation Review Form in Appendix will be helpful to research teams attempting to evaluate the translation and adaptation of educational and psychological measures before moving to the compilation of empirical evidence such as the comparability of factor structure in the source and target language versions of a test. Most of the questions on the Review Form would probably be obvious to many experienced translators themselves, but these are not always the persons leading the translation *review* process. In addition, limited funds or naïveté on the part of the researchers carrying out work involving translation and adaptation of an educational or psychological measure can also add logistical complications to the completion of a high-quality translation. All too often, the view is that anyone who knows the languages can do a good translation. This is one of the major misunderstandings in the field (Hambleton, 2005). The Review Form can serve as a aid to both inexperienced and experienced translation and adaptation reviewers and help to standardize the process of judgmental reviews.

Where necessary too, the Review Form can be shortened or extended or even edited to fit the particular needs of the translation and adaptation review team. We would recommend in practice that several reviewers work independently in completing the Review Form and then meet to share their item-level evaluations. Summarizing notes on the second page of the Review Form will be especially helpful for the discussion process. Note, however, that flawed items may not have more than a single problem – for example, the meaning of the test item may be quite different in the two language versions. Nonetheless, this single flaw is sufficient to justify a rewrite of the translated or adapted item. It is not a matter of expecting flawed items to receive a high number of ratings indicating problems. Agreement of reviewers on a single flaw is often sufficient to initiate a revision of the translation or, in some instances, discarding the item altogether.

REFERENCES

Allalouf, A. (2003). Revising translated differential item functioning items as a tool for improving cross-lingual assessment. *Applied Measurement in Education, 16*, 55–73.

Allalouf, A., Hambleton, R. K., & Sireci, S. G. (1999). Identifying the causes of DIF in translated verbal items. *Journal of Educational Measurement, 36*, 185–198.

Angoff, W. H., & Cook, L. L. (1988). *Equating the scores of the Prueba de Aptitud Academica and the Scholastic Aptitude Test* (Report No. 88–2). New York: College Entrance Examination Board.

Auchter, J. E., & Stansfield, C. W. (1997, June). *Developing parallel tests across languages: Focus on the translation and adaptation process.* Paper presented at the annual meeting of the Council of Chief State School Officers, Colorado Springs, CO.

Azocar, F., Areán, P., Miranda, J., & Muñoz, R. F. (2001). Differential item functioning in a Spanish translation of the Beck Depression Inventory. *Journal of Clinical Psychology, 57,* 355–365.

Beller, M., Gafni, N., & Hanani, P. (2005). Constructing, adapting, and validating admissions tests in multiple languages. In R. K. Hambleton, P. F. Merenda, & C. Spielberger (Eds.), *Adapting educational and psychological tests for cross-cultural assessment* (pp. 297–320). Mahwah, NJ: Erlbaum.

Bhushan, V. (1974). Adaptation of an intelligence test from English to French. *Journal of Educational Measurement, 11,* 43–48.

Binkley, M., & Pignal, J. (1997). An analysis of items with different parameters across countries. In S. Murray, I. Kirsch, & L. Jenkins (Eds.), *Adult literacy in OECD countries: Technical report on the First International Adult Literacy Survey.* Washington: U.S. Department of Education, National Center for Education Statistics (NCES 98-053; pp. 143–160). Retrieved from http://nces.ed.gov/pubs98/98053.pdf.

Butcher, J. N. (2004). Personality assessment without borders: Adaptation of the MMPI-2 across cultures. *Journal of Personality Assessment, 83,* 90–104.

Butcher, J. N., & Garcia, R. E. (1978). Cross-national application of psychological tests. *Personnel and Guidance Journal, 56,* 472–475.

Collazo, A. A. (2005). Translation of the Marlowe–Crowne Social Desirability Scale into an equivalent Spanish version. *Educational and Psychological Measurement, 65,* 780–806.

Drasgow, F., & Probst, T. (2005). The psychometrics of adaptation: Evaluating measurement equivalence across languages and cultures. In R. K. Hambleton, P. F. Merenda, & C. Spielberger (Eds.), *Adapting educational and psychological tests for cross-cultural assessment* (pp. 265–296). Mahwah, NJ: Erlbaum.

Ellis, B. B. (1989). Differential item functioning: Implications for test translation. *Journal of Applied Psychology, 74,* 912–921.

Elosúa, P., Hambleton, R. K., & Zenisky, A. L. (2008). *Improving the methodology for detecting biased test items* (Center for Educational Assessment Research Report No. 586). Amherst: University of Massachusetts, Center for Educational Assessment.

Elosúa, P., & López-Jaúregui, A. (2007). Potential sources of DIF in the adaptation of tests. *International Journal of Testing, 7,* 39–52.

Ercikan, K. (1998). Translation effects in international assessments. *International Journal of Educational Research, 29,* 543–553.

Ercikan, K. (1999, April). *Translation DIF on TIMSS.* Paper presented at the meeting of the National Council on Measurement in Education, Montréal, Canada.

Ercikan, K. (2002). Disentangling sources of differential item functioning in multilanguage assessments. *International Journal of Testing, 2,* 199–215.

Fitzgerald, C. (2005). Test adaptation in a large-scale certification program. In R. K. Hambleton, P. F. Merenda, & C. D. Spielberger (Eds.), *Adapting educational and psychological tests for cross-cultural assessment* (pp. 195–212). Mahwah, NJ: Erlbaum.

Gafni, N., & Canaan-Yehoshafat, Z. (1993). *An examination of differential item functioning for Hebrew- and Russian-speaking examinees in Israel.* Paper presented at the conference of the Israeli Psychological Association, Ramat-Gan, Israel.

Gierl, M., & Khaliq, S. (2001). Identifying sources of differential item and bundle functioning on translated achievement tests: A confirmatory analysis. *Journal of Educational Measurement, 38,* 164–187.

Gierl, M. J., Rogers, W. T., & Klinger, D. (1999). *Consistency between statistical and judgmental reviews for identifying translation DIF.* Paper presented at the meeting of the National Council on Measurement in Education, Montréal, Canada.

Gregoire, J., & Hambleton, R. K. (2009). Advances in test adaptation research [special issue]. *International Journal of Testing, 2,* 75–168.

Hambleton, R. K. (1994). Guidelines for adapting educational and psychological tests: A progress report. *European Journal of Psychological Assessment, 10,* 229–244.

Hambleton, R. K. (2001). The next generation of ITC test translation and adaptation guidelines. *European Journal of Psychological Assessment, 17,* 164–172.

Hambleton, R. K. (2005). Issues, designs, and technical guidelines for adapting tests in multiple languages and cultures. In R. K. Hambleton, P. F. Merenda, & C. Spielberger (Eds.), *Adapting educational and psychological tests for cross-cultural assessment* (pp. 3–38). Mahwah, NJ: Erlbaum.

Hambleton, R. K., & Kanjee, A. (1995). Increasing the validity of cross-cultural assessments: Use of improved methods for test adaptations. *European Journal of Psychological Assessment, 11,* 147–160.

Hambleton, R. K., Merenda, P. F., & Spielberger, C. (Eds.). (2005). *Adapting educational and psychological tests for cross-cultural assessment.* Mahwah, NJ: Erlbaum.

Hambleton, R. K., Yu, L., & Slater, S. C. (1999). Field-test of ITC guidelines for adapting psychological tests. *European Journal of Psychological Assessment, 15,* 270–276.

Hilton, A., & Skrutkowski, M. (2002). Translating instruments into other languages: Development and testing processes. *Cancer Nursing, 25,* 1–7.

Joldersma, K. B. (2004, April). *Cross-linguistic instrument comparability.* Paper presented at the meeting of the American Educational Research Association, San Diego, CA. Retrieved March 27, 2006, from http://www.ed-web3.educ.msu.edu/CEPSE/mqm/forms/KJ.doc.

Jones, D. V. (1998). National curriculum tests for mathematics in English and Welsh: Creating matched assessments. *Assessment in Education, 5,* 193–211.

Lin, J., & Rogers, W. T. (2005, April). *Validity of the simultaneous approach to the development of equivalent achievement tests in English and French (Stage II).* Paper presented at the meeting of the National Council on Measurement in Education, Montréal, Canada. Retrieved March 27, 2006, from http://www.education.ualberta.ca/educ/psych/crame/files/NCME%20paper%202005%20CRAME.pdf.

Lin, J., & Rogers, W. T. (2006, April). *Validity of the simultaneous approach to the development of equivalent achievement tests in English and French (Stage III).*

Paper presented at the meeting of the National Council on Measurement in Education, Montréal, Canada. Retrieved March 27, 2006, from http://www.education.ualberta.ca/educ/psych/crame/files/NCME06_JL.pdf.

Malak, B., & Trong, K. L. (2007). Translating the PIRLS 2006 reading assessment and questionnaires. In M. O. Martin, I. V. S. Mullis, & A. M. Kennedy (Eds.), *PIRLS 2006 technical report* (pp. 49–60). Chestnut Hill, MA: Boston College.

McQueen, J., & Mendelovits, J. (2003). PISA reading: Cultural equivalence in a cross-cultural study. *Language Testing, 20,* 207–223.

O'Connor, K. M., & Malak, B. (2000). Translation and cultural adaptation of the TIMSS instruments. In M. O. Martin, K. D. Gregory, & S. E. Stemler (Eds.), *TIMSS 1999 technical report* (pp. 89–100). Chestnut Hill, MA: Boston College.

Osterlind, S. J., Miao, D., Sheng, Y., & Chia, R. C. (2004). Adapting item format for cultural effects in translated tests: Cultural effects on construct validity of the Chinese versions of the MBTI. *International Journal of Testing, 4,* 61–73.

Sireci, S. G., & Allalouf, A. (2003). Appraising item equivalence across multiple languages and cultures. *Language Testing, 20,* 147–165.

Sireci, S. G., & Berberoglu, G. (2000). Evaluating translation DIF using bilinguals. *Applied Measurement in Education, 13,* 229–248.

Solano-Flores, G., Contreras-Niño, L. A., & Backhoff-Escudero, E. (2005, April). *The Mexican translation of TIMSS-95: Test translation lessons from a post-mortem study.* Paper presented at the meeting of the National Council on Measurement in Education. Montréal, Quebec, Canada. Retrieved March 27, 2006 from http://www.air.org/news/documents/NCME2005Mexican%20translation.pdf.

Solano-Flores, G., Trumbull, E., & Nelson-Barber, S. (2002). Concurrent development of dual language assessments: An alternative to translating tests for linguistic minorities. *International Journal of Testing, 2,* 107–129.

Stansfield, C. W. (2003). Test translation and adaptation in public education in the USA. *Language Testing, 20,* 188–206. Retrieved March 27, 2006, from http://www.2lti.com/Docs/PDF/Test%20Translation.pdf.

Tanzer, N. K. (2005). Developing tests for use in multiple languages and cultures: A plea for simultaneous development. In R. K. Hambleton, P. F. Merenda, & C. D. Spielberger (Eds.), *Adapting educational and psychological tests for cross-cultural assessment* (pp. 235–264). Mahwah, NJ: Erlbaum.

Van de Vijver, R. J. R. (2009, July). *Translating and adapting psychological tests for large scale projects.* Paper presented at the 11th European Congress of Psychology, Oslo, Norway.

Van de Vijver, F. J. R., & Hambleton, R. K. (1996). Translating tests: Some practical guidelines. *European Psychologist, 1,* 89–99.

Van de Vijver, F. J. R., & Poortinga, Y. H. (2005). Conceptual and methodological issues in adapting tests. In R. K. Hambleton, P. F. Merenda, & C. D. Spielberger (Eds.), *Adapting educational and psychological tests for cross-cultural assessment* (pp. 39–64). Mahwah, NJ: Erlbaum.

Van de Vijver, F. J. R., & Tanzer, N. K. (2004). Bias and equivalence in cross-cultural assessment: An overview. *European Review of Applied Psychology, 54,* 119–135.

Van Eeden, R., & Mantsha, T. R. (2007). Theoretical and methodological considerations in the translation of the 16PF into an African language. *South African Journal of Psychology, 37,* 62–81.

Van Haaften, E. H., & Van de Vijver, F. J. R. (2003). Human resilience and environmental degradation: The eco-cultural link in the Sahel. *International Journal of Sustainable Development and World Ecology, 10*, 85–99.

Wolf, R. M. (1998). Validity issues in international assessments. *International Journal of Educational Research, 29*, 491–501.

Yen, W. M. (1984). Effects of local item dependence on the fit and equating performance of the three-parameter logistic model. *Applied Psychological Measurement, 8*, 125–145.

APPENDIX

Item Translation and Adaptation Review Form

Directions: Read the 25 questions on the next two pages. These are the questions we would like you to answer for each of the test items in the assessment or questionnaire. There are four possible answers to each question: Y = Yes, N = No, U = Unsure, NR = Not Relevant. Show your answer to each question by circling one of the four possible answers in the column corresponding to the test item number. Now you are ready to begin with the ratings process. Read the test item, and then answer the 25 questions, providing your answers in the column marked "Item." Please use the back of this sheet if you would like to explain any of your responses.

Question Number = x Y = Yes N = No U = Unsure NR = Not Relevant

Category	Translation and adaptation questions	Item			
General	1. Does the item have the same or highly similar meaning in the two languages?	Y	N	U	NR
	2. Is the language of the translated item of comparable difficulty and commonality with respect to the words in the item in the source language version?	Y	N	U	NR
	3. Does the translation introduce changes in the text (omissions, substitutions, or additions) that might influence the difficulty of the item in the two language versions?	Y	N	U	NR
	4. Are there differences between the target and source language versions of the item related to the use of metaphors, idioms, or colloquialisms?	Y	N	U	NR
Item format	5. Is the item format, including physical layout, the same in the two language versions?	Y	N	U	NR

(continued)

(continued)

Category	Translation and adaptation questions	Item			
	6. Is the length of the item stem and, if applicable, answer choices about the same in the two language versions?	Y	N	U	NR
	7. Will the format of the item and task required of the examinee be equally familiar in the two language versions?	Y	N	U	NR
	8. If a form of word or phrase emphasis (bold, italics, underline, etc.) was used in the source language item, was that emphasis used in the translated item?	Y	N	U	NR
	9. For educational tests, is there one correct answer in both the source and target language version of the item?	Y	N	U	NR
Grammar and phrasing	10. Is there any modification of the item's structure such as the placement of clauses or other word order changes that might make this item more or less complex in the target language version?	Y	N	U	NR
	11. Are there any grammatical clues that might make this item easier or harder in the target language version?	Y	N	U	NR
	12. Are there any grammatical structures in the source language version of the item that do not have parallels in the target language?	Y	N	U	NR
	13. Are there any gender or other references that might make this item be cued in the target language version?	Y	N	U	NR
	14. Are there any words in the item that, when translated, change from having one meaning to having more than one common meaning?	Y	N	U	NR
	15. Are there any changes in punctuation between the source and target versions of the item that may make the item easier or harder in the translated version?	Y	N	U	NR
Passages (if present)	16. When the passage is translated from the source language to the target language, do the words and phrases of the translated version convey similar content and ideas to the source version?	Y	N	U	NR
	17. Does the passage depict any individual or groups in a stereotypic fashion through occupation, emotion, situation, or otherwise?	Y	N	U	NR
	18. Does the passage involve writing on a controversial or inflammatory topic, or might the passage be perceived as demeaning or offensive to anyone?	Y	N	U	NR

Category	Translation and adaptation questions	Item			
	19. Does the passage include content or require skills that may be unfamiliar to some students in either of the two language or cultural groups?	Y	N	U	NR
	20. Except for necessary translations of text or labels, are graphics, tables, and other item elements the same in the source and target language versions of the item?	Y	N	U	NR
Culture	21. Have terms in the item in one language been suitably adapted to the cultural environment of the second language version?	Y	N	U	NR
	22. Are there cultural differences that would have an effect on the likelihood of a response being chosen when the item is presented in the source or target language version?	Y	N	U	NR
	23. Are measurement and currency units (distance, etc.) from the source language version of the item in the appropriate convention for the country using the target language version?	Y	N	U	NR
	24. Are the concepts covered in the item at about the same level of abstraction in the two language versions?	Y	N	U	NR
	25. Does the concept or construct of the item have about the same familiarity and meaning in both the source and target language versions?	Y	N	U	NR

Question	Explanation for rating
1	
2	
3	
4	
5	
6	
7	
8	
9	
10	
11	
12	
13	
14	
15	
16	
17	
18	
19	
20	
21	
22	
23	
24	
25	

4

Making Scientific Sense of Cultural Differences in Psychological Outcomes: Unpackaging the *Magnum Mysterium*

MICHAEL HARRIS BOND AND FONS J. R. VAN DE VIJVER

THE PROBLEM AT HAND

Culture is the elephant of Sufi legend – complicated, obscure, and ponderous, a daunting Rorschach of puzzling complexity. Kynna, a character in Renault's (2002) *Funeral Games*, confronts an alien culture with this reaction:

> Kynna kept a cheerful countenance, but felt her spirits flag. The alien speech of the passersby, the inscrutable monuments, the unknown landscape, the vanishing of all she had pictured in advance, were draining her of certainty . . . she had known that the world was vast, but at home in her native hills, it had had no meaning. Now, on the threshold of the illimitable East, she felt like a desolate in its indifferent strangeness. (p. 74)

The use of culture as a variable of interest in scientific psychology yields studies reporting arresting differences between cultural groups in whatever response is of interest to the psychologist – be it pace of life, helping behavior, public staring, physical proximity, the content of complaint letters to government officials, or apologizing. These observed differences provoke intriguing speculations about their origins. Such speculations are often embedded in "thick description" and comparison of the social systems in question, are historically informed, and consider institutionally diverse factors that may lead to the different observed outcomes. Scholars present these "explanations" with experience and insight into the cultures involved. Because most readers are novices with respect to the cultures concerned, they are persuaded by the sophisticated argumentation on offer. But is it right?

This chapter describes how we can develop and test models of cross-cultural differences. We argue that an analytical approach to culture is adequate to explain cross-cultural differences but that we should try to be as specific as possible in such explanations. Saying that a particular Chinese person has a strong family orientation (compared with a Westerner) because he or she is Chinese does not tell us much. It is more informative to say that Chinese have a strong family orientation because they have been socialized for greater dependency on the family compared with persons in Western cultures. Our approach focuses on the identification of cultural elements that can explain such cross-cultural differences; we then show how these elements perform their explanatory role.

The focus of this chapter is on explaining cross-cultural differences. Those of us socialized to deal with individuals as our unit of statistical analysis may need to redefine our orientation; we are seeking a feature of culture, not of individuals, that associates with the psychological outcome or processes that we are trying to explain. We begin this chapter by describing a hypothetical example and then present a methodological framework that allows us to test expected cross-cultural differences.

A Mundane Example: A Collision of Cultures

The first author has lived in Hong Kong for 31 years. His professional work focuses on the psychology of the Chinese people and has resulted in three English-language publications that summarize what our discipline purports to know about the Chinese people (Bond, 1986, 1991, 1996). This background qualifies him to comment on a striking cultural difference that would presumably be confirmed by any observer from an Anglo culture like the first author – namely, that the number of collisions between people in Hong Kong swimming pools is greater than that between people in any Anglo culture one might choose.

This is a rather prosaic outcome to explore, one might argue, but there have been calls in our discipline to explore the psychological factors underlying the more mundane activities and behaviors that are part of daily life for most of us (Bond, 2005). Additionally, the first author has a personal interest in this topic because he has been pummeled by errant Hong Kong Chinese swimmers on innumerable occasions during his daily exercise. We have often argued that one could approach a culture through the analysis of any behavior, so why not collisions in a swimming pool?

We could easily construct a study comparing this type of spatial intrusion. Being competent cross-culturalists, we would control for the obvious factors that increase the frequency of such uninvited physical contact – the size of the pool, the number of persons using the pool, the presence of lane markers, and even the temperature of the water. We would also develop a reliable way of assessing the frequency of collisions, which is our outcome in question. This may be more problematic, however. If members of one cultural group regard physical contact in public settings as less polite, they may show more dramatic reactions to being struck by another individual. Thus, collisions in Anglo pools may be easier to detect given the same frequency of actual contact because Anglos regard such uninvited contact as impolite, however unintended it may be. Perhaps we could solve this measurement problem by observing how frequently swimmers approach one another within a given distance.

Having surmounted these challenges to our research design, we would run the experiment and collect our data. The analysis would be a straightforward comparison between cultural groups. Being careful statisticians, we will further note that swimming pools are nested within cultures and that this factor must be controlled in assessing cultural differences, just as we must do in cross-cultural studies of individual behavior occurring in dyads, groups, classrooms, departments, and organizations.

These conceptual and design considerations must be addressed in cross-cultural research and may account for the reluctance of many psychologists to grasp the nettle of culture. As seasoned researchers, however, we have persevered, addressed the scientific niceties, and attained the Golden Fleece of ancient cross-cultural psychology – that is, a scientifically confirmed difference in our outcome of interest, in this case, swimming pool collisions. Now we must explain this difference.

Explanations for Collision

As an expert in Chinese psychology, the first author could maintain that the difference in collision frequency arises because of differences in some relevant aspect of Anglo and Chinese personalities. In other words, the typical Hong Kong person is higher or lower in trait *X*, where *X* is any belief, value, conditioned response, self-construal, type of efficacy, or personality dimension, conscious or unconscious, that can be plausibly linked to indifference about physical contact with strangers. If he stayed closer to his initial training in social psychology, he might instead maintain that Hong Kong Chinese construe the social situation differently than do Anglos. Again, this difference must lie along any dimension that can be plausibly linked to indifference about physical contact with strangers: One plausible hypothesis might be that any time the Hong Kong Chinese are in a bounded space, be it an elevator, a train compartment, a bathroom, or a swimming pool, they construe others in that same space as in-group members, whereas Anglos do not. Hence, politeness norms applying to public spaces do not apply for the Hong Kong Chinese, who are then free to treat one another as members of one big, jostling family. Whether using an explanation based on personality or social psychology, the explanation could be made even more persuasive by grounding the psychological constructs involved as a logical adaptation to the different institutional regulations and structures encountered by typical Chinese or Anglos in their life courses. After all, self-ways come from folkways, as Markus and Kitayama (2003) have reminded us.

The Scientific Assessment of Cultural Differences

Any of these educated guesses may be right; so, too, could alternatives provided by informed and creative scholars working at the interface of culture and social behavior. It is not enough in science to assert; one must also confirm. However elegant, grounded, and persuasive the assertion, it remains a hypothesis to be tested empirically. That process requires us to operationalize the psychological reflection of culture that we believe to be shaping the observed outcome in question, to establish its metric equivalence, and to link it to that outcome (Lonner & Adamopoulos, 1997). Such a scientific procedure has been called "unpackaging culture" (Whiting, 1976) and "peeling the onion" (Poortinga, van de Vijver, Joe, & van de Koppel, 1987); another elegant metaphor is "dispelling the fog of culture," because, if we execute the scientific process correctly, the unpackaging enables us to see clearly and to identify specific features of a murky, complex landscape – what could be called the *magnum mysterium* of culture.

The various explanations of collision frequency in Chinese and Anglo pools can be reduced to different methodological frames used to describe a cross-cultural difference in outcome. Such a frame identifies ways in which cultural factors and psychological outcomes are related. Two kinds of schemes are common in cross-cultural psychology. The first involves mediating variables (Baron & Kenny, 1986). Suppose that the number of collisions could be entirely explained by either a smaller size of or more swimmers in Chinese pools. The causal scheme is as follows:

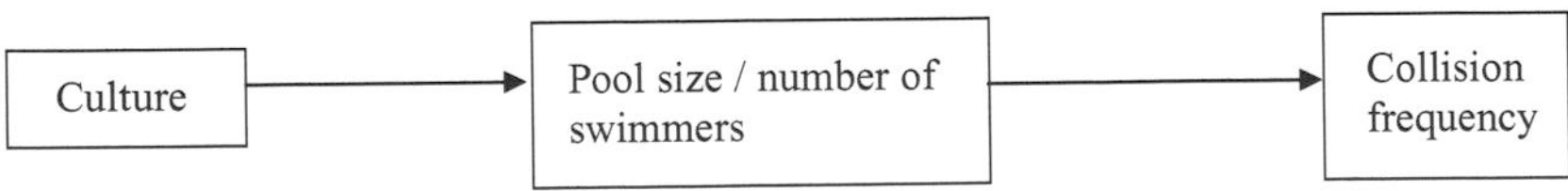

In this model, culture has an influence on pool size and number of swimmers, which in turn have an influence on collision frequency. If we control for pool size or number of swimmers, no cross-cultural difference remains.

One might want to argue that country differences in pool size also require an explanation. This reasoning would mean that there should be a box between culture and pool size in our scheme. The scheme could be made complex and possibly more realistic by adding more boxes, but the idea of a chain of explanatory variables that eventually leads to a psychological outcome should remain. If our explanatory variable is sufficient to explain all cross-cultural variation, we do not need a direct arrow from culture to collision frequency. Such a direct arrow would indicate that our mediational variable, pool size or number of swimmers, could not fully account for cross-cultural differences in collision frequency. If a direct arrow would still be significant, we would need other explanatory variables, such as norms about personal space, to unpackage the remaining cultural difference. The goal is to obtain a scheme in which a direct arrow from culture to collision frequency is no longer needed and can be replaced by an explanatory variable.

There is a common theme in all these explanations that is essential for all approaches that attempt to unpackage culture. We explain cross-cultural differences by referring to specific cultural factors, such as the acceptability of smaller personal space in Chinese culture, as explanations of differences in collision frequency between Anglo and Chinese pools. Culture is then the distal variable, which through our inquiry is replaced by more specific cultural factors. An explanation is more successful if it can statistically eliminate more of the cross-cultural difference.

In a second causal scheme, culture moderates the relationship between an input and an output variable. For example, Entwistle and Mason (1985) studied the relationship between socioeconomic status and fertility in different countries. In poorer countries, there tends to be a positive relationship between status and fertility, whereas a negative relationship is often found in richer countries. Statistically speaking, moderator effects can be modeled using interaction effects between culture and the explanatory variable – in this case, affluence.

However, an emphasis on the interaction component could detract attention from the core issue involved: A moderator indicates that the relationship between the explanatory and outcome variable varies across countries. Even if a statistical interaction could fully account for the cross-cultural variation observed, the conceptual issue of why culture and the explanatory variable interact is still not addressed. The statistical modeling, using an interaction with culture, can be successful, but the conceptual problem with the modeling is that culture has been used as a nominal or categorical variable.

Our plea to unpackage culture does not favor the use of culture as a nominal variable but is aimed at replacing the nominal (and global) concept of culture with more specific cultural factors, which usually can be measured at a more differentiated level.

It is more fruitful to view moderation as a third-variable problem. Extending our analysis of culture and fertility, we could argue that one of the reasons to have children, notably in poorer countries, is old-age security for the parents (Kagitcibasi, 2005). If we assume for the simplicity of the argument that old-age security is the only relevant third variable, a measure of this variable might be able to account for all cross-cultural differences in fertility and would enable us to model all cross-cultural variation without having to rely on culture as a moderator variable.

Contemporary Importance of Unpackaging Cultural Differences

This challenge of demystifying culture was lurking in the wings when the cross-cultural discipline was more primitive in its reach, involving simple, two-culture comparisons. The earliest stage of cross-cultural psychology was characterized by our accumulating such differences. By doing so, cross-culturalists sent continuous warning shots across the bow of the mainstream by showing that psychological outcomes were different from equivalent samples of persons socialized into different cultural traditions (Bond, 2009). These studies served an important function by providing the intellectual legitimization for continuing to do cross-cultural psychology.

However, we have moved beyond this initial stage of legitimizing the cross-cultural enterprise and shifted our emphasis from *exploring* to *explaining* cross-cultural differences. Some scholars have argued that our theorizing about how culture operates is primitive psychologically (see, e.g., Messick, 1988). Despite the dearth of available theories, the need to validate more sophisticated theorizing has become ever more pressing as the cross-cultural discipline begins producing multicountry comparisons and bicultural studies that use more sophisticated methods or procedures. Clearly, we must organize our findings theoretically before we drown in a welter of differences; we must dispel the thickening fog of culture.

TWO KINDS OF CROSS-CULTURAL STUDIES

The procedures we describe in this section outline the two broad strategies that have been developed to identify the features of culture that affect its psychologically revealing consequences. The relevant features of culture of ultimate concern to psychologists are the constructs we use to distinguish persons from one another – personality dispositions, constructions of the social situation, relational tendencies (Caralis & Haslam, 2004), and, ultimately, behavior (Bond, 2005). These constructs may themselves be derived from the more distal features characterizing the culture – its role dyads, its groups, its organizations, and its social institutions, each with its frequency of member engagement, its norms, and its regulatory strength. These in turn may derive from features of the culture's ecology and history. We have slowly begun to unravel this complex concatenation of interrelated factors and increasingly succeed in integrating these layers of influence in empirically testable ways (e.g., Gelfand, Nishii, & Raver, 2006).

The *Explicanda*

What are the "psychologically revealing consequences" of culture that we are trying to explain? For our present purposes, it is two research outcomes, what one might call the two "consequences of culture for psychologists": The first is the staple of early cross-cultural psychology mentioned earlier, that is, differences in the *level* of some psychological construct of interest shown by members from two or more cultural groups, be it holistic thinking (Nisbett, Peng, Choi, & Norenzayan, 2001), the value of integration (Bond, 1988), social dominance orientation (Pratto et al., 2000), the belief in fate control (Leung & Bond, 2004), the enactment of communal sharing across relationships (Haslam, Reichert, & Fiske, 2002), or indeed any other psychological construct thought to derive from some set of influences. We label this type of cultural consequence the *positioning effect* (Leung & Bond, 1989; van de Vijver & Leung, 1997, called these *level-oriented studies*) because different modes of socialization across the cultural groups may be regarded as raising or lowering the strength of that construct, positioning cultural groups differently with respect to one another. Thus, positioning influences the *mean score* of a culture on an instrument measuring that construct. Our goal is to "unpackage" the cultural differences by finding out what feature of culture may explain the relative positioning of cultural groups. Using our earlier example, we ask whether pool size or the number of swimmers can explain the cross-cultural differences in mean number of collisions in a pool.

The second consequence of culture is a difference in the *strength of linkage* between two constructs when comparing two or more cultural groups. Whereas the previous consequence affected the mean score of a culture, the focus here is on comparing the *correlation* of constructs within a culture across cultural groups. In the first identified cross-cultural difference of this sort, Bond and Forgas (1984) examined an actor's intention to associate with a partner whose character was varied by the experimental manipulation.

They found that willingness to associate with the other was predicted by that partner's perceived emotional stability for Australians but not for Hong Kong Chinese. The strength of connection between a dimension of person perception and its behavioral consequence was higher in one cultural group than in another. The input variable, emotional stability, was more relevant as a predictor of intentions to associate for members of one cultural group than for members of another. Two distinguishable psychological constructs, the neuroticism of a target person and intention to associate, related at different strengths in different cultural groups.

This type of cultural consequence may be labeled *linking effects* (van de Vijver & Leung, 1997, called these *structure-oriented studies*). Bond (2009) has argued that the discovery and explanation of such linkage effects distinguish the current stage of cross-cultural research as we have entered the 21st century. Such research assesses how psychological constructs influence one another *within* cultural groups, then explores their strength of linkage *across* cultural groups. Ultimately, we hope to explain scientifically why the strength of that influence varies. Such research is essential for building universal models of psychological process that include culture as one component among many influencing that outcome.

Cultural positioning effects and cultural linking effects are findings generated by doing cross-cultural research on an outcome of interest. Linking effects are more complex and require more sophisticated thinking about the dynamics driving the outcome. They are also less subject to the methodological challenges posed by cultural response styles or other sources of bias that affect all items of an instrument in a more or less uniform way. In general, studies of linking effects address correlations, which are not influenced by cross-cultural differences in mean scores. Thus, only biasing effects with an impact on correlations invalidate cross-cultural comparisons in studies of linking effects. Nonetheless, both positioning and linking effects are mere descriptions of the patterns emerging from our cross-cultural data, that is, results in search of an explanation. We now turn to the process of generating explanations for cultural effects and confirming our hypotheses empirically.

EXPLAINING CULTURAL POSITIONING EFFECTS

Two-Culture Comparisons of Positioning Effects

An outcome difference between two cultural groups was the first *explicandum* clamoring for empirical attention. Many of us cross-cultural psychologists were flushed with our early success at demonstrating cross-cultural differences in our psychological outcomes of interest and at providing plausible ex post facto explanations for them in the Discussion sections of our papers (e.g., Bond & Hewstone, 1988). Often the newsworthiness of these results was sufficient justification for their publication, so editorial boards were willing to print them despite the speculative explanations offered. Occasionally, we predicted the outcomes a priori using the available literature on culture (e.g., Leung & Bond, 1984), then explained the results by appealing to these cultural dynamics and the psychological processes we deemed to be responsible for the difference. Again, if the reasoning was sufficiently novel and embedded within a sound knowledge of the cultures involved, such cross-cultural comparisons passed muster for journal acceptance.

More seasoned mainstream critics sobered us with reminders of our ultimate scientific goal, however. Reviewing the progress of cross-cultural social psychology to that moment, Messick (1988) pointed out to us cultural enthusiasts that

> Whatever it is that we mean by culture – institutions, attitudes, personality traits, social environments, expectations, and so forth – what are the processes by means of which it influences behavior? This challenge involves an examination of what culture means psychologically, and the mechanisms and processes that express culture through action. (p. 289)

Meeting this challenge to the satisfaction of such alert skeptics required that we measure these psychological "mechanisms and processes that express culture through action." Then we had to use these measures to "lift the fog" of culture that surrounded the difference. Informed, creative social scientists could conjure up plausible explanations for almost any cross-cultural difference in outcome, but how could we validate that explanation scientifically?

An Exemplary Study?

For illustrative purposes, we focus on a study that can address the key issues involved. Kwan, Bond, and Singelis (1997) examined the average difference in life satisfaction between Americans and Hong Kong Chinese. Why were American university students more satisfied with their lives than comparable Hong Kong students? To answer any psychological "why" question involving culture, we must hypothesize about culture's impact on the psychological processes that lead to the outcome that may differ between the two cultural groups in question. All unpackaging requires such theorizing, however simple or complex it may be.

To simplify the Kwan et al. (1997) argument, we may focus on their hypothesis that being socialized into a collectivist cultural system such as that of the Chinese would lead a member of that culture to strive for and hence to achieve greater relationship harmony, compared with members of a more individualistic cultural system, such as that of Americans. Success in this life domain in turn would lead to greater life satisfaction. This argument was partly confirmed using confirmatory factor analyses and structural equation modeling: Relationship harmony predicted life satisfaction positively and equally well in both groups.

Complete Versus Incomplete Unpackaging?

The key result from Kwan et al. (1997) was the identical link between relationship harmony and life satisfaction in both countries. We had empirically confirmed our argument about the psychological importance of interpersonal support (relationship harmony) in affecting contentment with one's life (life satisfaction). However, did differing levels of relationship harmony *fully* account for the cultural difference in life satisfaction? Statistical tests revealed that they did not. They did in part but required the addition of self-esteem as a supplementary predictor to explain the cultural difference completely.

When we use single constructs to predict outcomes, sometimes we succeed in completely unpackaging the cultural difference, and sometimes we do not. Singelis, Bond, Sharkey, and Lai (1999), for example, fully unpackaged cultural differences between Americans and Hong Kong Chinese in self-embarrassability by using independent self-construal: Americans were less embarrassable through their own actions than were Hong Kong Chinese because the Americans in the study were on average more independent than the Hong Kong Chinese. When a respondent's level of independence as a psychological variable was entered into a hierarchical regression equation, the original cultural difference disappeared.

Even when not all the cross-cultural difference can be unpackaged, a study can be valuable. A supported explanation of cross-cultural differences, even if it is incomplete, is better than no explanation at all or a post hoc explanation that requires future testing. How much of the target outcome can be explained by the hypothesized psychological predictors depends on various factors. The first is the comprehensiveness of our models. The more comprehensive our models, the more we can expect to explain. The second is the specificity of the predicted variables. It is easier to predict the more focused outcome of self-embarrassability than to predict the broader concept of life satisfaction. The third is the breadth of the predictors. Broadband predictors tend to give us more statistical leverage than narrowband predictors. For example, the comprehensive variable of affluence (Georgas, van de Vijver, & Berry, 2004) tends to be a better predictor of cross-cultural differences in psychological outcomes than is the more specific variable of sex ratio.

We conclude with a caveat. We argued that the implicit aim of unpackaging culture is to account fully for country differences in psychological outcomes. There is a simple statistical way to increase the amount of variance explained – namely, by increasing the number of predictors. Our exhortation to unpackage culture is not meant as an invitation to include as many explanatory variables as possible in our studies. The choice of explanatory variables should be based on theoretical considerations. It is the combination of theoretical expectations and statistical testing of these expectations that will advance cross-cultural psychology as a field.

The Ultimate Goal of Model Development

The incompleteness of the unpackaging means we must conjure a more comprehensive model to account for the cultural difference. Our personal familiarity with the two cultural systems in question may be particularly fertile sources for ideas about which constructs are missing (Bond, 1997). Thus, Kwan et al. (1997) were inspired to add relationship harmony as a predictor of life satisfaction to the already established, pancultural link between self-esteem and life satisfaction (Diener & Diener, 1995). Similarly, Kam and Bond (2008) have added image loss, an important indigenous Chinese concept, to the well-established influence of blame judgments in predicting angry responses to being hurt. Our increasing accuracy in explaining the cultural difference thus becomes a litmus test for the success of our theorizing.

Disappearing Culture

Notice something important: If we have completely unpackaged the cultural difference by using a construct to predict the outcome, then we have effectively "made culture disappear." In this vein, Lam, Buehler, McFarland, Ross, and Cheung (2005) made cultural differences in affective forecasting disappear by unpackaging them with a culturally equivalent measure of focal thinking. As the authors concluded from their analysis, "defocused Euro-Canadians and East Asians made equally moderate affective forecasts" (p. 1296). For the purpose of their current study, there is no further mystery about the cultural difference; it has been completely explained. Such a successful application of the unpackaging approach leads to a seemingly paradoxical conclusion: Despite the significant cross-cultural difference in affective forecasting, we do not need to know a person's cultural background to predict his or her score on affective forecasting. Simply knowing the person's position on the explanatory variable is sufficient. European Canadians and East Asians with an equal standing on focal thinking have the same expected score on affective forecasting. The observed cross-cultural differences in affective forecasting are due to cross-cultural differences in focal thinking. "Explaining away" cross-cultural differences is the implicit aim of the unpackaging approach to cross-cultural psychology.

Even if we completely unpackage the cultural difference, there is no end to model elaboration, because there is always more outcome variance to predict – gender, education level, and other categorical factors may also relate to the outcome. The difference these categorical variables produce may suggest additional constructs for the model, and these categorical differences will need in turn to be unpackaged (Clark, 1987).

There are other sources of ideas about the relevant variables to incorporate into our models. Finding a cross-cultural or other categorical difference is only one source of provocation for generating new psychological constructs to include in our theorizing about outcomes of interest. After all, psychologists have long been practicing innovative science with single cultural groups, especially with that subculture known as the American college student, and generating a rich legacy. Becoming more creative in our psychologizing is a lifelong challenge for us psychologists (Bavelas, 1987), but "doing culture" exposes us to one provocative agent (Bond, 1997) in a host of many stimulants for creative thought (Perkins, 2000).

The Comparison of Positioning Effects Across Many Countries

Our *explicandum* in this case is differences across a large number of cultural groups in the level of some psychological outcome, be it the social axiom of religiosity (Leung & Bond, 2004), the value dimension of integration (Bond, 1988), the length of felt emotion (Wong & Bond, 2002), the size of gender stereotypes (Williams & Best, 1990), the pace of life (Levine &

Norenzayan, 1999), or helping behavior (Levine, Norenzayan, & Philbrick, 2001). Just as with two-culture differences, these differences cry out for explanations that are scientifically persuasive. Attaining that scientific Grail requires the availability of a culture-level metric that may be theoretically connected to the outcome of interest. Producing such culture-level metrics may be considered a second stage of cross-cultural work (Bond, 2009) and is continuing apace into this century.

Dimensions of Cultural Variation

In terms of money, time, energy, coordination costs, and other human resources, it is relatively easy to conduct a two-culture study. By contrast, orchestrating a study involving many countries is a labor of Herculean proportions and not advisable for anyone just starting out in academe. Fortunately, we can now benefit from the extant mapping of cultures, usually national groups, that has been stimulated by those founding heroes of a second stage in cross-cultural research – Sawyer (1967) and Hofstede (1980). They gave us, respectively, dimensions of "hard" or "soft" cultural variation, in which "hard" dimensions refer to those extracted from ecological, demographic, economic, medical, political, or social features of a cultural system and "soft" to those extracted from psychological measures such as values, beliefs, or self-efficacy (Schwarzer, 1993) and other dimensions of personality (see Smith, Bond, & Kagitcibasi, 2006, chap. 4, for a fuller recounting of such measures). These dimensions can then be used to pry open the portals of culture.

Unilevel and Multilevel Studies

If we look at the level of data that are commonly employed in cross-cultural psychology, three kinds of designs to unpackage cross-cultural differences can be distinguished. The first employs data at the individual level. For example, a questionnaire about family orientation has been administered in various countries, and the researcher assumes that cross-cultural differences in family orientation are influenced by modernity. Therefore, a questionnaire related to modernity has also been administered. It is a characteristic feature of these designs that both the dependent variable (family orientation) and the explanatory variable (modernity) have been collected at the individual level. The statistical analysis needs to address the question, "To what extent can cross-cultural differences in family orientation be accounted for by differences in individual levels of modernity?" Covariance analysis could be used to answer this question: Country is the independent variable, family orientation is the dependent variable, and modernity is the covariate. Assuming that the cross-cultural differences in family orientation were significant, the covariance analysis will tell us to what extent modernity can account for these differences. An alternative to covariance analysis is hierarchical regression analysis. Modernity is used to predict family orientation. The size of the cross-cultural differences in the latter is compared before and after the regression analysis.

The second type of analysis to unpackage differences in levels uses a combination of individual- and culture-level data. For example, data on family orientation and modernity are collected at the individual level, whereas additional country data are available on, for example, Hofstede's dimensions. Multilevel models are able to combine the individual- and culture-level data in a single analysis (Goldstein, 2003; Hox, 2002; Raudenbush & Bryk, 2002; see also Chapter 11 by Nezlek). Such an analysis could address the questions of to what extent the relation between family orientation and modernity varies across countries (an individual-level analysis) and how a country's level of modernity influences this relationship (a country-level analysis).

The third type of analysis deals with country-level data. Correlation- and covariance-based techniques can be used, such as Pearson correlations, regression analysis, and path analysis. Publications that attempt to understand the cross-cultural patterning of country means often employ two sets of data. The first set is formed by country-level indicators such as gross national product, educational expenditure, and life expectancy. Large international institutions such as the World Bank, the United Nations, and the World Health Organization have online databases available. Examples of relevant sites are http://www.worldbank.org, http://www.unesco.org, http://www.oecd.org, and http://www.who.org. These indicators are usually complemented by average scores of a cultural group's members on psychological variables reported in the literature. Leung and Bond (2004) have termed such a measure a *citizen score*, because it represents the typical level of that psychological construct among the members of the cultural system, usually a nation. The database with citizen scores is growing each year. Leung and Bond (2004) produced 40 citizen scores for the social axiom of religiosity, Bond (1988) produced 22 citizen scores for the value dimension of integration, Wong and Bond (2002) produced 30 citizen scores for the length of felt emotions, Williams and Best (1990) produced 30 citizen scores for the size of the difference in gender stereotypes, Levine and Norenzayan (1999) produced 33 citizen scores for the pace of life, and Levine et al. (2001) produced 23 citizen scores for helping behavior. Thus, whichever statistic of association we use, the number of pairs being related is the number of cultural groups in the study.

Correlation analyses have been reported most frequently. For example, Wong and Bond (2008) found that the length of felt emotion among the citizens of a nation correlated negatively with Schwartz's culture-level value of intellectual autonomy. This finding was consistent with their argument about the opposition between a society's emphasis on intellectual freedom and the interference of an individual's thought by disruptive emotional experience. Similarly, Levine and Norenzayan's (1999) citizen score for pace of life correlated strongly with a culture's level of affluence, a finding consistent with the hypothesis that time becomes money to be used judiciously in wealthier social systems.

A correlation of any sort assesses the linear relation between the relevant constructs. It is the most basic pattern of relationship tested in psychological theorizing. Other patterns, such as the famous U-curve, are possible, and may be tested using quadratic equations. Some sophisticated theorizing now involves the interaction of two cultural features in predicting a given cultural outcome (e.g., van de Vliert, Huang, & Levine, 2004). Regardless of the complexity of the model relating its constructs, the statistic used to test a model is determined by the hypothesized nature of the relationship being tested.

The Yield From Successful Unpackaging

No experiments are possible with cultures, and thus no causal statements can be made with scientific certainty about the relationship between features of culture and psychological outcomes. We can nonetheless embed these culture-level findings within a model of how culture exercises an influence on the given outcome. We can then use this model to inspire our thinking about the processes that drive the outcome at the individual level. Thus, for example, if cultural affluence is linked to citizen pace of life, then we may use this knowledge to speculate that feelings of time pressure may be a crucial individual-level variable driving a person's speed of walking or interpersonal exchanges. Being socialized into more affluent societies may result in more members of that society feeling more time pressure, a positioning of time pressure that may then account for the generally greater pace in such societies. Again, the Golden Fleece for which we strive when doing culture-level studies of positioning effects is to provoke the development of more comprehensive theory for these outcomes of interest. This theorizing can then be tested at the individual level of analysis.

Explaining Cultural Linking Effects

The *explicandum* for linking effects is not a difference across cultures in the *level* of a psychological outcome; it is the difference across cultures in the *strength of connection* between two variables in the model predicting that outcome. It is important to remember that in both these cases of unpackaging, we are testing a model by measuring the constructs involved and assessing whether the relationship among these constructs supports our theorizing. In the case of linking effects, our model grapples with the puzzle of why a feature of culture is more relevant for members of one cultural group than another, that is, why do we have a linking effect with these constructs? As before, we begin with two-culture comparisons, then move to multicountry comparisons in which we will discover that the scientific yield is much greater.

Two-Culture Comparisons

Let us refer back to our discussion of unpackaging a difference in the level of a psychological outcome across two cultural groups. We can use covariance analysis, multiple regression, or structural equation modeling to do so. When doing this unpackaging, we sometimes discover that some of the linkages among constructs in the two-culture model are of unequal strength. Thus, for example, Singelis et al. (1997) found that independent self-construal interacted with culture and was relatively more powerful in predicting self-embarrassabilty for the Americans than for the Hong Kong Chinese. This outcome implies that the model does better in the American culture in which the linkage between predictor and outcome is stronger. Although we may not have predicted such an interaction, this kind of outcome is a blessing in disguise.

Such a finding will provoke further theory development in two ways: First, it should inspire us to identify the missing construct in the second cultural group that could compensate for and make the elaborated model equally powerful in predicting self-embarrassability for both cultural groups. Such was the process leading Kwan et al. (1997) to propose relationship harmony as a supplementary construct to self-esteem that Diener and Diener (1995) had earlier found to be a relatively less powerful predictor of life satisfaction in collectivist cultural groups. Kwan et al. (1997) speculated that relationship harmony may be a relatively more powerful predictor of life satisfaction for the Hong Kong Chinese, thereby compensating for the relative weakness of self-esteem as a predictor in that culture. In this way, the cultural imbalance signaled by the interaction stimulated innovative thoughts about cultural dynamics.

Second, an interaction arising from a two-culture comparison is provocation for our thinking about the dynamics of culture in yet another way: Which aspect of cultural systems might be responsible for heightening the influence of the predictive construct in one culture compared with another? Why should self-esteem, for example, be more determinative of life satisfaction in America than in Hong Kong? What is it about social systems and socialization processes characterizing America and Hong Kong that produces a differential impact for self-esteem? One can, of course, speculate about possible candidates, but the thrust of this chapter is to use the cultural difference to focus us on conceptualizing the process involved, measuring its components, and then assessing the validity of our reasoning.

Working at the Level of Culture

We are now dealing with culture-level phenomena, that is, features of societal entities and their systems. The unit of analysis is no longer the individual but the cultural unit. To validate a stable and discriminating feature of culture that explains differences in linkage strength, we must move to multicountry samples in which we can quantify the hypothetical feature responsible for the shift in linkage strength and correlate this feature of the country with the strength of that linkage. Doing this work is predicated on having dimensionalized measures of cultural variation, a legacy of second-stage studies from cross-cultural psychology (Bond, 2009). We have already encountered these measures in considering cultural positioning effects across many cultural groups. We can now use them as aids to explain cultural linking effects in multicountry studies.

APPLICATIONS

Analysis of Covariance

The use of analysis of covariance is widespread in psychology as a tool for statistically controlling intergroup differences in background variables, such as age and education, which can confound cross-group differences in a target variable. This use of covariance analysis is also common in cross-cultural psychology. However, cross-cultural psychologists additionally use this technique to test the validity of specific explanations of intergroup differences. For example, covariance analysis can be used to examine to what extent cross-cultural differences in school achievement scores can be explained by differences in school quality. The latter variable is then the covariate; the significance and size of the cross-cultural differences are then compared before and after controlling for this covariate.

As an example, Earley (1989) was interested in the influence of individualism–collectivism on social loafing (individuals invest less effort when they work in a group than when they work alone). Americans showed more social loafing than did Chinese. After controlling for scores on individualism–collectivism as covariates, the difference in social loafing between these two groups disappeared.

Regression Analysis

The design assumes that data on a target variable and at least one explanatory variable have been measured in different cultures. The data analysis, consisting of a three-step procedure, starts with an analysis of variance to test for the presence of cultural differences in the dependent variable (cf., van de Vijver & Leung, 1997). If the *F* ratio of culture is not significant, there are no cross-cultural differences to be explained, and the analysis does not need to proceed. However, if the *F* ratio is significant, explanatory variables, which should have been measured at the individual level, are introduced in the second step (country-level explanatory variables such as gross domestic product should be tested in a multilevel model, described later). The independent variable is the explanatory variable in a regression analysis for which the target variable is the dependent variable. Residual scores are saved. In the third step, cross-cultural differences in the residual scores are tested.

To gain insight into the size of the cross-cultural differences at hand, effect sizes (eta square or omega square values) may be obtained, which are available in most statistical packages. If we call the *F* ratio of the first and third step F_{pre} and F_{post}, respectively, the analysis may show different outcomes. First, the explanatory variable may be unrelated to the cross-cultural differences, which is the case when both F_{pre} and F_{post} are significant and the effect sizes on the original and residual scores are more or less the same. Second, F_{pre} and F_{post} may be both significant, but the effect sizes have been reduced considerably. The explanatory variables then provide a partial explanation of the cross-cultural differences. Third, after the inclusion of context variables, F_{post} is no longer significant, and the effect size of the cross-cultural differences on the residual score is negligible. In this case, the cross-cultural difference has been completely unpackaged.

The cross-cultural differences in the target variable can be statistically accounted for by differences in the explanatory variable.

As an example, Poortinga (in Poortinga & van de Vijver, 1987) examined the habituation of the orienting reflex among illiterate Indian tribes and Dutch army conscripts. The amplitude of the skin conductance response, the dependent variable, was significantly larger in the Indian group. He hypothesized that intergroup differences in arousal could account for these differences. Arousal was operationalized as spontaneous fluctuations in skin conductance measured in a control condition. Cross-cultural differences in habituation of the orienting reflex then disappeared after statistically controlling for these fluctuations in a hierarchical regression analysis.

Correlation Analysis

Individual-level studies often address the question of whether a correlation has the same size in different cultures. The most simple case tests the difference of two correlations, whereas more advanced applications test the similarity of covariances, regression coefficients, or path coefficients (in structural equation modeling). As an example, Bond and Forgas (1984) found that variations in a target's level of conscientiousness led observers to trust these target persons more. The importance of conscientiousness in driving intentions to trust the other was, however, stronger for Hong Kong Chinese than for Australians. The researchers interpreted this significant difference in linkage strength as arising from collectivist cultural dynamics – in cultural systems in which institutions guaranteeing individual trustworthiness are less available, in-group members depend on one another's moral discipline to a greater extent in guiding their behavior toward that other.

Because this finding involves only two cultural groups, it is impossible to test this speculation. Hong Kong and Australia differ from one another on a host of dimensions, and it is therefore impossible to pinpoint which of these putative culture-level causes of the difference in linkage strength is responsible for the observed difference in outcome. To achieve that more satisfying conclusion, many more cultural groups than two are needed, and new statistical tools come into play.

Hierarchical Linear Modeling

Hierarchical linear (multilevel) modeling is an analytic tool used to treat data sets from various countries (at least 10) that explore the relationship between input and output variables at the individual level. It provides an assessment of the strength of relationship between the input (*X*) and the output (*Y*) variables, called Level 1 effects, but also assesses the degree to which the strength of the *X–Y* relationship varies across the cultural groups involved, called Level 2 effects. If the strength of the linkage is statistically similar across these groups, one can conclude that the *X–Y* linkage is pancultural, at least as far as this data set is concerned, and is a viable candidate for status as a universal relationship.

Culture as Relevance

If, however, we find a Level 2 effect, then we know that the *X* variable relates differently to the psychological output, *Y*, in different cultural groups, that is to say, *X* has more impact on *Y* in some cultures than in others. For example, Wong and Bond (2005) examined the effect of self-assessed control of emotional experience on the amount of self-reported verbal activity during episodes of anger. Using the Scherer, data set (Scherer, Wallbott, & Summerfield, 1986), they were able to examine the relationship between control and verbalizing in 30 of the 37 national groups meeting their numerical criterion. Across all groups, greater reported control was associated with less verbalization, a Level 1 effect. However, the Level 1 effect was qualified by a significant Level 2 effect. Thus, there was a cultural linking effect moderating the relationship between control and verbal activity for anger, such that the beta weight varied from a low of −.001 among the Portuguese to a high of −.810 among the Mainland Chinese. A respondent's culture of origin made a difference in how emotional control was translated into verbal activity during episodes of anger.

What feature of culture could account for the change in impact of control on verbal activity? Arguing that the exercise of control would be related to cultural value emphases, Wong and Bond examined the role of Schwartz's (2004) cultural value domain of hierarchy as a possible moderator of the Level 1 relationship they had discovered. They found that

> Hierarchy moderated the relationship between emotion control and verbal activity for the emotion of anger ($\beta = -.277, p < .01$). This negative relationship suggested that the stronger emphasis of hierarchy in a culture, the stronger the negative relationship between emotion control and verbal activity of individuals in anger emotion, i.e., the greater the attempt to control the verbal expression of anger in hierarchical societies, the less the verbal activity manifested. (p. 16)

What we have illustrated in this research appears to be an example of a relevance effect – in this case, a cultural relevance effect – such that, during episodes of anger, the control variable is more relevant as a suppressor of verbal activity in more hierarchical nations. How did Wong and Bond (2005) attempt to explain this cultural moderation effect? They argued that

> People in hierarchy-valuing cultures are socialized to contain their verbal expression in anger-eliciting situations in order to maintain the order created by social hierarchy. It appears that the spontaneous display of verbal expression in anger-provoking situations will create social conflicts by appearing to challenge the social hierarchy. Therefore, in cultures where social hierarchy is emphasized, there is a strong connection between emotion control and verbal expression when anger is felt, whereas such a connection is not as strong in cultures where hierarchy is less stressed. (pp. 21–22)

It is an intellectual challenge to explain such interactions, in part because interactions are always challenging but also because we cross-cultural psychologists are unused to contending with the influence of cultural as opposed to psychological variables. Organizational and educational psychologists have more experience integrating Level 2 effects into their models, because they frequently deal with smaller units at Level 2, such as companies or classrooms, respectively. However, even when these more experienced professionals build culture into their design, they find its effects a considerable challenge to explain (e.g., Fu et al., 2004).

It is worth noting that Wong and Bond (2005) examined 12 Level 1 relationships in their study. Of the 10 significant Level 1 results, 3 were qualified by an interaction with culture. The other 7 were not, instead showing pancultural effects and thus qualifying as possible universals. Thus, for example, interpersonal movement in response to anger was positively and equally related to the felt intensity of the emotion in all cultural groups. These pancultural effects, unqualified by interaction with culture, are basic building blocks in a universal psychology and provide assurance that theorizing and research conducted in one cultural system have widespread application. They are an important payoff for the investments required in organizing such multicountry research.

Cultural Features as Essential Input in Modeling Psychological Outcomes

Also important are the culturally variable relationships between predictor and outcome variables of interest. By providing such rare findings, we can begin incorporating culture into our models of psychological outcomes. Note that information about cultural features now becomes necessary in models predicting psychological outcomes. When there are no interactions with culture, then culture acts through the constructs of the model, positioning these constructs at higher or lower levels. When a cultural feature interacts with a construct in the model, however, that feature of culture becomes a necessary element in the model. Culture has not disappeared. Instead, information about the score of a cultural group on that feature becomes important in improving the predictability of the outcome across cultural groups. Culture has thereby been vindicated as an object of study by psychologists.

Complexifying Our Models

The examples in this section thus far have presented simple *X–Y* linkages of a hypothesized causal factor to a psychological outcome. The models that we test across cultures are becoming more complex. For example, Law, Bond, and Ohbuchi (2005) have developed a model for predicting the level of anger a person experiences when harmed by another. The joint proximal predictors of the target's response of anger are the degree of blame the target ascribes to the perpetrator and the amount of face loss incurred by the target. Blame in turn is driven by the target's assessment of the amount of harm done, the perpetrator's intention to harm, and the justification of the perpetrator in harming the target. Image loss in its turn is driven by the target's assessment of the amount of harm done.

In testing models of this or greater complexity across many cultural groups, structural equation modeling may be used. As a consequence of testing such models across many cultural groups, we begin to develop theories of cultural influence in which the beta weights connecting the many constructs in the model are found to vary by culture. When we have sufficiently useful measures of cultural features and sufficiently large multicountry samples, we will be able to identify those specific features of cultural systems that are reliably associated with the enhanced relevance of constructs in the model. Research with this potential is just beginning (see e.g., Matsumoto et al., 2008).

CONCLUSION

As psychologists, our lives-in-culture have been oriented toward bringing the nimbus of culture under intellectual control. For us, that control is achieved by treating what we call culture with conceptual articulation, scientific rigor, and model elaboration. This is a heroic undertaking, because it demands so much from those who venture into this mostly uncharted, still foggy night.

We have developed procedures of unpackaging to assist us in this exercise. As with all scientific procedures, their mastery serves the instrumental purpose of extending our intellectual range. For us developing cross-cultural psychologists, that intellectual range is assessed in terms of how well we build universal models in which a model is defined as the specification of constructs and their interrelationships in predicting a psychological outcome of interest.

We have found that culture exercises two effects on our models: It positions the respondents from a given culture at a higher or lower level on one of the constructs determining that outcome. Alternatively, culture moderates the impact of one construct on another in our model. This moderation must then be explained scientifically by finding some measurable feature of culture that associates with this degree of impact. The discovery of this cultural feature is crucial, because it then must be incorporated into our models of the psychological outcome to make that model more fully applicable in any given cultural group. Attaining this greater precision by embracing culture scientifically is the contemporary Golden Fleece of our Herculean labors, justifying the hardships encountered on our journeys into the *magnum mysterium.*

> The very point which appears to complicate a case is, when duly considered and scientifically handled, the one which is most likely to elucidate it.
>
> – Sherlock Holmes, *The Hound of the Baskervilles*

REFERENCES

Baron, R. M., & Kenny, D. A. (1986). The moderator–mediator variable distinction in social psychological research: Conceptual, strategic and statistical considerations. *Journal of Personality and Social Psychology, 51*, 1173–1182.

Bavelas, J. B. (1987). Permitting creativity in science. In D. N. Jackson & P. Rushton (Eds.), *Scientific excellence* (pp. 307–327). Newbury Park, CA: Sage.

Bond, M. H. (1986). *The psychology of the Chinese people.* Hong Kong: Oxford University Press.

Bond, M. H. (1988). Finding universal dimensions of individual variation in multicultural surveys of values: The Rokeach and Chinese value surveys. *Journal of Personality and Social Psychology, 55*, 1009–1015.

Bond, M. H. (1991). *Beyond the Chinese face: Insights from psychology.* Hong Kong: Oxford University Press.

Bond, M. H. (1996). (Ed.). *The handbook of Chinese psychology.* Hong Kong: Oxford University Press.

Bond, M. H. (1997). (Ed.). *Working at the interface of cultures: 18 lives in social science.* London: Routledge.

Bond, M. H. (2009). Circumnavigating the psychological globe: From yin and yang to starry, starry night. In S. Bekman & A. Aksu-Koc (Eds.), *Perspectives on human development, family, and culture* (pp. 31–49). Cambridge: Cambridge University Press.

Bond, M. H. (2005). A cultural-psychological model for explaining differences in social behavior: Positioning the belief construct. In R. M. Sorrentino, D. Cohen, J. M. Olsen, & M. P. Zanna (Eds.), *Culture and social behavior* (Vol. 10, pp. 31–48). Mahwah, NJ: Erlbaum.

Bond, M. H., & Forgas, J. P. (1984). Linking person perception to behavioral intention across cultures: The role of cultural collectivism. *Journal of Cross-Cultural Psychology, 15,* 337–352.

Bond, M. H., & Hewstone, M. (1988). Social identity theory and the perception of intergroup relations in Hong Kong. *International Journal of Intercultural Relations, 12,* 153–170.

Bond, M. H., Wan, W. C., Leung, K., & Giacalone, R. (1985). How are responses to verbal insult related to cultural collectivism and power distance? *Journal of Cross-Cultural Psychology, 16,* 111–127.

Caralis, C., & Haslam, N. (2004). Relational tendencies associated with broad personality dimensions. *Psychology and Psychotherapy: Theory, Research and Practice, 77,* 397–402.

Clark, L. A. (1987). Mutual relevance of mainstream and cross-cultural psychology. *Journal of Consulting and Clinical Psychology, 55,* 461–470.

Diener, E., & Diener, M. (1995). Cross-cultural correlates of life satisfaction and self-esteem. *Journal of Personality and Social Psychology, 68,* 653–663.

Earley, P. C. (1989). Social loafing and collectivism: A comparison of the United States and the People's Republic of China. *Administrative Science Quarterly, 34,* 565–581.

Entwistle, B., & Mason, W. M. (1985). Multi-level effects of socioeconomic development and family planning in children ever born. *American Journal of Sociology, 91,* 616–649.

Fu, P. P., Kennedy, J., Tata, J., Yukl, G., Bond, M. H., Peng, T.-K., et al. (2004). The impact of societal cultural values and individual social beliefs on the perceived effectiveness of managerial influence strategies: A meso approach. *Journal of International Business Studies, 35,* 284–305.

Gelfand, M. J., Nishii, L. H., & Raver, J. L., (2006). On the nature and importance of cultural tightness-looseness. *Journal of Applied Psychology, 91,* 1225–1244.

Georgas, J., Van de Vijver, F., & Berry, J. W. (2004). The ecocultural framework, ecosocial indices and psychological variables in cross-cultural research. *Journal of Cross-Cultural Psychology, 35,* 74–96.

Goldstein, H. (2003). *Multilevel statistical models.* London: Arnold.

Haslam, N., Reichert, T., & Fiske, A. P. (2002). Aberrant social relations in the personality disorders. *Psychology and Psychotherapy: Theory, Research and Practice, 75,* 19–31.

Hofstede, G. (1980). *Culture's consequences: International differences in work-related values.* Beverly Hills, CA: Sage.

Hox, J. (2002). *Multilevel analysis. Techniques and applications.* Mahwah, NJ: Erlbaum.

Inglehart, R., & Baker, W. E. (2000). Modernization, cultural change and the persistence of traditional values. *American Sociological Review, 65,* 19–51.

Kagitcibasi, C. (2005). Autonomy and relatedness in cultural context. Implications for self and family. *Journal of Cross-Cultural Psychology, 36,* 403–422.

Kam, C. C. S., & Bond, M. H. (2008). The role of emotions and behavioral responses in mediating the impact of face loss on relationship deterioration: Are Chinese more face-sensitive than Americans? *Asian Journal of Social Psychology, 11,* 175–184.

Kwan, V. S. Y., Bond, M. H., & Singelis, T. M. (1997). Pancultural explanations for life satisfaction: Adding relationship harmony to self-esteem. *Journal of Personality and Social Psychology, 73,* 1038–1051.

Lam, K. C. H., Buehler, R., McFarland, C., Ross, M., & Cheung, I. (2005). Cultural differences in affective forecasting: The role of focalism. *Personality and Social Psychology Bulletin, 31,* 1296–1309.

Law, R., Bond, M.H., & Ohbuchi, K. (2005). *A pancultural model for predicting the anger arising from interpersonal harm.* Manuscript submitted for publication.

Leung, K., & Bond, M.H. (1984). The impact of cultural collectivism on reward allocation. *Journal of Personality and Social Psychology, 47,* 793–804.

Leung, K., & Bond, M. H. (1989). On the empirical identification of dimensions for cross-cultural comparisons. *Journal of Cross-Cultural Psychology, 20,* 133–152.

Leung, K., & Bond, M. H. (2004). Social axioms: A model of social beliefs in multicultural perspective. In M. P. Zanna (Ed.), *Advances in experimental social psychology* (Vol. 36, pp. 119–197). San Diego, CA: Elsevier Academic Press.

Levine, R. V., & Norenzayan, A. (1999). The pace of life in 31 countries. *Journal of Cross-Cultural Psychology, 30,* 178–205.

Levine, R. V., Norenzayan, A., & Philbrick, K. (2001). Cross-cultural differences in helping strangers. *Journal of Cross-Cultural Psychology, 32,* 543–560.

Lonner, W. J., & Adamopoulos, J. (1997). Culture as antecedent to behavior. In J. W. Berry, Y. H. Poortinga, & J. Pandey (Eds.), *Handbook of cross-cultural psychology: Vol.1. Theory and method* (2nd ed., pp. 43–83). Needham Heights, MA: Allyn & Bacon.

Markus, H. R., & Kitayama, S. (2003). Culture, self, and the reality of the social. *Psychological Inquiry, 14,* 277–283.

Matsumoto, D., Yoo, S. H., Anguas-Wong, A. M., Arriola, M., Ataca, B., Bond, M. H., et al. (2008). Mapping expressive differences around the world: The relationship between emotional display rules and individualism versus collectivism. *Journal of Cross-Cultural Psychology, 39,* 55–74.

Messick, D. M. (1988). Coda. In M. H. Bond (Ed.), *The cross-cultural challenge to social psychology* (pp. 286–289). Newbury Park, CA: Sage.

Nisbett, R. E., Peng, K., Choi, I., & Norenzayan, A. (2001). Culture and systems of thought: Holistic versus analytic cognition. *Psychological Review, 108,* 291–310.

Perkins, D. (2000). *The Eureka effect: The art and logic of breakthrough thinking.* New York: Norton.

Poortinga, Y. H., & Van de Vijver, F. J. R. (1987). Explaining cross-cultural differences: Bias analysis and beyond. *Journal of Cross-Cultural Psychology, 18*, 259–282.
Poortinga, Y. H., Van de Vijver, F. J. R., Joe, R. C., & Van de Koppel, J. M. H. (1987). Peeling the onion called culture: A synopsis. In C. Kagitcibasi (Ed.), *Growth and progress in cross-cultural psychology* (pp. 22–34). Berwyn, PA: Swets North America.
Pratto, F., Liu, J. H., Levin, S., Sidanius, J., Shih, M., Bachrach, H., & Hegarty, P. (2000). Social dominance orientation and the legitimization of inequality across cultures. *Journal of Cross-Cultural-Psychology, 31*, 369–409.
Raudenbush, S. W., & Bryk, A. S. (2002). *Hierarchical linear models: Applications and data analysis methods* (2nd ed.). Thousand Oaks, CA: Sage.
Renault, M. (2002). *Funeral games.* New York: Vintage.
Sawyer, J. (1967). Dimensions of nations: Size, wealth, and politics. *American Journal of Sociology, 73*, 145–172.
Scherer, K. R., Wallbott, H. G., & Summerfield, A. B. (Eds.) (1986). *Experiencing emotion: A cross-cultural study.* Cambridge, MA: Cambridge University Press.
Schwartz, S. H. (2004). Mapping and interpreting cultural differences around the world. In V. Vinken, J. Soeters, & P. Ester (Eds.), *Comparing cultures: Dimensions of culture in a comparative perspective* (pp. 43–73). Leiden, The Netherlands: Brill.
Schwarzer, R. C. (1993). *Measurement of perceived self-efficacy. Psychometric scales for cross-cultural research.* Berlin: Freie Universitat.
Singelis, T. M., Bond, M. H., Sharkey, W. F., & Lai, S. Y. (1999). Unpackaging culture's influence on self-esteem and embarrassability: The role of self-construals. *Journal of Cross-Cultural Psychology, 30*, 315–341.
Smith, P. B., Bond, M. H., & Kagitcibasi, C. (2006). *Understanding social psychology across cultures.* London: Sage.
Van de Vijver, F. J. R., & Leung, K. (1997). *Methods and data analysis for cross-cultural research.* Newbury Park, CA: Sage.
Van de Vliert, E., Huang, X., & Levine, R. V. (2004). National wealth and thermal climate as predictors of motives for volunteer work. *Journal of Cross-Cultural Psychology, 34*, 62–71.
Whiting, B. B. (1976). The problem of the packaged variable. In K. A. Riegel & J. F. Meacham (Eds.), *The developing individual in a changing world* (Vol. 1, pp. 303–309). The Hague, NL: Mouton.
Williams, J., & Best, D. (1990). *Sex and psyche: Gender and self viewed cross-culturally.* Newbury Park, CA: Sage.
Wong, S., & Bond, M. H. (2002, August). Measuring emotionality across cultures: Self-reported emotional experiences as conceptualizations of self. In R. G. Craven, H. W. Marsh & K. B. Simpson (Eds.), *Self-concept research: Driving international research agendas.* Presented at the Self-concept Enhancement and Learning Facilitation (SELF) Research Centre International Conference, Sydney. Retrieved April 20, 2010, from http://www.self.ox.ac.uk/Conferences/2002_CD_Wong_&_Bond.pdf.
Wong, S., Bond, M. H., & Rodriguez Mosquera, P. M. (2008). The influence of cultural value orientations on self-reported emotional expression across cultures. *Journal of Cross-Cultural Psychology, 39*, 224–229.

5

Sampling: The Selection of Cases for Culturally Comparative Psychological Research

KLAUS BOEHNKE, PETRA LIETZ, MARGRIT SCHREIER, AND ADALBERT WILHELM

INTRODUCTION

Sampling is at the core of data collection, and a plethora of techniques and procedures have been described in the literature. Opinion polls and social science surveying are at the forefront of research and practical applications in this context. Despite a multitude of handbook articles (e.g., Schuman & Kalton, 1985) and – much rarer – textbook chapters (Häder & Gabler, 2003), the *lege artis* sampling of participants for psychological research remains a neglected topic. Among psychologists, commonsense convictions about the importance of the sampling topic range from implicitly declaring the question irrelevant for the discipline to accepting as sound science only studies that employ a rigid probability sampling approach.

Adherents to the first conviction base their view on the belief that all human beings are members of one and only one population. They argue that one simply needs to pick any member of this population and by default will have a "good" sample. This view is supported by work on measurement and factorial invariance (Meredith, 1964, 1993). Especially in the context of cross-cultural research, the Meredith selection theorem is used to argue that issues of sampling can be treated with lower priority because of the invariance of the underlying indicator-to-construct relations that exist under mild conditions on the selection procedure (Selig, Card, & Little, 2007). At the same time, there is a pragmatic component to the argument: Because the population consists of all human beings, it is practically impossible to create a complete sampling frame and draw a random sample without auxiliary information. Today most experimental general psychology and some experimental social psychology research take a convenience sampling approach, without, however, explicitly saying so (Howitt & Cramer, 2005; Owusu-Bempah & Howitt, 2000).

The counter-position states that only a random probability sample is a good sample. Adherents to this stance frequently refer to the classic chapter on sampling by Schuman and Kalton (1985) in the *Handbook of Social Psychology* (Lindsey & Aronson, 1985). By drawing a probability sample, the decision of who is selected as a case for a particular study does not rest in the hands of the researcher, but chance determines membership in the sample. It is assumed that probability sampling yields a sample that is representative of a previously specified population and that only such a representative sample allows for generalizing of results to the population.

In this chapter, we present these two extreme positions in more detail and try to reconcile them in the practical realm of (cross-)cultural psychological research. In this field, sampling is relevant not only at the micro-level of individuals but also at the macro-level of cultures. The typical situation in (cross-)cultural psychology requires selection of a number of cultures with a specific purpose or criterion in mind, which is only then followed by the selection of individuals within each culture. Sampling at the level of cultures typically involves yet another sampling strategy: purposive sampling. In this case, the goal is not necessarily to achieve a representative sample but one that satisfies other criteria related to the purpose of the study.

We first describe three sampling strategies in more detail (random, non-systematic, and purposive) and then take a closer look at the implications of sampling at the levels of culture and of the individual. Next, these general considerations are applied to cross-cultural psychology in particular. After an overview of the sampling strategies commonly employed in cross-cultural research, suggestions are made to optimize sampling at the individual and the cultural level.

SAMPLING: SOME KEY CONCEPTS

In psychology, the need for sampling arises for two reasons: cost and accessibility. A census of all human beings (even within a specific culture) is impossible because not all members are easily accessible, and in addition, the population is too large to be studied with a reasonable amount of money and time. Thus, it is straightforward to select a group of participants with the aim of having a sample that yields a fair representation of the population. A second quality criterion for sampling is the precision or accuracy of the sample estimates for the population characteristics under investigation. Probability samples are seen as the gold standard in both respects, and convenience sampling (the most typical form of nonsystematic sampling) is often viewed critically because of its potential to produce unrepresentative samples. In the most general terms, convenience sampling is discarded because it has huge potential to produce biased samples. The beauty of probability sampling is that the preferences of the researcher do not play a role in correctly designed and implemented probability samples because the case selection mechanism is governed solely by chance.

A crucial source of misunderstanding becomes clear here: Preventing sample bias is considered a means toward achieving the goal of representativeness. This, however, need not necessarily be the case. Although probability sampling clearly eliminates bias due to researcher preferences, a randomly generated sample may still not be representative. Moreover, the elusive term of *representativeness* can mean many things besides its primary connotation of providing "a fair representation of a population."

In this section, we give a description of three approaches to sampling and elicit the underlying rationale concerning representativeness. A summary overview of the various types of sampling is provided in Table 5.1.

Probability Sampling

Simple random sampling (SRS) is the purest form of probability sampling. It is often used in its own right but also forms the core random ingredient for other, more complex probability sampling schemes. Researchers using SRS define a population of individuals they want to study and then draw up a sampling frame, which is basically a listing of all individuals within the population. From the sampling frame, individuals are then randomly selected in a manner that ensures every member of the population has an equal chance of entering the sample. SRS is thus an equal probability selection method (epsem) (Barnett, 2002) in which any of the samples of size n drawn from a population of size N (N choose n) has the same probability of occurring.

SRS can be performed in various ways – for example, by drawing units randomly from "an urn," the common metaphor for a full list of the population under scrutiny, by drawing every so-and-so-manieth unit from a randomized list (this is usually called *systematic random sampling*; Neuman, 2006), or by following a randomly determined "visiting scheme" of sampling units (*random route* procedures).

Although giving each member of the population the same probability to be chosen for the sample makes intuitive sense with respect to representativeness following the democratic principle of one (wo)man, one vote, a close look at the second part of the epsem casts doubt on the representativity of simple random samples. Because all possible samples of the same

Table 5.1. *Types of sampling*

Type of sampling	Definition
Probability sampling	Sample selection by random procedure
• Simple random sampling	A sampling frame of all units in the population is constructed from which cases are randomly selected in a manner that ensures every member of the population has an equal chance of entering the sample.
• Multistage sampling	A simple random sampling procedure is applied twice in succession. For instance, in a first step, 50 cities are selected randomly from among all German cities. In a second step, 50 individuals from each of these 50 cities are randomly selected; they constitute the final sample.
• Cluster sampling	In a first step, a number of higher level units are selected by means of simple random sampling (e.g., 10 Grade 8 classes from schools in a given city). In a second step, all members of these units are included in the sample.
• Stratified sampling	If it is known that a given factor has an effect on the phenomenon under study (e.g., religious affiliation), the population is divided into strata before sampling, with each stratum corresponding to a value of that factor (e.g., a specific religious affiliation). Units are then selected randomly from each stratum. The number of units per stratum can be either proportional or disproportional to the percentage of units from the population in each stratum.
Nonsystematic sampling	Sample selection according to availability
• Convenience sampling	Units from the population that happen to be available to the researcher are included in the sample (e.g., by including those countries in a study where a researcher knows colleagues who are working on a similar topic).
• Quota sampling	As in stratified sampling, the population is first divided into strata. However, the selection of units from each stratum occurs by convenience, not randomly.
Purposive sampling	Sample selection is performed according to the information richness of cases.
• By type of case	Cases are selected according to the extent to which they manifest the phenomenon of interest. These sampling strategies involve selection on the dependent variable, and they require previous knowledge about the phenomenon under study.
– Typical case sampling	Units that are considered to be typical of the population are included in the sample (e.g., two countries from the ex-communist region that manifest survival and secular–rational values to the same degree as do most other countries in that region).

Type of sampling	Definition
– Extreme case sampling	Units that manifest the phenomenon of interest either to an unusually high or an unusually low degree are included in the sample (e.g., countries from the ex-communist region that manifest either an unusually high or an unusually low degree of survival and of secular–rational values compared with other countries in that region).
– Intensive case sampling	Units that manifest the phenomenon of interest to a high but not an unusually high degree are included in the sample (e.g., countries from the ex-communist region that manifest a high but not unusually high degree of survival and of secular–rational values compared with other countries in that region).
– Deviant case sampling	Units that are in some way unusual and that deviate from the norm are included in the sample (e.g., countries from the ex-communist region that are high on survival and low on secular–rational values compared with other countries in that region).
– Critical case sampling	Units that can be considered paradigmatic of the phenomenon of interest are included in the sample (e.g., a country such as Russia that epitomizes the ex-communist region).
• By sample composition	
– Homogeneous sampling	The sample is selected to consist of units that manifest the phenomenon of interest to a similar degree (e.g., persons high on empathy).
– Heterogeneous sampling	The sample is selected to consist of units that manifest the phenomenon of interest to varying degrees. A sample consisting of two contrasting cases (one person high and one person low on empathy) constitutes a special type of heterogeneous sample.
• By sampling procedure	
– Stratified purposive sampling	As in stratified sampling, relevant factors and strata are identified before sampling. Selection of units within each cell usually occurs by convenience, and each cell is filled only by a small number of units (this may be as small as $n = 1$).
– Theoretical sampling	Factors that influence the phenomenon of interest are identified in the course of ongoing research. Units are selected to be alternately high or low on these factors.
– Snowball sampling	Members of the population under study are contacted and requested to name other members of the population who might be willing to participate in the study. This sampling strategy is especially useful with hard-to-reach populations (drug users, elites, etc.).

size have the same probability to be chosen, a sample in which all members are White Anglo-Saxon males is – according to the logic just noted – considered as representative for the American society as a sample that matches exactly the gender and ethnic proportions in the population. SRS prevents obvious mistakes in representativeness, but it does not necessarily promote representativeness in all respects. This is the reason for the development of more complex sampling schemes such as stratified or multistage samples.

The major advantage of probability sampling – with SRS as its simplest form – is that the probability sampling scheme facilitates statistical analysis. When using a probability sample, we can at least conceptually consider the effect of different samples on the characteristic of interest. The random selection mechanism provides us with the means to quantify the impact of repeatedly taking samples on the estimators of interest. It is this replicability of sampling that is crucial for accuracy and precision in studying any sample. Nonsystematic samples (such as convenience samples) lack any objective sampling principle that lends itself to obtaining repeated estimates of a known accuracy of the population characteristic of interest. Repetition, in this context, is important because all estimates have known errors, but through the process of obtaining repeated estimates, the researcher gets closer to obtaining a value for the "true" population characteristic of interest. The statistical operationalization of "unbiasedness" also depends on the concept of replicability and on the knowledge of the probability distribution for all possible samples of a fixed size. It is this accessibility to the statistical machinery and logic that makes probability sampling – and, in particular, SRS – so attractive. From a statistical perspective, SRS is an ideal to which any other sampling scheme is compared. Nonsystematic samples are often disqualified because they do not lend themselves to a direct comparison with SRS.

Nonetheless, SRS also has some obvious shortcomings: Quite often, a population is divided into natural groups (such as women and men, extroverts and introverts, etc.), and the intuitive understanding of representativeness asks for a sample that "represents" these groups and their characteristics. In other words, the information about the various natural groups and their proportion in the population should be integrated into the sampling plan. This is achieved by stratified sampling: Stratified sampling limits the random process to each natural group within the population and combines the benefits of probability sampling with the auxiliary information on the stratification variables. Compared with SRS, stratified samples have potentially three advantages: (a) stratification may result in more efficient estimations of the population characteristics, (b) stratification increases representativeness of the sample because certain characteristics of the population are exactly matched by the design of the sample, and (c) stratification can lead to an improved accessibility of the sample. Sampling frames may actually be available only for the individual strata and not for the total population. Thus, for example, it might be possible to create a sampling frame based on the amount of school funding for government schools, for which information about finances is usually accessible, but not for private schools, for which such information is usually less easily accessible.

Even more complex sampling schemes such as cluster sampling or multistage sampling are likewise informed by the goals of accessibility and representativity. The idea is to incorporate additional information about the population to make the practical sampling process easier and cheaper and to improve the representativeness of the sample. The good news is that in many instances, the administrative improvements also lead to more efficient estimations, as in the case of the stratified sample. More details on multistage sampling can be found in Lehtonen and Pahkinen (1995).

Representativeness and statistical analysis are closely connected in all investigations that seek to make statements about the social entities (populations) from which the samples are drawn. In social surveys, we are usually interested in "the big picture," that is, the attitude and behavior of the group and not of a single individual. The population characteristic of interest is usually an average, a total, or a specific ratio that relates in some way to the average behavior of the average person in an average situation. Probability sampling is tailored to provide adequate information about such population characteristics and yields excellent results within this paradigm.

Nonsystematic Sampling

In the face of all the advantages of random sampling, why do psychologists nevertheless frequently work with nonsystematic samples, especially convenience samples? The main reason may be accessibility. Probability samples require a correct sampling frame at some level, and usually collecting information from randomly selected individuals is cost- and time-intensive. Moreover, psychological research often takes place in laboratory settings, and it is usually difficult to get random samples of the population to a particular place. Researchers back their pragmatic choice of sampling by substantive arguments. Usually, proponents of this research approach attempt to safeguard their studies against sample selectivity allegations by pointing to the fact that they are using subject randomization as an element of their study design. This means they distribute their conveniently selected subjects at random to an experimental or a control group. This strategy rules out a biased distribution of study participants to one or the other condition, but it does not eliminate the possibility that the entire sample of a study is biased or that effects shown in the experiment are found only in a particular conveniently selected sample. However, we have to consider two types of validity here: internal and external validity. A random distribution of subjects, sampled in whatever way, across an experimental and a control group helps make the study internally valid in the sense of neutralizing the effects of potential confounding factors. The sampling issue per se, however, pertains to external validity, that is, the extent to which the results of the study can be generalized to other members of the same population.

As pointed out earlier, the benefit of probability sampling is the availability of adequate statistical analyses, which goes hand in hand with representativeness for studies on social phenomena. Psychological research, however, is often more individualistic, focusing on special situations and contexts. Many psychologists are not interested in generalizing from the sample to the population in statistical terms, as, for example, in the following question: How many people are high, medium, or low on empathy? Their interest tends to be on testing a theory about empathy; for instance, a theory concerning the relation between certain child-rearing practices and the degree of empathy. From such a theory, one could predict that persons who were raised in an authoritarian fashion are lower on empathy in later life than those who were raised according to more "democratic" principles. Whereas the survey researcher would be interested in absolute values of empathy, the psychologist is often concerned with the relationship between the empathy scores of those raised according to authoritarian principles and those raised according to more democratic principles. Many psychologists would not be concerned with drawing conclusions about the distribution of the variable (e.g., empathy) in the population but with the relationship between two variables, which is assumed to hold across varying levels of both variables, that is, with drawing conclusions about the theory (i.e., whether the relationship between the empathy scores in the two groups follows the predicted pattern). This latter type of generalization has also been termed *generalization to a theory* (or *analytic generalization*).

Here the main concern is with the use of the experimental procedure involving the randomized assignment of participants to the experimental and control groups, thus ensuring the internal validity of the study. External validity is taken for granted under the assumption that, if humankind is the population, any member of that population is by definition representative; the exact sampling procedure is thus only of secondary importance. If a higher degree of external validity is considered desirable, convenience sampling can be extended to use additional information much in the same way as SRS is extended in stratified sampling. This sampling procedure is known as *quota sampling* and is widely used in market research and opinion surveys. As in stratified sampling, some strata are chosen to ensure representativity of the sample. However, instead of using a fully random procedure to determine sampling units within each stratum, interviewers and instructors are allowed to use personal choice and preferences to fill the required quota for each stratum. Hence, the principles of probability sampling can no longer be applied, and the effect of nonresponse can lead to a large bias. However, empirical evidence shows that quota sampling often works extremely well, despite its theoretical shortcomings (Walter, 1989).

Purposive Sampling

Because of the close association between strategies of random sampling and probability theory, the term *sampling* is often seen as pertaining exclusively to the quantitative research paradigm in psychology. Hence, researchers who prepare studies within the qualitative research paradigm sometimes reject the use of the term for the acquisition of participants to their research because of this connotation (see Denzin, 1997) and prefer to use the term *case selection* (Curtis, Gesler, Smith, & Washburn, 2000; Gobo, 2004). Case selection, however, is a more specific term that has been introduced in the context of the case study design, referring to an in-depth examination of a few instances of a phenomenon (Yin, 2003). Moreover, as in quantitative research, the qualitative researcher is faced with the situation of being unable to study every single member of the population of interest and having to select some members for empirical research. Thus, despite the terminological difficulties some qualitative researchers have with the term "sampling," it has recently become the generally applied term when discussing the strategies and techniques used for case selection in a psychological study, regardless of whether the study takes a qualitative or a quantitative methodological approach (Gobo, 2004; Quinn Patton, 2002).

Researchers engaging in qualitative studies are usually not concerned with generalizing to a population. Their research interests are more likely to focus either on the detailed description of a few instances of a phenomenon of interest (e.g., a few persons especially high in empathy) or on generating a theory about a phenomenon. Hence, they rarely use probability sampling techniques. They sometimes resort to convenience sampling, arguing that for the variables under scrutiny in their research, a small nonprobability sample is fully sufficient (Barlow & Hersen, 1984). More typically, however, case selection in qualitative research will be guided by the relevance of a case for a given research topic (Flick, 1998; Quinn Patton, 2002). This latter type of sampling for relevance is called *purposive sampling*. Its uses are by no means limited to the qualitative research paradigm where it originated but extend to all empirical studies in which representativeness of the sample cannot be achieved either by a nonsystematic convenience sampling strategy (because different members of the population yield different information) or by following a random sampling strategy (e.g., because the sample is so small that bias is likely to result despite the random procedure).

Because sampling in small *N* and qualitative research has been a neglected topic for so long, strategies of purposive sampling have been described and classified in many ways. The most common classification criterion refers to the type of case included in the sample (Quinn Patton, 2002). Cases can be such that they exemplify a given phenomenon of interest in a typical way (*typical case sampling*), they can exemplify the phenomenon to an extreme or to a considerable extent (*extreme* and *intensive case sampling*), they may in some way be unusual or contrast with the ways in which the phenomenon is usually present (*deviant case sampling*), or they may be of particular importance in the specific context (*critical case sampling*). A second criterion refers to the composition of the sample: The sample can consist of similar (*homogeneous sample*) or of contrasting cases (*heterogeneous sample*). Sample composition is closely related to the study purpose and the logic underlying the sampling strategy (discussed subsequently).

A third criterion concerns the procedure of sample selection (Johnson, 1990). Most sampling strategies work in such a way that as a first step, a decision is made concerning the composition of the sample, and then as a second step, the members of the sample are selected. This is also the strategy underlying many of the sampling procedures described in the previous sections. In stratified sampling (and likewise in quota sampling), for instance, the initial decision relates to the strata and the proportion to which they should be represented in the sample; a second step involves selecting members from each stratum. Such stratification strategies have also been used in purposive sampling (Kelle & Kluge, 1999). Here the first step consists of determining which factors are likely to affect the phenomenon of interest (with empathy, this might be a person's gender, the way in which a person was raised, etc.); the identification of such factors derives from previous knowledge about the phenomenon. On this basis, a sampling guide is constructed that specifies which factor combinations are to be included in the sample. In a second step, cases are selected that exemplify these factor combinations (e.g., women who were raised in an authoritarian manner, etc.). Whereas in SRS and convenience sampling, each factor combination is usually represented by a large number of cases, in *stratified purposive sampling*, there will be only a few cases per combination, sometimes only one. Other purposive sampling strategies, such as typical or extreme case sampling, also proceed such that a decision about the sample composition precedes sample selection.

In contrast to random and convenience sampling, in purposive sampling, strategies exist that work in a data-driven manner, that is, the composition of the sample and the criteria underlying the composition gradually emerge from the process of sample selection. The best known sampling strategy of this type is *theoretical sampling*, which was developed in the framework of grounded theory (e.g., Strauss & Corbin, 1998). As a first step, a few similar cases are selected. In a second step, some variation is introduced, and if this variation affects the phenomenon of interest, it is subsequently elaborated on by selecting additional cases. Other strategies that are characterized according to the procedure employed in sample selection include *snowball sampling*, in which one member of the population refers the researcher to other members, who in turn name still more members until a sample of sufficient size has been achieved (Neuman, 2006; Quinn Patton, 2002).[1] *Sequential sampling* (in which new cases are added on the basis of information obtained from previous cases; Neuman, 2006) constitutes a similar strategy. Both snowball and sequential sampling are especially useful strategies if the targeted population is difficult to reach. These types of populations are often found in the higher (top managers, politicians, etc.) or lower (drug users, homeless persons, etc.) strata of society; here the person who refers the researcher to other members of the population who might be willing to participate in the study acts as a gatekeeper.

[1] Snowballing techniques need not be restricted to the purposive sampling paradigm, in which a purposively selected case refers the researcher to another case on grounds of substantive considerations; these techniques can also be applied under the convenience sampling scheme, when, for example, a haphazardly selected study participant is requested to hand another copy of the study instrument to someone of his or her choice. One could even think of using a snowballing technique in probability sampling by, for example, asking a randomly selected study participant to phone the third-next person following his or her own phonebook entry and ask that person to participate in the study.

As we pointed out earlier, purposive sampling is usually not suitable for describing the distribution of a variable across a population and does not allow the researcher to generalize from the sample to the population. More often, the researcher will be interested in providing an in-depth description of a particular kind of case – for instance, a person who has displayed an unusual degree of empathy. The researcher would then be interested in obtaining an intensive, perhaps even extreme, case in terms of empathy. With a single case, however, there is always the danger that characteristics of the type of case (such as unusual degrees of empathy) are confounded with characteristics of this individual case. An analysis that is based on two or three cases that exemplify the phenomenon of interest would hence provide the researcher with a stronger basis for the purpose of case description than the examination of only one case. Therefore, the researcher would most likely select a few similar cases – that is, a homogeneous sample – and would expect these cases to yield similar results. The logic underlying this strategy of case selection has been termed the *logic of literal replication* (Yin, 2003).

The logic of literal replication has been used not only in research with a purely descriptive purpose but also in studies with an explanatory purpose in which the relationship between variables is at issue (e.g., which factors contribute to high degrees of empathy in adult life); explanatory designs making use of this logic have also been said to follow the *method of agreement* (Ragin, 1989). However, especially in an explanatory context, these designs have also been criticized on methodological grounds: As a rule, explanation requires some degree of variation. The result, for instance, that persons high on empathy were raised in a democratic family climate tells the researcher little if some persons low on empathy were similarly raised. Although the logic of literal replication eliminates such variation, the *logic of theoretical replication* (*method of difference*; Ragin, 1989; Yin, 2003) serves precisely to introduce variation into the design that permits explanation even on the basis of a small number of cases. To explore the relationship between the variables of interest, some similar cases are included in a first step and then, in a second step, contrasted with cases that differ on selected factors (e.g., persons who were raised in an authoritarian and persons who were raised in a democratic fashion, with their levels of empathy as the study variable). The strategies of purposive stratified sampling and theoretical sampling both follow this line of reasoning. The goal here is similar to that which is sometimes pursued with convenience sampling: to generalize to a theory on the basis of the variations of the relationships between variables of interest. Sample size, however, will usually be much smaller with purposive than with convenience sampling, and a statistical analysis of the data is thus typically not an option.

A special subtype of small-*N* research employing purposive sampling strategies is constituted by case study research (Ragin & Becker, 1992; Yin, 2003). Small-*N* research tends to be "small" compared with most quantitative research, working with samples of perhaps 7, 15, 25, or so cases, with psychopharmacological studies being an oft-cited example for this (see, e.g., Conners, Casat, & Gualtieri, 1996). Case study research in the narrow sense of the term, however, will often employ samples consisting of only two or three, and sometimes of one case only. This small sample size is the result of the holistic, in-depth analysis of each case both individually and in comparison to the other cases (which need not be characteristic of small-*N* research). Sampling strategies for case study research have usually been advanced in terms of the earlier provided descriptions of the logic of literal and theoretical replication, and issues of case selection are closely tied to design considerations (which is another difference compared with generic small-*N* research). Case study designs and hence the corresponding classification of sampling strategies according to a replication logic have been of particular importance in selecting cultures for cross-cultural research (discussed later).

Sampling Units and Levels of Analysis

Many types of social research, including cross-cultural research, involve a hierarchical or multilevel structure because societies are systems in which individuals are organized into groups. Thus, for example, people live in neighborhoods, neighborhoods combine into regions, regions form states, and states or administrative regions constitute a country. Another example consists of people who work in teams, which are part of a department, which form a division or a branch, and ultimately a company or organization. Students offer another example: They are taught in classes, which are set in schools that, in turn, are often run by state ministries. In all these instances, the numbers of cases become smaller the higher the level of grouping. The purpose of this section is to highlight the implication of collecting and analyzing data at different levels.

Consider, for example, a study of factors influencing empathy among undergraduate students in three countries. Within each country, a list of all universities offering courses at the undergraduate level is obtained, and 10 are selected in each to reflect the range of institutions offering tertiary education (e.g., in terms of providers, enrollment sizes, programs). These are the primary sampling unit. As the next step, a list of all undergraduate students for each university is obtained from which a simple random sample of, say, 150 students is drawn. Thus, students are the secondary sampling unit. This study results in a data structure in which 4,500 students are grouped within 30 universities, which are located in 3 countries.

What is the sample size in this study: 4,500, 30, or 3? Many analyses would proceed to consider 4,500 as the sample size. This has the advantage that many results of statistical tests will be significant because such tests are sensitive to sample size, which means that the more cases, the greater the likelihood of differences becoming significant. The disadvantage is that the primary sampling unit was not students but universities and that students in one university tend to be more like each other than students in another university. Hence, should the appropriate sample size be 30? The answer is no, because in this scenario, all data obtained from students would have to be aggregated to the level of the university. This, in turn, would mean that valuable and potentially crucial differences between students that are important for the study would disappear. An alternative would be to disaggregate university-level data such as enrollment size, student–teacher ratio, or student support service offerings. In this scenario, the variance between universities would be inflated because each data point for a university would be repeated 150 times. Finally, because this study is conducted across countries, chances are that the researchers also wish to make comparisons across countries. Again, either the information from the two lower levels would need to be aggregated, which would leave only three cases, or the country-level information – for example, gross domestic product or expenditure on tertiary education per capita – would need to be disaggregated to a lower level. Another option would be merely to describe differences between countries or between universities. The ultimate aim of researchers, however, is frequently to test the size of differences to make some statements as to whether the differences (here in empathy and its influencing factors) among students, universities, and countries are due to chance.

The answer to the most appropriate way in which to analyze data from such nested systems is the use of multilevel or hierarchical models (Goldstein, 1987, 2003; Muthén & Muthén, 1998–2005; Raudenbush, 1993; Raudenbush & Bryk, 2002). Given the data structure of the previous example, a three-level model would be constructed in which the information collected from 4,500 students would represent Level 1 data, the information about universities would represent Level 2 data, and country information would enter the model at Level 3. In this way, all data would be analyzed appropriately at the level at which they were obtained, and the nested structure would be taken into account in the analyses because students would be linked to the universities in which they are enrolled; universities, in turn, would be linked to the countries in which they operate. As a consequence, the effects of student-level factors, such as gender or personality traits, on empathy can be controlled for, while taking into account other potentially influential factors at the other two levels, such as size of university at Level 2 or educational expenditure at Level 3. Moreover, because such multilevel models consider the correct number of cases at each level, accurate estimates of significance for the effects under examination will be obtained.

It is hoped that this example has illustrated the importance of two things: First, the type of questions considered in much culturally comparative psychological research examines individuals who are nested within countries, resulting in different numbers of cases on at least two levels. Second, to take account of this nested data structure, multilevel models are appropriate forms of data analysis because they allow the complexities of the various contexts to be modeled while considering the different number of cases at each level.

RESEARCH AND SAMPLING IN CULTURALLY COMPARATIVE PSYCHOLOGICAL RESEARCH

What is it that researchers in (cross-)cultural psychology actually do, and what should they be doing? This section of the chapter first offers a brief typology of culturally comparative research and the importance of sampling strategies therein. It then proceeds to an overview of actual sampling practices in published cross-cultural research. It finally makes suggestions on specific sampling desiderata for culturally comparative psychological research.

Types of Culturally Focused Research

Before discussing the specifics of sampling for culturally comparative research, a brief look at a typology of such research is worthwhile. Kohn (1987) distinguished four types of comparative research: the case study approach, the cultural context approach, the cross-cultural approach, and the intercultural approach.

Research using the case study approach focuses on culture itself or on aspects thereof. Typically, no hypothesis about the impact of culture on behaviors, attitudes, or other phenomena of psychological interest is formulated. Qualitative research strategies are employed almost exclusively. There is little consideration of questions of cross-cultural functional or conceptual equivalence of the phenomena under scrutiny. Researchers "delve deeply into" a culture that is typically not their own, employing a field research strategy and trying to understand as much of the new culture (or in rare cases, their own culture; Barritt, Beekman, Bleeker, & Mulderij, 1983) as possible. After returning from "the field" the researcher compares his or her field knowledge with "book knowledge," for example, about his or her own culture or a third culture. In rare cases, the researcher starts a "second round" of research in yet another culture. The case study approach is often associated with the cultural psychology paradigm (Shweder, 1990). Typically one culture or only a few cultures are studied; cultures are sampled purposively (at best; often a convenience sampling based on accessibility criteria is used). Sampling of study participants will usually be purposive or employ another variety of nonprobability sampling such as that reported in *Narratives of Recovery From Disabling Mental Health Problems* (Lapsley, Nikora, & Black, 2002).

The cultural context approach focuses on the impact of culture on a certain phenomenon. No specific hypothesis is formulated, but the role of culture in a particular field of interest is studied. Research in this approach is predominantly but not exclusively qualitative; archival data pertaining to the phenomenon under investigation are also frequently used. This approach is more typical for qualitative sociology (H. Schwartz & Jacobs, 1979) than for psychological research. It is often used in political science as well to compare the role of political bodies across cultures. There is substantial consideration of equivalence problems. Here sampling of cultures must by definition be purposive. As with the case study approach, sampling of study participants will typically be purposive or employ another variety of nonprobability sampling, but archival data from random probability samples can be easily incorporated. Examples of this type of approach are studies of the race relations in adequately selected countries (e.g., Brazil, South Africa, the United States; Hamilton, Huntley, Alexander, Guimarães, & James, 2001; Marx, 1998).

The cross-cultural approach (in the narrow sense) focuses on a relational or a shift hypothesis. Culture or nation-state is usually treated as a quasi-experimental or a moderator variable. Studies almost exclusively use a quantitative research methodology. Often cross-cultural research understands comparisons as natural quasi-experiments. Equivalence of concepts and measures is a core issue. This approach has been used widely in educational performance research (e.g., Comber & Keeves, 1973; Mullis,

Martin, Gonzalez, & Chrostowski, 2004; Walker, 1976), which includes research on the impact of particular educational practices and resource provisions on performance (Lundberg & Lynnakylä, 1993; Postlethwaite & Ross, 1992), and in value research (S. H. Schwartz, 1992). In some of these research endeavors, a universality assumption serves as the starting point, whereas in others, it is the thought of what can be learned from each other. Sampling strategies on the culture level vary among convenience (i.e., based on accessibility criteria), purposive, and – in rare cases (discussed later) – stratified probability sampling. Sampling strategies on the individual level depend on the variables at stake. The use of random probability sampling is frequent in some fields of interest (cross-national studies on educational attainment can serve as an example), but rare in others, such as studies on the relation of family or context variables on offspring aggression. An example of this approach is testing the hypothesis that punitive parenting fosters aggressive child behavior across cultures (Scott et al., 1991).

The intercultural approach focuses on culture as an attribute of the individual and treats it as an exogenous variable like gender or age. Methodology will often be quantitative but can very well be qualitative. Equivalence is of lesser importance; it is largely taken for granted as in monocultural studies. The intercultural approach is often used in studies of intercultural communication, for example, in supranational organizations or units. Sampling units on the supra-individual level are typically organizations, not cultures. Here, sometimes, we even find studies of entire populations, like all branches of Company X in whatever culture they may be situated; Hofstede's study on culture's consequences (1980, 2001) aimed for this. Individual-level samples are generally drawn without consideration for cultural or national upbringing, but culture or nation of upbringing is noted. Examples of this approach can be found in job satisfaction studies of employees in multinational companies (Bernin et al., 2003).

Sampling Cultures

This section describes what psychologists actually do by taking a look at research published in the primary publication outlet in the field, the *Journal of Cross-Cultural Psychology (JCCP)*.[2]

[2] The authors thank Maheen Ahmed for coding the articles, with coding then cross-checked by the first author, who changed the coding of a mere four articles in this checking procedure. *JCCP* appears in six issues per volume, which on average encompasses six to seven articles, so altogether some 400 articles were coded.

Of all articles published in Volumes 27 (1996) through 36 (2005) of *JCCP*, none used a probability sampling approach to selecting cultures, 5% were classified as employing a convenience selection of cultures; 1% as quota-sampling cultures; 67% as having selected cultures purposively, but not theoretically; 0.5% used snowballing for selecting cultures; 1% used the deviant case approach; 4.5% used sequential sampling for selecting cultures; and 21% took a theoretical sampling approach as defined earlier in this chapter. In summary, no published study employed random probability sampling of cultures, approximately 6% used convenience sampling, and the remainder, some 94%, reported using purposive sampling for selecting the studied cultures. We note that this high percentage of purposive culture sampling seems vastly exaggerated. Experiential knowledge suggests that in many more than 6% of all cases, cultures were originally selected conveniently (by knowing a colleague in a country other than one's own), and the purposefulness of the selection procedure was only developed ex post facto. This is by no means illegitimate but should be stated more explicitly than is currently the case.

What are the central problems in sampling cultures? First of all, there is the lack of independence, sometimes called Galton's problem: In times of globalization, in particular, in which cultures can be considered increasingly less independent (resulting in the problem first named by Naroll [1961], that it is inappropriate to consider cultures as independent cases in a statistical analysis), should one not disregard culture altogether and always draw simple random samples? This question is not easily answered.

Attempting to answer it leads directly to the even more complex problems surrounding the term *culture*: Before looking in more detail at how to select cultures for psychological studies, it has to be pointed out that in a reiteration of how cultures can and should be selected for comparative research, the very concept of culture must only be taken as a fuzzy descriptor of the unit at the higher level of analysis (the lower level being the individual), the primary sampling unit, as it was labeled before. In cross-cultural psychology (in the narrower sense portrayed earlier), culture is regularly equated with nation-state or country. Only in particular cases, such as French- and English-speaking Canada; French- and Dutch-speaking Belgium; or French-, German-, and Italian-speaking Switzerland are nation-state/country and culture not seen as synonymous from a sampling point of view. Furthermore, although the authors of this chapter (like many other researchers) will avoid defining the term culture (because one could easily fill a monograph with the necessary considerations), a section dealing with the question of how to sample cultures for comparative psychological research must highlight the difficulties in identifying what a culture is. Only in the rare, probably increasingly outdated case that nation-states have an ethnically and linguistically homogeneous population does it seem acceptable simply to equate nation-state with culture. European nation-states that have been isolated for some time and are not yet a major destination for migrants might serve as an example here (e.g., Albania). Many other nation-states today encompass diverse ethnic groups, more than one language is spoken by significant parts of their – regular, nonmigrant – population, larger parts of a nation-state may adhere to different religions, and the like.

A possible solution to the delimitation of cultural zones has recently been proposed independently by S. H. Schwartz (2008) and Inglehart and Welzel (2005). Both have demonstrated empirically that on the basis of their unique approaches to studying human values around the world, a limited number of cultural regions can be distinguished: Inglehart and Welzel as well as Schwartz speak of some eight distinct cultural regions. Their typologies still suffer to some extent from the unavailability of larger sets of value preference data from non-Western parts of the world, such as sub-Saharan Africa, Oceania, parts of the Muslim world, or the Caribbean, but their typologies may nevertheless form a useful sampling frame for sampling cultures in future culturally comparative psychological research. The two world maps produced by Inglehart and by Schwartz are depicted in Figures 5.1a and 5.1b.

Inglehart and Welzel as well as Schwartz distinguished virtually the same eight cultural regions of the world. Inglehart and Welzel (2005) discussed Protestant Europe, English-speaking countries, Latin America, Africa, South Asia, Catholic Europe, ex-communist countries, and Confucian countries as distinguishable cultural regions. Schwartz's (2008) world map looks very similar. He distinguished Western Europe, English-speaking countries, Latin America, Protestant and Catholic East-Central and Baltic Europe, Orthodox East Europe, South and Southeast Asia, Muslim Middle East and Sub-Saharan Africa, and Confucian countries. Taking into consideration the degree of convergence of classifications of cultural regions obtained on the basis of distinctly different conceptual and methodological approaches, it does make sense to propose for future comparative multiculture studies to base the sampling of cultures on the findings of Schwartz and of Inglehart. In particular, such an approach can be fruitful in that values have been found to play an important role in many of the research topics of interest to (cross-)cultural psychologists (S. H. Schwartz, 1999).

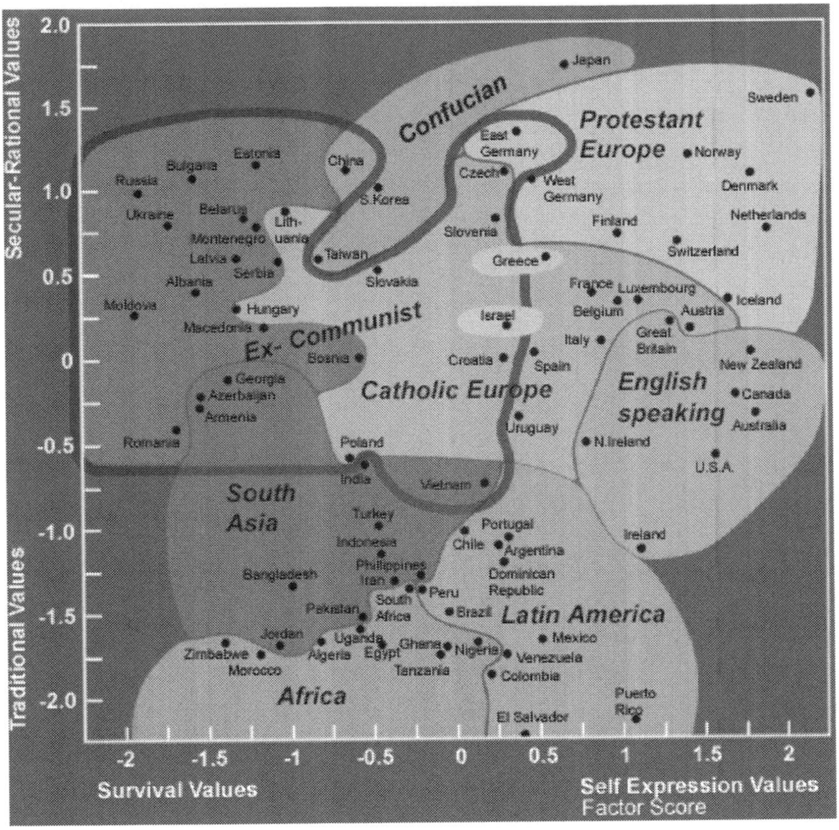

(a)

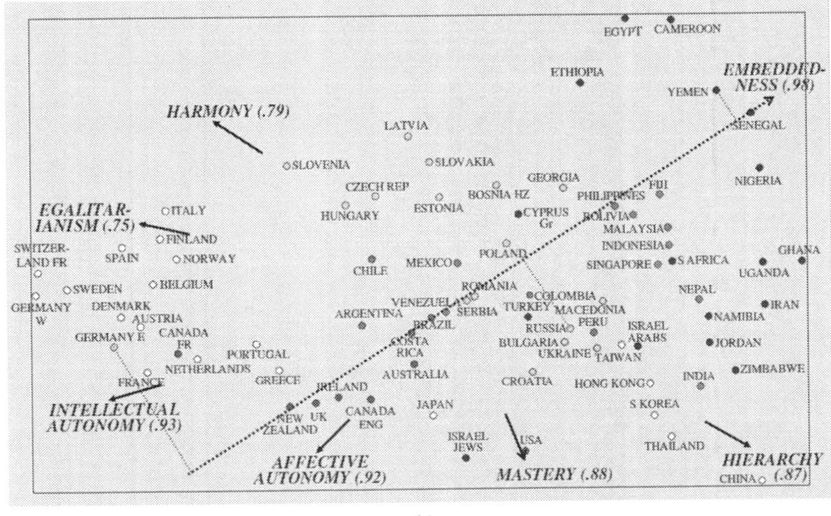

(b)

Figure 5.1. (a) Cultural regions according to Inglehart and Welzel (2005, p. 63). (b) Cultural regions according to Schwartz (2008, fig. 3).

Having reviewed the practice of sampling cultures for comparative psychological research and having pointed to some of its problems, we make the following suggestions for sampling cultures:

1. *Sample from cultural zones.* Researchers need not delve too deeply into a – likely futile – attempt to define culture as their sampling unit when they sample nation-states from the cultural zones as described by Schwartz and by Inglehart. A simple comprehensive list of the world's nation-states is, however, not a good frame for sampling cultures.
2. *Employ purposive sampling.* The sampling procedure should be purposive – for instance, in terms of selecting typical or intense cases. If no criteria for the selection of cultures are available, random probability sampling can also be employed, but because of the typically small sample size (on the level of the primary sampling unit), this will not yield a representative sample (of cultures). For sampling specific nation-states from within cultural zones, it might even be acceptable to select specific cultures on the grounds of convenience considerations, because using the cultural-zones approach already establishes a purposive sampling frame.
3. *Let your research goal guide the sampling strategy.* The exact culture-level sample composition must be guided by the type of research question at stake. In studies that test for a differentiating impact of "culture," a homogeneous sample of cultures produces a stronger test of such a hypothesis than a heterogeneous sample of cultures. Studying Germany, Austria, and German-speaking Switzerland can be a good choice when studying, for example, the importance of cultural context as a determinant of adolescent xenophobia. In studies that aim at testing cross-cultural similarity, the contrary holds true. In that case, one would want to select a heterogeneous sample of cultures to make the finding of similarity stronger. This would, for example, make sense in a study of the universality of the finding that punitive parenting leads to high aggression levels among offspring.
4. *Study more than just two cultures.* One other proposition can be made: The comparison of just two cultures, be it in case studies, cultural context studies, cross-cultural studies (in the narrower sense), or by only including participants from two cultures in an intercultural study, is problematic because similarities as well as differences are interpreted as such, without any knowledge of the size of differences

or the degree of similarity. The *tertium comparationis* is missing in such studies. The researcher is tempted to overemphasize – or in rare cases, underemphasize – differences that were found, because nothing is known about the size of the difference between Cultures A and B compared with the size of the differences between each of the two cultures and a third culture, C. Today, comparing the former East and the former West Germany to each other may still produce considerable differences on certain psychological variables, but when, for example, Poland is included in the study, the differences between the two Germanys tend to become minute. In other words, it is a question of relativity, in that, although the absolute difference between two cultures might seem large, this difference is smaller than the difference between those two cultures and a third.

Sampling Individuals

Here we once again take a look at research published in Volumes 27 to 36 of *JCCP*. When selecting individuals, 7% of all studies used a probability sampling approach, whereas 93% used a nonprobability sampling strategy. Among the – few – probability samples, approximately one third used a simple random or a cluster sampling approach; one quarter chose the stratified sampling approach, with the remainder using a systematic sampling approach. Among the studies using nonprobability sampling, almost 56% opted for convenience sampling of individual study participants. Studies resorting to a convenience selection of individuals constitute the majority of all studies published in *JCCP* (51%). Between 16% and 18% of the studies that used a nonprobability sampling strategy for sampling individuals drew a quota sample or opted for purposive selection. Altogether, 11 studies published in *JCCP* between 1996 and 2005 were classified as convenience samples at both the culture and individual levels.

In total, only 7% of all studies published in *JCCP* between 1996 and 2005 used random probability sampling of individuals. Is this evidence of mediocre professional standards of cross-cultural psychology? A majority of all studies published in the selected volumes of *JCCP* used convenience sampling of individual study participants. Is this an indicator that sampling needs to be addressed more rigidly in cross-cultural psychology? We argue no – and yes. In our eyes, there is no definitive reason why culturally comparative psychological studies must use random probability sampling of individuals as good practice for any kind of study.

Let us first turn to sampling for studies using a quantitative methodological approach. The reason random probability sampling is often seen as the silver bullet of sampling is that in quantitative psychological research, it seems to guarantee the generalizability of findings. However, this assertion is only valid for certain types of psychological studies. Psychologists using quantitative research methods typically do not want to generalize to the collective from which their sample was drawn but to other bearers of the psychological attribute under scrutiny in their research. Random probability sampling may indeed be the best choice for a comparison of the epidemiology of particular psychological phenomena in different cultures. However, even in these cases, a probabilistic sampling strategy is not needed from a statistical point of view. Following the saying that "to every sample there is a population," Rouanet, Bernard, and Lecoutre (1986) showed that no probabilistic considerations are necessary to test the adequacy of a sample for representing a population. The test of the adequacy of a sample for a population can be achieved in what statisticians call the set-theoretical paradigm, which is based entirely on the mathematics of permutations. It follows the same logic as randomization tests (see Bortz, Lienert, & Boehnke, 2008) in which all possible distributions of a variable are contrasted with a given distribution, the distribution of the sample under scrutiny. Of course, in cases in which nothing is known about parameters of the population, set-theoretical considerations will not be applicable, but such cases are rare in psychological research.

Whenever information about the parameters of the population is available from sources other than the sample, no random probability sampling is needed as long as the aim of the study is not to describe a collective – the population – but to enhance knowledge about the relationship of psychological phenomena in a given set of individuals. To check the plausibility of an assumption that a nonrandomly drawn sample can be used to gain psychological knowledge of individuals from a particular population, the researcher simply has to rely on a test of the extremes. Consider an example from Rouanet et al. (1986): A delegation of five men is unlikely to be a "good" sample of a larger political body with a gender distribution of 70% women and 30% men.

In summary, any sample can be a "good" sample for a population under scrutiny to a certain – ideally quantifiable – degree. Unlike for the typical research question of sociologists, psychologists must have typical, not representative, samples to follow the terminology of Rouanet et al. (1986). The ideal sample for a quantitative psychological study is one that allows generalizations about the psychological phenomenon at stake, about the dependent variable and its network of relationships with other psychological phenomena; it is not usually a sample that allows generalizations about the distribution of the dependent variable in a collective.

However, simply allowing any individual to enter a sample for a given study, as was the case in more than half of all studies published in *JCCP*, does not meet the requirement that psychologists must work with samples typical of the distribution of psychological phenomena under study. Convenience selection of individuals for culturally comparative psychological research is, on the contrary, jeopardizing the validity of such research. If effects of culture on psychological phenomena are to be tested (the purpose of many cross-cultural studies in the narrower sense discussed earlier), one must ensure that the selection of participants for a certain study is comparable across cultures and typical of the culture from which they originate. To include conveniently selected individuals is not sufficient unless one can show ex post facto that the samples included are both typical for the distribution of the psychological attribute in the culture they represent and that this is the case in all cultures included. This requirement is central, because – as has been shown for various types of volunteering behaviors (e.g., helping behavior; Levine, Norenzayan, & Philbrick, 2001) – volunteering for participation in psychological research is presumably related to culture in and of itself.

In summary, one can say that quantitative culturally comparative psychological research need not work with random probability samples unless its emphasis is epidemiological. Cross-cultural psychology should not, however, resort predominantly to convenience samples. Samples must be typical of the cultures from which they are drawn in that they show the culturally typical distribution of the *dependent* variable and must be comparable in their cultural typicality across cultures. Thus, sampling for quantitative research must be purposive or theoretical, as discussed earlier, if a random probability sampling approach is not taken.

This demand makes it clear that sampling strategies for quantitative and qualitative psychological research need not differ as greatly as is sometimes suggested. The usual aim of qualitative psychological research is the in-depth understanding of a psychological phenomenon, not the generalizability of findings to larger numbers of individuals. With this in mind, one must emphasize that for qualitative research, appropriate sampling strategies are at least as important as they are for quantitative research. As with quantitative research, qualitative investigations should not resort to studying convenient selections of research volunteers, but, even more so than when conducting quantitative research, should carefully consider the inclusion of every potential study participant vis-à-vis the aims of the study.

In light of these considerations, we make the following suggestions:

1. *Let generalization goals guide individual-level sampling.* If the goal of a study is generalization to the population (estimation of population parameters), representativeness and statistical adequacy of the sample are important and can be achieved through random sampling or by drawing on the set-theoretical paradigm – that is, by statistically testing the adequacy of a convenience sample vis-à-vis known population characteristics.
2. *Let the distribution of the study variable (the dependent variable) determine optimal sampling.* If the goal is generalization to a theory – for instance, in terms of the relationship between two variables – typicality of the sample is of greater concern than is representativeness. The distribution of the study variable *in the sample* is the determining factor; sole use of simple random sampling is inadequate. To use an extreme example, to cross-culturally compare the determinants of heroin addiction, it would not make sense to draw a simple random sample from a given population. A sufficient number of individuals who are addicted to heroin alongside comparable nonaddicts would be necessary in the sample. In such a case, we would ideally suggest a multistep procedure: (a) Obtain the best possible information on the distribution of the study variable in the population (e.g., "heroin addiction," but the same would apply for the variable "empathy") from existing data sets. (b) Examine the relationship between the study variable and other variables (e.g., heroin use or empathy and child-rearing practices). (c) Purposefully divide the population into strata depending on participants' values on the study variable (e.g., heroin intake, degree of empathy) and, if possible, the relational variables under scrutiny. (d) Draw similarly sized samples either randomly or purposefully from among each stratum; strategies may also be combined across strata (random sampling for typical values and purposive sampling for extreme values). It is important to include values from the entire range of the study variable, because relationships with other variables may change across the range.

CONCLUSIONS

Before summarizing the content of this chapter, several provisos are in order. The description of adequate sampling procedures for culturally comparative psychological research is something that in and of itself is subject to change.

Today, a global version of random route sampling can be described using the global positioning system; mobile phone access for most of the world's population may soon be a reality, and Internet access will reduce the social and global digital divide (Compaine, 2001). In step with these technological advances, sampling across cultures will also change. If theorists such as Fukuyama (1992) are correct in suggesting that the world is drifting toward a single global culture, incorporating the primary sampling unit "culture" into one's plans may become obsolete. Most, if not all, "culturally" comparative studies would then fall into the category of intercultural studies, in which one's place of upbringing is a measured variable included in models but no longer a sampling criterion. For the time being, however, considering culture as a primary sampling unit for culturally comparative psychological research seems more appropriate than ever before. Interest in the topic among the scientific community has greatly increased in recent years, with the *Journal of Cross-Cultural Psychology* having moved now and then into the Top 10 of all social psychology journals.

This chapter distinguished three types of sampling on two levels of case selection, the primary sampling unit being the level of culture, the secondary sampling unit being the individual within a culture. Guidelines for sampling strategies were outlined for both quantitative and qualitative research. On both levels of sampling, three general approaches to case selection were distinguished: probability sampling, nonsystematic sampling, and purposive sampling. It was argued that on the culture level, case selection should usually be purposive, with the cultural zones approach introduced by values researchers (S. H. Schwartz, Inglehart) serving as a promising sampling frame. With regard to the sampling of individuals within cultures, we argued that the case selection strategy should be guided by the generalization goals of a particular study. Studies that aim at generalization to a collective should employ random probability sampling. Researchers who aim at generalization to a theory by testing, for example, the generalizability of a close relationship between two or more variables should ensure the typicality of their samples for the dependent variable and the variables assumed to be related to it.

We also argued that sampling is of crucial importance for both qualitative and quantitative psychological research, and we called for greater attention to sampling issues in both approaches to studying psychological phenomena. The saying "there is a population to every sample" cannot legitimize the use of convenience sampling of arbitrary quality in quantitative research, nor can reference to the deep understanding of a few cases legitimize disregard for who the cases are in qualitative research.

Moreover, our "call to order" should be heard not only by psychologists working in a more narrowly defined cross-cultural paradigm; it also applies to cultural psychology, to intercultural research strategies, and to a culture-as-context approach that is often found in the neighboring disciplines of qualitative sociology and political science. The humanistic-sounding notion that all human beings are members of a single population and thereby represent the population equally well with regard to any thinkable phenomenon or variable under scrutiny prevents adequate knowledge acquisition in psychology and neighboring disciplines, and it should therefore be put to rest.

REFERENCES

Barlow, D. H., & Hersen, M. (1984). *Single case experimental designs. Strategies for studying behavior change.* New York: Pergamon Press.

Barnett, V. (2002). *Sample surveys: Principles and methods.* London: Oxford University Press.

Barritt, L., Beekman, T., Bleeker, H., & Mulderij, K. (1983). The world through children's eyes: Hide and seek and peekaboo. *Phenomenology and Pedagogy, 1*, 140–161.

Bernin, P., Theorell, T., Cooper, C. L., Sparks, K., Spector, P. E., Radhakrishnan, P., & Russinova, V. (2003). Coping strategies among Swedish female and male managers in an international context. *International Journal of Stress Management, 10*, 376–391.

Bortz, J., Lienert, G.-A., & Boehnke, K. (2008). *Verteilungsfreie Methoden in der Biostatistik.* Berlin: Springer.

Comber, L. C., & Keeves, J. P. (1973). *Science education in nineteen countries.* (International Studies in Evaluation, Vol. 1). New York: Wiley.

Compaine, B. M. (2001). *The digital divide: Facing a crisis or creating a myth?* Cambridge, MA: MIT Press.

Conners, C. K., Casat, C. D., & Gualtieri, C. T. (1996). Bupropion hydrochloride in attention deficit disorder with hyperactivity. *Journal of the American Academy of Child and Adolescent Psychiatry, 35*, 1314–1321.

Curtis, S., Gesler, W., Smith, G., & Washburn, S. (2000). Approaches to sampling and case selection in qualitative research: Examples in the geography of health. *Social Science and Medicine, 50*, 1001–1014.

Denzin, N. K. (1997). *Interpretative ethnography. Ethnographic practices for the 21st century.* London: Sage.

Flick, U. (1998). *An introduction to qualitative research.* London: Sage.

Fukuyama, F. (1992). *The end of history and the last man.* New York: Free Press.

Gobo, G. (2004). Sampling, representativeness, and generalizability. In C. Seale, G. Gobo, J. F. Gubrium, & D. Silverman (Eds.), *Qualitative research practice* (pp. 435–456). London: Sage.

Goldstein, H. (1987). *Multilevel models in educational and social research.* New York: Oxford University Press.

Goldstein, H. (2003). *Multilevel statistical models.* London: Edward Arnold; New York: Wiley.

Häder, S., & Gabler, S. (2003). *Sampling and estimation.* In J. A. Harkness, F. J. R. Van de Vijver, & P. P. Mohler (Eds.), *Cross-cultural survey methods* (pp. 117–134). Hoboken, NJ: Wiley.

Hamilton, C. V., Huntley, L., Alexander, N., Guimarães, A. S. A., & James, W. (2001). *Beyond racism: Race and inequality in Brazil, South Africa, and the United States.* Boulder, CO: Lynne Rienner.

Hofstede, G. (1980). *Culture's consequences: International differences in work-related values.* Newbury Park, CA: Sage.

Hofstede, G. (2001). *Culture's consequences: Comparing values, behaviors, institutions, and organizations across nations.* Newbury Park, CA: Sage.

Howitt, D., & Cramer, D. (2005). *Introduction to research methods in psychology.* Harlow: Pearson Education.

Inglehart, R., & Welzel, C. (2005). *Modernization, cultural change, and democracy: The human development sequence.* Cambridge: Cambridge University Press.

Johnson, J. C. (1990). *Selecting ethnographic informants.* Newbury Park, CA: Sage.

Kelle, U., & Kluge, S. (1999). *Vom Einzelfall zum Typus* [From single case to type]. Opladen, Germany: Leske & Budrich.

Kohn, M.L. (1987). Cross-national research as an analytic strategy. *American Sociological Review, 52,* 713–731.

Lapsley, H., Nikora, L., & Black, R. (2002). *"Kia Mauri Tau!" Narratives of recovery from disabling mental health problems.* Wellington, New Zealand: Mental Health Commission.

Lehtonen, R., & Pahkinen, E. J. (1995). *Practical methods for design and analysis of complex surveys.* Chichester, England: Wiley.

Levine, R. V., Norenzayan, A., & Philbrick, K. (2001). Cultural differences in the helping of strangers. *Journal of Cross Cultural Psychology, 32,* 543–560.

Lindsey, G., & Aronson, E. (1985). *The handbook of social psychology.* New York: Random House.

Lundberg, I., & Linnakylä, P. (1993). *Teaching reading around the world.* The Hague, the Netherlands: International Association for the Evaluation of Educational Achievement.

Marx, A. W. (1998). *Making race and nation: A comparison of South Africa, the United States, and Brazil.* Cambridge: Cambridge University Press.

Meredith, W. (1964). Notes on factorial invariance. *Psychometrika, 29,* 177–185.

Meredith, W. (1993). Measurement invariance, factor analysis and factorial invariance. *Psychometrika, 58,* 525–543.

Mullis, I. V. S., Martin, M. O., Gonzalez, E. J., & Chrostowski, S. J. (2004). *TIMSS 2003: International mathematics report: Findings from IEA's trends in international mathematics and science study at the fourth and eighth grade.* Chestnut Hill, MA: TIMSS & PIRLS International Study Center, Boston College.

Muthén, L. K., & Muthén, B. O. (1998–2005). *Mplus. User's guide* (3rd ed.). Los Angeles: Muthén & Muthén.

Naroll, R. (1961). Two solutions to Galton's problem. *Philosophy of Science, 28,* 15–29.

Neuman, W. L. (2006). *Social research methods: Qualitative and quantitative approaches.* Boston: Allyn & Bacon.

Owusu-Bempah, K., & Howitt, D. (2000). *Psychology beyond Western perspectives.* Leicester: BPS.

Postlethwaite, T. N., & Ross, K. N. (1992). *Effective schools in reading: Implications for educational planners.* The Hague, the Netherlands: IEA.

Quinn Patton, M. (2002). *Qualitative evaluation and research methods* (3rd ed.). Newbury Park: Sage.

Ragin, C. (1989). *The comparative method.* Berkeley, CA: University of California Press.

Ragin, C., & Becker, H. S. (Eds.). (1992). *What is a case? Exploring the foundations of social inquiry.* Cambridge: Cambridge University Press.

Raudenbush, S. W. (1993). Hierarchical linear models and experimental design. In L. K. Edwards (Ed.), *Applied analysis of variance in behavioral science.* New York: Marcel Dekker.

Raudenbush, S. W., & Bryk, A. S. (2002). *Hierarchical linear models: Applications and data analysis methods.* Thousand Oaks: Sage.

Rouanet, H., Bernard, J., & Lecoutre, B. (1986). Nonprobabilistic statistical inference: A set-theoretic approach. *The American Statistician, 40,* 60–65.

Schuman, H., & Kalton, G. (1985). Survey methods. In G. Lindzey & E. Aronson (Eds.), *The handbook of social psychology* (pp. 635–698). New York: Random House.

Schwartz, H., & Jacobs, J. (1979). *Qualitative sociology: A method to the madness.* New York: Free Press.

Schwartz, S. H. (1992). Universals in the content and structure of values: Theoretical advances and empirical tests in 20 countries. *Advances in Experimental Social Psychology, 25,* 1–65.

Schwartz, S. H. (1999). Cultural value differences: Some implications for work. *Applied Psychology: An International Review, 48,* 23–48.

Schwartz, S. H. (2008). *Cultural value orientations: Nature and implications of national differences.* Moscow: State University Higher School of Economics Press.

Scott, W. A., Scott, R., Boehnke, K., Cheng, S. W., Leung, K., & Sasaki, M. (1991). Children's personality as a function of family relations within and between cultures. *Journal of Cross-Cultural Psychology, 22,* 182–208.

Selig P., Card, N. A., & Little, T. D. (2007). Modeling individuals and cultures using multi-level SEM. In F. J. R. van de Vijver, D. A. van Hemert, & Y. H. Poortinga (Eds.), *Individuals and cultures in multilevel analysis.* Mahwah, NJ: Erlbaum.

Shweder, R. (1990). Cultural psychology – what is it? In J. Stigler, R. Shweder, & G. Herdt (Eds.), *Cultural psychology: Essays on comparative human development* (pp. 1–43). New York: Cambridge University Press.

Strauss, A., & Corbin, J. (1998). *Basics of qualitative research: Techniques and procedures for developing grounded theory.* London: Sage.

Walker, D. (1976). *The IEA six subject survey: An empirical study of education in twenty-one countries.* Stockholm: Almqvist & Wiksell.

Walter, S. D. (1989). The feasibility of matching and quota sampling in epidemiologic studies. *American Journal of Epidemiology, 130,* 379–389.

Yin, R. K. (2003). *Case study research. Design and methods.* Thousand Oaks: Sage.

6

Survey Response Styles Across Cultures

TIMOTHY P. JOHNSON, SHARON SHAVITT, AND
ALLYSON L. HOLBROOK

INTRODUCTION

Survey reports are susceptible to multiple forms of measurement error (Sudman & Bradburn, 1974; Tourangeau, Rips, & Rasinski, 2000). In this chapter, we consider some of the potential processes through which culture may be implicated in measurement error. In particular, we focus on cultural variability in several common survey response styles, including socially desirable responding (SDR), acquiescent response style (ARS), and extreme response style (ERS). Awareness of response styles is particularly important in the conduct of cross-cultural research. Systematic variance in response style behaviors across racial, ethnic, or national groups may be mistakenly interpreted as cultural differences (or similarities) in the substantive measures being compared (Johnson & van de Vijver, 2003; Keillor, Owens, & Pettijohn, 2001; Middleton & Jones, 2000; Si & Cullen, 1998). Response styles also may suppress or inflate associations among variables (Wells, 1961) differentially across cultural groups. Thus, the potential for cultural variability in survey reporting has direct implications for many academic disciplines that rely on survey research for measurement purposes, as well as for applied researchers working across many substantive fields. This review integrates evidence and experiences from many of these disciplines regarding three of the most common forms of response style that vary across cultures. Three types of evidence are considered: (a) evidence of differences across racial and ethnic groups within nations, (b) evidence of differences across countries, and (c) evidence of associations between direct

Preparation of this chapter was supported by Grant No. 1R01HD053636–01A1 from the National Institutes of Health, Grant No. 0648539 from the National Science Foundation, and Grant No. 63842 from the Robert Wood Johnson Foundation to the authors.

measures of cultural values and each response style. We also consider the potential cultural mechanisms underlying these processes. Methodological issues relevant to the measurement of response styles and proposed methods to compensate for cultural heterogeneity in these reporting processes are reviewed as well.

CULTURE AND SOCIALLY DESIRABLE RESPONDING

A widely studied topic in research methodology, SDR continues to be a serious concern in survey measurement because of its potential to introduce response bias (Johnson & van de Vijver, 2003; Paulhus, 1991; Tourangeau & Yan, 2007). SDR is the systematic tendency to give answers that make the respondent look good (Paulhus, 1991). Understanding how social desirability is viewed and pursued in different cultural contexts and groups is key to the validity of cross-cultural research efforts and many other research efforts involving self-reports. In general, research findings indicate that compared with individualists, collectivists have a greater tendency to give responses that make the self look good. This finding has emerged in multiple studies and has been shown across nations, across racial and ethnic groups within nations, and across individual-level cultural variables.

Importantly, recent research suggests that the nature of SDR is multidimensional and that collectivists and individualists may in fact engage in distinct forms of SDR (Lalwani, Shavitt, & Johnson, 2006). That is, there is increasing evidence that SDR comprises the tendency to engage in *impression management*, which is the tendency for people to intentionally misrepresent themselves to appear more favorable, and in *self-deceptive enhancement*, or the tendency for people to have inflated yet genuinely held views of themselves (Paulhus 1998a). Impression management reflects the traditional view of socially desirable responding (Paulhus, 1998a; Schlenker & Britt, 1999; Schlenker, Britt, & Pennington, 1996), a construct often associated with dissimulation or deception (Mick, 1996). We examine the implications of this distinction for cultural differences in SDR later in the chapter.

Definitions of Socially Desirable Responding

As noted, socially desirable responding has traditionally been defined in impression management terms: the reporting by survey respondents of information that projects a favorable image of themselves, sometimes at the expense of accuracy (Nederhof, 1985; Ross & Mirowsky, 1984a). This reporting style reflects the human propensity to emphasize and occasionally overstate positive qualities and behaviors while deemphasizing or understating negative ones. Survey validation studies generally support this presumption. It has been documented in the United States, for example, that voting (Sigelman, 1982), church attendance (Hadaway, Marler, & Chaves, 1993), and physical exercise (Adams et al., 2005) are overreported, whereas drug use (Fendrich, Johnson, Hubbell, & Spiehler, 2004) and sexually transmitted diseases (Clark, Brasseux, Richmond, Getson, & D'Angelo, 1997) are underreported during survey interviews. Marlowe and Crowne described social desirability in a manner that explicitly conceptualized it as being culturally conditioned, referring to SDR as "the need for social approval and acceptance and the belief that it can be attained by means of *culturally* acceptable and appropriate behaviors" (1961, p. 109) [emphasis added].

Podsakoff, MacKenzie, Lee, and Podsakoff (2003) distinguished between person-centered and survey-item-centered social desirability. They described the former as the tendencies of some individuals to respond to survey items "more as a result of their social acceptability than their true feelings." The latter they defined as "the fact that items may be written in such a way as to reflect more socially desirable attitudes, behavior, or perceptions" (p. 882).

Numerous other investigators have offered definitions of socially desirable responding. Stricker defined SDR as "conformity on items for which the social norms exist and are perceived; conformity on such items simply involves making responses approved by the social norms, i.e., socially desirable responses" (1963, p. 320). Messick defined it as "individual consistencies in the tendency to give answers that are considered desirable by social consensus, a tendency that has been taken by some to mean that the respondent is consciously or unconsciously attempting to place himself or herself in a favorable light" (1991, p. 165).

Measuring Socially Desirable Responding

Measures of social desirability can be placed in two overarching categories. The first type of measure is focused on identifying *individuals'* tendency to engage in socially desirable responding. These measures are based on the assumption that socially desirable responding is a tendency that is systematically greater in some individuals than in others. The second set of measures has focused on identifying social desirable *responding*. These approaches have focused on identifying questions that have social desirability connotations and conditions that foster or discourage socially desirable responding.

Both approaches have been used to identify the extent to which individuals with different characteristics (e.g., race, ethnicity, or cultural orientation) demonstrate socially desirable responding.

Individuals' Socially Desirable Response Tendencies

Several self-report measures have been developed to assess individual differences in socially desirable response tendencies (Crowne & Marlowe, 1964; A. L. Edwards, 1957; Eysenck & Eysenck, 1964; Paulhus, 1998a; Stöber, 2001). These measures have been shown to be associated with reports of favorable and unfavorable opinions and behaviors. For example, persons scoring highly on such measures as the Marlowe–Crowne scale have been found less likely to report unfavorable behaviors and values, such as alcohol consumption, intoxication, and marijuana use (Bradburn & Sudman, 1979), as well as materialism (Mick, 1996).

Some of these measures conceptualize socially desirable responding as a single construct, whereas others conceptualize it as having multiple components. For example, the Paulhus Deception Scales measure both impression management and self-deceptive enhancement (Paulhus 1998a). Impression management is tapped by items such as "I sometimes drive faster than the speed limit" (reverse scored) and "I have never dropped litter on the street" (Paulhus, 1998a). Self-deceptive enhancement is assessed by items such as "My first impressions of people usually turn out to be right" and "I am very confident of my judgments."

In contrast, the Marlowe–Crowne scale measures primarily impression management (Paulhus, 1991). It includes items such as "My table manners at home are as good as when I eat out in a restaurant" and "If I could get into a movie without paying and be sure I was not seen, I would probably do it" (reverse scored). Recent research, however, suggests that the Marlowe–Crowne scale may not tap a single dimension reliably (Leite & Beretvas, 2005).

These scales for tapping SDR have been used to measure differences in the tendency to engage in socially desirable responding across cultural groups (e.g., Johnson & van de Vijver, 2003; Lalwani, Shavitt, & Johnson, 2006) as well as across contexts that heighten the salience of cultural self-views (Lalwani & Shavitt, 2009). However, one difficulty with using these measures in cross-cultural research is that the scales themselves may not be equally applicable across cultural groups. For example, the reliability of the Marlowe–Crowne scale sometimes differs across Western versus Eastern contexts (e.g., internal consistency coefficients of 0.72 vs. 0.43, respectively; Middleton & Jones, 2000).

Most social desirability scales ask respondents to report the extent to which they agree that a series of statements describes them (some for which agreement means greater SDR and others for which agreement means less SDR). An additional approach is to use scenario measures. These measures generally present respondents with a situation (e.g., being offered the opportunity to cheat on a difficult and important class assignment) and then ask them the likelihood that they would engage in a particular response (e.g., choosing to cheat). Such scenario measures have been developed to assess both impression management and self-deceptive enhancement (Lalwani et al., 2006; Lalwani & Shavitt, 2009). One difficulty with using such measures in cross-cultural research is that the measures themselves must be comparable across cultures. Furthermore, the development of scenario measures is difficult and time-consuming, and the final measures may not be useful in populations different from those in which they were developed. For example, a scenario about cheating on a class assignment is reasonable in a study of college students but unlikely to work in a general population study or community sample.

Socially Desirable Response Behavior

Other measures of SDR have focused on measuring socially desirable response behavior. These studies compare answers to questions that do versus those that do not have social desirability connotations. In many studies, questions with social desirability connotations have been identified via face validity (e.g., Aneshensel, Frerichs, Clark, & Yokopenic, 1982; Aquilino, 1998; Groves, 1977; Groves & Kahn 1979; Locander, Sudman, & Bradburn, 1976). A downside to this is that the researcher is determining which questions are likely to be subject to SDR bias within the population being studied. Although this assessment is clear for some questions (e.g., illegal drug use), the social desirability connotations of other questions (e.g., experiencing different types of problems) are more ambiguous and likely to vary across cultures.

One approach to dealing with this difficulty has been to collect empirical data on the social desirability connotations of different questions (e.g., Holbrook, Green, & Krosnick, 2003). Some studies ask respondents which questions they believe others would or would not feel comfortable answering (e.g., Blair, Sudman, Bradburn, & Stocking, 1977; see Johnson & van de Vijver, 2003, for a review). Another approach involves conducting a pretest in which a randomly selected subset of respondents is asked to "fake bad" by giving socially undesirable answers, whereas other respondents are randomly assigned to "fake good" by giving socially desirable answers.

If these two groups give significantly different answers to a question, this indicates that there is a generally agreed-on desirable answer to the question and that it has social desirability connotations (e.g., Holbrook et al., 2003; Wiggins, 1959). Although such approaches allow researchers to identify which questions have social desirability connotations, they require a pretest to do so. Furthermore, cross-cultural research on socially desirable responding would require pretests that establish that the social desirability connotations of questions are consistent across cultures.

Another approach to identifying social desirability connotations has been to examine whether responses to questions are affected by conditions that foster or discourage socially desirable responding. For example, a great deal of evidence indicates that people are more willing to report unfavorable attitudes, beliefs, and behaviors when the reporting circumstances ensure anonymity (Himmelfarb & Lickteig, 1982; Paulhus, 1984; Warner, 1965; see Bradburn, Sudman, & Wansink, 2004, for a review) or greater privacy (e.g., Tourangeau & Smith, 1996; see also Puntoni & Tavassoli, 2007) or when respondents believe researchers have other access to information revealing the truth of their thoughts and actions (e.g., Evans, Hansen, & Mittlemark, 1977; Pavlos, 1972; Sigall & Page, 1971). These approaches have also been used to reduce social desirability response bias (and are discussed later in more detail).

Techniques that increase respondents' anonymity or privacy are useful to identify questions that are likely affected by social desirability connotations. However, they cannot be used to identify specific individuals who are demonstrating socially desirable responding. The characteristics of individuals showing socially desirable responding only can be inferred by comparing the effect of a manipulation (e.g., mode or anonymity) across subgroups of respondents.

Finally, socially desirable responding has been assessed by comparing survey self-reports to "gold standard" validation measures. For example, studies examining reports of voter turnout have compared self-reports of turnout to both official records of whether individual respondents voted (Traugott & Katosh, 1979) and to official reports of turnout in a given election (Clausen, 1968; Traugott & Katosh, 1979). Studies of drug use have compared self-reports of drug use to laboratory tests of drugs found in respondents' hair, saliva, urine, or blood (Colon, Robles, & Sahai, 2001; Fendrich et al., 2004). A variant of this approach involves selecting respondents for a study based on a known characteristic (e.g., having been arrested for driving under the influence) and examining the proportion of respondents who report the behavior (e.g., Locander et al., 1976). This approach allows researchers to assess whether each individual's response is accurate. However, such gold standards are not available for many of the constructs of interest to researchers (e.g., attitudes, beliefs, and perceptions). Furthermore, in many cases, gold standards such as public records or laboratory tests are not free from error themselves (e.g., errors in turnout records may vary systematically across voting precincts; Traugott, Traugott, & Presser 1992).

Cultural Variables and Socially Desirable Responding

Cross-Cultural Differences in Socially Desirable Responding

There is considerable evidence for differences in SDR as a function of racial and ethnic groups within nations. In the United States, Mexican American and Mexican respondents have been found to provide more socially desirable answers compared with Whites (Ross & Mirowsky, 1984b; Warnecke et al., 1997). Those retaining a strong Mexican identity also are more likely to give socially approved responses, suggesting that social desirability may be mediated by acculturation (Ross & Mirowsky, 1984a). Ross and Mirowsky speculated that the greater tendency to provide socially desirable answers among Mexican Americans (compared with Anglos in the United States) was a consequence of the strong family ties found in Mexican society and related pressures to conform and present a "good face to the outside world" (1984b, p. 190).

U.S.-based research has also documented SDR differences between non-Hispanic Whites and other racial and ethnic populations. Several studies have demonstrated that African American respondents in the United States typically score higher on SDR measures than do non-Hispanic whites (Crandall, Crandall, & Katkovsky, 1965; Fisher, 1967; Klassen, Hornstra, & Anderson, 1975; Warnecke et al., 1997). Similar findings have been reported in South Africa, where Black respondents have been shown to score higher on SDR, compared with White South Africans (D. Edwards & Riordan, 1994).

Validation studies in the United States have also found Black–White differences in the likelihood that self-reported information can be validated using external information sources, such as biological testing and official records. Johnson and Bowman (2003), for example, found that African Americans were consistently less likely to provide accurate information regarding substance use behaviors when compared with non-Hispanic Whites across several dozen studies that they reviewed. African Americans have also been found to underreport abortions (Jones & Forrest, 1992) and to overreport voting behavior (Abramson & Claggett, 1986; Katosh & Traugott, 1981).

Differences between White and Asian samples in the United States have been reported as well. Non-native Asian college students at an American university have been shown to endorse more Marlowe–Crowne social desirability items than do native White U.S. students (Abe & Zane, 1990). Furthermore, Middleton and Jones (2000) observed more socially desirable answers among college students from East Asian countries studying in the United States compared with U.S.- and Canadian-born students. Keillor et al. (2001) reported higher social desirability scores among Malaysian graduate students compared with students from both the United States and France.

Cross-national studies also have noted SDR differences across nations. Sri Lankan respondents have been shown to provide more socially desirable answers compared with English respondents (Perera & Eysenck, 1984). Malaysian respondents also have been found to express more socially desirable answers than either U.S. or French respondents (no differences in SDR were found between the French and U.S. samples). G. M. Chen (1995) found that Chinese college students disclose less information compared with a sample of American counterparts. Such unwillingness to self-disclose also can reflect an effort to respond desirably (P. B. Smith & Bond, 1998). Finally, in a large multination study, Bernardi (2006) reported lower impression management scores among U.S. college students compared with those from 11 other countries.

However, the nature of the relation between cultural variables and SDR is also dependent on the type of socially desirable responding in question. Lalwani et al. (2006) argued that two distinct response patterns should emerge as a function of cultural orientations or backgrounds – impression management and self-deceptive enhancement (Gur & Sackeim, 1979; Paulhus, 1991; Sackeim & Gur, 1979). Each of these response styles corresponds to different culturally relevant goals. As noted earlier, subscales measuring these dimensions comprise the Paulhus Deception Scales (Paulhus, 1984, 1991, 1998b). Impression management refers to an attempt to present one's self-reported actions in the most positive manner to convey a favorable image (Paulhus, 1998a; Schlenker & Britt, 1999; Schlenker et al., 1996). Concerns about one's social relationships, predominant in collectivistic cultural contexts, likely give rise to a tendency to present oneself in such ways to "fit in" harmoniously and gain social approval.

In contrast, self-deceptive enhancement refers to the tendency to describe oneself in inflated and overconfident terms. It is a predisposition to see one's skills in a positive light and has been described as a form of "rigid overconfidence" (Paulhus, 1998a). Such a response style is adaptive for individualistic cultural contexts, in which the motive to see oneself as competent and self-reliant predominates because achieving independence is a central goal.

Lalwani et al. (2006) showed that U.S. respondents (individualistic context), compared with those from Singapore (collectivistic context), scored higher in self-deceptive enhancement and lower in impression management. Similarly, European American respondents, compared with Korean American respondents, scored higher in self-deceptive enhancement and lower in impression management. Parallel findings emerged in multicultural student samples when features of the context were manipulated to make salient either an independent self-view (individualistic context) or an interdependent self-view (collectivistic context) (Lalwani & Shavitt, 2009).

Moreover, data in the United States as a function of cultural orientation shed light on the specific cultural goals served by these response styles (Lalwani et al., 2006). Specifically, people with a cultural orientation that emphasizes sociability, benevolence, and cooperation tended to engage in impression management. However, people with a cultural orientation that emphasizes self-competence, self-direction, and independence tended to engage in self-deceptive enhancement. (See Triandis & Gelfand, 1998, and Shavitt, Lalwani, Zhang, & Torelli, 2006, for more on these specific cultural orientations.) The observed response styles thus appear to reflect distinct self-presentational goals – to be seen as sociable and benevolent (impression management) versus self-reliant and capable (self-deceptive enhancement).

Although the evidence for cultural differences in SDR is considerable, some research has failed to find differences in SDR across nations or across ethnic groups within nations. Lai and Linden (1993) reported no differences in social desirability between Asian Canadian and European Canadian respondents on measures of both self-deceptive enhancement and impression management. Heine and Lehman (1995) also reported no differences between samples of European Canadian and Japanese university students in SDR using these same measures. Further, research comparing U.S. and Philippine students failed to identify differences in socially desirable responding (Grimm & Church, 1999). In a nationwide survey of adults in the United States, Gove and Geerken (1977) found no differences in mean social desirability scores between White, African American, and Hispanic respondents. No racial differences in SDR were identified in a probability sample of adults in Erie County, New York, reported by Welte and Russell (1993). Furthermore, Tsushima (1969) reported no differences in

SDR scores between medical patients in New York City of Italian and Irish ethnicity, and Okazaki (2000) found no differences in SDR between White and Asian American college students. Given that several studies have found no SDR differences, research is needed to address more comprehensively the conditions under which cultural and ethnic group differences in SDR would be expected.

Cultural Processes and Socially Desirable Responding

To some extent, the differences in SDR that have emerged can be seen as reflecting cultural differences in the need to maintain harmonious interpersonal relations. This has been identified as an important value within numerous collectivistic cultures, as exemplified by the smooth interpersonal relations style of Filipinos (Church, 1987), the Latino cultural script of *simpatia* (Triandis, Marín, Lisanski, & Betancourt, 1984), and the East Asian courtesy bias (Deutcher, 1973). Indeed, Middleton and Jones (2000) offered several hypotheses linking Hofstede's (2001) cultural constructs with SDR behaviors within the context of Eastern versus Western cultures. They suggested that individuals embedded within high power distance cultures might be more likely to provide socially desirable responses, whereas persons within low power distance environments might feel fewer constraints to self-expression. Uncertainty avoidance, they postulated, might also be associated with SDR, given that individuals in Eastern nations that are characterized by high uncertainty avoidance might be expected to offer socially desirable responses when confronted with ambiguous situations. Persons within feminine cultures might be expected to have higher SDR as well, because those cultures emphasize the maintenance of harmonious social relationships. Members of individualistic societies are expected to feel weaker social pressures to conform and hence be less prone to provide socially desirable answers. In addition, members of societies that emphasize a long-term time orientation, including the long-term maintenance of social relationships, might be expected to feel social pressures to respond in a socially desirable manner.

Bernardi (2006) has offered several hypotheses regarding potential associations between SDR and Hofstede's cultural classifications. He proposed relationships similar to those outlined by Middleton and Jones (2000) with regard to SDR associations with individualism, uncertainty avoidance, and power distance. However, in contrast to Middleton and Jones's expectations, Bernardi proposed that SDR will be greater among more masculine cultures in which competition and the drive for success will produce greater levels of corruption and "an atmosphere of success at any cost" (p. 45). Although

Bernardi reported support at the national level that SDR decreased with sampled countries' individualism scores and increased with uncertainty avoidance, power distance and masculinity were not found to be independently associated with SDR.

Other evidence is available with which to examine some of these hypothesized processes. Van Hemert, van de Vijver, Poortinga, and Georgas (2002) reported significant negative correlations between a nation's individualism score and mean scores on the Lie scale of the Eysenck Personality Inventory (Eysenck & Eysenck, 1964) across 23 nations. In addition, researchers have identified greater propensities among collectivists toward conformity (Bond & Smith, 1996) and unwillingness to self-disclose (P. B. Smith & Bond, 1998), characteristics also likely to be associated with socially desirable reporting (see Johnson & van de Vijver, 2003). Schwartz, Verkasalo, Antonovsky, and Sagiv (1997) reported significant correlations between scores on the Marlowe–Crowne scale and the values of conformity and tradition. In line with this, as noted earlier, collectivistic values have been linked with a tendency to present oneself in normatively appropriate ways (Lalwani et al., 2006).

Another line of research has compared conceptions of what is perceived to be socially desirable (or not) across cultures. High correlations of the perceived social desirability of items between cultural groups have been reported (Diers, 1965; Gough & Heilbrun, 1980; Iwawaki & Cowen, 1964; Williams, Satterwhite, & Saiz, 1998). Strong but variable within-group correlations also have been reported between the perceived desirability of items and their likelihood of being endorsed by respondents within several ethnic and national groups (Dohrenwend, 1966; Iwawaki, Fukuhara, & Hidano, 1966; Phillips & Clancy, 1970; Turk Smith, Smith, & Seymour, 1993). These findings suggest that social desirability may well be a pancultural or etic concept, albeit one that nonetheless reflects varying degrees of cultural conditioning (Johnson & van de Vijver, 2003).

CULTURE AND ACQUIESCENCE

Differences in the propensity to give acquiescent responses have been identified both within racial and ethnic subgroups within nations and also across countries. A great deal of evidence indicates that acquiescent responding is more typical of ethnic minority or non-White respondents than of White Anglo respondents. At the national level, respondents in Asian, Mediterranean, or African societies generally engage in more acquiescent responding than do respondents in North American or Western European countries.

Overall, then, the evidence consistently points to more acquiescent responding among those with collectivistic cultural backgrounds. However, findings for other dimensions of culture, such as uncertainty avoidance and power distance, are somewhat contradictory and variable depending on whether the nation or the respondent is the unit of analysis.

Definitions of Acquiescent Responding

The ARS, also known as "yea-saying," was identified early in the 1900s (Fritz, 1927). Lentz defined it as "the tendency to agree rather than disagree to propositions in general" (1938, p. 659), and Stricker viewed acquiescent response style as one that reflected conformity "on items for which . . . social norms do not exist" (1963, p. 320). In contrast to survey questions for which social norms are more evident and thus invite socially desirable responses, survey items *not* containing obvious social desirability cues, he postulated, may be more likely to elicit acquiescent responses.

Knowles and Condon (1999) outlined two alternative approaches to interpreting acquiescence. According to one approach, acquiescence is a motivational problem of deliberate impression management (Leary & Kowalski, 1990). According to the other approach, acquiescence is the "uncritical acceptance of an item" (Knowles & Condon, 1999, p. 380). Ross and Mirowsky (1984b) agreed with this impression-management interpretation, viewing acquiescence, along with SDR, as an image management technique deliberately used by some respondents in low power positions within a society. However, empirical research has failed to demonstrate an association between ARS and measures of impression management or self-deceptive enhancement (Knowles & Nathan, 1997), although it has been associated with measures of conformity (Heavan, 1983).

The latter view outlined by Knowles and Condon (1999) regarding uncritical acceptance reflects Cronbach's (1942, 1950) earlier conceptualization, which emphasized suboptimal cognitive processing rather than conscious deception. Krosnick's (1991) analysis supports this conceptualization, suggesting that acquiescence is a form of satisficing. In this regard, Knowles and Nathan (1997) have suggested that the cognitive demands that are associated with some survey tasks, such as distractions, audiences, and time pressures, may increase acquiescent responding.

Various elements of the survey itself are thought to be predictive of ARS as well. It has long been believed that survey respondents may be more prone to acquiesce when questions are ambiguous or when respondents are otherwise uncertain of the task (Bass, 1955; Cronbach, 1950; Jackman, 1973;

Moscovici, 1963; Ray, 1983). Stricker (1963) classified ambiguity and readability as two question characteristics that may be associated with the tendency to provide acquiescent answers. Banta (1961) and Bass (1955) demonstrated empirically that acquiescent responding increased with the ambiguity of survey items. Stricker (1963) also found that acquiescent answers increased for more difficult-to-read attitude, but not personality, questions.

Finally, some have associated acquiescence with demographic characteristics of the respondent. For example, ARS has been found to be more common among persons with lower levels of education (Greenleaf, 1992a; Heavan, 1983; McClendon, 1991; Mirowsky & Ross, 1991; Narayan & Krosnick, 1996; Schuman & Presser, 1981; Watson, 1992).

Measuring Acquiescent Responding

Unlike SDR, there are no multipurpose measures of ARS. A number of approaches have been used in practice to measure this tendency. Most researchers have employed one of the approaches described in this section, but some have combined two or more types of measures into an index of acquiescence response bias (e.g., Baumgartner & Steenkamp, 2001).

Acquiescent responding has been captured most commonly as agreement with heterogeneous sets of survey items, although there is some variation in how "agreement" has been operationalized (e.g., Bachman & O'Malley, 1984). For example, acquiescence has been measured as the percentage of agree–disagree or yes–no questions to which a respondent answered "agree" or "yes" (e.g., Holbrook et al., 2003) or the proportion of statements to which a respondent reported they agreed or strongly agreed (Ross & Mirowsky, 1984b). It also has been measured as the number of "strongly agree" responses minus the number of "strongly disagree" responses to a series of Likert-type questions (Bachman & O'Malley, 1984).

Theoretically, any survey question with positive (e.g., approve, yes, favor, agree) response options and negative (e.g., disapprove, no, oppose, disagree) response options could be subject to acquiescence, but questions using some variant of agree–disagree response options are most common. One difficulty with this agreement-focused approach is that the actual attitude or dimension being measured may contaminate the metric of agreement. In other words, respondents may score high (or low) on such a measure of ARS at least in part because of their attitudes rather than their tendency to acquiesce.

One approach to minimizing contamination of ARS measures has been to examine items on a scale in which some items are reverse coded (e.g., Ross

& Mirowsky, 1984b; Watson, 1992). If the items in a scale all measure a single underlying construct, respondents should be unlikely to agree with both positively worded items (e.g., those for which greater agreement means being higher on the dimension being measured) and negatively worded items (e.g., those for which greater agreement means being lower on the dimension being measured). Although this approach addresses contamination of the ARS measure by the focal dimension being measured, the content of positive and negatively worded items is different.

To address this issue more systematically, researchers have used two approaches to attempt to eliminate contamination. One approach has been to assess ARS by randomly assigning one half of respondents to report whether they agree or disagree with one statement (e.g., "Please tell me whether you agree or disagree with this statement: Individuals are more to blame than social conditions for crime and lawlessness in this country") and the other half to respond to the opposite statement (e.g., "Please tell me whether you agree or disagree with this statement: Social conditions are more to blame than individuals for crime and lawlessness in this country"; Javeline, 1999). Acquiescence is present if the proportion of respondents who agree with one statement is greater than the proportion who disagree with the second. Cross-cultural differences in acquiescent reporting would be assessed by examining whether the effect of question form varies across respondents of different cultural groups or with different cultural values. This method requires that the researcher has control of the content of the questionnaire (i.e., it cannot typically be used to analyze acquiescence in existing data). Furthermore, it is sometimes difficult to ensure that the statements being used are true opposites.

A different approach to measuring ARS has been to compare the responses to an agree–disagree question to responses to a parallel question using a forced-choice response format (e.g., Javeline, 1999; Narayan & Krosnick, 1996; Schuman & Presser, 1981). For example, Schuman and Presser (1981) analyzed a series of survey experiments in which one half of respondents were randomly assigned an agree–disagree question (e.g., "Please tell me whether you agree or disagree with this statement: Individuals are more to blame than social conditions for crime and lawlessness in this country") and the other half were asked a forced-choice question (e.g., "Which in your opinion is more to blame for crime and lawlessness in this country – individuals or social conditions?"; see also Narayan & Krosnick, 1996). Acquiescence is assessed as the difference in the proportion of respondents who agree with the statement in the agree–disagree formatted question and the proportion of respondents who choose the parallel forced-choice option (e.g., "individuals" in our example). As with the previously described method, the challenge with this approach is to make the responses as comparable as possible across the two formats. This assessment approach has not been widely employed for cross-cultural comparisons (although see Javeline, 1999).

Cultural Variables and Acquiescent Responding

Cross-Cultural Differences in Acquiescent Response Style

Within the United States, one of the earliest studies to document ethnic variability in ARS propensity was reported by Lenski and Leggett (1960). In sampling a cross-section of adults in Detroit, they found that 20% of African American respondents gave mutually contradictory answers to survey questions, compared with 5% of White respondents. Subsequent research has confirmed that African Americans generally are more likely to provide acquiescent answers than Whites (Bachman & O'Malley, 1984; Dohrenwend, 1966; Johnson et al., 1997). Latino respondents in the United States have also been found to be more likely to acquiesce (Marín, Gamba, & Marín, 1992; Ross & Mirowsky, 1984b), with the level of acquiescence decreasing with increasing levels of acculturation (Marín et al., 1992). In analyses of a national survey of health care access conducted in the mid-1970s, Aday, Chiu, and Andersen (1980) found higher rates of ARS among Spanish-heritage persons in response to a single pair of positively and negatively worded questions. They reported that 24% of the Spanish-heritage group exhibited "some" tendency to acquiesce, compared with 13% of non-Hispanic Whites and 17% to 18% of other non-White populations. Using a balanced scale to construct a measure of acquiescence, Warnecke et al. (1997) also documented a greater propensity to provide acquiescent responses among African American and Mexican American respondents in the United States, compared with non-Hispanic Whites. Although the trend did suggest elevated levels of ARS among Puerto Ricans relative to non-Hispanic Whites in this study, the difference was not significant. Also, in comparing responses to a questionnaire concerned with beliefs about mental health, Arkoff, Thaver, and Elkind (1966) found that Asian graduate students in Hawaii provided more acquiescent responses than did Whites.

Across countries, evidence is accumulating that acquiescent response styles may be more typical of collectivistic societies (Harzing, 2006; Hofstede, 2001; Johnson, Kulesa, Cho, & Shavitt, 2005; P. B. Smith, 2004; P. B. Smith & Fisher, 2008; van de Vijver, Ploubidis, & van Hemert, 2004). For instance, across a sample of six European nations, van Herk, Poortinga, and Verhallen (2004) reported higher values on an acquiescence measure among respondents from several Mediterranean countries (Greece, Italy, and Spain), relative to samples of respondents from northwestern European countries (England, France, and Germany). Similar findings were reported by Baumgartner and Steenkamp (2001), who reported that Greek and Portuguese respondents exhibited greater acquiescence than respondents from other European nations. Greeks also were found to have a greater propensity to acquiesce compared with British and Belgian respondents (Steenkamp & Baumgartner, 1998) and U.S. respondents (Triandis & Triandis, 1962). England and Harpaz (1983), in examining large samples of respondents from the United States and Israel, found that differences in response patterns between these two nations also suggested the presence of systematically higher levels of acquiescence among Israeli respondents, which the authors indicated "certainly weakens any inference about meaningful country differences" (p. 55). Further, differences in acquiescent responding have been observed between Kazakh and Russian respondents, a finding interpreted to be a consequence of greater "deference" within the Kazakh culture (Javeline, 1999). In a study reported by Grimm and Church (1999), Philippine college students studying in the United States were found, on average, to acquiesce somewhat more than their U.S. counterparts, but only when the survey instruments were written in English and fewer scale points were provided. South African women also have been reported to acquiesce in their responses more frequently than Canadian adolescent females (Mwamwenda, 1993). Korean college students have also been found to acquiesce more than U.S. college students (Locke and Bail, 2009). In comparing acquiescence scores across 26 nations, analyses by Harzing (2006) found the highest ARS scores among students in Taiwan, Malaysia, India, and Mexico. Taken together, these findings are consistent with the notion of greater ARS among respondents in collectivistic compared with individualistic cultures.

Recent research also provides evidence that the person-level self-construal of independence–interdependence and the cultural-level context of individualism–collectivism may have an interactive effect on ARS. In one of the few studies that investigated the effects of both individual- and cultural-level effects, P. B. Smith and Fisher (2008) reported cross-national and cross-level analyses that demonstrate that interdependent persons are most acquiescent when embedded within collectivistic cultural environments. These findings are useful in specifying more precisely the conditions under which respondents are most likely to respond in an acquiescent manner.

Cultural Processes and Acquiescent Response Style

The findings referenced in the previous section indicate that researchers have begun to identify cultural dimensions that may underlie cross-group variability in ARS. Consistent with this evidence, acquiescence would appear to be more common in collectivistic cultures because they value deference, politeness, and hospitality (Javeline, 1999) and because their belief systems are characterized by holistic and dialectical thinking, which may be more tolerant of contradictory ideas (Choi & Choi, 2002; Minkov, 2008; Watkins & Cheung, 1995; Wong, Rindfleisch, & Burroughs, 2003).

P. B. Smith (2004) has also proposed that acquiescence may be more common within more uncertain and anxiety-prone cultures. Findings linking acquiescence with uncertainty avoidance, however, have been mixed. Smith found that nations scoring high in uncertainty avoidance also scored higher across several measures of acquiescence. He hypothesized that uncertainty-avoidant cultures are more anxiety prone and have less tolerance for ambiguity and that these traits may be associated with this response style. Similar national-level findings have been reported by van de Vijver et al. (2004). Individual-level analyses conducted by Harzing (2006) also suggest a positive association between ARS and uncertainty avoidance. In contrast, hierarchical analyses have found acquiescent responding to be higher within cultures that score low in uncertainty avoidance (Johnson et al., 2005), a finding that supports the view that acquiescence is more common in social environments with greater tolerance for ambiguity and uncertainty.

Findings relevant to potential associations between power distance and ARS are contradictory as well. Multination analyses by Harzing (2006) revealed a positive association between the acquiescent response style and one of three measures of power distance examined in her student samples. These findings were interpreted as suggesting that persons in high power distance cultures would be more likely to defer to persons in positions of authority, an interpretation reinforced by the power disparities in this study between student respondents and faculty investigators. Van de Vijver et al. (2004) reported a similar positive correlation between power distance and acquiescence, but contrary findings were reported by Johnson et al. (2005), who observed a negative relationship between these two constructs in employee samples that were examined via hierarchical models. At the national level, and consistent with other researchers who have examined national-level associations between these measures (Hofstede, 2001; P. B. Smith, 2004; P. B. Smith & Fisher, 2008; van Hemert et al., 2002), they noted a positive association between Hofstede's measure of power distance and ARS in their sample of nations ($r = 0.21$). However, they found a negative relationship between national-level power distance and individual-level ARS when examined in cross-level models.

Further, Johnson et al. (2005) identified an inverse relationship between cultural masculinity and acquiescent responding. Such findings are consistent with the emphasis placed on assertiveness and decisiveness within masculine cultures (Hofstede, 1998). Other research, however, has failed to find a relationship between this dimension of national culture and ARS at the national level (P. B. Smith, 2004; P. B. Smith & Fisher, 2008; van Hemert et al., 2002).

CULTURE AND EXTREME RESPONSE STYLES

The presence of extreme response propensities has been recognized for many decades (Cronbach, 1946) and is known to vary across racial and ethnic groups and across nations. Within the United States, for example, Latino and African Americans consistently have been shown to exhibit more ERS than do non-Hispanic Whites. Cross-nationally, U.S. samples have been demonstrated to respond in a more extreme manner than East Asian samples, and less so than South Asian samples. Several potential cultural processes are believed to contribute to extreme responding. Among those proposed are differential cultural emphases on sincerity, moderation, modesty, willingness to be judgmental, clarity, assertiveness, and decisiveness during interpersonal communications, as well as familiarity with survey instruments developed within Western scientific traditions.

Definitions of Extreme Responding

Clarke has described ERS as "the tendency for some individuals to consistently use the extreme ends of response scales in a multiple category response format" (2001, p. 302). Similarly, Baumgartner and Steenkamp defined ERS as the "tendency to endorse the most extreme response categories regardless of content" (2001, p. 145). Some earlier psychological research had conceptualized ERS as an indicator of intolerance of ambiguity, suggesting that "a social group with a higher tension level would earn a higher extreme response score than a social group with a lower tension level" (Soueif, 1958, p. 329). Over subsequent decades, however, few researchers have defined ERS in this manner.

Less educated respondents are known to endorse extreme responses more frequently than do those with more education (Greenleaf, 1992a; Marín et al., 1992; Warnecke et al., 1997), as are older respondents (Greenleaf, 1992a; Holbrook et al., 2006). Extreme responding also is believed to be more common when the topics being discussed are more salient to the respondent (Gibbons, Zellner, & Rudek, 1999). Given that the relevance of particular topics is, in many cases, likely to vary across cultures, it is perhaps not surprising that levels of ERS might vary as well.

As with the other response styles discussed in this chapter, cultural variability in ERS propensities may produce differences in empirical findings that are artifactual rather than substantive. Findings from various analytic procedures consequently may become biased. Score frequencies, standard deviations, interitem correlations, and factor structures, for example, may be influenced to differing degrees across groups (Arce-Ferrer, 2006; Arce-Ferrer & Ketterer, 2003; Chun, Campbell, & Yoo, 1974), introducing serious measurement confounds.

Measuring Extreme Response Style

There are several approaches to measuring extreme responding. Most commonly, it is assessed as the proportion of survey items for which a respondent selects an extreme response option. This often is assessed using a measure that was developed for other purposes (Bachman & O'Malley, 1984; Biggs & Das, 1973; Crandall, 1982; Das & Dutta, 1969). However, this approach to measuring ERS only reflects preference for the most extreme response options and does not capture additional variance in respondents' preferences for extremity or moderate response options. Furthermore, using items for which the true response may be correlated may contaminate these measures of ERS (Clarke, 2000; Rutten, De Beuckelaer, & Weijters, 2008). Such ERS indices should be treated in analysis as a binomial proportion, although this usually has not been done (Gold, 1975a, 1975b; Greenleaf, 1992b).

Another approach involves evaluating the variance around mean responses (Greenleaf, 1992a; Hui & Triandis, 1989; Kiesler & Sproull, 1986), again typically using responses to multi-item scales intended for other purposes (e.g., for measuring individual differences). However, this approach also typically involves examining variance across related items (e.g., items in an existing scale that all measure the same underlying construct) and therefore may result in contamination.

Greenleaf (1992b) recommended that existing survey items not be used to measure ERS but that a special set of items be included in a survey to do so. Accordingly, he developed a measure that seeks to avoid the issue of contamination via a scale in which (a) the items are minimally intercorrelated, (b) the items have similar and known proportions of respondents who chose responses of a given extremity, and (c) "established stochastic techniques and statistical models" can be applied to assess internal reliability or convergent validity (p. 331).

Although it enables measurement of ERS without contamination, the utility of this measure is limited in a number of ways. First and most obviously, it cannot be used to assess ERS in existing data sets that do not include the scale. Second, using this measure necessitates adding a 16-item scale to a survey or study, which is sometimes not financially feasible. In addition, the generalizability of conclusions based on this scale may be limited. For instance, the scale uses 6-point Likert-type response options and "is not intended to measure ERS for scales with different anchors or a different number of response intervals" (Greenleaf, 1992b, p. 330). Furthermore, the items were administered in a mail survey and may not be generalizable to other modes. Thus, it is unclear whether this scale measures a general tendency to select extreme responses across formats or modalities. Researchers using other modes or response formats may need to use the procedures described by Greenleaf (1992b) to develop a new ERS scale. Finally, it is unlikely that all items in the Greenleaf scale are associated with equivalent norms across cultural groups.

Other approaches to measuring ERS have used structural equation modeling (SEM) and item response theory procedures to create a latent factor representing ERS. DeJong, Steenkamp, Fox, and Baumgartner (2008), for example, employed item response theory to develop a measure of ERS that does not assume that all items are equally useful for measuring ERS or require that an item's usefulness for measuring ERS be constant across groups (e.g., countries or racial groups). The authors argued that this approach also allows researchers to use existing survey items to measure ERS even if those items are related (DeJong et al., 2008). This allows researchers to measure ERS without including items (such as those developed by Greenleaf) developed specifically for that purpose.

Cheung and Rensvold (2000) used SEM to assess whether the measurement model for ERS was invariant across cultural groups. Holbrook et al. (2006) argued that although ERS has been defined as a preference for extreme response options regardless of content, measures of ERS used in previous research do not reduce contamination from the content of items used to measure ERS. A measure of ERS was introduced that uses confirmatory factor analysis. With this measure, the extremities of responses to a series of questions are treated as measured variables that reflect a latent variable representing ERS (with the impact of the latent variable on each measured variable being set to 1.0). Individual differences in ERS were indicated if the variance of this factor was significantly different from zero (Holbrook et al., 2006). In a comparison of this new measure to a measure based on the traditional approaches described earlier, this measure of ERS showed more theoretically sensible associations with demographic and personality variables. Using SEM to measure ERS is a relatively new approach in the literature, but it shows promise for assessing ERS in cross-cultural contexts.

Cultural Variables and Extreme Responding

Cross-Cultural Differences in Extreme Response Style

Several studies have documented variations in extreme responding across racial and ethnic groups within the United States. Early work by Berg and Collier (1953) reported higher levels of ERS among African American versus White male college students. No differences were found, however, for African American versus White females. Using several nationally representative samples of youth participating in the Monitoring the Future project, Bachman and O'Malley (1984) also documented the finding that African American youth were more likely than White youth to select the extreme response categories across several Likert-type scales. Further, Holbrook et al. (2006) reported more extreme responding among African American and Latino samples compared with White non-Hispanic respondents in an analysis of data from the 2004 National Election Survey. Similar findings of higher ERS among African American and Latino than among White college students in the United States were reported by Clarke (2001). In a sample of adults in Chicago, Warnecke et al. (1997) also reported higher ERS among Mexican American and Puerto Rican respondents, relative to non-Hispanic White respondents. Comparisons of patient ratings of medical care have also documented more extreme responding among Hispanic, compared to non-Hispanic, samples (Weech-Maldonado et al., 2008). Additionally, a comparison of Hispanic versus non-Hispanic U.S. Navy recruits reported by Hui and Triandis (1989) indicated higher levels of extreme responding among Hispanics, but only when reporting on 5-point measurement scales; no differences in extreme responding were found when 10-point scales were employed.

ERS differences have also been observed across the few available international comparisons between West and South Asian samples. Stening and Everett (1984) found more extreme responding among Indonesians, Malaysians, Filipinos, and Thais, relative to U.S. respondents. A seven-nation study conducted by Marshall and Lee (1998) also reported cross-national differences, with samples scoring highest on ERS in the nations of Indonesia and Malaysia and lowest in Australia, the United States, and Singapore (New Zealand and South Korea had intermediate scores). No differences were observed, however, in ERS scores between Philippine and U.S. college students (Grimm & Church, 1999).

In contrast, comparisons between Western and East and Asian samples generally have revealed greater levels of ERS among Western respondents. For example, Chun et al. (1974) identified more ERS within a sample of U.S. college students, compared with a similar sample of Korean students. C. Lee and Green (1991) reported similar findings. C. Chen, Lee, and Stevenson (1995) found increased use of extreme response categories among U.S. students when compared with students from Japan and China. Zax and Takahashi (1967) and Wang et al. (2008) reported similar findings. Among samples of consumers in four nations, those from the United States were found to be more likely to use the full range of 9-point scales, compared with consumers from China, Korea, and Thailand (Yeh et al., 1998). Comparisons between Australian and Asian (predominantly Chinese) samples conducted by Dolnicar and Grun (2007) found higher ERS scores among Australians. Findings consistent with these have also been reported within the United States, where Grandy (1996) reported that Asian American students tended to avoid the extreme endpoints of response scales in comparison to Whites. Gibbons, Hamby, and Dennis (1997) similarly found that U.S.-born college students had higher ERS scores than did a sample of primarily East Asian international students at the same university. J. W. Lee, Jones, Mineyama, and Zhang (2002) found similar results in comparing samples of Caucasian and East Asian (Chinese and Japanese) consumers in Southern California.

Similar findings have been reported in a study by Iwata, Roberts, and Kawakami (1995) that compared samples of Japanese and U.S. adult responses to the Centers for Epidemiologic Studies Depression Scale (CES-D). However, this research noted greater ERS among U.S. respondents for positive items (e.g., symptoms such as feeling good, happy) only. There were no differences in the selection of extreme values when responding to negatively worded depression questions (e.g., feeling fearful or a failure). Iwata and colleagues interpreted these findings as being a consequence of Japan's traditional (and collectivistic) emphasis on the maintenance of social harmony by modestly understating one's personal qualities. Therefore, Iwata et al.'s research suggests that group differences may be driven more by cultural variability in self-presentation styles than by familiarity with survey question response formats. Consistent with these findings, other research has noted higher levels of nonresponding to positively worded items among Chinese Americans (Ying, 1989).

The pattern of findings reported across the various cultures reviewed in this section are consistent with those obtained from a recent large-scale study by Harzing (2006) that examined response styles across 26 nations. Specifically, she noted more ERS among respondents of the United States, relative to East Asian samples from Taiwan, Japan, Hong Kong, and China. She also observed more extreme responding among South Asians in Malaysia and India and among persons from Mexico and several other Latin American countries, compared with persons in the United States.

Across regions of Europe, Harzing (2006) found higher levels of ERS in southern European and Latin nations, compared with the nations of northern, western, and eastern Europe. These findings also support those from several studies that have included samples from European nations. Among these was one of the earliest comparative investigations of ERS, conducted by Brengelmann (1959), who compared response styles across English and German samples. Results suggested that German respondents systematically provided more extreme responses than did English respondents. Another early cross-national study by Triandis and Triandis (1962) found more extreme responses among Greek students than among U.S. students. A more recent study that examined survey data from six European nations (van Herk et al., 2004) concluded that ERS was more common in the Mediterranean countries of Greece, Italy, and Spain than in the northwestern European nations of France, Germany, and the United Kingdom. A student sample from France, however, engaged in more extreme responding than did one from Australia (Clarke, 2001).

Few studies have examined ERS patterns among African and Middle Eastern populations. Moors (2003) reported that immigrants in Belgium of Moroccan nationality were more likely to select extreme responses than were those with a Turkish background (Moors, 2003). Members of these two minority groups having an oral or reading proficiency (or both) in one of Belgium's languages were more likely to endorse extreme response options. In contrast, a study in Israel by Shapiro, Rosenblood, Berlyne, and Finberg (1976) found greater ERS among Bedouin youth than among their Moroccan Arab peers, who were presumed to have a more Western orientation. These findings were hypothesized to be a consequence of differential exposure to the English language. These discrepant findings are difficult to reconcile in the absence of additional empirical evidence from similar populations.

Cultural Processes and Extreme Response Style

Several mechanisms have been proposed to underlie the associations between cultural factors and ERS. C. Chen et al. (1995) suggested that a lower propensity to endorse extreme response options in survey questionnaires may be a consequence of East Asians being influenced by the concept of moderation, as emphasized by Confucian philosophy, and by beliefs that individuals should not stand out from their social group. Si and Cullen (1998) have made a similar point, observing that Asian cultures emphasize taking middle positions and avoiding extremes. This is also consistent with East Asian emphases on being interdependent (Markus & Kitayama, 1991), nonjudgmental (Riordan & Vandenberg, 1994), shy (Hoy, 1993), and modest in one's self-presentation (Farh, Dobbins, & Cheng, 1991; Kitayama, Markus, Matsumoto, & Norasakkunit, 1997). It also has been suggested that cultures with a high propensity to respond using extreme response options are those in which sincerity and conviction are emphasized (Arce-Ferrer & Ketterer, 2003; Clarke, 2001; Gibbons et al. 1999) and those with higher tension levels and a corresponding intolerance for ambiguity (Soueif, 1958). East-West cultural differences in dialectical thinking have also been discussed as an explanation for variability in extreme responding (Hamamura, Heine, & Paulhus, 2008; Minkov, 2009).

Observations of acculturation processes may contribute insights to our understanding of how culture influences ERS as well. English–Spanish bilinguals, for example, have been shown to exhibit a greater preference for extreme responses when interviewed in Spanish than in English (Gibbons et al., 1999). Consistent with this, Marín et al. (1992) reported that ERS was inversely correlated with acculturation levels among Latinos in the United States. That is, as Latino immigrants become more acculturated to U.S. society, their propensity to endorse extreme response categories diminished. Marín and colleagues interpreted these findings as being consistent with a fundamental Latino cultural script known as *simpatia* (Triandis et al., 1984), which they argue permits interpersonal interactions "to be more fluid and more responsive to a group's needs when individuals use extreme responses that reflect their unmoderated feelings" (Marín et al., 1992, p. 508). Wang et al. (2008) reported similar trends, finding that U.S.-born

Asian students selected scale endpoints more frequently than did foreign born Asian students.

Arce-Ferrer (2006) further hypothesized that higher ERS propensity among Latinos may be a consequence of an incongruity between collectivist communication patterns that emphasize high-context messages and the more direct individualistic principles underlying survey question construction. Indeed, common survey question design recommendations emphasize the importance of clear, unambiguously worded survey questions (Bradburn et al., 2004) and assume a commonality of direct communication style that is likely to be unwarranted when collecting survey data within high-context cultural groups (Oyserman, Coon, & Kemmelmeier, 2002). Consequently, Arce-Ferrer suggested that among more collectivistic populations, less familiarity with Western-style survey rating scales and the ambiguity inherent in their decontextualized format may result in reduced precision in language use and reduced sophistication in the use of ordinal-style Likert-type response scales. McQuiston, Larson, Parrado, and Flaskerud (2002) also presented evidence suggesting that Likert-type survey question formats may be overly confusing to recently arrived Mexican immigrants. Similar concerns have been expressed by Flaskerud, who, after observing that both Central American and Vietnamese immigrants had difficulty using the response options presented in Likert scales, commented that "the degree of variation Likert-type scales attempt to measure is meaningless to some cultural groups" (1988, p. 186).

Several of Hofstede's (2001) cultural dimensions have been empirically associated with extreme response style as well. An individual-difference measure of intolerance of uncertainty developed by Naemi, Beal and Payne (2009) has, for example, been found to be associated with extreme responding within a sample of U.S. college students. Marshall and Lee (1998) reported a positive correlation between ERS and responses to both a three-item measure of individualism and a six-item measure of religiosity. C. Chen et al. (1995) also found a positive association between a measure of individualism and the likelihood of endorsing extreme response options among students in Japan, Taiwan, and the United States. Other evidence comes from a study by Gibbons et al. (1997), who reported a correlation between ERS and less traditional attitudes toward women's roles, a finding consistent with the suggestion that the use of extreme response options is associated with an individualistic orientation. In a study using scales measuring cultural models of parenting, Lamm and Keller (2007) found more ERS among mothers living in countries with interdependent orientations than among those in countries with independent or autonomous orientations. This finding was interpreted as being consistent with an understanding of ERS as an expression of "axiomatic, rule-like beliefs that are communally shared" (2007, p. 54). DeJong et al. (2008) also reported a positive association between individualism and ERS in a multilevel analysis conducted with samples representing 26 countries. However, in a more complex finding involving hierarchical models, P. B. Smith and Fisher (2008) reported that *inter*dependent persons were less likely to select extreme responses but that this was especially the case when they were embedded within individualistic cultural environments.

Positive associations with ERS have also been found for national-level measures of uncertainty avoidance (DeJong et al., 2008; Harzing, 2006; van de Vijver et al., 2004), power distance (Johnson et al., 2005), and masculinity (DeJong et al., 2008; Johnson et al., 2005). Taken together, these findings suggest that extreme responding is characteristic of cultures that value distinctive, independent, competitive, assertive, decisive, and sincere behavior and that have a low tolerance for ambiguity (Hamilton, 1968; Marín et al., 1992). Preferences for middling response options – another response style not otherwise discussed in this chapter – may be more common within cultures that value modesty, moderation, interpersonal harmony, and subtlety (Chia, Allred, & Jerzak, 1997). For a review of the middling response style literature, see Yang, Harkness, Chin, and Villar (2010).

STRATEGIES FOR CONFRONTING CULTURAL VARIABILITY IN RESPONSE STYLES

A variety of strategies have been suggested as possible approaches to adjusting for group differences in survey response styles. Three general sets of strategies have been considered. One set emphasizes careful attention to the design of survey items and scales in hopes of eliminating or minimizing the effects of response styles. A second is concerned with addressing elements of the social environment within which survey data are collected that may encourage ARS and SDR. The third set includes several analysis strategies designed to detect or adjust for response style differences across groups. A brief overview of these proposed solutions is provided here. Researchers concerned with cultural variability in response styles would be advised to address this problem when designing measurement instruments and when collecting their data, in addition to employing analytic solutions.

Questionnaire Design Strategies

There are a variety of questionnaire design recommendations intended to minimize cross-group differences in response styles. To minimize socially desirable responding, Jones (1963) suggested avoiding the use of questions that are likely to invite socially desirable responses. T. W. Smith (2003) recommended framing questions to minimize threat and the likelihood that socially desirable responses will be provided, and Mitchell (1973) suggested that "moral" words should not be used when developing survey questions, because they are also likely to encourage socially desirable responding. See also Bradburn et al. (2004) for detailed recommendations.

To avoid ARS, Converse and Presser (1986) recommended that agree–disagree question response formats not be used when constructing survey items. Krosnick (1999) observed that yes–no and true–false formats are vulnerable to ARS as well and recommended using a forced-choice response format to minimize acquiescence. Also commonly suggested is the use of measurement scales that contain balanced sets of positively and negatively worded questions to eliminate or minimize the effects of acquiescence (Cloud & Vaughan, 1970; Jackson, 1967; Javeline, 1999; Knowles & Nathan, 1997; Messick, 1991; Mirowsky & Ross, 1991; Ray, 1979; Watson, 1992). However, Triandis (1972) cautioned that reversed items may have different neutral points across cultures that will further complicate analyses and comparisons. Using an established U.S. consumer scale, Wong et al. (2003) reported that whereas positively worded items and reverse-worded items appear to be largely equivalent in the United States (as assessed by item intercorrelations), they appear to represent different constructs for respondents in Thailand, Japan, Singapore, and Korea. Thus, the authors urged caution in the use of mixed-worded scales cross-culturally.

Other recommendations for minimizing ERS include the use of ranking rather than rating response formats (van Herk, 2000), although respondents may have more difficulty answering ranking items. Research by Diamantopoulos, Reynolds, and Simintiras (2006) also has found differences in ERS to be associated with the types of personal pronouns employed in survey items, suggesting that third-person items may be less susceptible to extreme responding than first-person items. Another suggestion put forth by several researchers is to reduce the length of Likert-type scales to a binary format (Cronbach, 1946, 1950; T. W. Smith, 2003). Interestingly, there is also some evidence that increasing, rather than decreasing, the number of response categories may be the best strategy for minimizing ERS. Experimental work by Hui and Triandis (1989) has suggested that ERS differences across cultural groups can be decreased or eliminated altogether when the number of response options presented to respondents is increased from 5 to 10 options. Similar research by Clarke (2001), however, indicated that cross-national variability in extreme responding actually may increase with the number of response choices available to respondents.

Data Collection Strategies

A rich literature is available suggesting that the race and ethnicity of survey respondents may interact with the race and ethnicity of interviewers to produce acquiescent or socially desirable responses, particularly when questions focus on topics that are racially or ethnically relevant (Anderson, Silver, & Abramson 1988; Schuman & Converse 1971; Stokes-Brown, 2006). Potential explanations include the possibility that respondents defer to the perceived thoughts, feelings, or opinions of interviewers from different cultural backgrounds when answering such questions (Lenski & Leggett, 1960); that respondents wish to portray themselves in a positive or socially desirable manner (Crowne & Marlowe, 1960); because racial stereotypes are activated for the racial or ethnic group of the interviewer (Davis & Silver, 2003); or because of cultural values that dictate politeness to strangers (Jones, 1963). To address these issues, many survey researchers deliberately match respondents with interviewers of a similar racial or ethnic background (Schaeffer, 1980; Vernon, Roberts, & Lee, 1982) or with indigenous interviewers (Bloom & Padilla, 1979) in hopes of placing respondents at greater ease, fostering greater candor, and minimizing the uncertainties of cross-cultural communication (Brislin, 1986). Although that is a common approach, some have argued that employing interviewers from outside may be preferable when conducting research in communities where the need for privacy is strong (Ferketich, Phillips, & Verran, 1993).

Another common strategy for addressing SDR is increasing respondents' privacy and anonymity when answering survey questions; much evidence suggests that social desirability response bias is lessened under conditions of greater privacy or anonymity (e.g., Himmelfarb & Lickteig, 1982; Paulhus, 1984; Tourangeau & Smith, 1996; Warner, 1965). The anonymity and privacy with which respondents are able to answer survey questions have been manipulated in a variety of ways, including the mode in which the survey questions are administered and the use of techniques such as the randomized response technique (RRT; e.g., Warner, 1965) and the item-count technique (ICT; e.g., Droitcour et al., 1991; Miller, Harrel, & Cisin, 1986) that allow respondents to answer a survey question anonymously without an interviewer or researcher knowing their responses. There is considerable evidence that self-administered surveys result in greater reports of unfavorable attitudes, beliefs, and behaviors and fewer reports of favorable attitudes, beliefs, and behaviors (e.g., Aquilino, 1992; Aquilino & LoSciuto, 1990; Tourangeau & Smith, 1996; see Bradburn et al., 2004, for a review). Similarly, techniques like the RRT and ICT have been shown to reduce socially desirable responding compared with direct self-reports (e.g., Buchman & Tracy, 1982; Dalton, Wimbush, & Daily, 1994; Franklin, 1989; Himmelfarb & Lickteig, 1982). However, applications of these techniques to address SDR concerns in cross-cultural research are rare.

Statistical Adjustment Strategies

More than 40 years ago, D. H. Smith (1967) recognized the importance of addressing the problem of cross-cultural variability in response styles when analyzing survey data. Today, several statistical approaches, many of which were initially developed in monocultural settings, are available as possible strategies for adjusting for cross-group differences in SDR, ARS, and ERS.

Statistical adjustments using standardized measures of social desirability (Middleton & Jones, 2000; Paulhus, 1981, 1991; Pleck, Sonenstein, & Ku, 1996), ARS (Vernon et al., 1982), or ERS (Greenleaf, 1992b) are a simple and commonly employed approach to attempting to compensate for differential response styles across groups. However, some investigators have found this to be an ineffective strategy (Dijkstra, Smit, & Comijs, 2001; Ellingson, Sackett, & Hough, 1999). Latent modeling approaches also have been used. Watson (1992), Billiet and McClendon (2000), and Mirowsky and Ross (1991) each have identified a general ARS dimension via SEM that could be included as a covariate in substantive analyses. Welkenhuysen-Gybels, Billiet, and Cambre (2003) have demonstrated a similar approach to controlling for ARS when assessing measurement equivalence across cultural groups. A related latent-class factor approach has been employed by Moors (2003) to identify and adjust for ERS.

Another popular approach is to apply corrections directly to measures believed to be affected by response style bias. For example, Greenleaf (1992a) described a method that applies a mean correction to item scores to adjust for ARS. Other forms of item and scale standardization have been employed by Leung and Bond (1989), Hofstede (2001), and P. B. Smith (2004). Harzing (2006), however, cautioned that these approaches also may eliminate true substantive differences. Others have attempted to avoid acquiescence and extreme responding effects by developing rescaled ipsative (i.e., ranking) measures that are believed to be less susceptible to these forms of bias (Cunningham, Cunningham, & Green, 1977; Schuman & Presser, 1981; Toner, 1987). Fischer (2004), Hofstee, ten Berge, and Hendriks (1998), and van de Vijver and Leung (1997) each provided in-depth reviews of these and additional procedures for scoring questionnaires to correct for acquiescence and extreme responding.

Emerging Topics

Despite the rapidly accumulating evidence about the role of culture in survey response styles, much of the evidence can be linked to the broad-based distinction between individualist and collectivist societies. This distinction is profoundly important and thus represents the most broadly used dimension of cultural variability for cross-cultural comparison (Gudykunst & Ting-Toomey, 1988). However, there are limitations to the insights afforded by any broad dimension. Further refinement can stimulate new insights and afford a more nuanced understanding of the link between culture and consumer phenomena (Maheswaran & Shavitt, 2000).

For instance, recent research points to the importance of a relatively new cultural distinction. Triandis and his colleagues (Singelis, Triandis, Bhawuk, & Gelfand, 1995; Triandis, 1995; Triandis, Chen, & Chan, 1998; Triandis & Gelfand, 1998) have proposed that, nested within each individualistic or collectivistic cultural category, some societies are *horizontal* (valuing equality) whereas others are *vertical* (emphasizing hierarchy). This distinction resembles the nation-level power distance construct (Hofstede, 1980, 2001), but there are important conceptual and structural distinctions (see Shavitt et al., 2006).

Although the contribution of the horizontal–vertical distinction is sometimes obscured by methods that conflate it with other dimensions, its impact is distinct from that associated with individualism–collectivism. Across numerous studies, results support the utility of examining distinctions in hierarchy and status motives for the understanding of personal and cultural values, social perceptions, and self-presentational patterns (e.g., Shavitt, Johnson, & Zhang, in press; Torelli & Shavitt, in press; see also Shavitt et al., 2006, for a review). For instance, people with a horizontal collectivistic cultural orientation, who emphasize sociability, benevolence, and cooperation, are characterized by a tendency to engage in impression management across multiple survey measures of this tendency. However, people with a vertical collectivistic orientation, who emphasize stature, duty, and conformity, are not especially likely to be concerned with impression management

(Lalwani et al., 2006). One might speculate that the vertical collectivistic orientation would instead be more predictive of deferential responding, perhaps including acquiescent responding, particularly if a survey is fielded by a person or organization toward which the respondent feels a sense of obligation or duty.

People with a horizontal individualistic orientation, who emphasize self-competence, self-direction, and independence, have a tendency to engage in self-deceptive enhancement (SDE). In contrast, those with a vertical individualistic orientation, who put emphasis on status, achievement, and personal power (Torelli & Shavitt, in press) are not likely to exhibit SDE (Lalwani et al., 2006). Instead, one may speculate that the vertical individualistic orientation would be more predictive of desirable self-presentations concerning one's achievements and competitive success, as well as a greater tendency to employ extreme response categories and a lesser inclination to provide acquiescent answers.

Recent research on a closely related construct, *status differentiation* (Matsumoto, 2007), suggests that this dimension also accounts for unique variance in cross-national differences beyond the role of other values such as collectivism. In this research, a 20-item scale was developed to address how individuals differentiate their self-regulation and their assertive behaviors toward others depending on the status inequalities between them. The results point to cultural distinctions in how differently people claim to treat those above them versus those below them in status, with Japanese showing a more hierarchical form of status differentiation than U.S. and South Korean participants. Therefore, status differentiation may be associated with a tendency to acquiesce in response to interviewers or survey organizations that one perceives to be above oneself in status. It may also be associated with assertive and extreme responding in response to interviewers or survey organizations that one perceives to be below oneself in status.

In sum, the constructs of horizontal and vertical individualism and collectivism, and the related dimension of status differentiation, hold promise for illuminating how power and status motivations influence survey response styles. The impact of these variables on survey response styles across cultures is a topic worthy of future research.

DISCUSSION

This chapter has reviewed a growing body of evidence suggesting that culture is an important mediator of several commonly recognized survey response styles, including acquiescent, extreme, and socially desirable responding.

This research, distilled from a diverse range of disciplines, has produced generally consistent patterns of findings, which are all the more impressive given the multiple levels and diverse types of cultural indicators that have been examined. For example, it would appear that SDR, broadly defined, is more common both among less powerful cultural groups within societies and among more traditional (i.e., collectivistic) cultures across nations. Similarly, acquiescent responding is more common both among cultural minority groups within nations and among respondents from more collectivistic and uncertainty-avoidant nations. Systematic differences in extreme responding also appear between Western and East Asian cultures. These may represent different degrees of individualism and uncertainty avoidance. (ERS differences between White and minority populations in the United States, however, are less well understood.)

The largely consistent nature of these findings is noteworthy given the multiple measures of each of these response styles that have been employed in practice. However, some of the cultural variability in response styles identified so far may be confounded with culture-based differences in how survey questions are interpreted or in substantive differences across cultures. A general limitation, then, is that most of the cross-cultural comparisons of response style measures reviewed have not investigated the role of measurement equivalence. Although this is a general concern, it would appear to be particularly problematic when comparing measures of social desirability across cultures. It will be important for future research to address this oversight.

It is also important to recognize that nearly all research concerned with cultural variability in survey response styles has been opportunistic in nature. We are aware of few studies that were designed explicitly to investigate response style variability cross-culturally (c.f., Lalwani et al., 2006). Rather, most research appears to have comprised creative secondary analyses of substantive survey data that were primarily collected for other purposes. Although these analyses have been highly informative, it may be difficult to make further advances without specifically designing research to confront these issues. Perhaps of primary importance would be research that clearly documents how failure to recognize or properly adjust for cross-cultural differences in survey response styles contributes erroneous inferences. Although such problems undoubtedly exist in the literature, the research reviewed here is only able to document cultural differences successfully using scales designed specifically to measure one or more response styles. Examples in which these differences actually altered interpretations of substantive measures are relatively rare (although see Iwata et al., 1995).

Finally, it should be acknowledged that several other survey-related response styles exist that were not reviewed in this chapter. Some of these include a middling response style (Chia et al., 1997; Si & Cullen, 1998), dis-acquiescence (Baumgartner & Steenkamp, 2001), nondifferentiation (Holbrook et al., 2003) and random, or noncontingent, responding (Watkins & Cheung, 1995). To date, these have received comparatively little attention; thus, little is known about the role of culture in these survey response patterns.

REFERENCES

Abe, J. S., & Zane, N. W. S. (1990). Psychological maladjustment among Asian and White American college students: Controlling for confounds. *Journal of Counseling Psychology, 37*, 437–444.

Abramson, P. R., & Claggett, W. (1986). Race-related differences in self-reported and validated turnout in 1984. *Journal of Politics, 48*, 412–422.

Adams, S. A., Matthews, C. E., Ebbeling, C. B., Moore, C. G., Cunningham, J. E., Fulton, J., et al. (2005). The effect of social desirability and social approval on self-reports of physical activity. *American Journal of Epidemiology, 161*, 389–398.

Aday, L. A., Chiu, G. Y., & Andersen, R. (1980). Methodological issues in health care surveys of the Spanish heritage population. *American Journal of Public Health, 70*, 367–374.

Anderson, B. A., Silver, B. D., & Abramson, P. R. (1988). The effects of race of the interviewer on measures of electoral participation by blacks in SRC National Election Studies. *Public Opinion Quarterly, 52*, 53–83.

Aneshensel, C. S., Frerichs, R. R., Clark, V. A., & Yokopenic, P. A. (1982). Measuring depression in the community: A comparison of telephone and personal interviews. *Public Opinion Quarterly, 46*, 110–121.

Aquilino, W. S. (1992). Telephone versus face-to-face interviewing for household drug use surveys. *International Journal of Addiction, 27*, 71–91.

Aquilino, W. S. (1998). Effects of interview mode on measuring depression in younger adults. *Journal of Official Statistics, 14*, 15–29.

Aquilino, W. S., & LoSciuto, L. A. (1990). Effects of interview mode of self-reported drug use. *Public Opinion Quarterly, 54*, 362–395.

Arce-Ferrer, A. J. (2006). An investigation into the factors influencing extreme-response style: Improving meaning of translated and culturally adapted rating scales. *Educational and Psychological Measurement, 66*, 374–392.

Arce-Ferrer, A. J., & Ketterer, J. J. (2003). The effect of scale tailoring for cross-cultural application on scale reliability and construct validity. *Educational and Psychological Measurement, 63*, 484–501.

Arkoff, A., Thaver, F., & Elkind, L. (1966). Mental health and counseling ideas of Asian and American students. *Journal of Counseling Psychology, 13*, 219–223.

Bachman, J. G., & O'Malley, P. M. (1984). Yea-saying, nay-saying, and going to extremes: Black–White differences in response style. *Public Opinion Quarterly, 48*, 491–509.

Banta, T. J. (1961). Social attitudes and response styles. *Educational and Psychological Measurement, 21*, 543–557.

Bass, B. M. (1955). Authoritarianism or acquiescence? *Journal of Abnormal and Social Psychology, 51*, 616–623.

Baumgartner, H., & Steenkamp, J.-B. E. M. (2001). Response styles in marketing research: A cross-national investigation. *Journal of Marketing Research, 38*, 143–156.

Berg, I. A., & Collier, J. S. (1953). Personality and group differences in extreme response sets. *Educational and Psychological Measurement, 13*, 164–169.

Bernardi, R. A. (2006). Associations between Hofstede's cultural constructs and social desirability response bias. *Journal of Business Ethics, 65*, 43–53.

Biggs, J. B., & Das, J. P. (1973). Extreme response set, internality–externality, and performance. *British Journal of Social and Clinical Psychology, 12*, 99–210.

Billiet, J. B., & McClendon, M. J. (2000). Modeling acquiescence in measurement models for two balanced sets of items. *Structural Equation Modeling, 7*, 608–628.

Blair, E., Sudman, S., Bradburn, N. M., & Stocking, C. (1977). How to ask questions about drinking and sex: Response effects in measuring consumer behavior. *Journal of Marketing Research, 14*, 316–321.

Bloom, D., & Padilla, A. M. (1979). A peer interviewer model in conducting surveys among Mexican-American youth. *Journal of Community Psychology, 7*, 129–136.

Bond, R., & Smith, P. B. (1996). Culture and conformity: A meta-analysis of studies using Asch's (1952b, 1956) line judgment task. *Psychological Bulletin, 119*, 111–137.

Bradburn, N. M., & Sudman, S. (1979). Reinterpreting the Marlowe–Crowne scale. In N. M. Bradburn & S. Sudman (Eds.), *Improving interview method and questionnaire design* (pp. 85–106). San Francisco: Jossey-Bass.

Bradburn, N., Sudman, S., & Wansink, B. (2004). *Asking questions: The definitive guide to questionnaire design – For market research, political polls, and social and health questionnaires* (rev ed.). San Francisco: Jossey-Bass.

Brengelmann, J.C. (1959). Differences in questionnaire responses between English and German nationals. *Acta Psychologica, 16*, 339–355.

Brislin, R. W. (1986). The wording and translation of research instruments. In W. J. Lonner & J. W. Berry (Eds.), *Field methods in cross-cultural research* (pp. 137–164). Beverly Hills, CA: Sage.

Buchman, T. A., & Tracy, J. A. (1982). Obtaining responses to sensitive questions: Conventional questionnaire versus randomized response technique. *Journal of Accounting Research, 20*, 263–271.

Chen, C., Lee, S.-Y., & Stevenson, H. W. (1995). Response style and cross-cultural comparisons of rating scales among East Asian and North American students. *Psychological Science, 6*, 170–175.

Chen, G.-M. (1995). Differences in self-disclosure patterns among Americans versus Chinese: A comparative study. *Journal of Cross-Cultural Psychology, 26*, 84–91.

Cheung, G. W., & Rensvold, R. B. (2000). Assessing extreme and acquiescence response sets in cross-cultural research using structural equations modeling. *Journal of Cross-Cultural Psychology, 31*, 187–212.

Chia, R. C., Allred, L. J., & Jerzak, P. A. (1997). Attitudes toward women in Taiwan and China. *Psychology of Women Quarterly, 21*, 137–150.

Chun, K.-T., Campbell, J. B., & Yoo, J. H. (1974). Extreme response style in cross-cultural research: A reminder. *Journal of Cross-Cultural Psychology, 5*, 465–480.

Church, A. T. (1987). Personality research in a non-Western culture: The Philippines. *Psychological Bulletin, 102*, 272–292.

Clark, L. R., Brasseux, C., Richmond, D., Getson, P., & D'Angelo, L. J. (1997). Are adolescents accurate in self-report of frequencies of sexually transmitted diseases and pregnancies? *Journal of Adolescent Health, 21*, 91–96.

Clarke, I., III. (2000). Extreme response style in cross-cultural research: An empirical investigation. *Journal of Social Behavior & Personality, 15*, 137–152.

Clarke, I., III. (2001). Extreme response style in cross-cultural research. *International Marketing Review, 18*, 301–324.

Clausen, A. R. (1968). Response validity – Vote report. *Public Opinion Quarterly, 32*, 588–606.

Cloud, J., & Vaughan, G. M. (1970). Using balanced scales to control acquiescence. *Sociometry, 33*, 193–202.

Colon, H. M., Robles, R. R., & Sahai, H. (2001). The validity of drug use responses in a household survey in Puerto Rico: Comparison of survey responses of cocaine and heroin use with hair tests. *International Journal of Epidemiology, 30*, 1042–1049.

Converse, J. M., & Presser, S. (1986). *Survey questions: Handcrafting the standardized questionnaire.* Thousand Oaks, CA: Sage.

Crandall, J. E. (1982). Social interest, extreme response style, and implications for adjustments. *Journal of Research in Personality, 16*, 82–89.

Crandall, V. C., Crandall, V. J., & Katkovsky, W. (1965). A children's social desirability questionnaire. *Journal of Consulting Psychology, 29*, 27–36.

Cronbach, L. J. (1942). Studies of acquiescence as a factor in the true–false test. *Journal of Educational Psychology, 33*, 401–415.

Cronbach, L. J. (1946). Response sets and test validity. *Educational and Psychological Measurement, 6*, 475–494.

Cronbach, L. J. (1950). Further evidence on response sets and test design. *Educational and Psychological Measurement, 10*, 3–31.

Crowne, D. P., & Marlowe, D. (1960). A new scale of social desirability independent of pathology. *Journal of Consulting Psychology, 24*, 349–354.

Cunningham, W., Cunningham, I. C., & Green, R. T. (1977). The ipsative process to reduce response set bias. *Public Opinion Quarterly, 41*, 379–394.

Dalton, D. R., Wimbush, J. C., & Daily, C. M. (1994). Using the unmatched count technique (UCT) to estimate base rates for sensitive behavior. *Personnel Psychology, 47*, 817–828.

Das, J. P., & Dutta, T. (1969). Some correlates of extreme response set. *Acta Psychologica, 29*, 85–92.

Davis, D. W., & Silver, B. D. (2003). Stereotype threat and race of interviewer effects in a survey on political knowledge. *American Journal of Political Science, 47*, 33–45.

DeJong, M. G., Steenkamp, J.-B. E. M., Fox, J. P., & Baumgartner, H. (2008). Using item response theory to measure extreme response style in marketing research: A global investigation. *Journal of Marketing Research, 45*, 104–115.

Deutcher, I. (1973). Asking questions: Linguistic comparability. In D. Warwick & S. Osherson (Eds.), *Comparative research methods* (pp. 163–186). Englewood Cliffs, NJ: Prentice-Hall.

Diamantopoulos, A., Reynolds, N. L., & Simintiras, A. C. (2006). The impact of response styles on the stability of cross-national comparisons. *Journal of Business Research, 59*, 925–935.

Diers, C. J. (1965). Social-desirability ratings of personality items by three subcultural groups. *Journal of Social Psychology, 67*, 97–104.

Dijkstra, W., Smit, J. H., & Comijs, H. C. (2001). Using social desirability scales in research among the elderly. *Quality & Quantity, 35*, 107–115.

Dohrenwend, B. (1966). Social status and psychological disorder: An issue of substance and an issue of method. *American Sociological Review, 31*, 14–34.

Dolnicar, S., & Grun, B. (2007). Cross-cultural differences in survey response patterns. *International Marketing Review, 24*, 127–143.

Droitcour, J., Caspar, R. A., Hubbard, M. L., Parsley, T. L., Visscher, W., & Ezzati, T. M. (1991). The item count technique as a method of indirect questioning: A review of its development and a case study application. In P. B. Biemer, R. M. Groves, L. E. Lyberg, N. A. Mathiowetz, & S. Sudman (Eds.), *Measurement errors in surveys* (pp. 185–210). New York: Wiley.

Edwards, A. L. (1957). *The social desirability variable in personality assessment and research.* New York: Druiden Press.

Edwards, D., & Riordan, S. (1994). Learned resourcefulness in Black and White South African university students. *Journal of Social Psychology, 134*, 665–675.

Ellingson, J. E., Sackett, P. R., & Hough, L. M. (1999). Social desirability corrections in personality measurement: Issues of applicant comparison and construct validity. *Journal of Applied Psychology, 84*, 155–166.

England, G. W., & Harpaz, I. (1983). Some methodological and analytic considerations in cross-national comparative research. *Journal of International Business Studies, 14*, 49–59.

Evans, R. I., Hansen, W. B., & Mittlemark, M. B. (1977). Increasing the validity of self-reports of smoking behavior in children. *Journal of Applied Psychology, 62*, 521–523.

Eysenck, H. J., & Eysenck, S. B. G. (1964). *The manual of the Eysenck Personality Inventory.* London: University of London Press.

Farh, J., Dobbins, G. H., & Cheng, B. (1991). Cultural relativity in action: A comparison of self-ratings made by Chinese and U.S. workers. *Personnel Psychology, 44*, 129–147.

Fendrich, M., Johnson, T. P., Hubbell, A., & Spiehler, V. (2004). The utility of drug testing in epidemiological research: Results from an ACASI general population survey. *Addiction, 99*, 197–208.

Ferketich, S., Phillips, L., & Verran, J. (1993). Development and administration of a survey instrument for cross-cultural research. *Research in Nursing & Health, 16*, 227–230.

Fischer, R. (2004). Standardization to account for cross-cultural response bias: A classification of score adjustment procedures and review of research in JCCP. *Journal of Cross-Cultural Psychology, 35*, 263–282.

Fisher, G. (1967). The performance of male prisoners on the Marlowe–Crowne social desirability scale: II. Differences as a function of race and crime. *Journal of Clinical Psychology, 23*, 473–475.

Flaskerud, J. (1988). Is the Likert scale format culturally biased? *Nursing Research, 37*, 185–186.

Franklin, L. A. (1989). Randomized response sampling from dichotomous populations with continuous randomization. *Survey Methodology, 15*, 225–235.

Fritz, M. F. (1927). Guessing in a true-false test. *Journal of Educational Psychology, 18*, 558–561.

Gibbons, J. L., Hamby, B. A., & Dennis, W. D. (1997). Researching gender-role ideologies internationally and cross-culturally. *Psychology of Women Quarterly, 21*, 151–170.

Gibbons, J. L., Zellner, J. A., & Rudek, D. J. (1999). Effects of language and meaningfulness on the use of extreme response style by Spanish-English bilinguals. *Cross-Cultural Research: The Journal of Comparative Social Science, 33*, 369–381.

Gold, B. (1975a). A comment on Shulman's "Comparison of two scales on extremity response bias." *Public Opinion Quarterly, 39*, 123–124.

Gold, B. (1975b). Reply to Art Shulman. *Public Opinion Quarterly, 39*, 126–127.

Gough, H. G., & Heilbrun, A. B. (1980). *The adjective check list manual.* Palo Alto, CA: Consulting Psychologists Press.

Gove, W. R., & Geerken, M. R. (1977). Response bias in surveys of mental health: An empirical investigation. *American Journal of Sociology, 82*, 1289–1317.

Grandy, J. (1996). *Differences in the survey responses of Asian American and White science and engineering students* (GRE Board Report No. 93-25P). Princeton, NJ: Educational Testing Service.

Greenleaf, E. A. (1992a). Improving rating scale measures by detecting and correcting bias components in some response styles. *Journal of Marketing Research, 29*, 176–188.

Greenleaf, E. A. (1992b). Measuring extreme response style. *Public Opinion Quarterly, 56*, 328–351.

Grimm, S. D., & Church, A. (1999). A cross-cultural study of response biases in personality measures. *Journal of Research in Personality, 33*, 415–441.

Groves, R. M. (1977). An experimental comparison of national telephone and personal interview surveys. In *Proceedings of the Section on Social Statistics: American Statistical Association* (pp. 232–241). Washington, DC: American Statistical Association.

Groves, R. M., & Kahn, R. L. (1979). *Surveys by telephone: A national comparison with personal interviews.* New York: Academic Press.

Gudykunst, W. B., & Ting-Toomey, S. (1988). *Culture and interpersonal communication.* Newbury Park, CA: Sage.

Gur, R. C., & Sackeim, H. A. (1979). Self-deception: A concept in search of a phenomenon. *Journal of Personality and Social Psychology, 37*, 147–169.

Hadaway, K., Marler, P., & Chaves, M. (1993). What the polls don't show: A closer look at U.S. church attendance. *American Sociological Review, 58*, 741–752.

Hamilton, D. L. (1968). Personality attributes associated with extreme response style. *Psychological Bulletin, 69*, 192–203.

Hamamura, T., Heine, S.J., & Paulhus, D.L. (2008). Cultural differences in response styles: The role of dialectical thinking. *Personality and Individual Differences, 44*, 932–942.

Harzing, A. W. (2006). Response styles in cross-national survey research: A 26-country study. *International Journal of Cross-Cultural Management, 6*, 243–266.

Heavan, P. C. L. (1983). Authoritarianism or acquiescence? South African findings. *Journal of Social Psychology, 119*, 11–15.

Heine, S. J., & Lehman, D. R. (1995). Social desirability among Canadian and Japanese students. *Journal of Social Psychology, 135*, 777–779.

Himmelfarb, S., & Lickteig, C. (1982). Social desirability and the randomized response technique. *Journal of Personality and Social Psychology, 43*, 710–717.

Hofstede, G. H. (1980). *Culture's consequences: International differences in work-related values.* Newbury Park: Sage.

Hofstede, G. H. (1998). *Masculinity and femininity: The taboo dimension of national cultures.* Thousand Oaks, CA: Sage.

Hofstede, G. H. (2001). *Culture's consequences: Comparing values, behaviors, institutions, and organizations across nations.* Thousand Oaks, CA: Sage.

Hofstee, W., ten Berge, J., & Hendriks, A. (1998). How to score questionnaires. *Personality and Individual Differences, 25*, 897–909.

Holbrook, A. L., Green, M. C., & Krosnick, J. A. (2003). Telephone vs. face-to-face interviewing of national probability samples with long questionnaires: Comparisons of respondent satisficing and social desirability response bias. *Public Opinion Quarterly, 67*, 79–125.

Holbrook, A. L., Johnson, T. P., & Cho, Y. I. (2006, May). *Extreme response style: Style or substance?* Paper presented at the 61st Annual Meeting of the American Association for Public Opinion Research, Montreal, Canada.

Hoy, R.R. (1993). A 'model minority' speaks out on cultural shyness. Science, *262*, 1117–1118.

Hui, C., & Triandis, H. C. (1989). Effects of culture and response format on extreme response style. *Journal of Cross-Cultural Psychology, 20*, 296–309.

Iwata, N., Roberts, C. R., & Kawakami, N. (1995). Japan–U.S. comparison of responses to depression scale items among adult workers. *Psychiatry Research, 58*, 237–245.

Iwawaki, S., & Cowen, E. L. (1964). The social desirability of trait-descriptive terms: Applications to a Japanese sample. *Journal of Social Psychology, 63*, 199–205.

Iwawaki, S., Fukuhara, M., & Hidano, T. (1966). Probability of endorsement of items in the Yatabe–Guilford Personality Inventory: Replication. *Psychological Reports, 19*, 249–250.

Jackson, D. N. (1967). Acquiescent response styles: Problems of identification and control. In I. A. Berg (Ed.), *Response set in personality assessment* (pp. 71–114). Chicago: Aldine.

Jackman, M. R. (1973). Education and prejudice or education and response set? *American Sociological Review, 38*, 327–339.

Javeline, D. (1999). Response effects in polite cultures. *Public Opinion Quarterly, 63*, 1–28.

Johnson, T. P., & Bowman, P. J. (2003). Cross-cultural sources of measurement error in substance use surveys. *Substance Use & Misuse, 38*, 1447–1490.

Johnson, T. P., Kulesa, P., Cho, Y. I., & Shavitt, S. (2005). The relation between culture and response styles: Evidence from 19 countries. *Journal of Cross-Cultural Psychology, 36*, 264–277.

Johnson, T. P., O'Rourke, D., Chávez, N., Sudman, S., Warnecke, R., Lacey, L., et al. (1997). Social cognition and responses to survey questions among culturally diverse populations. In L. Lyberg, P. Biemer, M. Collins, E. de Leeuw, C. Dippo, N. Schwarz, & D. Trewin (Eds.), *Survey measurement and process quality* (pp. 87–113). New York: Wiley.

Johnson, T. P., & Van de Vijver, F. J. (2003). Social desirability in cross-cultural research. In J. A. Harkness, F. J. Van de Vijver, & P. P. Mohler (Eds.), *Cross-cultural survey methods* (pp. 195–204). New York: Wiley.

Jones, E. L. (1963). The courtesy bias in South-East Asian surveys. *International Social Science Journal, 15*, 70–76.

Jones, E. L., & Forrest, J. D. (1992). Underreporting of abortion in surveys of U.S. women: 1976 to 1988. *Demography, 29*, 113–126.

Katosh, J. P., & Traugott, M. W. (1981). The consequences of validated and self-reported voting measures. *Public Opinion Quarterly, 45*, 519–535.

Keillor, B., Owens, D., & Pettijohn, C. (2001). A cross-cultural/cross-national study of influencing factors and socially desirable response biases. *International Journal of Market Research, 43*, 63–84.

Kiesler, S., & Sproull, L. S. (1986). Response effects in the electronic survey. *Public Opinion Quarterly, 50*, 402–413.

Kitayama, S., Markus, H. R., Matsumoto, H., & Norasakkunkit, V. (1997). Individual and collective processes in the construction of the self: Self-enhancement in the United States and self-criticism in Japan. *Journal of Personality and Social Psychology, 72*, 1245–1267.

Klassen, D., Hornstra, R. K., & Anderson, P. B. (1975). Influence of social desirability on symptom and mood reporting in a community survey. *Journal of Consulting and Clinical Psychology, 43*, 448–452.

Knowles, E. S., & Condon, C. A. (1999). Why people say "yes": A dual-process theory of acquiescence. *Journal of Personality and Social Psychology, 77*, 379–386.

Knowles, E. S., & Nathan, K. T. (1997). Acquiescent responding in self-reports: Cognitive style or social concern? *Journal of Research in Personality, 31*, 293–301.

Krosnick, J. A. (1991). The stability of political preferences: Comparisons of symbolic and non-symbolic attitudes. *American Journal of Political Science, 35*, 547–576.

Krosnick, J. A. (1999). Survey research. *Annual Review of Psychology, 50*, 537–567.

Lai, J., & Linden, W. (1993). The smile of Asia: Acculturation effects on symptom reporting. *Canadian Journal of Behavioural Science, 25*, 303–313.

Lalwani, A. K., & Shavitt, S. (2009). The "me" I claim to be: Cultural self-construal elicits self-presentational goal pursuit. *Journal of Personality and Social Psychology, 97*(1), 88–102.

Lalwani, A. K., Shavitt, S., & Johnson, T. (2006). What is the relation between cultural orientation and socially desirable responding? *Journal of Personality and Social Psychology, 90*, 165–178.

Lamm, B., & Keller, H. (2007). Understanding cultural models of parenting: The role of intracultural variation and response style. *Journal of Cross-Cultural Psychology, 38*, 50–57.

Leary, M.R., & Kowalski, R.M. (1990). Impression management: A literature review and two component model. *Psychological Bulletin, 107*, 34–47.

Lee, C., & Green, R. T. (1991). Cross-cultural examination of the Fishbein behavioral intentions model. *Journal of International Business Studies, 22*, 289–305.

Lee, J. W., Jones, P. S., Mineyama, Y., & Zhang, X. E. (2002) Cultural differences in responses to a Likert scale. *Research in Nursing & Health, 25*, 295–306.

Leite, W. L., & Beretvas, S. N. (2005). Validation of scores on the Marlowe–Crowne Social Desirability Scale and the Balanced Inventory of Desirable Responding. *Educational and Psychological Measurement, 65*, 140–154.

Lenski, G. E., & Leggett, J. C. (1960). Caste, class, and deference in the research interview. *American Journal of Sociology, 65*, 463–467.

Lentz, T. (1938). Acquiescence as a factor in the measurement of personality. *Psychological Bulletin, 35*, 659.

Leung, K., & Bond, M. H. (1980). On the empirical identification of dimensions for cross-cultural comparisons. *Journal of Cross-Cultural Psychology, 20*, 133–151.

Locander, W., Sudman, S., & Bradburn, N. (1976). An investigation of interview method, threat, and response distortion. *Journal of the American Statistical Association, 71*, 269–275.

Locke, J.D., & Baik, K.-D. (2009). Does an acquiescent response style explain why Koreans are less consistent than Americans? *Journal of Cross-Cultural Psychology, 40*, 319–323.

Maheswaran, D., & Shavitt, S. (2000). Issues and new directions in global consumer psychology. *Journal of Consumer Psychology, 9*, 59–66.

Marín, G., Gamba, R. J., & Marín, B. V. (1992). Extreme response style and acquiescence among Hispanics: The role of acculturation and education. *Journal of Cross-Cultural Psychology, 23*, 498–509.

Markus, H. R., & Kitayama, S. (1991). Culture and the self: Implications for cognition, emotion, and motivation. *Psychological Review, 98*, 224–253.

Marlowe, D. and Crowne, D. P. (1961). Social desirability and response to perceived situational demands. *Journal of Consulting Psychology* 25, 109–115.

Marshall, R., & Lee, C. (1998). A cross-cultural, between-gender study of extreme response style. *European Advances in Consumer Research, 3*, 90–95.

Matsumoto, D. (2007). Individual and cultural differences on status differentiation: The status differentiation scale. *Journal of Cross-Cultural Psychology, 38*, 413–431.

McClendon, M. J. (1991). Acquiescence and recency response-order effects in survey interviews. *Sociological Methods & Research, 20*, 60–103.

McQuiston, C., Larson, K., Parrado, E. A., & Flaskerud, J. H. (2002). AIDS knowledge and measurement considerations with unacculturated Latinos. *Western Journal of Nursing Research, 24*, 354–372.

Messick, S. (1991). Psychology and methodology of response styles. In R. E. Snow & D. E. Wiley (Eds.), *Improving inquiry in social science: A volume in honor of Lee J. Cronbach* (pp. 161–200). Hillsdale, NJ: Erlbaum.

Mick, D. G. (1996). Are studies of dark side variables confounded by socially desirable responding? The case of materialism. *Journal of Consumer Research, 23*, 106–119.

Middleton, K. L., & Jones, J. L. (2000). Socially desirable response sets: The impact of country culture. *Psychology & Marketing, 17*, 149–163.

Miller, J. D., Harrel, A. V., & Cisin, I. A. (1986, May). *A new technique for surveying deviant behavior: Item-count estimates of marijuana, cocaine, and heroin.* Paper presented at the annual meeting of the American Association for Public Opinion Research, St. Petersburg, FL.

Minkov, M. (2008). Self-enhancement and self-stability predict school achievement at the national level. *Cross-Cultural Research, 42*, 172–196.

Minkov, M. (2009). Nations with more dialectical selves exhibit lower polarization in life quality judgments and social opinions. *Cross-Cultural Research, 43*, 230–250.

Mirowsky, J., & Ross, C. E. (1991). Eliminating defense and agreement bias from measures of the sense of control: A 2 × 2 index. *Social Psychology Quarterly, 54*, 127–145.

Mitchell, R. E. (1973). Survey materials collected in the developing countries: Sampling, measurement, and interviewing obstacles to intro- and inter-national comparisons. In D. P. Warwick & S. Osherson (Eds.), *Comparative research methods* (pp. 204–226). Englewood Cliffs, NJ: Prentice-Hall.

Moors, G. (2003). Diagnosing response style behavior by means of a latent-class factor approach. Socio-demographic correlates of gender role attitudes and perceptions of ethnic discrimination reexamined. *Quality & Quantity: International Journal of Methodology, 37*, 277–302.

Moscovici, S. (1963). Attitudes and opinions. *Annual Review of Psychology, 14*, 231–260.

Mwamwenda, T. S. (1993). A comparison of two samples, South Africans and Canadians, on social desirability. *Psychological Reports, 72*, 965–966.

Naemi, B. D., Beal, D. J., & Payne, S. C. (2009). Personality predictors of extreme response style. *Journal of Personality, 77*, 261–286.

Narayan, S., & Krosnick, J. A. (1996). Education moderates some response effects. *Public Opinion Quarterly, 60*, 89–105.

Nederhof, A. J. (1985). Methods of coping with social desirability bias: A review. *European Journal of Social Psychology, 15*, 263–280.

Okazaki, S. (2000). Asian American and White American differences on affective distress symptoms: Do symptom reports differ across reporting methods? *Journal of Cross-Cultural Psychology, 31*, 603–625.

Oyserman, D., Coon, H. M., & Kemmelmeier, M. (2002). Rethinking individualism and collectivism: Evaluation of theoretical assumptions and meta-analyses. *Psychological Bulletin, 128*, 3–72.

Paulhus, D. L. (1981). Control of social desirability in personality inventories: Principal-factor deletion. *Journal of Research in Personality, 15*, 383–388.

Paulhus, D. L. (1984). Two-component models of socially desirable responding. *Journal of Personality and Social Psychology, 46*, 598–609.

Paulhus, D. L. (1991). Measurement and control of response bias. In J. P. Robinson & P. R. Shaver (Eds.), *Measures of personality and social psychological attitudes* (pp. 17–59). San Diego, CA: Academic Press.

Paulhus, D. L. (1998a). Interpersonal and intrapsychic adaptiveness of trait self-enhancement: A mixed blessing? *Journal of Personality and Social Psychology, 74*, 1197–1208.

Paulhus, D. L. (1998b). *Paulhus Deception Scales: User's manual.* North Tonawanda, NY: Multi-Health Systems.

Pavlos, A. J. (1972). Racial attitude and stereotype change with bogus pipeline paradigm. *Proceedings of the 80th Annual Convention of the American Psychological Association, 7*, 291–292.

Perera, M., & Eysenck, S. B. G. (1984). A cross-cultural study of personality: Sri Lanka and England. *Journal of Cross-Cultural Psychology, 15*, 353–371.

Phillips, D. L., & Clancy K. J. (1970). Response biases in field studies of mental illness. *American Sociological Review, 35*, 503–515.

Pleck, J. H., Sonenstein, F. L., & Ku, L. (1996). Black–White differences in adolescent males' substance use: Are they explained by underreporting by Blacks? *Journal of Gender, Culture, and Health, 1*, 247–265.

Podsakoff, P. M., MacKenzie, S. M., Lee, J., & Podsakoff, N. P. (2003). Common method variance in behavioral research: A critical review of the literature and recommended remedies. *Journal of Applied Psychology, 88*, 879–903.

Puntoni, S., & Tavassoli, N.T. (2007). Social context and advertising memory. *Journal of Marketing Research, 44* (2), 284–96.

Ray, J. J. (1979). Is the acquiescent response style problem not so mythical after all? Some results from a successful balanced F scale. *Journal of Personality Assessment, 4*, 638–643.

Ray, J. J. (1983). Reviving the problem of acquiescent response bias. *Journal of Social Psychology, 121*, 81–96.

Riordan, C., & Vandenberg, R. (1994). A central question in cross-cultural research: Do employees of different cultures interpret work-related measures in an equivalent manner? *Journal of Management, 20*, 643–671.

Ross, C. E., & Mirowsky, J. (1984a). The worst place and the best face. *Social Forces, 62*, 529–536.

Ross, C. E., & Mirowsky, J. (1984b). Socially-desirable response and acquiescence in a cross-cultural survey of mental health. *Journal of Health and Social Behavior, 25*, 189–197.

Rutten, A., De Beuckelaer, A., & Weijters, B. (2008, June). *Between-method convergent validity of three alternative methods to quantify response styles: A case-based comparison.* Paper presented at the International Conference on Survey Methods in Multinational, Multiregional and Multicultural Contexts, Berlin.

Sackeim, H. A., & Gur, R. C. (1979). Self-deception, other-deception, and self-reported psychopathology. *Journal of Consulting and Clinical Psychology, 47*, 213–215.

Schaeffer, N. C. (1980). Evaluating race-of-interviewer effects in a national survey. *Sociological Methods & Research, 8*, 400–419.

Schlenker, B. R., & Britt, T. W. (1999). Beneficial impression management: Strategically controlling information to help friends. *Journal of Personality and Social Psychology, 76*, 559–573.
Schlenker, B. R., Britt, T. W., & Pennington, J. (1996). Impression regulation and management: Highlights of a theory of self-identification. In R. M. Sorrentino & E. T. Higgins (Eds.), *Handbook of motivation and cognition*, Vol. 3: *The foundations of social behavior.* New York: Guilford.
Schuman, H., & Converse, J. (1971). The effects of black and white interviewers on black responses in 1968. *Public Opinion Quarterly, 35*, 44–68.
Schuman, H., & Presser, S. (1981). *Questions and answers in attitude surveys: Experiments in question form, wording, and context.* New York: Academic Press.
Schwartz, S. H., Verkasalo, M., Antonovsky, A., & Sagiv, L. (1997). Value priorities and social desirability: Much substance, some style. *British Journal of Social Psychology, 36*, 3–18.
Shapiro, A. H., Rosenblood, L., Berlyne, G. M., & Finberg, J. (1976). The relationship of test familiarity to extreme response styles in Bedouin and Moroccan boys. *Journal of Cross-Cultural Psychology, 7*, 357–364.
Shavitt, S., Johnson, T. P., & Zhang, J. (in press). Horizontal and vertical cultural differences in the content of advertising appeals. *Journal of International Consumer Marketing.*
Shavitt, S., Lalwani, A. K., Zhang, J., & Torelli, C. J. (2006). The horizontal/vertical distinction in cross-cultural consumer research. *Journal of Consumer Psychology, 16*, 325–356.
Si, S. X., & Cullen, J. B. (1998). Response categories and potential cultural bias: Effects of an explicit middle point in cross-cultural surveys. *International Journal of Organizational Analysis, 6*, 218–230.
Sigall, H., & Page, R. (1971). Current stereotypes: A little fading, a little faking. *International Journal of Psychology, 25*, 1–12.
Sigelman, L. (1982). The nonvoting voter in voting research. *Public Opinion Quarterly, 26*, 47–56.
Singelis, T. M., Triandis, H. C., Bhawuk, D., & Gelfand, M. J. (1995). Horizontal and vertical dimensions of individualism and collectivism: A theoretical and measurement refinement. *Cross-Cultural Research: The Journal of Comparative Social Science, 29*, 240–275.
Smith, D. H. (1967). Correcting for social desirability response sets in opinion-attitude survey research. *Public Opinion Quarterly, 31*, 87–94.
Smith, P. B. (2004). Acquiescent response bias as an aspect of cultural communication style. *Journal of Cross-Cultural Psychology, 35*, 50–61.
Smith, P. B., & Bond, M. H. (1998). *Social psychology across cultures* (2nd ed.). Hemel Hempstead, England: Harvester Wheatsheaf.
Smith, P. B., & Fisher, R. (2008). Acquiescence, extreme response bias and culture: A multilevel analysis. In F. J. van de Vijver, D. A. van Hemert, & Y. H. Poortinga (Eds.), *Multilevel analysis of individuals and cultures* (pp. 285–314). New York: Erlbaum.
Smith, T. W. (2003). Developing comparable questions in cross-national surveys. In J. A. Harkness, F. J. van de Vijver, & P. P. Mohler (Eds.), *Cross-cultural survey methods* (pp. 69–91). New York: Wiley.

Soueif, M. I. (1958). Extreme response sets as a measure of intolerance of ambiguity. *British Journal of Psychology, 49*, 329–333.

Steenkamp, J.-B. E. M., & Baumgartner, H. (1998). Assessing measurement invariance in cross-national consumer research. *Journal of Consumer Research, 25*, 78–90.

Stening, B. W., & Everett, J. E. (1984). Response styles in a cross-cultural managerial study. *Journal of Social Psychology, 122*, 151–156.

Stöber, J. (3002). The social desirability scale-17 (SDS-17): Convergent validity, discriminant validity, and relationship with age. *European Journal of Psychological Assessment, 17*, 222–232.

Stokes-Brown, A. K. (2006). Racial identity and Latino vote choice. *American Politics Research, 34*, 627–652.

Stricker, L. J. (1963). Acquiescence and social desirability response styles, item characteristics, and conformity. *Psychological Reports, 12*, 319–341.

Sudman, S., & Bradburn, N. M. (1974). *Response effects in surveys.* Chicago: Aldine.

Torelli, C., & Shavitt, S. (in press). Culture and concepts of power. *Journal of Personality and Social Psychology.*

Toner, B. (1987). The impact of agreement bias on the ranking of questionnaire response. *Journal of Social Psychology, 127*, 221–222.

Tourangeau, R., Rips, L., & Rasinski, K. (2000). *The psychology of survey response.* Cambridge: Cambridge University Press.

Tourangeau, R., & Smith, T.W. (1996). Asking sensitive questions: The impact of data collection mode, question format, and question context. *Public Opinion Quarterly, 60*, 275–304.

Tourangeau, R., & Yan, T. (2007). Sensitive questions in surveys. *Psychological Bulletin, 133*, 859–883.

Traugott, M. W., & Katosh, J. P. (1979). Response validity in surveys of voting behavior, *Public Opinion Quarterly, 43*, 359–377.

Traugott, M. W., Traugott, S. & Presser, S. (1992). *Revalidation of self-reported vote* (ANES Technical Report Series, No. nes010160). Ann Arbor, MI: American National Election Studies.

Triandis, H. C. (1972). *The analysis of subjective culture.* New York: Wiley-Interscience.

Triandis, H. C. (1995). *Individualism and collectivism.* Boulder, CO: Westview Press.

Triandis, H. C., Chen, X. P., & Chan, D. K. S. (1998). Scenarios for the measurement of collectivism and individualism. *Journal of Cross-Cultural Psychology, 29*, 275–289.

Triandis, H. C., & Gelfand, M. J. (1998). Converging measurement of horizontal and vertical individualism and collectivism. *Journal of Personality and Social Psychology, 74*, 118–128.

Triandis, H. C., Marín, G., Lisanski, J., & Betancourt, H. (1984). *Simpatia* as a cultural script of Hispanics. *Journal of Personality and Social Psychology, 47*, 1363–1375.

Triandis, H. C., & Triandis, L. M. (1962). A cross-cultural study of social distance. *Psychological Monographs, 76*(21, Whole No. 540).

Tsushima, W. T. (1969). Responses of Irish and Italians of two social classes on the Marlowe-Crowne social desirability scale. *Journal of Social Psychology, 77*, 215–219.

Turk Smith, S., Smith, K. D., & Seymour, K. (1993). Social desirability of personality items as a predictor of endorsement: A cross-cultural analysis. *Journal of Social Psychology, 133*, 43–52.

Van de Vijver, F. J. R., & Leung, K. (1997). *Methods and data analysis for cross-cultural research.* Thousand Oaks, CA: Sage.

Van de Vijver, F. J. R., Ploubidis, G., & Van Hemert, D. A. (2004). *Toward an understanding of cross-cultural differences in acquiescence and extremity scoring.* Paper presented at the Sheth/Sudman Symposium on Cross-Cultural Survey Research Methodology, Urbana, IL.

Van Hemert, D. A., Van de Vijver, F. J. R., Poortinga, Y. H., & Georgas, J. (2002). Structural and functional equivalence of the Eysenck Personality Questionnaire within and between countries. *Personality and Individual Differences, 33*, 1229–1249.

Van Herk, H. (2000). *Equivalence in a cross-national context: Methodological & empirical issues in marketing research.* Unpublished doctoral dissertation, Catholic University, Brabant, The Netherlands.

Van Herk, H., Poortinga, Y. H., & Verhallen, T. M. (2004). Response styles in rating scales: Evidence of method bias in data from six EU countries. *Journal of Cross-Cultural Psychology, 35*, 346–360.

Vernon, S. W., Roberts, R. E., & Lee, E. S. (1982). Response tendencies, ethnicity, and depression scores. *American Journal of Public Health, 116*, 482–495.

Wang, R., Hempton, B., Dugan, J.P., & Komives, S.R. (2008). Cultural differences: Why do Asians avoid extreme responses? *Survey Practice* (published online at: http://surveypractice.org/2008/10/30/cultural-differences/).

Warnecke, R. B., Johnson, T. P., Chávez, N., Sudman, S., O'Rourke, D., Lacey, L., et al. (1997). Improving question wording in surveys of culturally diverse populations. *Annals of Epidemiology, 7*, 334–342.

Warner, S. L. (1965). Randomized response: A survey technique for eliminating evasive answer bias. *Journal of the American Statistical Association, 60*, 62–69.

Watkins, D., & Cheung, S. (1995). Culture, gender, and response bias: An analysis of responses to the self-description questionnaire. *Journal of Cross-Cultural Psychology, 26*, 490–504.

Watson, D. (1992). Correcting for acquiescent response bias in the absence of a balanced scale: An application to class consciousness. *Sociological Methods & Research, 21*, 52–88.

Weech-Maldonado, R., Elliott, M. N., Oluwole, A., Schiller, K. C., & Hays, R. D. (2008). Survey response style and differential use of CAHPS rating scales by Hispanics. *Medical Care, 46*, 963–968.

Welkenhuysen-Gybels, J., Billiet, J., & Cambre, B. (2003). Adjustment for acquiescence in the assessment of the construct equivalence of Likert-type score items. *Journal of Cross-Cultural Psychology, 34*, 702–722.

Wells, W. D. (1961). The influence of yea-saying response style. *Journal of Advertising Research, 1*, 5–6.

Welte, J. W., & Russell, M. (1993). Influence of socially desirable responding in a study of stress and substance abuse. *Alcoholism: Clinical and Experimental Research, 17*, 758–761.

Wiggins, J. S. (1959). Interrelationships among MMPI measures of dissimulation under standard and social desirability instructions. *Journal of Consulting Psychology, 23*, 419–427.

Williams, J. E., Satterwhite, R. C., & Saiz, J. L. (1998). *The importance of psychological traits.* New York: Plenum Press.

Wong, N., Rindfleisch, A., & Burroughs, J. E. (2003). Do reverse-worded items confound measures in cross-cultural consumer research? The case of the Material Values Scale. *Journal of Consumer Research, 30*, 72–91.

Yang, Y., Harkness, J. A., Chin T.-Y., & Villar, A. (2010). Response styles in culture. In J. A. Harkness, M. Braun, B. Edwards, T. P. Johnson, L. Lyberg, P. Ph. Mohler, B.-E. Pennell, & T. W. Smith (Eds.), *Survey methods in multinational, multiregional, and multicultural contexts* (pp. 203–223). New York: Wiley.

Yeh, L. L., Kim, K. O., Chompreeda, P., Rimkeeree, H., Yau, N. J. N., & Lundahl, D. S. (1998). Comparison in use of the 9-point hedonic scale between Americans, Chinese, Koreans, and Thai. *Food Quality and Preference, 9*, 413–419.

Ying, Y. (1989). Nonresponse on the Center for Epidemiological Studies-Depression scale in Chinese Americans. *International Journal of Social Psychiatry, 35*, 156–163.

Zax, M., & Takahashi, S. (1967). Cultural influences on response style: Comparisons of Japanese and American college students. *Journal of Social Psychology, 71*, 3–10.

PART II

DATA ANALYSIS AND INTERPRETATION

7

Methods for Investigating Structural Equivalence

RONALD FISCHER AND JOHNNY R. J. FONTAINE

This chapter focuses on data analytic methods to investigate whether the internal structures of measurement instruments are equivalent between cultural groups. For example, is the structure of values that guide individuals' lives similar between Western and Far Eastern countries? Do employees use the same dimensions to evaluate their organization and their supervisors in different cultural groups? Is the structure of personality between the United States and China the same, or are there culture-specific personality dimensions? This chapter introduces the four most commonly used data analytic methods to investigate the equivalence of the internal structure between cultural groups – namely, multidimensional scaling (MDS), principal component analysis (PCA), exploratory factor analysis (EFA), and confirmatory factor analysis. Before presenting these four data analytic methods, the concept of structural equivalence is explained and situated within the equivalence framework. Moreover, at the end of this chapter two general issues about sample size and data transformation before the analyses are discussed.

THE CONCEPT OF STRUCTURAL EQUIVALENCE

The investigation of the internal structure forms a key element in the validation process of a measurement instrument within a cultural group (e.g., Messick, 1989). The question is whether the item responses adequately capture the underlying dimensions or factors of the domain one wants to assess. For instance, the responses to the items of a Big Five personality instrument should be captured by five underlying factors, and each of the items has to contribute to the assessment of the specific personality factor it has been constructed for. Thus, the investigation of the internal structure answers two questions: (a) what are the underlying dimensions or factors that capture the interrelationships between the observed item responses and (b) how does each item relate to these underlying dimensions or factors? The more the expected underlying dimensions emerge from the observed item–response relationships and the more each item relates to the expected underlying dimension, the more evidence there is for the construct validity of the instrument.

Evidence for the validity of an instrument collected in one cultural group does not necessarily generalize to other cultural groups. Methodological artifacts, such as familiarity with the assessment context or social desirability, could invalidate the use of the instrument in other cultural settings (e.g., van de Vijver & Leung, 1997). Moreover, it is possible that the cultural context shapes the way in which universal underlying psychological traits and processes emerge into the repertoire of cultural groups that requires the use of culture-specific items. It is even possible that the underlying psychological traits and processes are culturally constructed (e.g., Berry et al., 2002; Fontaine, 2008). In all these cases, the interrelationships between the item responses will not be same among cultural groups. Different underlying dimensions emerge, and the relationships between specific items and the underlying dimensions change across cultural groups. Thus, equivalence of the internal structure must be investigated in each new cultural group where the instrument is applied. The results of this investigation can range from a perfect identity of the internal structure (with the same dimensions structuring the responses to the instrument and the same items being nontrivially related to these dimensions), over a few items that shift in meaning, up to a fundamental difference in the dimensions that structure the domain. In the latter case, the instrument is measuring different psychological constructs in each of the cultural groups.

The investigation of equivalence of the internal structure is relevant from both theoretical and applied perspectives. From a theoretical perspective, there is a vigorous debate about the universality of psychological traits and processes and the way they emerge in the repertoire of a cultural group. The demonstration that the same internal structure emerges on the basis of the observed interitem relationships in two or more cultural groups contributes to a universalistic stance, whereas the observation of different underlying structures contributes to the relativistic stance. From a practical perspective, the demonstration of structural equivalence is a necessary condition to use validly a (translated) measurement instrument in another cultural context.

Structural equivalence forms a key aspect in the larger equivalence framework. Within that framework, four major levels of equivalence have been distinguished: functional equivalence, structural equivalence, metric equivalence, and full score equivalence (e.g., Fontaine, 2005; van de Vijver & Leung, 1997). Functional[1] equivalence means that the same construct exists within each of the cultural groups. Structural equivalence means that the same indicators can be used to measure the theoretical construct. Metric equivalence entails the possibility to make relative comparisons between cultural groups (for instance, comparing the relative difference between males and females on aggression between cultural groups). Full score equivalence is the highest form of equivalence and implies that cultural groups can be directly compared.

The investigation of the internal structure gives necessary, but insufficient, evidence for the validity of a measurement instrument within a cultural group. Demonstrating that the content of the measurement instrument is relevant and representative for the domain one intends to assess is a prerequisite for validity (e.g., Messick, 1989). Because the behavioral repertoires can differ between cultural groups, it is necessary to demonstrate the relevance and representativeness of the content of an assessment instrument within each of the cultural groups where the instrument is applied. An analysis of the internal structure can detect irrelevance (irrelevant items turn out not to be an indicator of the presumed underlying dimension or factor). However, an analysis of the internal structure cannot detect a lack of representativeness (also called construct underrepresentation). What has not been included in the instrument cannot be analyzed and evaluated. Construct underrepresentation is more than a theoretical threat. Because repertoires can differ between cultural groups, the relevance and representativeness of an instrument in one cultural group do not necessary generalize to other cultural groups. For instance, it has been argued that the construct of filial piety is much more extended in China than in Western countries (Ho, 1996). The investigation of the internal structure of a translated Western filial piety instrument in a Chinese sample will not reveal the underrepresentation of the construct in China. To justify construct equivalence, evidence of structural equivalence must be complemented with evidence for the relevance and especially the representativeness of the content of the instrument in each of the cultural groups.

Within the equivalence framework, it is also clear that structural equivalence is an insufficient condition for justifying indirect or direct comparisons

[1] Van de Vijver and Leung (1997) used the term *construct equivalence*, which included functional and structural equivalence. We prefer to separate the measurement aspect of structural equivalence from the theoretical discussion of functional equivalence of the theoretical construct (Fontaine, 2005). Functional equivalence is a prerequisite for structural equivalence.

between cultural groups. Structural equivalence only means that the same underlying dimensions emerge and that the item responses are nontrivially related to these dimensions in each of the cultural groups. It contributes to the valid use of the instrument in cultural contexts other than where it was developed. However, it does not imply that the underlying dimensions are measured on the same quantitative scales. As mentioned earlier, two more restrictive forms of equivalence are necessary for indirect or direct cross-cultural comparisons: metric and full score equivalence (e.g. Fontaine, 2005; van de Vijver & Leung, 1997). Metric equivalence means that the intervals between the numeric values of the scale have the same meaning in all cultural groups. This type of equivalence justifies indirect comparisons between cultural groups. For instance, if temperature is measured on a Celsius scale in one cultural group and on a Kelvin scale in another cultural group, the temperature cannot be directly compared between them. However, the intervals have the same meaning, and it is thus possible to validly compare the two groups with respect to the difference between average summer and winter temperature. Thus, with a metrically equivalent aggression scale, it is possible to compare cultural groups with respect to the average differences between men and women in aggression. Full score equivalence exists if the scale of the underlying dimension shares the same metric and the same origin between cultural groups. In the latter case, however, the same observed score refers to the same position on the underlying dimension in each of the cultural groups. For the investigation of metric and full score equivalence, the reader is referred to Chapter 10.

We can thus conclude that structural equivalence plays a key role in cross-cultural measurement because it contributes to the universalism–relativism debate and to the validation of an instrument within each of the cultural groups where it is used, and it is a necessary condition for demonstrating metric and full score equivalence.

STEPWISE APPROACH FOR USING THE DATA ANALYTIC METHODS

In this section, the four most commonly used data analytic methods for the demonstration of structural equivalence are presented in a stepwise way. We first briefly present the key features of each method as it is applied in monocultural, mostly Western research. We then introduce the type of data that can be analyzed with the data analytic method and possibly the preprocessing of the data. We discuss the application of the method within one reference group. Most cross-cultural research starts within one cultural group, which can be treated as the reference group, and is then applied in

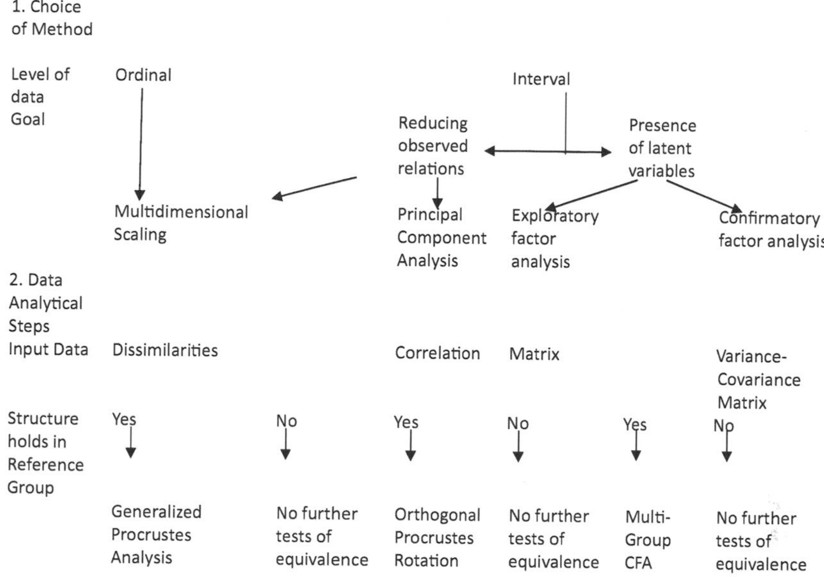

Figure 7.1. Decision tree for structural equivalence.

other cultural groups. The identification of a structure that fits well and is interpretable in the reference cultural group is a precondition for structural equivalence. If no such structure can be found in the reference group, lack of structural equivalence can be attributed to a lack of validity of the measurement approach, rather than to cultural differences in the assessed domain. The decision tree is schematically represented in Figure 7.1. We then present how the data analytic method can be used to assess structural equivalence between cultural groups. Finally, we discuss the strengths and weaknesses of each data analytic method.

Multidimensional Scaling

MDS is a scaling technique that represents observed associations between items as distances between points in a geometrical representation in such a way that the distances between the points represent as well as possible the associations between the items (e.g., Borg & Groenen, 2005; Kruskal & Wish, 1978). Large positive associations are represented by small distances; large negative associations are represented by large distances. For a recent, thorough overview, the reader is referred to the work of Borg and Groenen (2005).

As a guiding example of the application for this approach, we use recent research by Fontaine et al. (2006) on guilt and shame in Peru, Hungary, and Belgium (Figure 7.2). Guilt and shame scenarios were constructed, and participants in each cultural group were asked to rate the probability of 24 guilt and shame reactions (e.g., thinking about the damage one has caused, feeling guilty, or wanting to disappear). Within each cultural group, the ratings were averaged per scenario across the respondents. The application of multidimensional scaling on the dissimilarities between the 24 reactions revealed a two-dimensional structure. On the first dimension, guilt and shame reactions were opposed to one another. On the second dimension, interpersonal reactions (e.g., thinking about the damage one has caused) were opposed to intrapersonal reactions (wanting to improve oneself). In that two-dimensional representation, the items *guilt* and *regret* were for instance represented near one another, and were represented oppositely of the reactions *shame* and *embarrassment*.

Step 1. Preparing the Data

MDS can be used to work with a broad range of data. To apply this method, one only needs ordinal information about the associations between pairs of stimuli or items. This ordinal information can be collected directly or obtained by computing ordinal association measures between item scores. This technique has much appeal for cross-cultural research because it is the most flexible of the four techniques presented here. For instance, the internal structure of the emotion domain can be studied by asking participants to do a simple similarity sorting task on emotion terms (e.g., Fontaine, Poortinga, Setiadi, & Suprapti, 2002; Shaver, Wu, & Schwartz, 1992). Similar emotion terms are sorted into the same pile when they are similar or into different piles when they are not.

The input for MDS consists of (dis)similarities between pairs of stimuli or items. All (dis)similarities must be nonnegative (which may require some transformation). Before executing the MDS, a (dis)similarity matrix has to be created for each cultural group. In the case of a similarity sorting task, the similarities can be computed as the number of participants who sorted two pairs of stimuli into the same pile. If the data consist of rating data, a similarity or dissimilarity matrix must be created from the associations between the items. In the guilt and shame example, the Euclidian distances between the 24 standardized emotional reactions were used as dissimilarities. The Euclidean distances between standardized variables are inversely monotonically related to the Pearson correlations between those variables.

Step 2. Multidimensional Scaling Within the Reference Cultural Group
After the (dis)similarity matrices are constructed per cultural group, a MDS is executed on the reference cultural group. Two important decisions have to made here: (a) whether to apply a metrical or a nonmetrical MDS analysis and (b) the number of dimensions in which the structure has to be represented. With respect to the first decision, a nonmetrical MDS is indicated if the (dis)similarities only contain ordinal information about the associations between the stimuli. This is the case, for example, with the similarities obtained from a similarity sorting task. If the (dis)similarities are measured at an interval level, such as Euclidean distances, metrical MDS can be applied. For the second decision, there are four main criteria for selecting the dimensionality of the representation within each group – namely, the a priori theoretical expectation, the stress of the configuration, the scree plot, and the interpretability of the configuration. If one has an a priori hypothesis about the dimensionality and the position of the items, that geometrical solution should be checked first. In absence or nonconfirmation of the theoretical hypotheses, the three data-driven procedures (stress, scree test, interpretability) can be used. Borg and Groenen (2005) discussed these issues in greater detail. In the guilt and shame example (Fontaine et al., 2006), the Dutch-speaking Belgian sample was taken as a point of reference. As the dissimilarities were measured on an interval level (they were computed as Euclidian distances), metrical MDS was performed. The scree plot pointed to a two-dimensional solution that fit well.

The MDS configuration can be interpreted in two ways. First, there is the regional interpretation of the MDS configuration. It is visually investigated whether items that belong conceptually together are also represented in the same region within the geometrical representation. For instance, in the guilt and shame research, the emotion features that related to the interpersonal forms of guilt (such as focusing on the damage caused and wanting to repair) were represented in one region of the two-dimensional configuration (see Figure 7.1). A second form of interpretation focuses on the dimensions that span the geometrical representation. In the guilt and shame example, the first dimension could be interpreted as guilt versus shame and the second dimension as an inter- versus intrapersonal dimension.

We note here that all transformations on the coordinate system that preserve the relative distances between the points do not affect the fit of the geometrical representation. This means that rotation, reflection, shrinkage or dilation, and transposing of the coordinate system lead to mathematically equivalent structures. For MDS, it is, for example, not important whether the first or second dimension captures the guilt versus shame distinction or whether guilt is positioned at the positive or negative end of a dimension, as long as the relative position of stimuli remains unchanged. Thus, for the interpretation of the dimensions of the configuration, it is not necessary to work with the principal axis-rotated coordinate system that is generated by MDS programs. Rotation, reflection, shrinkage or dilation, and transposing of the coordinate system can be applied for generating optimally interpretable dimensions.

Step 3. Evaluating Structural Equivalence by Means of Generalized Procrustes Analysis

In the remaining cultural groups, an MDS configuration is computed with the same dimensionality as in the reference cultural group. The resulting coordinate systems, however, are not necessarily comparable between groups. Sampling fluctuations and small shifts of the stimuli in the representation can lead to a very different coordinate system. Thus, the possibility that the apparent differences can be attributed to rotation, reflection, shrinkage or dilation, or transposing of the coordinate system must be ruled out. This can be investigated by applying a generalized Procrustes analysis (GPA). There are two freeware programs that can execute GPA. The first program is the GPA program of Commandeur (1991).[2] This program rotates, reflects, transposes, and dilates or shrinks the MDS configurations from different cultural groups so that the coordinates maximally resemble one another.

GPA also creates a centroid configuration, which is the average geometrical configuration across groups. GPA offers a fit measure – namely, the proportion of squared distances in the culture-specific configurations that is accounted for by the centroid configuration. After GPA, the coordinates and also the position of individual stimuli can be directly compared with each other. The coordinates of the dimensions can be correlated with one another to obtain a more classical measure of congruence. For instance, Fontaine et al. (2006) correlated the coordinates of the emotion dimensions after GPA with the coordinates on the centroid (averaged) structure. In each of the three groups, the correlations were higher than .90 and most were even higher than .95. This clearly indicated that the culture-specific configurations were well reflected by the centroid configuration.

A second GPA freeware program is Orthosim2 by Barrett (2005). Orthosim2 can only work with two configurations (a target and a

[2] The GPA program can be requested from the author: Professor Dr. J. J. F. Commandeur, Faculteit der Economische Wetenschappen en Bedrijfskunde, Econometrie, De Boelelaan 1105, 1081 HV Amsterdam, the Netherlands.

comparison configuration). The program allows investigation of the congruence of both geometrical (MDS) and factor (PCA/EFA) structures.

If the fit of the configuration is inadequate in the different cultural groups, or if the GPA reveals substantial cultural differences in the position of most or all items along the dimensions, it is advisable to analyze the internal structure within each cultural group separately.

Alternative Approaches

With data from different cultural groups, it is also possible to compute a consensus geometrical configuration across all samples with replicated MDS, instead of computing a culture-specific configuration first and then applying a GPA (e.g., Fontaine, 2003). The advantage of this approach is that one directly has a fit measure of the consensus configuration with respect to the dissimilarity data in each of the cultural groups. This approach was taken by Fontaine, Poortinga, Delbeke, and Schwartz (2008) and Fischer, Milfont, and Gouveia (in press) to examine the stability of the structure of human values. They then used the fit measures to identify deviations from the consensus configuration. They found that the fit of the consensus value structure was lower in less developed countries or states.

If the researcher has a clear hypothesis about which structure is to be expected, the coordinates of the hypothetical structure can be used as starting values for the computation of the geometrical configuration. This overcomes the issue of sample-specific local minima and should allow a more direct comparison of configurations across cultural groups (see Bilsky, Janik, & Schwartz, in press).

Extensions

It is not necessary for MDS to use exactly the same stimuli or items in each of the cultural groups. Both replicated MDS and GPA can handle easily data structures with only partial overlap between the stimuli. This property is especially interesting for cross-cultural psychology, in which there are often good reasons to add culture-specific stimuli. It is possible with MDS to investigate whether these culture-specific stimuli can be best represented as culture-specific points in a universal space or whether these stimuli require an additional culture-specific dimension (e.g., Fontaine, 2003).

Strengths and Weaknesses

The strengths of MDS are that it can handle a broad range of data (from similarity data up to classical questionnaire data), that it imposes few restrictions (ordinal information is sufficient), that it can handle partially overlapping data sets (which is especially interesting for cross-cultural psychology), and that it leads to easy-to-interpret configurations (psychological associations are represented by distances). The major weakness of MDS is that it does not offer a measurement model for measuring individual differences. This means that MDS does not give information about whether and how individuals could be ordered along these dimensions. It only represents observed (dis)similarities as distances in a geometric space. To circumvent this problem, scales are constructed on the basis of the MDS results, which are then further investigated by means of classical test theory (e.g., Schwartz, 1992). Another weakness is that it is a descriptive technique. It generates an internal structure that best represents the observed associations given a selected dimensionality. Moreover, the GPA gives only descriptive information about the differences between the configurations. It offers no statistical test for observed structural differences between cultural groups.

Principal Component Analysis and Exploratory Factor Analysis

We present PCA and EFA together in this chapter. PCA is a reduction technique. It computes new variables, called components, as linear combinations of the observed items, in such a way that these components retain as much as possible of the total variance present in the original item responses. EFA is a measurement model that treats items as indicators of underlying constructs. It assumes that the observed relationships between the items have to be attributed to latent variables. EFA looks exploratively for the underlying variables that can account maximally for the common variance between the items. Despite their conceptual differences, with PCA being a reduction technique and EFA being a measurement model (e.g., Borsboom, 2006; Tabachnick & Fidell, 2007), these data analytic methods have a lot in common. For both methods, Pearson correlations between item responses are used as input, and a component or factor loading matrix is the most important output. The latter contains the correlations between the observed items and the components (reduced variables) or factors (latent variables). Furthermore, they are implemented in the same way in software packages such as SPSS and SAS. Finally, both methods often yield similar results, but it may be possible that both the number and the composition of the components or factors can be different, especially for the smaller factors. Programs such as SPSS use PCA as the default option, and it is generally a safe option to use PCA for explorative purposes. In the remainder of the text, the term *factor* refers to both components in a PCA and factors in an EFA. More detailed treatment of these methods can be found in, for instance, Field (2009) and Tabachnick and Fidell (2007).

In the following, we are using an example from organizational research (Fischer, 2004a; see also Fischer et al., 2007). Managers in organizations can use various principles to decide how to allocate rewards (pay raises, promotions, bonuses, etc.) to employees. The central criteria are equity (work performance; employees who work harder get more rewards), equality (all people are rewarded equally), need (people in need will receive more bonuses, money, etc.), or seniority (those people who have been with the organization longer and are older will receive more rewards). Employees were asked to indicate to what extent their managers had used these criteria when making recent decisions. PCA was applied to find out how many factors were needed to represent the covariation between these criteria.

Step 1. Preparing the Data

PCA and EFA work with continuous, or at least interval, data. Often, the ratings of questions on a Likert scale are treated as interval data. These methods are executed on the Pearson product-moment correlations between the items.[3] The Pearson product-moment correlations are computed by default in the factor procedures of the major statistical packages such as SPSS and SAS. In our example, employees completed a survey in which they indicated to what extent their managers had used equity, equality, need, or seniority criteria when making decisions about pay raises, promotions, or dismissals. The correlation matrix based on these answers was computed by default and used as an input.

Step 2. Principal Component Analysis and Exploratory Factor Analysis Within the Reference Group

As with the MDS, researchers must decide how many factors in the reference group should be extracted and how these factors should be interpreted. Also like MDS, four main criteria are used to select the number of factors: the a priori theoretical expectation, the variance accounted for by the factor structure, the scree plot, and the interpretability of the factor structure. A more in-depth treatment can be found in Field (2009) and Tabachnick and Fidell (2007).

After deciding how many factors should be extracted, the solution needs to be interpreted. The interpretation is made on the basis of the factor

[3] Although seldom performed, PCA (and EFA) can also be executed on the variance–covariance matrix.

loading matrix. As a general rule of thumb, loadings of less than .30 on any single factor should not be interpreted. However, more precise cutoffs for factor loadings are often reflective of researcher preferences. Cross-loadings may indicate that an item taps more than one construct or factor (item complexity), problems in the data structure, or circumplex structures, or it may indicate factor or component overlap (see Field, 2009; Tabachnick & Fidell, 2007).

If more than one component or factor has been identified, an infinite number of solutions exist that are all mathematically identical. These solutions can be represented graphically as a rotation of a coordinate system with the dimensions representing the factors and the points representing the loadings of the items on the factors. All these solutions account for the same percentage of total (PCA) or common (EFA) variance.

If a strong theoretical expectation exists about the factor structure, it can be rotated toward the theoretically expected structure. This theoretical structure may be represented in the form of zeros and ones (indicating which item should load on which factor). This rotation is called a Procrustean rotation. McCrae et al. (1996) suggested this technique is an alternative to confirmatory factor analysis for complex data sets.

Without a strong theoretical expectation, it is often preferred that the factor structure is characterized by a simple structure in which each item has a high (positive or negative) loading on one factor and zero loadings on the other factors; each factor is characterized by zero or high (positive or negative) loadings, and by a different profile of loadings. To obtain a simple structure, a varimax or Oblimin rotation is often applied. The former method assumes that factors are independent (orthogonal rotation); the latter method allows for factors to correlate (oblique rotation). Because all rotations account for the same amount of the total or the common variance, one rotation is not necessarily superior to others. The optimal rotation is therefore sometimes heavily debated. For instance, in the measurement of current affect, there is a vigorous debate about whether a valance–arousal or a positive affectivity–negative affectivity rotation best represents the underlying psychological mechanisms (e.g., Russell & Carroll, 1999; Watson, Wiese, Vaidya, & Tellegen, 1999).

In our example, the experimental literature had treated these four allocation criteria as independent (see reviews by Fischer, 2008; Fischer & Smith, 2003; Leung, 1997, 2005). At the same time, there may be some overlap. Seniority can be seen as an egalitarian principle (everyone can obtain rewards as long as they remain within the organization) or as a differential principle (because it differentiates among employees). Therefore, an exploratory analysis with oblique rotation was run, and both

Table 7.1. *Computational forms for most often used factorial congruence coefficients*

Coefficient	Computational form
Identity	$e_{xy} = \dfrac{2\sum x_i y_i}{\sum x_i^2 + \sum y_i^2}$
Additivity	$a_{xy} = \dfrac{2s_{xy}}{s_x^2 + s_y^2}$
Proportionality (Tucker's coefficient)	$p_{xy} = \dfrac{\sum x_i y_i}{\sqrt{\sum x_i^2 + \sum y_i^2}}$
Linearity (correlation coefficient)	$r_{xy} = \dfrac{s_{xy}}{s_x s_y}$

s_x the standard deviation of *x*; s_y the standard deviation of *y*; s_{xy} covariance of *x* and *y*.

the scree plot and the interpretability of the structure were considered when deciding on how many factors to extract (Fischer, 2004a; Fischer et al., 2007). The resulting four factors corresponded to equity, equality, need, and seniority criteria.

Step 3. Evaluating Structural Equivalence by Orthogonal Procrustes Rotation
In each of the remaining cultural groups, a factor structure is generated with the same number of factors as in the reference group. Because there is rotational freedom, this implies that factor structures that are structurally equivalent could look very different at first sight. Sampling fluctuations or small shifts in meaning of specific items can lead to a different factor loading matrix compared with the reference group. This can be overcome by an orthogonal Procrustes rotation toward the factor structure of the reference cultural group. After orthogonal Procrustes rotation, the factor structures can be directly compared between the cultural groups. The technical process for comparing two samples in SPSS is described in more detail in Box 7.1.

Once the solutions have been rotated, the congruence between the factor loadings for pairs of cultural groups can be computed. Four congruence measures have been proposed in the literature: the linearity, the proportionality (Tucker's phi), the additivity, and the identity coefficient (see Table 7.1). The most lenient coefficient is the linearity coefficient, which is the simple product-moment correlation between the factor pattern of the first and the factor pattern of the second cultural group. It is not influenced by addition or multiplication of the factor loadings. The most commonly used procedure is

Box 7.1. *A SPSS routine to carry out target rotation (adapted from van de Vijver & Leung, 1997)*

The following routine can be used to carry out a target rotation and evaluate the similarity between the original and the target-rotated factor loadings. One cultural group is being assigned as the source (entry from table inserted in loadings matrix below), and the second group is the target group (entry from table inserted in norms matrix below). The rotated or unrotated factor loadings for at least two factors obtained in two groups must be inserted. The loadings need to be inserted, separated by commas, and each line ends with a semicolon, except the last line, which ends with a bracket (}). Failure to pay attention to this will result in an error message, and no rotation will be carried out. Fischer and Smith (2006) measured self-reported extra-role behavior in British and East German samples. Extra-role behavior is related to citizenship behavior – voluntary and discretionary behavior that goes beyond what is expected of employees but helps the larger organization to survive and prosper. These items were supposed to measure a more passive component (Factor 1) and a more proactive component (Factor 2). The selection of the target solution is arbitrary; in this case, we rotated the East German data toward the U.K. matrix.

	UK		Germany	
	Factor 1	Factor 2	Factor 1	Factor 2
I am always punctual.	.783	−.163	.778	−.066
I do not take extra breaks.	.811	.202	.875	.081
I follow work rules and instructions with extreme care.	.724	.209	.751	.079
I never take long lunches or breaks.	.850	.064	.739	.092
I search for causes for something that did not function properly.	−.031	.592	.195	.574
I often motivate others to express their ideas and opinions.	−.028	.723	−.030	.807
During the last year I changed something in my work.	.388	.434	−.135	.717
I encourage others to speak up at meetings.	.141	.808	.125	.738
I continuously try to submit suggestions to improve my work.	.215	.709	.060	.691

The input for the SPSS syntax is as follows:

```
matrix.

compute LOADINGS={
  .778,    -.066;
  .875,     .081;
  .751,     .079;
  .739,     .092;
  .195,     .574;
 -.030,     .807;
 -.135,     .717;
  .125,     .738;
  .060,     .691 }.

compute NORMs = {
  .783,    -.163;
  .811,     .202;
  .724,     .209;
  .850,     .064;
 -.031,     .592;
 -.028,     .723;
  .388,     .434;
  .141,     .808;
  .215,     .709}.

compute s=t(loadings)*norms.
compute w1=s*t(s).
compute v1=t(s)*s.
call eigen (w1,w,evalw1).
call eigen (v1,v,evalv1).
compute o=t(w)*s*v.
compute q1=o &/abs(o).
compute k1=diag(q1).
compute k=mdiag(k1).
compute ww=w*k.
compute t1=ww*t(v).
compute procrust=loadings*t1.
compute cmlm2=t(procrust)*norms.
compute ca=diag(cmlm2).
```

(*continued*)

Box 7.1 (*continued*)

```
compute csum2m1=cssq(procrust).
compute csum2m2=cssq(norms).
compute csqrtl1=sqrt(csum2m1).
compute csqrtl2=sqrt(csum2m2).
compute cb=t(csqrtl1)*csqrtl2.
compute cc=diag(cb).
compute cd=ca&/cc.
compute faccongc=t(cd).
compute rm1m2=procrust*t(norms).
compute ra=diag(rm1m2).
compute rsum2m1=rssq(procrust).
compute rsum2m2=rssq(norms).
compute rsqrtl1=sqrt(rsum2m1).
compute rsqrtl2=sqrt(rsum2m2).
compute rb=rsqrtl1*t(rsqrtl2).
compute rc=diag(rb).
compute faccongr=ra&/rc.
compute cross1=procrust&*norms.
compute sumcross=csum(cross1).
compute mssqproc=cssq(procrust)/nrow(procrust).
compute mssqnorm=cssq(norms)/nrow(norms).
compute prop=sumcross/(sqrt(mssqproc&*mssqnorm)).
compute cross2=sumcross/nrow(procrust).
compute meanproc=csum(procrust)/nrow(procrust)).
compute sdproc=sqrt(mssqproc-meanproc&*meanproc).
compute meannorm=csum(norms)/nrow(norms)).
compute sdnorm=sqrt(mssqnorm – meannorm&*meannorm).
compute covar=sumcross/nrow(procrust)-meannorm&*meanproc.
compute correl=covar/(sdproc&*sdnorm).
compute addit=2*covar/(sdnorm&*sdnorm + sdproc&*sdproc).
compute idcoef=2*sumcross/(cssq(procrust)+cssq(norms)).
compute rowsqdif=sqrt(rssq(procrust-norms)/ncol(procrust)).
compute colsqdif=sqrt(cssq(procrust-norms)/nrow(procrust)).
compute dif={procrust-norms}.
print procrust /title = "FACTOR LOADINGS AFTER TARGET
   ROTATION"/ format f5.2.
print dif /title = "DIFFERENCE IN LOADINGS AFTER TARGET
   ROTATION"/format f5.2.
```

```
* the following two vectors express the difference between source loadings
* and target-rotated loadings. In the first the difference is taken between
* the loadings of two corresponding loadings and the difference is
  squared.
* For each item the squared differences are summed across all factors.
  The square
* root of these differences is then taken. The second vectors adds the
  squared
* differences across variables for each variable.
print rowsqdif /title = "Square Root of the Mean Squared Difference"
+ " per Variable (Item)" /format f5.2.
print colsqdif/title ="Square Root of the Mean Squared Difference"
+ " per Factor" / format f5.2.
print idcoef/title = "IDENTITY COEFFICIENT per Factor" /format f5.2.
print addit/title = "ADDITIVITY COEFFICIENT per Factor" /format f5.2.
print faccongc/title = "PROPORTIONALITY COEFFICIENT per Factor"
   /format f5.2.
print correl/title = "CORRELATION COEFFICIENT per Factor"
   /format f5.2.
end matrix.
```

The edited output for this example is:
Run MATRIX procedure:

```
FACTOR LOADINGS AFTER TARGET ROTATION
  .77  -.10
  .88   .04
  .75   .05
  .74   .06
  .22   .57
  .00   .81
 -.10   .72
  .16   .73
  .09   .69

DIFFERENCE IN LOADINGS AFTER TARGET ROTATION
 -.01   .06
  .07  -.16
  .03  -.16
```

(*continued*)

Box 7.1 (*continued*)

−.11	.00
.25	−.03
.03	.08
−.49	.29
.02	−.08
−.13	−.02

Square Root of the Mean Squared Difference per Variable (Item)

.05
.12
.12
.08
.18
.06
.40
.05
.09

Square Root of the Mean Squared Difference per Factor

.19 .13

IDENTITY COEFFICIENT per Factor

.94 .97

ADDITIVITY COEFFICIENT per Factor

.86 .92

PROPORTIONALITY COEFFICIENT per Factor

.94 .97

CORRELATION COEFFICIENT per Factor

.86 .93

The output shows the factor loadings following rotation, the difference in loadings between the original structure, and the rotated structure as well as the differences of each loading squared and then averaged across all factors (square root of the mean squared difference per variable column). A low value indicates good correspondence.

The important information is reported in the last four lines – namely, the various agreement coefficients. As can be seen there, the values are all above .85 and generally are beyond the commonly accepted value of .90. It is also worth noting that the first factor shows lower congruence. An examination of the differences between the loadings shows that one item (During the last year, I changed something in my work. . . .) in particular shows somewhat different loadings. In the U.K. sample, it loads moderately on both factors, whereas it loads highly on the proactivity factor in the German sample. Therefore, among the U.K. participants, making some changes in their workplace is a relatively routine and passive task, whereas for German participants, this is a behavior that is associated more with proactivity and initiative (e.g., Frese et al., 1996).

Tucker's coefficient of agreement or Tucker's phi (Tucker, 1951; cited in van de Vijver & Leung, 1997). This coefficient is not affected by multiplications of the factor loadings (e.g., factor loadings in one group are multiplied by a constant) but is sensitive to additions (e.g., when a constant is added to loadings in one group). The additivity coefficient resembles the Tucker's phi, except that this coefficient is not affected by simple addition of a constant in one group; it is sensitive to multiplications. The identity coefficient is the most stringent and is affected by both types of transformations. These congruence coefficients can be maximally 1. To judge similarity, some rules of thumb have been proposed. Conventionally, values larger than .95 are seen as showing acceptable factor similarity (van de Vijver & Leung, 1997), whereas values lower than .85 (ten Berge, 1986) are indicative of incongruence. However, these cutoff criteria might vary for different instruments, and no statistical test is associated with these indicators.

Tucker's phi is the most common index, but it may be enlightening to report all indices and compare their values. This may provide a more detailed and complete picture than one index alone. High values across indices indicate that the factor structure is similar. If low values are found or large differences exist between the various indices (e.g., more stringent indices showing substantially lower values), the similarity or replicability of the factor structure may be questioned. An investigation of the discrepancies in factor loadings and potential explanations for these differences would be necessary.

In our example, it was found that for the equity, equality, need, and seniority allocation factors, the congruence coefficients were generally in a range that indicates sufficient similarity.

Alternative Approaches

An alternative approach is to work with simultaneous component analysis (SCA). With SCA, a component analysis is performed on all cultural groups at once (Kiers, 1990; Kiers & ten Berge, 1989). It is a reduction technique that computes components as linear combinations of the observed items in such a way that maximally captures the variation in all cultural groups. Thus, SCA generates one internal structure for all cultural groups. How well the SCA structure represents the structure in each of the cultural groups can be investigated by comparing the variance accounted for by the SCA structure with the variance accounted for by the PCA structure per cultural group. An application of this approach in cross-cultural research can be found in Caprara, Barbaranelli, Bermúndez, Maslach, and Ruch (2000).

Extensions

Chan, Ho, Leung, Chan, and Yun (1999) proposed a bootstrap procedure to evaluate factor invariance statistically. With this method, a distribution of congruence coefficients is computed, which can then be used to derive a critical cutoff value. This empirical approach circumvents the need for adequate rules of thumb for Tucker's phi and other congruence measures.

Strengths and Weaknesses

The great strength of these techniques is that they are easy to use and well known. The implementation of Procrustean rotation in SPSS or SAS requires running a short syntax file (see Box 7.1). Congruence coefficients are available and are well accepted in the cross-cultural community. Moreover, both PCA and EFA allow for the computation or the estimation of the position of individuals on the factors. Furthermore, the factor scores for individuals can be saved.

A weakness is that the procedure focuses on the congruence at a factorial level, answering whether similar structures are found in each group compared with the reference group. Individual items may still show substantial loading differences, and the overall factorial similarity might be misleading. Research on the structure of the Eysenck Personality Questionnaire has shown that this issue is not without debate (Bijnen & Poortinga, 1988; Bijnen, van der Net, & Poortinga, 1986; Eysenck, 1986). It is possible and always useful to examine the target and rotated loadings as well as the difference between the target loadings and the loadings in a norm group to identify potential anomalies in addition to examining any congruence coefficient. This may reveal important and useful information of cross-cultural similarities and differences (see Box 7.1).

Confirmatory Factor Analysis

Confirmatory factor analysis (CFA) is a measurement model like EFA that treats items as indicators of underlying constructs. CFA is a theory-driven approach (e.g., Bollen, 1988; Long, 1983). The investigator indicates a priori which items are indicators of which latent variables. It is then statistically tested to which extent the a priori–specified measurement model represents the observed covariances between the item responses. For instance, Beirens and Fontaine (2010) could confirm five interrelated but distinct somatic complaint factors using 18 somatic complaint items. A measurement model in which each item was treated as an indicator of only one somatic complaint factor represented the observed covariances between the items well. Fischer et al. (2009) tested whether a four-component model of individualism–collectivism norms as proposed by Triandis (1995) could be measured in samples from 11 countries. Triandis had argued that the defining attributes of individualism–collectivism are whether (a) people see themselves as independent or as part of a larger group, (b) whether the structure of their goals is compatible with the group goals or not, (c) whether individuals are guided more by their personal attitudes or by their group norms, and (d) whether people emphasize the rational aspect of group membership or feel more relationally attached to groups. Fischer et al. (2009) created items that were thought to measure these four attributes and then were able to test whether the empirical data conformed to their theoretical prediction (which it did).

The three techniques discussed previously assume continuous, or at least interval, data. CFA additionally assumes multivariate normality of the data (although procedures have been developed to correct for a violation of this assumption). The issue of multivariate normality is particularly problematic in cross-cultural research in which it has been shown that score distributions vary systematically across cultures (Au, 1997).

CFA is a model-testing technique in which a theoretical model is compared with the observed structure in a sample. The model to be tested (e.g., the relationship between observed items and latent factors) can be graphically represented (see Figure 7.3 for an example of a CFA in one cultural group). CFA models are traditionally labeled with Greek letters. Programs such as EQS, AMOS, and LISREL have graphical interfaces that do not require this notation; however, LISREL still employs this notation in its output, and multigroup options (discussed later) require some basic familiarity with the Greek symbols. For this reason, we introduce the

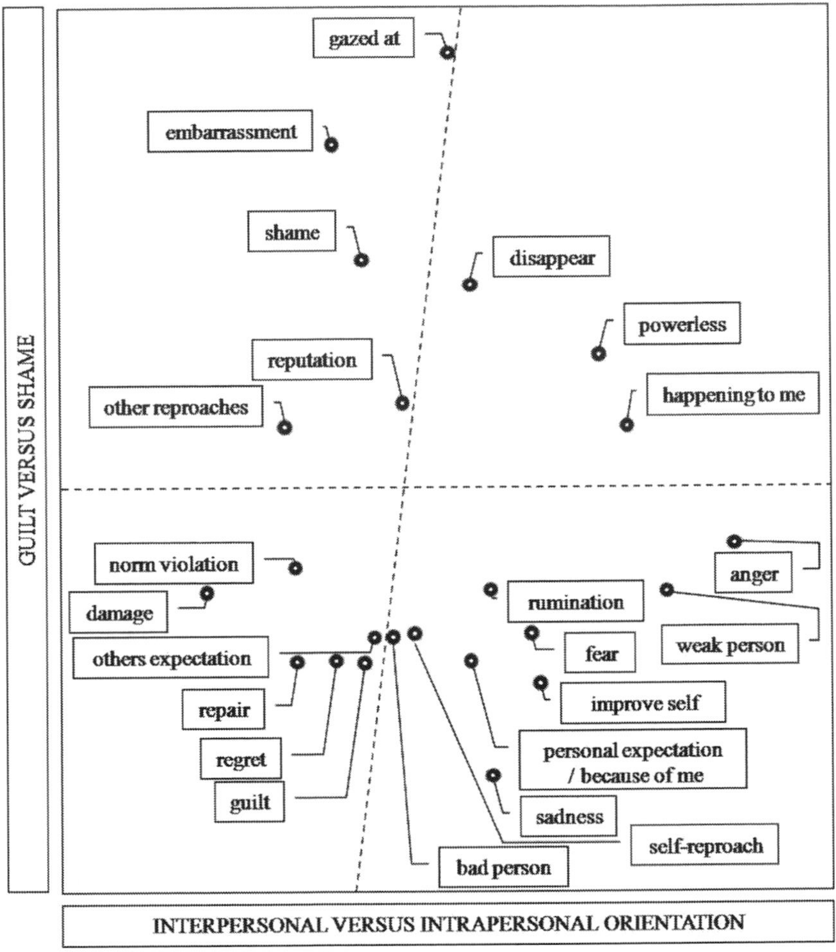

Figure 7.2. Two-dimensional representation of guilt and shame reactions in Peru, Belgium, and Hungary.

most important notation. For example, a researcher measured six items with a random sample of students. The first three items are expected to measure self-construals (observed variables are labeled with Latin letters, e.g., x_1 to x_3), whereas the other three items measure the structure of one's goals (x_4 to x_6). These items are thought to be indicators of two of the four defining attributes of individualism–collectivism mentioned by Triandis. It is expected that these two underlying and unobserved factors (called Ksi: ξ_1, ξ_2) cause the relationship among the observed variables. Because both

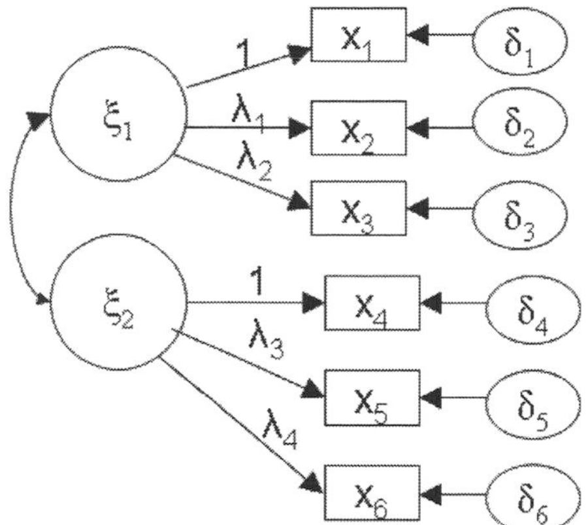

Figure 7.3. Example of a confirmatory factor analysis model. Latent and unobserved variables are represented by circles or ovals, whereas manifest variables are represented by squares or boxes. The relationship between the variables is indicated by lines. Lines with one arrow pointing to a specific variable represent a hypothesized direct relationship in which the variable with the arrow pointing to it is the dependent variable. Variables linked by lines with arrows at both ends indicate that the variables simply covary with no implied direction of the effect. The latent variables are represented by ξ (ksi); the observed variables are labeled x, the loadings of the observed variables on the latent variables are represented by λ (lambda), and the errors of measurement or unique factors or residuals are δ (delta). The loading of one item per latent factor has been constrained to zero. This is the most common option for allowing identification of the latent factors.

relate to individualism–collectivism, these factors are expected to covary, whereas the unique factors or residuals (measurement error) are expected to be independent. In a cross-cultural study with two cultural groups, one would have two models, one for each group.

Step 1. Preparing the Data

CFA can handle a number of input formats. Standard CFA programs such as LISREL, EQS, and AMOS now accept raw data files from other programs such as SPSS or Excel. Some programs such as Mplus require text files that were created in programs such as SPSS. It is best to use the variance–covariance matrix for modeling CFAs (Cudeck, 1989). For cross-cultural analyses, an analysis of the mean–variance–covariance matrix is particularly interesting (Cheung & Rensvold, 2000). The correlation matrix should not be used, especially not for cross-cultural comparisons, because standardizing the variance to unity in each group might conceal important information about cross-cultural differences or similarities. Fischer et al. (2009) used the mean–variance–covariance matrix for each cultural group for the analyses. They followed the example syntax provided in Cheung and Rensvold (2000), which required them to create a text file in SPSS containing the means, variances, and covariances.

Step 2. CFA Within the Reference Group

The next step involves testing the theoretically proposed model. In CFA, it is important to evaluate the model in this reference group. If the model does not perform well in this reference group, the process stops, and no further cross-cultural equivalence tests are possible. Fischer et al. (2009) selected one cultural group randomly and tested the model in this group (New Zealand) first.

The evaluation of model fit is done using various fit indices. The oldest and most commonly cited indicator is the chi-square statistic. The smaller the value, the less the model deviates from the sample covariance matrix; therefore, it is sometimes called an exact fit test (see Barrett, 2007). A good model would yield a nonsignificant chi-square statistic. However, chi-square is problematic for assessment of goodness of fit. In social sciences, it is implausible to assume that a null hypothesis about no significant differences between the model and the population is true. Obviously, individualism–collectivism norms cannot be reduced to three or four items each that load onto four latent factors. The models tested are nothing more than an approximation to reality, and it is counterintuitive to test a model that is a priori known to be false (Browne & Cudeck, 1992). Models that approximate the covariance matrix closely will be rejected given a sufficiently large sample size (Bentler & Bonnett, 1980; Bollen, 1989). Violation of assumptions underlying the chi-square statistic leads to incorrect probability levels (Ullman, 2007). Consequently, various alternative measures have been proposed. Bollen (1989); Browne and Cudeck (1992); Hu and Bentler (1998, 1999); Marsh, Balla, and McDonald, (1988); Marsh, Hau and Wen (2004); and Tanaka (1993) have discussed various fit indices, their cutoff criteria, and limitations.

Most fit indices are a derivation of the chi-square statistic. Researchers generally report these so-called approximate fit indices, which can be grouped into (a) incremental or comparative and (b) lack-of-fit indices.

First, incremental or comparative fit indices assume that there are a number of possible models that are all subsets of one another. At one end, there is the independence model where no related variances between the observed variables are assumed. At the other end, there is the saturated or full model with zero degrees of freedom (all variables are related with each other). The estimated model is expected to fall somewhere in between the two extremes. Consequently, the fit of the model is compared with an alternative model (mostly the independence model). Two of the more common approaches are the Tucker–Lewis Index (TLI) or nonnormed fit index (NNFI) and the comparative fit index (CFI; Bentler, 1990). Values ranging from the high 0.80s to 0.90s have been traditionally accepted as indicators of a good fit (Marsh et al., 1988). Hu and Bentler (1998, 1999) have called for more stringent parameters, suggesting cutoff parameters of .95 as acceptable.

The second group is lack-of-fit indices. The standardized root mean square residual (SRMR; Bollen, 1989), for example, compares the discrepancy between the sample matrix and the estimated population matrix (as implied by the model). Smaller values indicate better fit, with values less than .08 seen as acceptable in most recent simulation studies (Hu & Bentler, 1998). Hu and Bentler (1998, 1999) recommended this fit index because it is robust and sensitive to misspecifications. The root mean square error of approximation (RMSEA; Browne & Cudeck, 1992) is similar to the SRMR but also takes degrees of freedom into account and punishes less parsimonious models (more complex models). A value of less than 0.05 is ideal, values ranging between 0.06 and 0.08 are acceptable, and values greater than 0.10 indicate poor fit. On the basis of their simulation analysis, Hu and Bentler (1998, 1999) suggested that these parameters are too lenient and advocated .06 as an appropriate criterion.

The issue of appropriate fit indices cutoff criteria is highly contentious and remains an issue of debate. Most of the cutoff criteria suggested in the literature are based on intuition and have little statistical justification (Marsh et al., 2004). Marsh et al. also noted shortcomings of blindly adopting cutoff values suggested by simulations of studies such as Hu and Bentler's (1998, 1999). Marsh (in a 2001 posting on an e-mail network dedicated to structural equation modeling, SEMNET@UA1vm.ua.edu; see also the 2007 special issue in *Personality and Individual Differences*) posted a claim that it is nearly impossible to obtain these fit indices for multifactor rating instruments when conducted at an item level, with at least 5 to 10 items loading on a moderate number of factors (5 or more). Despite an invitation to provide counterexamples, none of the 1,500 members were able to provide such an example, highlighting that most traditional personality instruments would fail these strict criteria even in monocultural research.

The issue of potential underrepresentation in cross-cultural research should lead researchers to include larger numbers of items in their measures, therefore exacerbating the problem encountered in monocultural research. The question of appropriate fit in cross-cultural comparisons has not been addressed in the literature, which has been dominated by monocultural research. An uncritical application of these criteria may lead to an erroneous rejection of models in cross-cultural research. It is a good practice for cross-cultural researchers to examine the residuals and parameter estimates in each sample to identify variables that may function differently within and across cultural groups. In addition, all these fit indicators may perform well when comparing nested models. It should be standard practice to compare a number of possible theoretical models and then compare their respective fit. The best fitting model therefore must be evaluated against substantive and theoretical issues (MacCallum & Austin, 2000; Marsh et al., 2004). A good discussion of the various issues is provided in a special issue of *Personality and Individual Differences* (http://www.elsevier.com/wps/find/journaldescription.cws_home/603/description#description).

In our individualism–collectivism example, Fischer et al. (2009) evaluated the structure in the New Zealand sample (to be used as a reference group in the following multigroup CFA). The fit indices were acceptable (with the exception of one item that showed a large residual, suggesting a different loading pattern), and therefore the model could be tested across cultures. It is advisable to test the model in each group separately before attempting CFA. This can give one a feel for the data and may highlight potential problems. As already noted in the New Zealand sample, one item showed different loading patterns in all samples compared with the expected loading, and therefore, this item was allowed to load on the other factor. This revised model provided acceptable fit in all samples. However, these separate analyses do not address whether the loadings are comparable across all samples. For this, a multigroup analysis is necessary.

Step 3. Multigroup Confirmatory Factor Analysis

After the model fits acceptably in the reference group, it can be tested to what extent the structure is similar across groups. In this case, the reference group serves as the norm (New Zealand sample), and the fit in all other groups is compared with the structure in that group. This can be performed routinely in standard CFA programs such as LISREL, EQS, and AMOS. Parameters are then increasingly constrained to estimate how well the model fits across cultural groups. In this section, we discuss the lowest level of invariance that is equivalent to the tests described for MDS, PCA, and EFA and that is routinely used as a first step to estimate full measurement equivalence (e.g., Cheung & Rensvold, 2000; Meredith, 1993).

Form invariance (Cheung & Rensvold, 2000) or configural invariance (Byrne, Shavelson & Muthén, 1989) assumes that the same indicators (items) load on the same latent factor. This just tests whether the same items have the same nontrivial relationships with the underlying factor across cultures. If this test fails (by showing poor fit indices or large residuals), it would be advisable to run CFAs in each group separately to identify the problem (if this has not yet been performed). Fischer et al. (2009) demonstrated that all items loaded on their respective factor in the revised model. Therefore, the form or pattern of loadings was similar across all groups. However, the real power of CFA and multigroup CFA is the availability of other constraints that go beyond the focus of the current chapter (structural equivalence, or form invariance). In fact, most researchers are not interested in form invariance and only use this model as a baseline to examine the fit of more constrained models. We briefly discuss them in the next section.

Extensions

The procedure just described can be extended to impose further constraints in the data and allow for more sophisticated and informative analyses. The second level of invariance is factorial invariance (Cheung & Rensvold, 2000) or metric invariance (Byrne et al., 1989). Here, the factor loadings are constrained to be equal across groups. When factorial invariance is rejected, researchers must decide how to proceed. It may be possible to identify the reasons for differences in factor loading. This could indicate meaningful cultural differences but would preclude comparability of structures across cultures. It may be possible to remove these items (assuming there are only a few and that removing the items does not threaten domain underrepresentation). A third option might be to proceed with tests of partial invariance (Byrne et al., 1989) and constrain only those items that have been found to be invariant. Items showing differences are left to vary, and research may proceed with substantive testing of hypotheses.

The next higher level of restrictions constrains the item intercepts to be equal (Cheung & Rensvold, 2000; Vandenberg & Lance, 2000) in what is called scalar invariance (Vandenberg & Lance, 2000) or intercept invariance (Cheung & Rensvold, 2000). In the equivalence and bias literature, this is often referred to as scalar or full score equivalence (Fontaine, 2005; van de Vijver & Leung, 1997). If these constrained models are not rejected, it implies full score equivalence, and scores can be directly compared across groups. For example, if there was a group difference in levels of self-construals between two groups (Chinese and U.S. Americans) and scalar invariance was found, then the scores can be directly and unambiguously compared between the two samples.

As before, we need to evaluate the relative fit of these models. It is important to estimate to what extent model fit deteriorates because of increasing restrictions. This is possible because we are dealing with nested models, in which each subsequent test is a more restricted model than the previous one (Anderson & Gerbig, 1989). The most commonly used statistic is the chi-square difference test. The chi-square of the more restricted model is taken away from the chi-square of the previous model. Using the difference in degrees of freedom, the resulting chi-square follows the general chi-square distribution. A significant chi-square indicates that the fit is significantly worse in the more restricted model (Anderson & Gerbig, 1989). As discussed before, the chi-square is problematic, and it has been suggested also to consider changes in the other fit indices (Cheung & Rensvold, 2000; Little, 1997). Little (1997) suggested that a difference in the NNFI/TLI of less than 0.05 indicates equivalence. More recently, the criteria have been made more strict with differences in NNFI/TLI exceeding .01 indicating nonequivalence across cultural groups (Cheung & Rensvold, 2000). A difference of equal or less than .01 therefore indicates that the fit is not substantially worse between models. Little, Card, Slegers, and Ledford (2007) suggested that if the RMSEA of the more restrictive model is within the 90% confidence interval of the RMSEA of the more lenient model, the restrictive model can be selected. Selig, Card, and Little (2008) provide an overview of this group of techniques for cross-cultural work.

Coming back to our example, Fischer et al. (2009) were able to show that individualism–collectivism norms showed full score equivalence across all 11 samples included in their study. Therefore, the scores were directly comparable across samples. Being able to compare scores directly across cultural groups and to interpret the differences in terms of the latent underlying constructs (e.g., intelligence, motivation patterns, self-construals, individualism–collectivism norms) is obviously the aim of many if not most cross-cultural studies. This option therefore has much theoretical appeal for cross-cultural researchers. Little (1997) and Cheung and Rensvold (2000) discussed this option and provide examples of how it can be implemented in LISREL. However, these extensions already deal with level-oriented tests that are discussed more completely in Chapter 10.

The standard order is to constrain the pattern of loadings first, then the factor loadings, and finally the item intercepts. Additional interesting options include restrictions on factor intercorrelations (which is an indirect test of construct equivalence), the error terms (testing whether the error is invariant across cultures), and the latent means (testing whether the means on the latent construct are different across cultural groups). Vandenberg and Lance (2000) provided an overview and discussion of these various restrictions in cross-cultural organizational research. Their step-by-step procedures are directly applicable to cross-cultural research in general.

Strengths and Weaknesses

CFA is a theory-driven approach. A researcher should have a theory on how the observed variables are influenced by one or more latent variables. Therefore, the researcher has to specify a priori which items measure which factors. In the absence of theory, CFA should not be run. It is also appealing because it deals elegantly with all measurement questions simultaneously (both level- and structure-oriented questions in one comprehensive model).

However, it should be clear that testing models with CFA is more technical and, in particular, that the problem of how to assess model fit and what constitutes it is hotly debated in the literature. In addition to assumptions presented in the discussion of PCA and EFA, multivariate normality must be shown. Furthermore, apparent lack of fit can be due to technical problems (e.g., sample size, violation of normality, missing data) that contribute little to an understanding of the construct at hand. Given the editorial policies of major international journals, it has become increasingly popular to use CFA in cross-cultural research, but because of the concerns noted here, sample sizes in each cultural group should be large (with relatively arbitrary numbers of $N > 200$ being suggested; e.g., Barrett, 2007) and nonnormality and missing data within and across cultural groups should be examined. Popular software such as LISREL, EQS, AMOS, and Mplus can routinely fit many of these models, making cross-cultural CFAs easier to compute and evaluate. It is therefore an appealing technique for cross-cultural research, but its ultimate utility for psychological research continues to be critically examined (e.g., Borsboom, 2006).

A NOTE ON SAMPLE SIZES AND DATA TRANSFORMATION BEFORE THE INTERNAL STRUCTURE ANALYSES

Researchers should think about the sample size or, perhaps more important, the ratio of respondents to variables being measured. Guidelines vary widely, with a common recommendation to have samples of 200 (Barrett, 2007), 300, or more participants to yield a stable factor solution (Tabachnick & Fidell, 2007) or having at least 10 to 15 participants per variable (Field, 2009). Obviously, this is a major constraint for many cross-cultural comparisons that are based on small samples. Factor structures might appear different, because solutions in individual samples were unstable due to small sample sizes. It is paramount for cross-cultural researchers to have large enough samples to obtain stable factor structures that can then be examined for equivalence.

Another issue is that we assumed in the previous sections that researchers are using raw data. However, cross-cultural research is often threatened by differential response styles across cultures. This has led to recommendations of score transformations before analyses on the basis of the assumption that cultural response styles introduce particular biases in the data that need to be removed (e.g., Leung & Bond, 1989; Schwartz, 1992). The two most common and typical ones are ipsatization and double standardization (Fischer, 2004b). For ipsatized scores, the average across all variables for a particular individual is subtracted from the individual's raw score on a specific variable (Hofstede, 1980). Scores can be adjusted using only the means or means and variances. In the latter case, the mean-adjusted score is divided by the variance for each individual. The rationale for using ipsatization using means is that it removes acquiescent responding. If the ipsatization process takes the variance of the measures into account, the scores are also thought to be adjusted for extreme responding. The resulting adjusted score can be interpreted as the relative endorsement of this item or the relative position of the individual on a variable in relation to the other scores (Hicks, 1970). Double standardization then continues by subtracting the group mean score from each individual score (Leung & Bond, 1989). Double standardized scores have been recommended in the cross-cultural literature for detecting so-called culture-free (Hasegawa & Gudykunst, 1998; Leung & Bond, 1989; Singelis, Bond, Sharkey, & Lai, 1999) or etic dimensions (Yamaguchi, Kuhlman, & Sugimori, 1995).

The problem is that these techniques have some undesirable properties for most commonly used multivariate statistical techniques and introduce dependencies in the data (Hicks, 1970), which precludes the use of most multivariate techniques. MDS is the only technique that can adequately deal with ipsatized scores without problems. Ipsatization can lead to great distances if the original scales are highly negatively correlated. It may also be possible that circular structures are more pronounced. However, the overall structure should not be affected.

PCA can deal with ipsatization because components are linear combinations of observed variables. The dependencies in the data set introduced by ipsatization will nevertheless lead to bipolar factors, which may not have substantive meaning. Factor congruence between PCA based on raw data and ipsatized data can be low, especially for smaller factors (e.g., Fischer, 2004b). Therefore, the results in cross-cultural studies might lead to conflicting conclusions depending on whether ipsatized or nonipsatized data were used.

EFA should not be used with ipsatized data. It is inconsistent with the underlying theory, and the dependencies in the data create problems with the extraction of factors (Chan, 2003). The solutions may not have substantive meaning.

Standard CFA with ipsatized scores faces similar problems as EFA. Chan (2003) proposed a method that allows for the use of ipsative data matrices. This procedure involves a number of constraints to be placed on the factor loading and error covariance matrix. Chan reported an adequate recovery of the initial factor structure; however, the fit indices differ considerably between the raw and standardized matrix solution. This procedure is rather complex; however, it may be a promising option for dealing with ipsatized matrices.

An alternative method for dealing with acquiescence responding is to use a standard CFA but to model an independent method factor (Welkenhuysen-Gybels, Billiet, & Cambre, 2003). This technique can effectively control for any acquiescent responding and does not involve any of the problems associated with ipsatization.

Other standardization procedures are less frequently used (Fischer, 2004b) and do not have the same problematic statistical properties as ipsative scores. Group-mean centering or *z*-transformation across items within each group can be used to remove patterning effects (e.g., Leung & Bond, 1989; see Chapter 10). Some programs (e.g., Mplus) routinely do this centering. EFA, PCA, CFA, and MDS can all deal with data that have been centered.

CONCLUSIONS

This chapter presented techniques in which internal structure is compared in two or a few cultural groups. This means that in the research design, culture is treated as a fixed effect.

The steps discussed are essential for cross-cultural comparisons to be meaningful. However, these techniques have mistakenly been associated with only a measurement perspective. The question of structural equivalence is a research topic in its own right. Relativists have often proposed that psychological constructs cannot be compared across cultural groups, whereas universalists assume that structures hold irrespective of culture. With the techniques outlined here, it would be possible to address these fundamental questions empirically. First, it would need to be evaluated whether tests include all culturally relevant indicators for any given construct. Thus, constructed tests and instruments could be tested for cultural equivalence, which would address the question of human universality versus cultural determinancy. Work on emotions is a good case in point. Research has shown that the structure of emotions is similar, even in contexts in which specific language groups do not have words for certain emotions (e.g., Breugelmans & Poortinga, 2006). Therefore, these techniques can contribute significantly to an ongoing debate between cultural anthropologists and cultural psychologists and mainstream psychologists.

REFERENCES

Anderson, J. C., & Gerbig, D. W. (1988). Structural equation modelling in practice: A review and recommended two-step approach. *Psychological Bulletin, 103*, 411–423.

Au, K. Y. (1997). Another consequence of culture – intra-cultural variation. *International Journal of Human Resource Management, 8*, 743–755.

Barrett, P. (2005). Orthosim 2 [statistical software]. Retrieved September 9, 2009, from http://www.pbarrett.net/orthosim2.htm.

Barrett, P. (2007). Structural equation modeling: Adjudging model fit. *Personality and Individual Differences: Special Issue on Structural Equation Modeling, 42*, 815–824.

Beirens, K. & Fontaine, J. R. J. (2010). Development of the Ghent Multidimensional Somatic Complaints Scale. *Assessment, 17*, 70–80.

Bentler, P. M. (1990). Comparative fit indexes in structural models. *Psychological Bulletin, 107*, 238–246.

Bentler, P. M., & Bonnett, D. G. (1980). Significance tests and goodness of fit in the analysis of covariance structures. *Psychological Bulletin, 88*, 588–606.

Berry, J. W., Poortinga, J. H., Segall, M. H. & Dasen, P. R. (2002). *Cross-cultural psychology:Research and applications* (2nd ed.). Cambridge: Cambridge University Press.

Bijnen, E. J., & Poortinga, Y. H. (1988). The questionable value of cross-cultural comparisons with the Eysenck Personality Questionnaire. *Journal of Cross-Cultural Psychology, 19*, 193–202.

Bijnen, E. J., Van Der Net, T. Z. J., & Poortinga, Y. H. (1986). On cross-cultural comparative studies with the Eysenck Personality Questionnaire. *Journal of Cross-Cultural Psychology, 17*, 3–16.

Bilsky, W., Janik, M., & Schwartz, S. H. (2010). The structural organization of human values. *Journal of Cross-Cultural Psychology.*

Bollen, K. A. (1989). *Structural equations with latent variables.* New York: Wiley.

Borg, I., & Groenen, P. (2005). *Modern multidimensional scaling: Theory and applications* (2nd ed.). New York: Springer.

Borsboom, D. (2006). The attack of the psychometricians. *Psychometrika, 71*, 425–440.

Breugelmans, S. M., & Poortinga, Y. H. (2006). Emotion without a word: Shame and guilt among Rarámuri Indians and rural Javanese. *Journal of Personality and Social Psychology, 91*, 1111–1122.

Browne, M. W., & Cudeck, R. (1992). Alternative ways of assessing model fit. *Sociological Methods and Research, 21*, 230–258.

Byrne, B. M., Shavelson, R. J., & Muthén, B. (1989). Testing for the equivalence of factor covariance and mean structures: The issue of partial measurement invariance. *Psychological Bulletin, 105*, 456–466.

Caprara, G. V., Barbaranelli, C., Bermúndez, J., Maslach, C., & Ruch, W. (2000). Multivariate methods for the comparison of factor structures in cross-cultural research: An illustration with the Big Five Questionnaire. *Journal of Cross-Cultural Psychology, 31*, 437–464.

Chan, W. (2003). Analyzing ipsative data in psychological research. *Behaviormetrika, 30*, 99–121.

Chan, W., Ho, R., Leung, K., Chan, D. K., & Yung, F. (1999). An alternative method for evaluating congruence coefficients with Procrustes rotation. *Psychological Methods, 4*, 378–402.

Cheung, G. W., & Rensvold, R. B. (2000). Assessing extreme and acquiescence response sets in cross-cultural research using structural equations modeling. *Journal of Cross-Cultural Psychology, 31*, 160–186.

Commandeur, J. J. F. (1991). *Matching configurations.* Leiden, the Netherlands: DSWO Press. Retrieved from http://three-mode.leidenuniv.nl/bibliogr/commandeurjjf_thesis/front.pdf. Last accessed May 10, 2010.

Cudeck, R. (1989). Analysis of correlation matrices using covariance structure model. *Psychological Bulletin, 705*, 317–327.

Eysenck, H. J. (1986). Cross-cultural comparisons: The validity of assessment by indices of factor comparison. *Journal of Cross-Cultural Psychology, 17*, 506–515.

Field, A. (2009). *Discovering statistics using SPSS* (3rd ed.). Thousand Oaks, CA: Sage.

Fischer, R. (2004a). Organizational reward allocation principles: Testing organizational and cross-cultural differences. *International Journal for Intercultural Relations, 28*, 151–164.

Fischer, R. (2004b). Standardization to account for cross-cultural response bias: A classification of score adjustment procedures and review of research in *JCCP. Journal of Cross-Cultural Psychology, 35*, 263–282.

Fischer, R. (2008). Organizational justice and reward allocation. In P. B. Smith, M. Peterson, & D. Thomas (Eds.), *Handbook of cross-cultural management* (pp. 135–150). Thousand Oaks, CA: Sage.

Fischer, R., Ferreira, M. C., Assmar, E., Redford, P., Harb, C., Glazer, S., et al. (2009). Individualism–collectivism as descriptive norms: Development of a subjective norm approach to culture measurement. *Journal of Cross-Cultural Psychology, 40*, 187–213.

Fischer, R., Milfont, T., & Gouveia, V. V. (in press). Does social context affect value structures? Testing the intra-cultural stability of value structures with a functional theory of values. *Journal of Cross-Cultural Psychology.*

Fischer, R., & Smith, P. B. (2003). Reward allocation and culture: A meta-analysis. *Journal of Cross-Cultural Psychology, 34*, 251–268.

Fischer, R., & Smith, P. B. (2006). Justice criteria in the work place: The importance of values for perceptions of justice. *Applied Psychology: International Review, 55*, 541–562.

Fischer, R., Smith, P. B., Richey, B. E., Ferreira, M. C., Assmar, E. M. L., Maes, J., & Stumpf, S. (2007). Organizational reward allocation principles: Testing organizational and cross-cultural differences. *Journal of Cross-Cultural Psychology, 38*, 1–16.

Fontaine, J. R. J. (2003). Multidimensional scaling. In J. Harkness, F. J. R. van de Vijver, & P. Ph. Mohler (Eds.), *Cross-cultural survey methods* (pp. 235–246). Hoboken, NJ: Wiley.

Fontaine, J. R. J. (2005). Equivalence. In K. Kempf-Leonard (Ed.), *Encyclopedia of social measurement* (Vol. 1, pp. 803–813). New York: Academic Press.

Fontaine, J. R. J. (2008). Traditional and multilevel approaches in cross-cultural research: An integration of methodological frameworks. In F. J. R. van de Vijver, D. A. van Hemert & Y. Poortinga (Eds.), *Individuals and cultures in multi-level analysis*, pp. 65–92. Mahwah, NJ: Erlbaum.

Fontaine, J. R. J., Luyten, P., De Boeck, P., Corveleyn, J., Fernandez, M., Herrera, D., et al. (2006). Untying the Gordian knot of guilt and shame: The structure of guilt and shame reactions based on situation and person variation in Belgium, Hungary, and Peru. *Journal of Cross-Cultural Psychology, 37*, 273–292.

Fontaine, J. R. J., Poortinga, Y. H., Delbeke, L., & Schwartz, S. H. (2008). Structural equivalence of the values domain across cultures: Distinguishing sampling fluctuations from meaningful variation. *Journal of Cross-Cultural Psychology, 39*, 345–365.

Fontaine, J. R. J., Poortinga, Y. H., Setiadi, B., & Suprapti, S. M. (2002). Cognitive structure of emotion terms in Indonesia and The Netherlands. *Cognition and Emotion, 16*, 61–86.

Frese, M., Kring, W., Soose, A. & Zempel, J. (1996). Personal initiative at work: Differences between East and West Germany. *Academy of Management Journal, 39*, 37–63.

Hasegawa, T., & Gudykunst, W. B. (1998). Silence in Japan and the United States. *Journal of Cross-Cultural Psychology, 29*, 668–684.

Hicks, L.E. (1970). Some properties of ipsative, normative and forced-choice normative measures. *Psychological Bulletin, 74*, 167–184.

Ho, D. Y. F. (1996). Filial piety and its psychological consequences. In M. H. Bond (Ed.), *Handbook of Chinese psychology* (pp. 155–165). Hong Kong: Oxford University Press.

Hofstede, G. (1980). *Culture's consequences: International differences in work-related values.* Beverly Hills, CA: Sage.

Hu, L. T., & Bentler, P. M. (1998). Fit indices in covariance structure modeling: Sensitivity to underparameterized model misspecification. *Psychological Methods, 3*, 424–453.

Hu, L., & Bentler, P. M. (1999). Cutoff criteria for fit indexes in covariance structure analysis: Conventional criteria versus new alternatives. *Structural Equation Modeling, 6*, 1–55.

Kline, R. B. (2005). *Principles and practice of structural equation modeling.* New York: Guilford Press.

Kiers, H. A. L. (1990). *SCA: A program for simultaneous components analysis of variables measured in two or more populations.* Groningen, the Netherlands: ProGAMMA.

Kiers, H. A. L., & Ten Berge, J. M. F. (1989). Alternating least squares algorithms for simultaneous component analysis with equal weight matrices in two or more populations. *Psychometrica, 54*, 467–473.

Kruskal, J. B., & Wish, M. (1978). *Multidimensional scaling* (Sage University Paper No. 07). London: Sage.

Leung, K. (2005). How generalizable are justice effects across cultures? In J. Greenberg & J. A. Colquitt (Eds.), *Handbook of organizational justice* (pp. 555–588). Mahwah, NJ: Erlbaum.

Leung, K. (1997). Negotiation and reward allocation across cultures. In P. C. Earley & M. Erez (Eds.), *New perspectives on international industrial/organizational psychology* (pp. 640–675). San Francisco: New Lexington.

Leung, K., & Bond, M. H. (1989). On the empirical identification of dimensions for cross-cultural comparisons. *Journal of Cross-Cultural Psychology, 20*, 133–151.

Little, T. D. (1997). Mean and covariance structures (MACS) analysis of cross-cultural data: Practical and theoretical issues. *Multivariate Behavioral Research, 32*, 53–76.

Little, T. D., Card, N. A., Slegers, D. W., & Ledford, E. C. (2007). Representing contextual effects in multiple-group MACS models. In T. D. Little, J. A. Bovaird, & N. A. Card (Eds.), *Modeling contextual effects in longitudinal studies* (pp. 121–148). Mahwah, NJ: Erlbaum.

Long, J.S. (1983). *Confirmatory factor analysis* (Sage University Paper No. 33). Newbury Park, CA: Sage.

MacCallum, R. C., & Austin, J. T. (2000). Applications of structural equation modelling in psychological research. *Annual Review of Psychology, 51*, 201–226.

Marsh, H. W., Balla, J. R., & McDonald, R. P. (1988). Goodness of fit indexes in confirmatory factor analysis: The effect of sample size. *Psychological Bulletin, 103,* 391–410.

Marsh, H. W., Hau, K. T., & Wen, Z. L. (2004). In search of golden rules: Comment on hypothesis testing approaches to setting cutoff values for fit indexes and dangers in overgeneralising Hu & Bentler (1999) findings. *Structural Equation Modeling, 11,* 320–341.

McCrae, R. R., Zonderman, A. B., Costa, P. T., Jr., Bond, M. H., & Paunonen, S. V. (1996). Evaluating replicability of factors in the Revised NEO Personality Inventory: Confirmatory factor analysis versus Procrustes rotation. *Journal of Personality and Social Psychology, 70,* 552–566.

Meredith, W. (1993). Measurement invariance, factor analysis and factorial invariance. *Psychometrika, 58,* 525–543.

Messick, S. (1989). Validity. In R. L. Linn (Ed.), *Educational measurement* (3rd ed., pp. 13–103). New York: Macmillan Publishing Company.

Russell, J. A., & Carroll, J. M. (1999). On the bipolarity of positive and negative affect. *Psychological Bulletin, 125,* 3–30.

Schwartz, S. H. (1992). Universals in the content and structure of values: Theoretical advances and empirical tests in 20 countries. *Advances in Experimental Social Psychology, 25,* 1–65.

Selig, J. P., Card, N. A., & Little, T. D. (2008). Latent variable structural equation modeling in cross-cultural research: Multigroup and multilevel approaches. In F. J. R. van de Vijver, D. A. van Hemert, & Y. H. Poortinga (Eds.), *Individuals and cultures in multilevel analysis* (pp. 93–120). Mahwah, NJ: Erlbaum.

Shaver, P. R., Wu, S., & Schwartz, J. C. (1992). Cross-cultural similarities and differences in emotion and its representation: A prototype approach. In M. S. Clark (Ed.), *Review of personality and social psychology: Vol. 13. Emotion* (pp. 175–212). Newbury Park, CA: Sage.

Singelis, T. M., Bond, M. H., Sharkey, W. F., & Lai, C.S.Y. (1999). Unpackaging cultures's influence on self-esteem and embarrassability. *Journal of Cross-Cultural Psychology, 30,* 315–341.

Tabachnick, B. G., & Fidell, L. S. (2007). *Using multivariate statistics* (5th ed.). Boston: Allyn & Bacon.

Ten Berge, J. M. F. (1986). Some relationships between descriptive comparisons of components from different studies. *Multivariate Behavioral Research, 21,* 29–40.

Triandis, H. C. (1995). *Individualism & collectivism.* Boulder, CO: Westview Press.

Ullman, J. B. (2007). Structural equation modeling. In B. G. Tabachnick & L. Fidell (Eds.), *Using multivariate statistics* (5th ed., pp. 676–781). Boston: Allyn & Bacon.

Van de Vijver, F. J. R., & Leung, K. (1997). *Methods and data analysis for cross-cultural research.* London: Sage.

Vandenberg, R. J., & Lance, C. E. (2000). A review and synthesis of the measurement invariance literature: Suggestions, practices, and recommendations for organizational research. *Organizational Research Methods, 3,* 4–70.

Watson, D., Wiese, D., Vaidya, J., & Tellegen, A. (1999). The two general activation systems of affect: Structural findings, evolutionary considerations, and psychobiological evidence. *Journal of Personality and Social Psychology, 76,* 820–838.

Welkenhuysen-Gybels, J., Billiet, J., & Cambre, B. (2003). Adjustment for acquiescence in the assessment of the construct equivalence of Likert-type score items. *Journal of Cross-Cultural Psychology, 34*, 702–722.

Yamaguchi, S., Kuhlman, D. M., & Sugimori, S. (1995). Personality correlates of allocentric tendencies in individualist and collectivist cultures. *Journal of Cross-Cultural Psychology, 26*, 658–672.

8

Evaluating Test and Survey Items for Bias Across Languages and Cultures

STEPHEN G. SIRECI

INTRODUCTION

The world is growing smaller at a rapid rate in this 21st century, and it is little wonder that interest and activity in cross-cultural research are at their peak. Examples of cross-cultural research activities include international comparisons of educational achievement, the exploration of personality constructs across cultures, and investigations of employees' opinions, attitudes, and skills by multinational companies. In many, if not all, of these instances, the research involves measuring psychological attributes across people who have very different cultural backgrounds and often function using different languages. This cultural and linguistic diversity poses significant challenges for researchers who strive for standardization of measures across research participants. In fact, the backbone of scientific research in psychology – standardization of measures – may lead to significant biases in the interpretation of results if the measuring instruments do not take linguistic and cultural differences into account.

The International Test Commission (ITC) has long pointed out problems in measuring educational and psychological constructs across languages and cultures. Such problems are also well documented in the *Standards for Educational and Psychological Testing* (American Educational Research Association [AERA], American Psychological Association, & National Council on Measurement in Education, 1999). For example, the *Guidelines for Adapting Educational and Psychological Tests* (Hambleton, 2005; ITC, 2001) provide numerous guidelines for checking the quality of measurement instruments when they are adapted for use across languages. These guidelines include careful evaluation of the translation process and statistical analysis of test and item response data to evaluate test and item comparability. Many of these guidelines are echoed by the aforementioned *Standards*. Table 8.1

Table 8.1. *Selected excerpts from professional guidelines related to cross-lingual assessment*

Standards for Educational and Psychological Testing (AERA et al., 1999)	Guidelines for Test Adaptations (Hambleton, 2005)
A clear rationale and supporting evidence should be provided for any claim that scores earned on different forms of a test may be used interchangeably. (p. 57)	Instrument developers/publishers should compile judgmental evidence, both linguistic and psychological, to improve the accuracy of the adaptation process and compile evidence on the equivalence of all language versions. (p. 22)
When substantial changes are made to a test, the test's documentation should be amended, supplemented, or revised to keep information for users current and to provide useful additional information or cautions. (p. 70)	When a test is adapted for use in another population, documentation of the changes should be provided, along with evidence to support the equivalence of the adapted version of the test. (p. 23)
When a test is translated from one language to another, the methods used in establishing the adequacy of the translation should be described, and empirical and logical evidence should be provided for score reliability and the validity of the translated test's score inferences for the uses intended in the linguistic groups to be tested. (p. 99)	Test developers/publishers should ensure that the adaptation process takes full account of linguistic and cultural differences in the intended populations. (p. 22)
When multiple language versions of a test are intended to be comparable, test developers should report evidence of test comparability. (p. 99)	Test developers/publishers should apply appropriate statistical techniques to (a) establish the equivalence of the language versions of the test, and (b) identify problematic components or aspects of the test that may be inadequate in one or more of the intended populations. (p. 22)
When there is credible evidence of score comparability across regular and modified tests . . . no flag should be attached to a score. When such evidence is lacking, specific information about the nature of the modification should be provided. (p. 98)	Comparisons across populations can only be made at the level of invariance that has been established for the scale on which the scores are reported. (p. 23)

Note: AERA = American Educational Research Association.

presents some brief excerpts from the *Guidelines* and *Standards* that pertain to maximizing measurement equivalence across languages and cultures while ruling out issues of measurement bias. As can be seen from Table 8.1, both qualitative and quantitative procedures are recommended to comprehensively evaluate test comparability across languages. The qualitative procedures involve use of careful translation and adaptation designs and comprehensive evaluation of the different language versions of a test. Quantitative procedures include the use of dimensionality analyses to evaluate construct equivalence, differential predictive validity to evaluate the consistency of test-criterion relationships across test versions, and differential item functioning procedures to evaluate potential item bias.

BIAS AND EQUIVALENCE IN CROSS-CULTURAL ASSESSMENT

The ITC *Guidelines* and the AERA et al. *Standards* warn against the significant threats to the validity of inferences derived from measurement instruments used across diverse languages and cultures. These threats have also been pointed out by many cross-cultural researchers, who tend to categorize them in terms of bias or equivalence. Van de Vijver and colleagues, for example, identified three general categories of potential bias in cross-lingual assessment: method bias, construct bias, and item bias (e.g., van de Vijver & Leung, this volume; van de Vijver & Poortinga, 2005; van de Vijver & Tanzer, 1997). In terms of equivalence, such threats can be examined by evaluating linguistic equivalence, structural equivalence, construct equivalence, metric equivalence, or scalar equivalence (e.g., Geisinger, 1994; Hambleton, 1993; Sireci, 2005). I briefly describe these terms, but it should be noted that there are some differences across researchers in how they are defined.

Van de Vijver and colleagues describe *method bias* as a systematic source of error affecting scores that is due to a bias inherent in the measurement process. Examples of measurement bias in cross-cultural assessment include test administrator bias (e.g., interviewer bias and translator bias when a test is being administered orally by a bilingual translator), differential familiarity with item formats (e.g., multiple-choice items, Likert-type items), differential social desirability (e.g., social desirability interacts with culture), and other response sets such as acquiescence that would be more prevalent in one cultural group than another. The key concept behind method bias is that it typically affects all items within an assessment.

Distinguished from method bias, *construct bias* refers to inconsistency in the attribute being measured across groups. This concept refers to both measurement of a unitary concept across cultural groups who take the test within a single language (e.g., African Americans and European Americans in the United States taking a test in English), as well as measurement of the same construct across different adaptations of the test (e.g., Francophones and Anglophones taking French- or English-language versions of a test in Canada). Van de Vijver and others point out that a construct may be legitimate in one cultural group but not another. Thus, before cross-cultural assessment can commence, it must be determined that the construct exists in all groups to be measured and that it is conceptualized in the same way across all groups. In educational testing, departure from construct equivalence can be seen when curricula differ across countries or other jurisdictions (e.g., 8th-grade math includes algebra in one curriculum but not another).

In considering *item bias*, we move from the total test score level to the item level. Item bias refers to problems with a specific test item, such as when an item is not translated properly or provides some type of advantage or disadvantage to members of a particular linguistic or cultural group. Biases associated with an item must be attributed to a source that is not relevant to the construct measured. For example, an arithmetic test item that uses a game of cricket as its frame of reference may confuse test takers not familiar with the game and affect their performance. The context of the item (a cricket game) is irrelevant to the construct measured (arithmetic knowledge or skill). However, differential performance on an item that has high content validity may reflect true differences and not bias. Therefore, when conducting statistical analyses to identify potentially biased items, it must be borne in mind that *bias* involves a subjective decision that the cause of differential performance on an item is due to construct-irrelevant factors. Statistical evaluation of item bias is a focus of this chapter.

Bias can also be evaluated from the perspective of equivalence. Van de Vijver and Poortinga (1997) differentiated linguistic equivalence from psychological equivalence. When test items are translated from one language to another, one may achieve linguistic equivalence (each translated word appropriately matches its translated counterpart) without achieving psychological equivalence (consistency of meaning across languages). Hambleton (1993) described a striking example of this difference in which the idiom "out of sight, out of mind" was translated into "invisible, insane." Obviously, the literal translation holds up, but the intended meaning of the idiom was lost in translation

A more global perspective on equivalence is *construct equivalence*. When construct equivalence exists across groups defined by language, culture, or disability, the same construct is being measured with equal precision across all groups. Thus, construct equivalence involves a uniform definition of the construct measured (i.e., identical construct definition and test specifications) and uniform measurement of the construct. These criteria imply that the construct exists in all studied groups, it is conceptualized the same way in all groups, and it is manifested in the same way for all groups. Establishing construct equivalence across groups is a daunting and complex task, and thus different aspects of construct equivalence are often studied.

One of the most common aspects of construct equivalence that is studied is *structural equivalence*, which is consistency of test dimensionality across groups of examinees. Methods for evaluating structural equivalence include exploratory factor analysis, confirmatory factor analysis, and, my personal favorite, multidimensional scaling (see Day & Rounds, 1998; Robin, Sireci, & Hambleton, 2003; Sireci, Harter, Yang, & Bhola, 2003). Structural equivalence is the most common method for evaluating construct equivalence because the data required for analysis – an examinee-by-item response matrix – are easily available. However, it should be remembered that the study of common dimensionality across test forms or subgroups of examinees is just one lens through which we can view construct equivalence. More comprehensive evaluations of construct equivalence would also include criterion-related studies such as analysis of differential predictive validity and more complex comparisons of the nomological network (Cronbach & Meehl, 1955) surrounding the construct. Unfortunately, such comprehensive evaluations of construct equivalence are rarely conducted because of the difficulty in acquiring valid criterion data.

When comparisons are made across examinees who take different versions of an assessment, such as different language versions of a test, the most stringent type of equivalence is *scalar equivalence*. Scalar equivalence means that the measurement scale is identical across versions of the assessment. For example, scalar equivalence across Flemish- and French-language versions of a test would mean that a score of 55 on the Flemish version of the test "means the same thing" (i.e., represents the same location on the construct continuum) as a score of 55 on the French version of the test.

Establishing item, construct, and scalar equivalence (or ruling out the aforementioned biases) are perhaps the most difficult challenges faced by contemporary psychometricians involved in cross-cultural research. In the remainder of this chapter, I focus on statistical methods for evaluating item bias. However, it is extremely important for cross-cultural researchers to realize that evaluating item bias is insufficient for evaluating equivalence or comparability of scores derived from multiple forms of an assessment or across culturally diverse groups of examinees. Analysis of bias and equivalence at the item level must first rule out systematic bias at the total test score level, because total test score (or a projection of it such as a latent trait estimate) is typically used as the matching variable in analysis of differential item functioning. Therefore, analysis of structural equivalence is a valuable means for justifying subsequent analysis of differential item functioning and item bias. Methods for evaluating structural equivalence can be found in Reise, Widaman, and Pugh (1993); Robin et al. (2003); Sireci, Bastari, and Allalouf (1998); Sireci et al. (2003); and Sireci, Patsula, and Hambleton (2005).

METHODS FOR EVALUATING ITEM BIAS

Defining Item Bias

Before describing methods for evaluating *item bias*, the term must be distinguished from two others – *item impact* and *differential item functioning* (DIF). Item impact refers to a significant group difference on an item, for example, when one group has a higher proportion of students answering an item correctly than another group.[1] Such differences do not necessitate bias, because they could reflect "true" group differences on the attribute measured. DIF is a statistical observation that involves *matching* test takers from different groups on the characteristic measured and then looking for performance differences on an item. The logic behind this matching is that test takers from different groups who have similar proficiency (i.e., who are matched) should respond similarly to a given test item. If they do not, the item is said to "function differently" across groups. However, such differential functioning does not necessarily signify item bias. It merely flags the item for a statistical difference; it does not explain the cause of the difference.[2] Item *bias* is present when an item has been statistically flagged for DIF *and the reason for the DIF is traced to a factor irrelevant to the construct the test is intended to measure.* Therefore, for item bias to exist, a characteristic of the item that is unfair (construct-irrelevant) to one or more groups must be identified. DIF is a necessary, but insufficient, condition for item bias.

[1] Or, in the context of attitude, opinion, or personality research, a higher endorsement rate on one or more points on a rating scale can be substituted for a higher proportion correct.

[2] The logic in DIF analysis is similar to that of analysis of covariance (ANCOVA; i.e., looking at differences after controlling for another variable), and thus like any other nonexperimental design, cause cannot be inferred. The DIF procedures described in this chapter are specifically designed to analyze dichotomous and ordinal (e.g., Likert-type) data because applications of ANCOVA to this area have tended to violate the underlying assumptions of the model, such as heteroscedasticity and interval-level data.

Table 8.2. *Common methods for evaluating differential item functioning*

Method	Description	Sources	Cross-lingual applications
Delta plot	Scatter plot of transformed item difficulties	Angoff (1972)	Angoff & Modu (1973); Muniz et al. (2001); Robin et al. (2003)
Standardization index	Weighted conditional *p* value difference	Dorans & Kulick (1986); Dorans & Holland (1993)	Muniz et al. (2001); Sireci, Fitzgerald, & Xing (1998)
Mantel–Haenszel	Contingency table approach	Holland & Thayer (1988); Dorans & Holland (1993)	Allalouf et al. (1999); Budgell, Raju, & Quartetti (1995); Muniz et al. (2001)
Lord's chi-square	IRT-based approach	Lord (1980)	Angoff & Cook (1988)
IRT likelihood ratio	Test-nested IRT models	Thissen et al. (1988, 1993)	Sireci & Berberoglu (2000)
IRT area	Test area between ICCs	Raju (1988, 1990)	Budgell et al. (1995)
Logistic regression	Test conditional group difference	Swaminathan & Rogers (1990)	Allalouf et al. (1999); Hauger & Sireci (2008)
SIBTEST	Weighted conditional *p* values; can be aggregated across items	Shealy & Stout (1993)	Gierl & Khaliq (2001)

Note: ICC = intraclass correlation coefficient; IRT = item response theory; SIBTEST = simultaneous item bias test.

Classifying Differential Item Functioning Detection Methods

There are numerous methods for evaluating DIF (for other comprehensive discussions of DIF methods, see Camilli & Shepard, 1994; Clauser & Mazor, 1998; Holland & Wainer, 1993; Millsap & Everson, 1993; or Potenza & Dorans 1995). Many of these methods have been applied to evaluate item comparability across translated or adapted measurement instruments. Table 8.2 presents a list of eight of the more common methods and provides citations for each method. The first citation listed is one of the classic references to the procedure. The second citation gives one or more applications of the method to the problem of evaluating items adapted for use across languages. These methods can be classified as graphical (delta plot), contingency table-based (standardization, Mantel–Haenszel, simultaneous item bias test [SIBTEST]), item response theory (IRT)-based (Lord's chi-square, IRT likelihood ratio, IRT area), or regression-based (logistic regression).

In this chapter, I focus on five methods for evaluating DIF: delta plot, standardization, Mantel–Haenszel, IRT likelihood ratio, and logistic regression. These five methods provide a wide variety of options for evaluating DIF, and the choice of method depends on several factors, including sample sizes, type of test item (dichotomous or polytomous), and concerns regarding types of DIF. The delta plot method is introduced because of its simplicity and its place in the history of DIF methodology. The Mantel–Haenszel method is included because it is one of the most popular methods used by educational testing programs and is widely discussed in the literature. The IRT likelihood ratio test is perhaps the most powerful test of DIF but has more stringent requirements regarding model assumptions and sample sizes. The logistic regression approach represents a nice compromise of the strengths and limitations of the other methods and is currently one of the most popular.

Applications of DIF methodology may focus on comparing two groups of examinees or more than two groups. In either instance, one group is typically chosen as the "reference group," which is usually some type of majority group (e.g., Caucasians). When a test is translated from one language to another, the reference group is typically the group taking the version of the test written in the original language. The other groups studied are called the "focal" groups, which typically represent minority groups of test takers or a target language version of an assessment.

Delta Plot

The delta plot method for evaluating DIF (Angoff, 1972; Angoff & Modu, 1973) provides a visual comparison of item difficulty statistics to allow the identification of items that function differentially across groups. This relatively early procedure was designed to identify potentially biased educational test items that were scored dichotomously (i.e., correct or incorrect). The procedure involves first calculating the proportions of examinees in the reference and focal groups who answer an item correctly. These proportions are typically called "p values." Angoff (1972) realized these group-specific p values do not account for the overall differences across groups, and he recommended transforming them to a common metric, which is called the delta metric at the Educational Testing Service (ETS). The delta metric is a normal transformation of these *p* values onto a scale with a mean of 13 and standard deviation of 4, although any other convenient mean and standard deviation could be used. The transformed *p* values are typically called *transformed item deltas.* The delta plot involves plotting the group-specific deltas against one another, with the reference group on the horizontal axis and the focal group on the vertical axis. If the relative difficulties (or endorsement rates) of the items are consistent across groups, they will fall on a 45-degree line. If any item's difficulty is different in the two groups, that item will deviate from this line.

When producing a scatter plot of delta values, the intercept of the regression line running through the plot reflects the overall difference between the groups in terms of proficiency. If the intercept is at zero, the two groups have the same distribution. If the intercept on the focal group's axis deviates from zero (e.g., 1.0), it means that the mean of the focal group's ability distribution is one delta (e.g., one fourth of a standard deviation) lower than the mean of the reference group. Items on the delta plot that fall within a narrow ellipse reflect items that have approximately equal difficulty in both cultures and thus can be considered as equivalent. Items that deviate significantly from this line are said to demonstrate DIF.

An example of a delta plot is presented in Figure 8.1, which presents the delta values for 100 items that were originally developed in English and translated into a target language (described further in Robin et al., 2003). The fact that the 45-degree line does not emanate from the origin reflects the overall difference in proficiency between the two groups, which is 4.0 (in favor of the English-language group) in this case. A confidence band was drawn around this line, and it can be seen that there are many items falling outside the band. These are the items flagged for DIF. In this case, the confidence bands were derived by taking random draws from the English-language sample. However, other procedures, such as forming the interval based on standard errors, are also common.

The delta plot method is relatively easy to do and interpret. However, it may miss items that function differently across groups if the discriminating power of the item is low, and erroneously flag items for DIF, if the discriminating power of the item is high (Dorans & Holland, 1993). For these reasons, although it is of historical interest, the delta plot is not widely recommended, unless it is used primarily as a preliminary check before doing more comprehensive DIF analyses (e.g., to identify items to remove from the matching variable in a more comprehensive analysis).

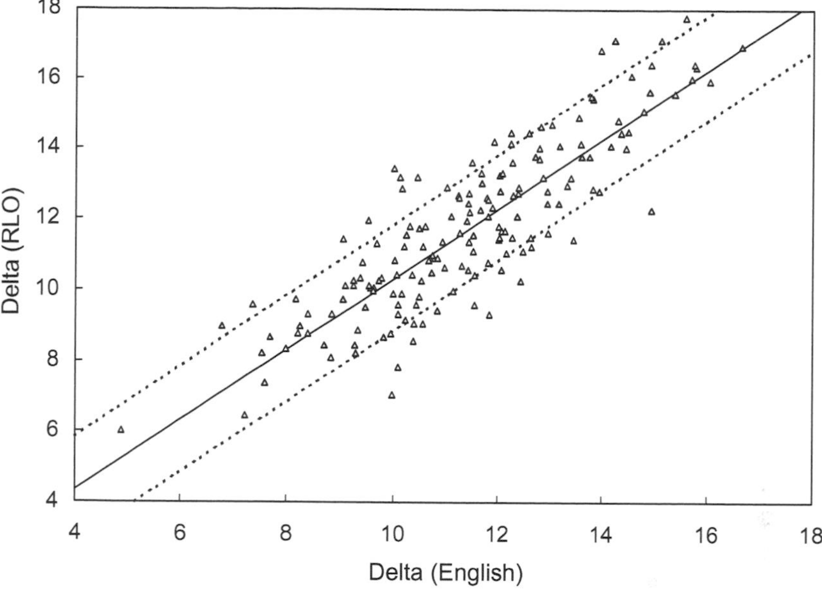

Figure 8.1. Example of a delta plot.

Standardization

Dorans and Kulick (1986) suggested using traditional standardization methods to construct an index for detecting DIF. This standardization approach is a conditional p value procedure, in which separate p values are computed for each item, conditional on the total test score. The difference between these estimates is calculated between the reference and the focal groups, and a summary statistic is calculated by summing up these differences, weighted by the score distribution of the reference group. In practice, test score intervals are computed to match examinees (i.e., thick matching) so that the sample sizes per test score interval are not too small. The standardized index proposed by Dorans and Kulick (STD-P) is computed as:

$$STD - P = \frac{\sum_m w_m(E_{fm} - E_{rm})}{\sum_m w_m} \tag{8.1}$$

in which w_m = the relative frequency of the reference group at score level m, and E_{fm} and E_{rm} are the proportion of examinees at score level m who answered the item correctly in the focal and reference groups, respectively.

Equation 8.1 is known as the "signed" version of the statistic because positive differences at one point of the scale can be offset by negative differences at another point. The "unsigned" version of the statistic is

$$STD - P = \frac{\sum_{m} \left| w_m (E_{fm} - E_{rm}) \right|}{\sum_{m} w_m} \tag{8.2}$$

and can be used to identify "nonuniform" DIF (i.e., DIF that is inconsistent across the matching variable, described further in a later section of this chapter).

The signed version of the standardization index ranges from −1 to 1. For example, if STD-P is .10, it means that, on average, examinees in the reference group who are matched to examinees in the focal group have a 10% greater chance of answering the item correctly. An STD-P value of ±.10 has been used as a criterion for flagging items for DIF (Sireci, Fitzgerald, & Xing, 1998). Using this criterion, if 10 items on a test were flagged for DIF and they were all in favor of one of the two groups, the aggregate level of DIF on the test would be approximately 1 point on the total raw test score scale in favor of the reference group. Using real and simulated data, Muniz, Hambleton, and Xing (2001) concluded that the standardization index was effective for flagging adapted versions of items for DIF when sample sizes were as small as 100.

Mantel–Haenszel

The Mantel–Haenszel (MH) method for identifying DIF is similar to the standardization index in that examinees from two groups are matched on the proficiency of interest, and the likelihood of success on the item is compared across groups. Mantel and Haenszel (1959) extended the chi-square test of independence to examine the efficacy of a cancer treatment. Patients were stratified by the severity of their illness, and at each level of severity a two-by-two frequency table was constructed. One factor of this table was "treatment" or "control" and the other factor was "survival" (survived vs. died). Mantel and Haenszel derived a clever weighting scheme to combine the results of all of these two-by-two tables across the severity strata in a statistically optimal fashion. The resulting summary statistic has become known as the Mantel–Haenszel statistic in their honor (Wainer & Sireci, 2005).

Holland and Thayer (1988) applied the MH statistic to the problem of estimating DIF in the context of dichotomously scored items, and more

Table 8.3. *Frequencies required to compute Mantel–Haenszel statistic at each level of conditioning variable*

Group	Correct	Incorrect	Total
Reference	A_j	B_j	N_{rj}
Focal	C_j	D_j	N_{fj}
Total	M_{1j}	M_{0j}	T_j

Note: *j* denotes one level of the matching criterion, and the capital letters refer to cell, row, or column frequencies.

recent extensions on the method were developed for polytomous items (e.g., Potenza & Dorans, 1995; Zwick, Donoghue, & Grima, 1993). MH is similar to the standardization index in that examinees from two groups are matched on the proficiency of interest, and the likelihood of success on the item is compared across groups. It is different however, in that it looks at the odds ratio of success on each item rather than the difference in the proportions. To compute the MH statistic, the following frequencies are calculated *at each level of the conditioning variable*: the total numbers of examinees in each group, the numbers of examinees in each group who answered the item correctly, and the number who answered the item incorrectly. An example of the necessary data at just one level of the conditioning variable (denoted by the subscript *m*) for the dichotomous case is presented in Table 8.3.

The null hypothesis tested is that the ratios of the proportions correct to incorrect for each group are the same. Using the notation in Table 8.3, the common odds ratio α_{MH} is estimated by

$$\alpha MH = \frac{\sum_{j} \frac{A_j\, D_j}{T_j}}{\sum_{t} \frac{B_j\, C_j}{T_j}}. \tag{8.3}$$

When $\alpha_{\text{MH}} = 1$, the likelihood of responding correctly to the item is the same for both the focal and reference group, across *J* score levels. The significance of the deviation of the MH statistic is determined through a one degree of freedom chi-square statistic:

$$\text{MH-}\chi^2 = \frac{\left[\left|\sum_{j} A_j - \sum_{j} E(A_j)\right| - .5\right]^2}{\sum_{j} Var(A_j)} \tag{8.4}$$

where

$$Var(A_j) = \frac{N_{rj} N_{fj} M_{1j} M_{0j}}{T_j^2 (T_{j-1})} \tag{8.5}$$

In addition to providing a test for statistical significance, an effect size can also be computed, and rules of thumb exist for classifying these effect sizes into small, medium, and large DIF (Dorans & Holland, 1993). Assuming that MH-χ^2 shows a significant value ($p < .05$), items are defined as "large DIF" if the absolute value of MH-χ^2 is at least 1.5, items are defined as "medium DIF" if the absolute value of MH-χ^2 is between 1.0 and 1.5, and all other items are classified as "small DIF." Items classified in this last category are not flagged as functioning differentially across groups.

The MH method has been shown to be particularly powerful in detecting DIF. For this reason, it is often used as the standard for comparison in studies involving dichotomous items that compare DIF detection methods. The MH statistic achieves its power by focusing all evidence on the detection of a single parameter (hence, the single degree of freedom), which is the extent to which the log odds ratio is consistently different from one across all strata. It is typically successful in detecting what has come to be known as uniform DIF. However, it is unable to detect successfully more complex types of DIF that systematically vary across strata (i.e., "nonuniform" DIF). Like the standardization method, determining the score intervals on which to match examinees (i.e., how thin or thick the matching should be) is another limitation of the method.[3]

Item Response Theory Likelihood Ratio

The three methods for DIF detection described previously all use an observed test score to match examinees across groups, and thus they do not posit a strong model for item responses. There are several methods for detecting DIF that are based on IRT models. Essentially, all IRT DIF detection methods test whether a common set of item parameters can be used to describe the functioning of an item in each cultural group. If different parameters are needed to describe the functioning of the item in each group, then the item is flagged for DIF.

In the IRT likelihood ratio method for evaluating DIF (Thissen, Steinberg, & Wainer, 1988, 1993), two IRT models are fit to examinee response

[3] Fischer (1993) provided an interesting demonstration of the relationship of the MH statistic and other chi-square-based indices to the Rasch IRT model.

data, and the difference between the fit of these models to the data is evaluated for statistical significance. The first model fit to the data is a "no-DIF" (compact) model in which the same item parameters are used to calibrate the item in each group. The second model fit to the data is a "DIF" (augmented) model in which separate parameters are used to calibrate the item in each group. Each model has an associated likelihood. The difference between these likelihoods is used to test whether the improvement in fit from the additional parameters in the augmented model is statistically significant (Thissen et al., 1988). The difference between the likelihoods of each model is distributed as chi-square,[4] and the degrees of freedom associated with this chi-square test are the difference in the number of parameters estimated by each model.

An item is considered to function differentially if the value of the likelihood ratio test is significantly different from zero, in which case additional separate likelihood ratio tests for each item *parameter* are carried out to determine which parameter(s) is (are) causing the DIF.

The IRT likelihood ratio test has been widely applied to the investigation of DIF across subgroups of examinees using both dichotomous and polytomous IRT models (Thissen et al., 1988; Wainer, Sireci, & Thissen, 1991). There have also been several applications of this method to the problem of detecting flaws in test adaptations (e.g., Sireci & Berberoglu, 2000). Advantages of this method are its statistical power, its flexibility in handling both dichotomous and polytomous data, and its ability to simultaneously test multiple groups. Traditionally, the procedure had one major drawback: It was extremely time-consuming to apply. For each item, multiple IRT models must be fit to the data. When the assessment comprises a large number of items and the no-DIF model is rejected, isolating the specific DIF items can an arduous process. Thankfully, however, Thissen (2001) developed a macro version of his Multilog IRT software that makes this task easier. His IRTLRDIF software is described in the Appendix to this chapter. IRTLRDIF first tests the no-DIF model, and if the difference is statistically significant, it sequentially tests all model parameters for DIF. This program is recommended for cross-cultural researchers interested in investigating DIF using the IRT likelihood ratio procedure.

The IRT likelihood ratio procedure has both power and flexibility. It is powerful in that it has all of the optimality of maximum likelihood estimation. It is flexible in that it can assess differences in item behavior in any

[4] Specifically, it is the log of the likelihood that is distributed as chi-square, and in practice – 2 times the log of the likelihood is used to compare fit across the models.

way that can be characterized by the model. For example, like the logistic regression method for evaluating DIF (described next), IRT-based methods can identify both *uniform* and *nonuniform* DIF. Uniform DIF is present if one group performs differently on an item relative to matched members in the other group throughout the entire range of proficiency. Nonuniform DIF occurs when there is a systematic difference in performance across matched groups, but the direction of the difference changes at different points along the range of proficiency. Uniform DIF is similar to a main effect, for example, when females systematically outperform matched males on a test item. Nonuniform DIF represents an interaction between proficiency and performance differences across groups – for example, when high-proficiency males outperform high-proficiency females, but low-proficiency females outperform low-proficiency males (see Jodoin & Gierl, 2001; Swaminathan & Rogers, 1990; or Zumbo, 1999, for further discussion of uniform and nonuniform DIF).

Although the IRT likelihood ratio procedure is powerful and flexible, it has some drawbacks. First, IRT models require a relatively large sample size for accurate item parameter estimation. Thus, to apply a method based on IRT, sample sizes of at least 200 in all studied groups are needed for the simplest IRT models (e.g., Rasch model), and sample sizes of 1,000 or more may be needed for more complex models. Also, most IRT models in use today assume the test is measuring a unidimensional construct, and therefore the models are not appropriate for multidimensional data. Determining the appropriateness of the fit of an IRT model to the data may also be a drawback, because expertise in IRT is needed. Such expertise is also needed to run the sophisticated software required for IRT DIF analysis. Another limitation of an IRT approach is there are no effect size indices to help us distinguish between statistically significant and substantive DIF.

Logistic Regression

Logistic regression has been widely regarded as one of the best statistical methods for evaluating DIF (Rogers & Swaminathan, 1993; Swaminathan & Rogers, 1990; Zumbo, 1999). As with methods based on IRT, logistic regression provides advantages over contingency-table-based methods such as standardization and MH because there is no need to divide a continuous score scale into categories, and it is possible to detect both uniform and nonuniform DIF. Also like IRT-based methods, logistic regression has performed well in both simulation and applied research on DIF (e.g., Jodoin & Geirl, 2001; Sireci et al., 2003), and it can be used for both dichotomous and polytomous test items (Zumbo, 1999). Furthermore, because logistic regression is based on observed scores rather than "true" (latent trait) scores, there are fewer assumptions underlying the model, and it can be fit using smaller sample sizes, relative to models based on IRT.

In using logistic regression to detect DIF, the analysis proceeds in stepwise fashion, similar to hierarchical multiple regression. The item score is the criterion variable in the regression equation, overall proficiency (typically total test score) is the conditioning variable (covariate), and group membership is the predictor variable. The analysis typically has three stages representing three separate analyses. It begins by entering the conditioning variable into the prediction equation first, then entering a variable that indicates group membership, and, finally, entering a variable that represents group-by-conditioning variable interaction. Uniform DIF is evaluated by examining the statistical significance of the regression coefficient for the group variable during the second stage. Nonuniform DIF is assessed by examining the significance of the slope associated with the group-by-conditioning variable interaction. For binary (dichotomous) items, the logistic regression formula for the third stage of the analysis is:

$$\ln\left[\frac{p_i}{(1-p_i)}\right] = b_0 + b_{tot} + b_{group} + b_{tot^*group} \tag{8.6}$$

where p_i refers to the probability of responding to item i correctly, $1 - p_i$ refers to the probability of responding to item i incorrectly, b_{tot} is the regression coefficient for the conditioning variable (e.g., total score), b_{group} is the regression coefficient for group membership, and b_{tot^*group} is the coefficient for the group-by-conditioning variable interaction.

Effect sizes are also available for logistic regression DIF analyses. Zumbo (1999) proposed effect sizes based on the proportion of variance (R^2) accounted for by the group membership and interaction terms. Jodoin and Gierl (2001) refined Zumbo's effect size criteria and established criteria equivalent to those used by the ETS for the MH method (Dorans & Holland, 1993). The Jodoin and Gierl DIF effect size classification criteria are as follows:

Negligible or small DIF: $R^2 < 0.035$
Moderate or medium DIF: statistically significant AND $0.035 \leq R^2 \leq 0.070$
Large or C-level DIF: statistically significant AND $R^2 > 0.070$

Note that the effect size for uniform DIF involves computing the incremental R^2 between the first and second stages of analysis, and the effect size for non-uniform DIF involves computing the incremental R^2 between the first and third stages of analysis.

DATA COLLECTION DESIGNS AND VALIDITY ISSUES

In the previous section, five methods for evaluating DIF were discussed. In this section, the limitations of DIF analyses in the context of cross-lingual assessment are considered, and data collection designs for evaluating DIF are discussed.

It should be understood from the outset that evaluating the equivalence of items translated or adapted across languages is, technically, an unsolvable problem. When an item is translated from one language to another and the two separate versions are administered to different groups of examinees, there is nothing to link the data across the separate groups. We cannot assume that the groups are equivalent, because the examinees come from different backgrounds; thus, equating or linking based on an assumption of randomly equivalent groups is typically not defensible. Similarly, we cannot consider the items to be equivalent because they are adaptations of one another. In fact, the purpose of the DIF analysis is to test their equivalence. Hence, equating or linking designs based on common items is also not defensible in this situation (Sireci, 1997).

For this reason, application of DIF methodology to translated test items is different from the problem DIF methods are designed to address. In a typical application of a DIF detection method, examinees from different groups (e.g., European Americans and African Americans) are compared on the same set of test items. In cross-lingual DIF assessment, examinees from different groups are compared on different items.

In earlier considerations of this problem, I proposed that carefully selected anchor items could be identified to form a matching variable across groups of examinees that differ with respect to language. In Sireci (1997), I suggested using nonverbal items or items with little verbal loading. In Sireci (2005), I advocated the use of bilingual designs for identifying items that do not function differently across languages. I believe both approaches can be useful to help achieve comparability in cross-lingual assessment, although no approach can unequivocally guarantee comparability.

A brief discussion on the use of bilingual examinees for evaluating test and item comparability is warranted. A common situation in cross-cultural research is when a test is developed in one language and adapted for use in another. If groups of examinees who are proficient in both languages are available to the researchers, then the separate language versions of the test can be administered to these examinees to evaluate the items and test scores. This analysis can use a repeated-measures design (in which the bilingual examinees take both language versions of the assessment in counterbalanced fashion) or a randomly equivalent groups design (in which the language version of the assessment is randomly assigned to each examinee). In these designs, DIF analyses and comparisons of total test scores can be conducted, and the grouping variable is defined by the language version of the test. The expectation under the null hypothesis is one of equivalence. That is, the groups can be considered to be randomly equivalent, and thus there should be no differences in item or test performance across languages.

Although the use of bilingual examinees presents sound experimental methodology for evaluating translated versions of tests and items, the Achilles' heel of the approach is that the bilingual examinees may not represent the examinee groups to which the test results are typically generalized. That is, these examinees may not represent the test behavior of either of the monolingual groups of interest. In addition, the idea of a truly bilingual examinee may not exist, and there are surely variations across examinees in their proficiencies in one or both languages, as well as differences in which language they are most dominant. Thus, bilingual examinees cannot *solve* the problem of evaluating the comparability of different language versions of a test. However, such examinees represent at least a portion of the population of interest, and they can be used to identify problematic items. After all, if different language versions of an item function differentially when administered to bilinguals, it is likely the psychological meaning of the item is not invariant across languages.

SUMMARY AND FUTURE RESEARCH DIRECTIONS

In this chapter, I briefly touched on issues of bias and equivalence in cross-cultural assessment, described methods for evaluating potential item bias, and discussed the applicability of these methods to cross-lingual assessment. Both pessimistic and optimistic perspectives were raised. On the pessimistic side, a strict determination that translated or adapted versions of an item are equivalent is impossible. On the positive side, however, there are several statistical, qualitative, and data collection techniques that can be used to evaluate item equivalence and bias in cross-lingual assessment in such a way that we can have moderate confidence in our conclusions regarding equivalence or nonequivalence across languages. In this section, I elaborate on this positive perspective.

On the basis of lessons learned in conducting cross-lingual research, and from the literature, I believe there are several steps cross-cultural researchers can take to maximize the comparability of test items across languages, including the application of DIF detection methods to evaluate translated or adapted test items. These steps include the following.

Use Careful and Comprehensive Translation and Adaptation Processes

As pointed out in the ITC *Guidelines*, the equivalence of tests and items across languages is likely to be maximized through the use of careful and comprehensive adaptation procedures. Brislin, Hambleton, van de Vijver, and others have discussed the pros and cons of different models for adapting tests from one language to another (e.g., Brislin, 1970, Hambleton, 1994; Hambleton, Sireci, & Robin, 1999; van de Vijver & Tanzer, 1997). These models include forward-translation, back-translation, forward-translation with subsequent review and revision (iterative forward translation), as well as parallel test development, although no single model is recommended as best. It is generally recommended that test adaptations involve separate teams of bilingual translators with independent translations and reviews, including discussions to resolve any differences of opinion regarding translation equivalence (i.e., invariance of psychological meaning across languages).

Statistically Evaluate Adapted Items Using Differential Item Functioning Detection Methods

Although DIF detection methods cannot unequivocally determine item invariance across languages, they can be used to evaluate different language versions of items, and when systematic biases across languages and cultures have been ruled out (e.g., through dimensionality analysis), they can provide a useful tool for identifying items that have different psychological meanings across languages. DIF analyses, particularly when applied to data from bilingual examinees, can be useful for identifying sets of items that are likely to be variant or invariant across languages. When bilingual designs are used in such DIF analyses, different types of bilingual examinees should be considered (Sireci, 2005).

Conduct Other Analyses of Test and Item Score Comparability

Evaluation of item bias is just one type of statistical analysis that can be done to evaluate bias and equivalence in cross-cultural assessment. Other studies that could and should be conducted include analyses to evaluate common structure in the item response data from different groups of examinees (i.e., the aforementioned structural analyses), evaluation of the score variability and measurement precision across groups (e.g., reliability estimates, standard errors, test information functions, etc.), and differential predictive validity studies (where applicable). Quality translation and adaptation procedures and construct equivalence studies should be conducted to rule out a systematic bias before doing DIF studies.

Target Analyses to Support the Types of Inferences Made From Test Scores

In many instances of test translation and adaptation, a test is adapted for use from one language to another, but comparisons of individuals across languages are not conducted. In such situations, the validity of comparative inferences is not an issue, and scalar equivalence is not needed. Thus, empirical analyses should focus on the psychometric properties of the adapted test instrument, relative to the original instrument (e.g., dimensionality analyses, analysis of measurement precision, etc.). When comparisons of examinees who took different language versions of an assessment are made – for example, in international comparisons of educational achievement or international credentialing testing – empirical analyses should target score comparability. These analyses should include investigation of DIF, in addition to the other analyses mentioned. That is, construct equivalence and item equivalence should be evaluated.

Follow-Up Differential Item Functioning Analyses With Qualitative Analysis

The majority of this chapter focused on statistical evaluation of tests and items. Obviously, statistical evaluation is only part of the process. As mentioned earlier, DIF techniques are used to flag items, but subjective evaluation of the reasons for DIF should determine whether item bias is present. An important lesson learned from analyses of cross-lingual DIF is that reasons why flagged items functioned differentially are often attainable, which is not always true in DIF analyses conducted within a single language. These explanations typically stem from translation problems noticed only after an item was flagged or from differential cultural familiarity across languages (Allalouf, Hambleton, & Sireci, 1999). It is recommended that the results from subjective evaluations of DIF be communicated to test developers and translators so that such problems can inform future test development and adaptation efforts.

Select Differential Item Functioning Detection Methods Best Suited to Situation

Several specific DIF detection methods were described in this chapter, but it may not be clear which methods are best for any particular situation. Factors that will affect choice of DIF detection method include type of item (dichotomous, polytomous), sample sizes, statistical software, and psychometric expertise. In considering these and other factors, the logistic regression approach appears to be applicable in the widest variety of situations. Most statistical software packages include logistic regression, binary and ordinal methods are available, and it can be conducted with sample sizes as small as 200 per group (Zumbo, 1999). Situations involving smaller sample sizes may consider the delta plot and standardization methods (Muniz et al., 2001).

CONCLUSION

The world is becoming smaller, yet nothing separates people from different cultural backgrounds more than language. For cross-cultural researchers, cross-lingual assessment provides significant challenges because it is difficult to ensure the same construct is being measured across all research participants. In most cases of cross-lingual assessment, translated or adapted versions of assessment instruments are used. Research and professional guidelines suggest that (a) careful and comprehensive translation procedures be used to ensure the same psychological meaning is represented in both languages, (b) the translated items undergo several rounds of review by bilingual translators, and (c) statistical procedures be used to evaluate the statistical characteristics of items and test scores after examinees have responded to the items. By performing these qualitative and statistical analyses, researchers can better evaluate measurement bias and equivalence across cultures, which will lead to more valid inferences about examinees and about differences in the construct measured across cultures.

REFERENCES

Allalouf, A., Hambleton, R. K., & Sireci, S. G. (1999). Identifying the sources of differential item functioning in translated verbal items. *Journal of Educational Measurement, 36*, 185–198.

American Educational Research Association, American Psychological Association, & National Council on Measurement in Education. (1999). *Standards for educational and psychological testing.* Washington, DC: American Educational Research Association.

Angoff, W. H. (1972). Use of difficulty and discrimination indices for detecting item bias. In R. A. Berk (Ed.), *Handbook of methods for detecting test bias* (pp. 96–116). Baltimore: Johns Hopkins University Press.

Angoff, W. H., & Cook, L. L. (1988). *Equating the scores of the Prueba de Aptitud Academica and the Scholastic Aptitude Test* (Report No. 88-2). New York: College Entrance Examination Board.

Angoff, W. H., & Modu, C. C. (1973). *Equating the scores of the Prueba de Aptitud Academica and the Scholastic Aptitude Test* (Research Report No. 3). New York: College Entrance Examination Board.

Brislin, R. W. (1970). Back-translation for cross-cultural research. *Journal of Cross-Cultural Psychology, 1*, 185–216.

Budgell, G., Raju, N., & Quartetti, D. (1995). Analysis of differential item functioning in translated assessment instruments. *Applied Psychological Measurement, 19*, 309–321.

Camilli, G., & Shepard, L. A. (1994). *Methods for identifying biased test items.* Thousand Oaks, CA: Sage.

Clauser, B. E., & Mazor, K. M. (1998). Using statistical procedures to identify differentially functioning test items. *Educational Measurement: Issues and Practice, 17*, 31–44.

Cronbach, L. J., & Meehl, P. E. (1955). Construct validity in psychological tests. *Psychological Bulletin, 52*, 281–302.

Day, S. X., & Rounds, J. (1998). Universality of vocational interest structure among racial and ethnic minorities. *American Psychologist, 53*, 728–736.

Dorans, N. J., & Holland. P. W. (1993). DIF detection and description: Mantel–Haenszel and standardization. In P. W. Holland & H. Wainer (Eds.), *Differential item functioning* (pp. 35–66). Hillsdale, NJ: Erlbaum.

Dorans, N. J., & Kulick E. (1986). Demonstrating the utility of the standardization approach to assessing unexpected differential item performance on the Scholastic Aptitude Test. *Journal of Educational Measurement, 23*, 355–368.

Fischer, G. (1993). Notes on the Mantel–Haenszel procedure and another chi-squared test for the assessment of DIF. *Methodika, 7*, 88–100.

Geisinger, K. F. (1994). Cross-cultural normative assessment: Translation and adaptation issues influencing the normative interpretation of assessment instruments. *Psychological Assessment, 6*, 304–312.

Gierl, M. J., & Khaliq, S. N. (2001). Identifying sources of differential item and bundle functioning on translated achievement tests: A confirmatory analysis. *Journal of Educational Measurement, 38*, 164–187.

Hambleton, R. K. (1993). Translating achievement tests for use in cross-national studies. *European Journal of Psychological Assessment, 9*, 57–68.

Hambleton, R. K. (1994). Guidelines for adapting educational and psychological tests: A progress report. *European Journal of Psychological Assessment, 10*, 229–244.

Hambleton, R. K. (2005). Issues, designs, and technical guidelines for adapting tests into multiple languages and cultures. In R. K. Hambleton, P. Merenda, & C. Spielberger (Eds.), *Adapting educational and psychological tests for cross-cultural assessment* (pp. 3–38). Hillsdale, NJ: Erlbaum.

Hambleton, R. K., Sireci, S. G., & Robin, F. (1999). Adapting credentialing exams for use in multiple languages. *CLEAR Exam Review, 10*, 24–28.

Hauger, J. B., & Sireci, S. G. (2008). Detecting differential item functioning across examinees tested in their dominant language and examinees tested in a second language. *International Journal of Testing, 8*, 237–250.

Holland, P. W., & Thayer, D. T. (1988). Differential item functioning and the Mantel–Haenszel procedure. In H. Wainer & H. I. Braun (Eds.), *Test validity* (pp. 129–145). Hillsdale, NJ: Erlbaum.

Holland, P. W., & Wainer, H. (Eds.). (1993). *Differential item functioning*. Hillsdale, NJ: Erlbaum.

International Test Commission. (2001). *International Test Commission guidelines for test adaptation*. London: Author.

Jodoin, M. G., & Gierl, M. J. (2001). Evaluating power and Type I error rates using an effect size with the logistic regression procedure for DIF. *Applied Measurement in Education, 14*, 329–349.

Lord, F. M. (1980). *Applications of item response theory to practical testing problems*. Hillsdale, NJ: Erlbaum.

Mantel, N., & Haenszel, W. (1959). Statistical aspects of the analysis of data from retrospective studies of disease. *Journal of the National Cancer Institute, 22*, 19–48.

Millsap, R. E., & Everson, H.T. (1993). Methodology review: Statistical approaches for assessing measurement bias. *Applied Psychological Measurement, 17*, 297–334.

Muniz, J., Hambleton, R. K., & Xing, D. (2001). Small sample studies to detect flaws in test translation. *International Journal of Testing, 1*, 115–135.

Penfield, R. D. (2005). DIFAS: Differential item functioning analysis system. *Applied Psychological Measurement, 29*, 150–151.

Potenza, M. T., & Dorans, N. J. (1995). DIF assessment for polytomously scored items: A framework for classification and evaluation. *Applied Psychological Measurement, 19*, 23–37.

Raju, N. S. (1988). The area between two item characteristic curves. *Psychometrika, 53*, 495–502.

Raju, N. S. (1990). Determining the significance of estimated signed and unsigned areas between two item response functions. *Applied Psychological Measurement, 14*, 197–207.

Reise, S. P., Widaman, K. F., & Pugh, R. H. (1993). Confirmatory factor analysis and item response theory: Two approaches for exploring measurement invariance. *Psychological Bulletin, 114*, 552–566.

Robin, F. (1999). *SDDIF: Standardization and delta DIF analyses* [computer program]. Amherst: University of Massachusetts, Laboratory of Psychometric and Evaluative Research.

Robin, F., Sireci, S. G., & Hambleton, R. K. (2003). Evaluating the equivalence of different language versions of a credentialing exam. *International Journal of Testing, 3*, 1–20.

Rogers, H. J., & Swaminathan, H. (1993). A comparison of logistic regression and Mantel-Haenszel procedures for detecting differential item functioning. *Applied Psychological Measurement, 17*, 105–116.

Shealy, R., & Stout, W. (1993). A model-based standardization differences and detects test bias/DTF as well as item bias/DIF. *Psychometrika, 58*, 159–194.

Sireci, S. G. (1997). Problems and issues in linking tests across languages. *Educational Measurement: Issues and Practice, 16*, 12–19.

Sireci, S. G. (2005). Using bilinguals to evaluate the comparability of different language versions of a test. In R. K. Hambleton, P. Merenda, & C. Spielberger (Eds.), *Adapting educational and psychological tests for cross-cultural assessment* (pp. 117–138). Hillsdale, NJ: Erlbaum.

Sireci, S. G., Bastari, B., & Allalouf, A. (1998, August). *Evaluating construct equivalence across adapted tests.* Invited paper presented at the annual meeting of the American Psychological Association (Division 5), San Francisco, CA.

Sireci, S. G., & Berberoglu, G. (2000). Evaluating translation DIF using bilinguals. *Applied Measurement in Education, 13*, 229–248.

Sireci, S. G., Fitzgerald, C., & Xing, D. (1998). Adapting credentialing examinations for international uses. *Laboratory of Psychometric and Evaluative Research Report No. 329.* Amherst, MA: University of Massachusetts, School of Education.

Sireci, S. G., Harter, J., Yang, Y., & Bhola, D. (2003). Evaluating the equivalence of an employee attitude survey across languages, cultures, and administration formats. *International Journal of Testing, 3*, 129–150.

Sireci, S. G., Patsula, L., & Hambleton, R. K. (2005). Statistical methods for identifying flawed items in the test adaptations process. In R. K. Hambleton, P. Merenda, & C. Spielberger (Eds.), *Adapting educational and psychological tests for cross-cultural assessment* (pp. 93–115). Hillsdale, NJ: Erlbaum.

Swaminathan, H., & Rogers, H. J. (1990). Detecting differential item functioning using logistic regression procedures. *Journal of Educational Measurement, 27*, 361–370.

Thissen, D. (2001). *IRTLRDIF v2.0b: Software for the computation of the statistics involved in item response theory likelihood-ratio tests for differential item functioning.* Retrieved from http://www.unc.edu/~dthissen/dl.html.

Thissen, D., Steinberg, L., & Wainer, H. (1988). Use of item response theory in the study of group differences in trace lines. In H. Wainer & H. I. Braun (Eds.), *Test validity* (pp. 147–169). Hillsdale, NJ: Erlbaum.

Thissen, D., Steinberg, L., & Wainer, H. (1993). Detection of differential item functioning using the parameters of item response models. In P. W. Holland & H. Wainer (Eds.), *Differential item functioning* (pp. 67–114). Mahwah, NJ: Erlbaum.

Van de Vijver, F. J. R., & Poortinga, Y. H. (1997). Towards an integrated analysis of bias in cross-cultural assessment. *European Journal of Psychological Assessment, 13*, 29–37.

Van de Vijver, F. J. R., & Poortinga, Y. H. (2005). Conceptual and methodological issues in adapting tests. In R. K. Hambleton, P. Merenda, & C. Spielberger (Eds.), *Adapting educational and psychological tests for cross-cultural assessment* (pp. 39–63). Hillsdale, NJ: Erlbaum.

Van de Vijver, F., & Tanzer, N. K. (1997). Bias and equivalence in cross-cultural assessment. *European Review of Applied Psychology, 47*, 263–279.

Wainer, H., & Sireci, S. G. (2005). Item and test bias. *Encyclopedia of social measurement* (Vol. 2, pp. 365–371). San Diego, CA: Elsevier.

Wainer, H., Sireci, S. G., & Thissen, D. (1991). Differential testlet functioning: Definitions and detection. *Journal of Educational Measurement, 28*, 197–219.

Waller, N. G. (1998). EZDIF: The detection of uniform and non-uniform differential item functioning with the Mantel–Haenszel and logistic regression procedures. *Applied Psychological Measurement, 22*, 391.

Zumbo, B. D. (1999). *A handbook on the theory and methods of differential item functioning (DIF): Logistic regression modeling as a unitary framework for binary and Likert-type (ordinal) item scores.* Ottawa, Canada: Directorate of Human Resources Research and Evaluation, Department of National Defense.

Zwick, R., Donoghue, J. R., & Grima, A. (1993). Assessment of differential item functioning for performance tasks. *Journal of Educational Measurement, 30*, 233–251.

APPENDIX

Statistical Software for Differential Item Functioning Analysis

Several software packages are available for conducting differential item functioning (DIF) analyses, and many analyses can be done using standard statistical software packages such as SAS or SPSS. Camilli and Shepard (1994) and Zumbo (1999) provided some code for conducting DIF analyses in SPSS, and some code for conducting a logistic regression DIF analysis using SPSS is provided in this Appendix. In addition, at the time of this writing, several DIF software packages are available for free on the Internet. I list some of them here. I would thank the authors of these programs for allowing free access to these packages. They are helpful to those of us who wish to investigate DIF, and we remain grateful to them.

FREE DIFFERENTIAL ITEM FUNCTIONING SOFTWARE AVAILABLE ON THE INTERNET

1. Item Response Theory Likelihood Ratio DIF Software

Dave Thissen created an excellent piece of software that makes item response theory (IRT) likelihood ratio DIF analysis much easier. I really like this package. At the time of this writing, IRTLRDIF v. 2 for windows can be downloaded at http://www.unc.edu/~dthissen/dl/irtlrdif201.zip, and for MAC at http://www.unc.edu/~dthissen/dl/IRTLRDIF201.sit.

2. Logistic Regression

Bruno Zumbo (1999) developed a terrific handbook on understanding and interpreting DIF in which he focuses on the logistic regression procedure. The handbook can be downloaded from http://educ.ubc.ca/faculty/zumbo/DIF. It includes some code for running logistic regression analyses in SPSS.

Although the code still works, it is a bit dated. Here is some code for running a logistic regression analysis in SPSS on a dichotomously scored item:

```
LOGISTIC REGRESSION VAR=item5
/METHOD=ENTER tot
/CRITERIA PIN(.05) POUT(.10) ITERATE(20) CUT(.5).
LOGISTIC REGRESSION VAR=item5
/METHOD=ENTER tot group
/CRITERIA PIN(.05) POUT(.10) ITERATE(20) CUT(.5).
LOGISTIC REGRESSION VAR=item5
/METHOD=ENTER tot group group*tot
/CRITERIA PIN(.05) POUT(.10) ITERATE(20) CUT(.5).
```

As described in this chapter, the analysis actually involves three separate logistic regression runs. In this example, "item5" is the item being analyzed for DIF, "tot" is the total score, and "group" is the dichotomous variable that indicates the reference or focal group. The first analysis gives us a baseline for gauging the increase in variance accounted for by the second and third analyses. The second analysis adds the grouping variable (to test for uniform DIF), and the third analysis adds the group-by-total score interaction, to test for nonuniform DIF. Note that default values are used in this code for inclusion and exclusion criteria and for the number of iterations. The code for analyzing DIF on a polytomous (e.g., Likert-type) item uses polytomous logistic regression and is similar:

```
PLUM
Item5 BY group WITH tot
/CRITERIA = CIN(95) DELTA(0) LCONVERGE(0) MXITER(100)
  MXSTEP(5)
PCONVERGE(1.0E-6) SINGULAR(1.0E-8)
/LINK = LOGIT
/PRINT = FIT PARAMETER SUMMARY.
```

Again, the default inclusion–exclusion and iteration criteria are used, and "item5" refers to the item of interest. However, this time the item may have more than two response categories.

3. Multiple DIF Procedures
   a) Over the years, various faculty and students at the University of Massachusetts Amherst (UMASS) have developed useful psychometric software programs including DIF software. DIF software available from UMASS includes SDDIF (Robin, 1999), which

contains the standardization and delta-plot procedures. Software from UMASS can be downloaded from http://www.umass.edu/remp/main_software.html.

b) Randall Penfield at the University of Miami developed a Windows-based program called DIFAS (Penfield, 2005) that is extremely comprehensive and user-friendly. DIFAS includes multiple DIF detection methods including the Mantel–Haenszel procedure, generalized Mantel–Haenszel for polytomous items, and nonparametric approaches. At the time of this writing, DIFAS is available by contacting the author at penfield@miami.edu.

c) *EZDIF*: This software was developed by Niels Waller (1998) and performs both Mantel–Haenszel and logistic regression DIF analyses. At the time of this writing, it is available at http://www.psych.umn.edu/faculty/waller/downloads/dif/dif.zip.

9

Effect Sizes in Cross-Cultural Research

DAVID MATSUMOTO, JOHN J. KIM, ROBERT J. GRISSOM, AND DALE L. DINNEL

EFFECT SIZES IN CROSS-CULTURAL RESEARCH

Comparison is a cornerstone of cross-cultural research. A standard methodology in conducting these comparisons begins with the selection of measures of psychological constructs that produce quantitative data from two or more cultures or countries. The usual statistical analysis of data from two cultures involves testing a null hypothesis (H_0) that conflicts with the research hypothesis either by positing that a correlation between two variables is zero in the population or that there is no difference between the means of two populations. Differences are tested by comparing variance among the culture means relative to the variance within the cultures, typically using *t* or *F* tests. When the chance probability of obtaining *t* or *F* values is sufficiently low ($\leq$5%), the result is considered statistically significant. The *p* level represents the probability that a result at least as extreme as the obtained result would occur if the H_0 were true. This attained *p* value primarily indicates the strength of the evidence that the H_0 is wrong (but the *p* value does not by itself indicate sufficiently how wrong H_0 is).

Statistical significance does not necessarily reflect differences among people of the different cultures, however. The sole computation of *t*s or *F*s precludes our ability to interpret meaningful differences among people, because *p* values merely indicate the strength of the evidence against the null hypothesis of no difference between population means. Statistical significance, assuming no Type I error, only reflects some unknown, nonzero difference between the population means. Furthermore, the larger the sample

Portions of this chapter appeared in Matsumoto, Grissom, and Dinnel (2001) and Grissom and Kim (2005).

sizes, the easier it is for smaller differences to become statistically significant. Therefore, a statistically significant difference may actually reflect a trivially small difference between population means. Interpretations of cultural differences *among people* based on "statistically significant" findings may be based on "practically insignificant" differences between means. "Practically insignificant" means that the nonzero difference between culture means is so small that it is of little or no practical significance. A synonymous phrase would be "substantively insignificant."

For example, observe in Formula 9.1 for t that the part of the formula that is usually of greatest interest in research is the overall numerator, the difference between means. However, Formula 9.1 reveals that whether or not t is large enough to attain statistical significance is not merely a function of how large this numerator is but depends on how large this numerator is relative to the overall denominator. For any given difference between means, an increase in sample sizes will increase the absolute value of t and thus decrease the magnitude of p. Therefore, a statistically significant t may indicate a large difference between means or perhaps a less important small difference that has been elevated to the status of statistical significance because the researcher had the resources to use relatively large samples. Large sample sizes are to be encouraged because they are more likely to be representative of populations, are more likely to produce replicable results, increase statistical power, and also perhaps increase robustness to violation of statistical assumptions. These same ideas are applicable to the computation of the F ratio and its corresponding p values.

$$t = \frac{\overline{Y}_a - \overline{Y}_b}{\left[\dfrac{s_a^2}{n_a} + \dfrac{s_b^2}{n_b}\right]^{1/2}} \tag{9.1}$$

The phrase *statistically significant*, however, can be misleading because synonyms of *significant* in the English language, but not in the language of statistics, are *important* and *large*, and a statistically significant result may not be a large or important result. In the phrase *statistically significant*, significant means "signifying," signifying that there is sufficient evidence against a null hypothesis of no difference. In the phrase *practically significant*, significant means "large" or "important." An example would be a statistically significant difference between boys and girls that is so small it does not warrant separate instructional practice for teaching.

A significant t or F in a cross-cultural study therefore does not necessarily mean that most people of one culture have an appreciably greater score than most people of another, nor that the average person from one culture will have a substantially higher score than the average person from the other, nor that a randomly selected individual from one culture will likely have a higher score than a randomly selected individual from the other. In short, statistical significance may not have any meaningful implications for predicting differences on the level of individuals, and those who consider it as indicating such meaningful differences may in fact create or perpetuate stereotypes about those people and cultures. Although most researchers are aware of these limitations of significance testing, most reports rely solely on significance tests, largely ignoring the practical significance of the results.

These possible mistakes have several implications. Theoretically, they may lead to the construction of knowledge based on stereotypes. Research is then created to test this bias, which is perpetuated because of the continued use of limited data analytic techniques. Practically, programs for intercultural sensitivity, training, competence, adjustment, and the like are based on cultural stereotypes, providing consumers with incorrect guidelines that may be more harmful than helpful.

To examine the degree to which cross-cultural data are indicative of meaningful differences among individuals based on culture group membership, further analyses are needed to estimate the otherwise unknown degree of difference between two or more cultures' populations. Collectively, these techniques are known as measures of effect size, and when used in cross-cultural research, we refer to them as cultural effect size. Although their importance has long been recognized, their use in cross-cultural research is still limited. We argue here for their incorporation in cross-cultural work, a position that is consistent with the recommendation of the American Psychological Association's Task Force on Statistical Inference (Wilkinson et al., 1999).

In the remainder of this chapter, we first define effect size, discuss controversies surrounding traditional null hypothesis significance testing (NHST), and describe some assumptions about effect sizes. We describe the use of confidence intervals, which, although not technically an effect size (ES), can complement interpretations of results with ESs. We then introduce several measures of ES that we believe are most appropriate for cross-cultural research. We selected them for their ease of computation and interpretation and for their relevance. Using these measures, we analyze data from a recent study to demonstrate their efficacy. Finally, we argue for the incorporation of ES statistics to complement traditional NHST.

AN INTRODUCTION

Definition of Effect Size

Let's assume the case of the typical null hypothesis that implies that there is no effect or no relationship between variables. Whereas a test of statistical significance provides the quantified strength of evidence (attained p level) that a null hypothesis is wrong, *an ES is a statistic that measures the degree to which a null hypothesis is wrong*. ES measures typically involve some form of correlation or its square, some form of standardized difference between means, or the degree of overlap of distributions; however, there are many ES measures that do not fit into these categories. Again, we use the label *effect size* for measures of the degree to which results differ from what is implied for them by a typical null hypothesis. Although ES is not synonymous with practical significance, knowledge of a result's ES can inform judgments about practical significance.

Often the relationship between the numerical value of a test statistic and an estimator of ES is ES_{EST} = test statistic/f(N), where f(N) is some function of total sample size, such as degrees of freedom. Specific forms of this formula are available for many test statistics, including t, F, and chi-square, so that reported test statistics can be approximately converted to indirect estimates of ES by a reader of a research report without access to the raw data that would be required to estimate an ES directly. However, researchers who work with their own raw data, unlike those who work with sets of previously reported test statistics (meta-analysts), can estimate ESs directly, so they do not need to use an approximate conversion formula.

Many measures of ES are available (Cohen, 1988; Feingold, 1992, 1995; Feingold & Mazzella, 1998; Hedges & Olkin, 1985; Rosenthal, 1991; Wilcox, 1997), as well as informative overviews and summaries of them (e.g., Grissom & Kim, 2005; Rosenthal, Rosnow, & Rubin, 2000). Some provide information that is highly relevant in cross-cultural studies, in which researchers are concerned with the representation of group-level cultural differences on the individual level. By *individual level*, we allude to the fact that significance tests only tell us what proportions of t or F distributions are beyond the value attained by our t or F result. The measures of ES recommended here do not address proportions of such distributions; rather, they inform us about outcomes in terms of proportions of members of a culture or in terms of the performance of the average member of a culture relative to proportions of members of another culture.

Controversy About Null-Hypothesis Significance Testing

Discussions concerning the limitations of *t*, *F*, and of NHSTs are not new. One of the first concerns about NHST is its dependence on sample size, which is also relevant for cross-cultural research. In addition, Cohen (1962) pointed out the utility of power analysis in psychological research and highlighted the high error rates that are typically associated with NHST. Mistakes commonly cited include accepting the null hypothesis when it fails to be rejected, automatically interpreting rejected null hypotheses as theoretically or practically meaningful, and failing to consider the likelihood of Type II errors (Loftus, 1996; Shrout, 1997; see also Wilcox, 1998). Some writers (e.g., Hunter, 1997) have recommended outright bans on NHST, arguing that error rates are as high as 60%, not the 5% traditionally thought.[1] Others have argued for the continued use of NHST in addition to the incorporation of ES statistics and confidence intervals (e.g., Abelson, 1997; Harris, 1997).

Statisticians have long urged researchers to report ESs, but researchers have been slow to respond. Fisher (1925) was an early, largely unheeded, advocate of such estimation. It can even be argued that readers of a report of applied research that involves control or placebo groups, or that involves treatments whose costs are different, have a right to see estimates of ESs. Some might even argue that not reporting such estimates in an understandable manner to those who might apply the results of research in such cases (e.g., educators, health officials, managers of trainee programs, clinicians, governmental officials) may be a kind of withholding of evidence. Increasingly, editors of journals that publish research are recommending, or requiring, the reporting of estimates of ESs. For example, the American Psychological Association recommends the reporting of such estimates; the *Journal of Educational and Psychological Measurement* and at least 22 other journals as of the time of this writing require such reporting.

There is a range of professional opinion regarding when estimates of ESs should be reported. On one hand is the view that NHST is meaningless because no null hypothesis can be literally true. For example, according to

[1] This argument is based on the fact that if the null hypothesis is false, Type I error is impossible; the only type of error that could possibly occur would be Type II. In these cases, the maximum potential error rate for the significance test is thus 97.5% for two-tailed tests and 95% for one-tailed tests. Hunter (1997) cited studies that have computed the error rate for the statistical significance test in leading psychological journals and that conclude that the error rate was about 60% at the time of the study. For more information, see Hunter (1997).

this view, no two or more population means can be exactly equal to many decimal places. Therefore, from this point of view, the task of a researcher is to estimate the size of this "obviously" nonzero effect. The opposite opinion is that significance testing is paramount and that ESs are to be reported only when results are found to be statistically significant.

Many estimators of ES tend to overestimate ESs in the population (called "positive" or "upward bias"), and a question arises concerning whether this upward bias of estimators of ES is large enough so that the reporting of a bias-based nonzero estimate of ES will seriously inflate the overall estimate of ES in a field of study when the null hypothesis is true (i.e., actually zero effect in the population) and results are statistically insignificant. Those who are not concerned about such bias urge the reporting of all ESs, significant or not significant, to improve the accuracy of meta-analyses. Their reasoning is that such reporting will avoid the problem of meta-analyses inflating overall estimates of ES that would result from not including the smaller ESs that arise from primary studies with results that did not attain statistical significance.

Some are of the opinion that ESs are more important in applied research, in which one might be interested in whether the ES is estimated to be large enough to be of practical use. In contrast, in theoretical research, one might be interested not only in whether results support a theory's prediction but to what degree. These latter questions require ES.

Assumptions of Test Statistics and Effect Sizes

When statisticians create a new test statistic or measure of ES, they often do so for populations that have certain characteristics. For the *t*, *F*, and some common examples of ESs, two of these assumed characteristics, called assumptions, are that the populations from which the samples are drawn are normally distributed and have equal variances. The latter assumption is called homogeneity of variance or homoscedasticity. When data actually come from populations with unequal variances this violation of the assumption is called heterogeneity of variance or heteroscedasticity. Often a researcher asserts that an ES that involves the degree of difference between two means is significantly different from zero because significance was attained when comparing the two means by a *t* test (or an *F* test with one degree of freedom in the numerator). However, nonnormality and heteroscedasticity can result in the shape of the actual sampling distribution of the test statistic departing sufficiently from the theoretical sampling distribution of *t* or *F* so that, unbeknownst to the researcher, the actual *p* value for the result is not the same as the observed p value in a table or printout. For example, an observed $p < .05$ may actually represent a true $p > .05$, an inflation of Type I error. Also, violation of assumptions can result in lowered statistical power. These kinds of violations of assumptions can also affect estimation and interpretation of ESs.

Unfortunately, violations of assumptions, often in combination, are common in real data. In a review of the literature, Grissom (2000) noted that there are theoretical reasons to expect, and empirical results to document, heteroscedasticity throughout various areas of research, and there is no reason not to suspect this to be the case with cross-cultural data as well. Distributions for samples with larger means often have larger variances than those for samples with smaller means, resulting in the possibility of heteroscedasticity. These characteristics may not be accurately reflected by comparison of variances of samples taken from those populations because the sampling variability of variances is high. Also, sample distributions with greater positive skew tend to have the larger means and variances, again suggesting possible heteroscedasticity.

Heteroscedasticity may also result from ceiling or floor effects, because these result in greater reductions in variabilities in measurements of variables, because the measurement may not cover the full range of the variable as it exists in the sample. Heteroscedasticity can also result from outliers – atypically high or low scores. Outliers may merely reflect recording errors or another kind of research error, but they are common and should be reported as possibly reflecting an important effect of a treatment on a minority of participants or an indication of an important characteristic of a small minority of the participants.[2]

It is important to understand heteroscedasticity because it may make the use of certain measures of ES problematic. A full discussion of these issues is beyond the scope of this chapter; interested readers are referred to Grissom and Kim (2005) for a more complete discussion of the issues.

CONFIDENCE INTERVALS IN CROSS-CULTURAL COMPARISONS

Although confidence intervals are not ESs, there are connections between them, and both can provide useful perspectives on data. The confidence intervals that are discussed here provide information that relates to the amount of difference between two populations' means. When the dependent

[2] Precise definitions and rules for detecting outliers vary (Brant, 1990; Davies & Gather, 1993; Staudte & Sheather, 1990). Wilcox (2001, 2003) discussed a simple method for detecting outliers and also provided an S-PLUS software function for such detection (Wilcox, 2003).

variable is a commonly understood variable that is scaled in familiar units, a confidence interval and an ES can provide useful and complementary information about the results.

The most important part of the formula for the *t* statistic that tests the usual null hypothesis about two population means is the numerator, $\overline{Y}_a - \overline{Y}_b$. Using $\overline{Y}_a - \overline{Y}_b$ to estimate the size of the difference between μ_a and μ_b can provide an informative result. The procedure for constructing a confidence interval uses the data from Groups a and b to estimate a range of values that is likely to contain the value of $\mu_a - \mu_b$ within them, with a specifiable degree of confidence in this estimate.

Theoretically, although any given population of scores has a constant mean, equal-sized random samples from a population have varying means (sampling variability). Therefore, $\overline{Y}_a$ and $\overline{Y}_b$ might each be either overestimating or underestimating their respective population means. Thus, $\overline{Y}_a - \overline{Y}_b$ may well be larger or smaller than $\mu_a - \mu_b$. In other words, there is a margin of error when using $\overline{Y}_a - \overline{Y}_b$ to estimate $\mu_a - \mu_b$. If there is such a margin of error, it may be positive, $(\overline{Y}_a - \overline{Y}_b) > (\mu_a - \mu_b)$, or negative, $(\overline{Y}_a - \overline{Y}_b) < (\mu_a - \mu_b)$. The larger the sample sizes and the less variable the populations of raw scores, the smaller the absolute value of the margin of error will be. That is, as is reflected in Formula 9.2, the margin of error is a function of the standard error. In the present case, the standard error is the standard deviation of the distribution of differences between two populations' sample means.

Another factor that influences the amount of margin of error is the level of confidence that one wants to have in one's estimate of a range of values that is likely to contain $\mu_a - \mu_b$. The more confident one wants to be in this estimate, the greater the margin of error will have to be. Thus, a procedure that greatly decreases the margin of error without excessively reducing our level of confidence in the truth of our result would be useful. The tradition is to adopt what is called the 95% (or .95) confidence level that leads to an estimate of a range of values that has a .95 probability of containing the value of $\mu_a - \mu_b$. When expressed as a decimal value (e.g., .95), the confidence level of an accurately calculated confidence interval is also called the probability coverage of a confidence interval. To the extent that a method for constructing a confidence interval is inaccurate, the actual probability coverage will depart from what it was intended to be and appears to be (e.g., depart from the nominal .95). Although 95% confidence may seem to some readers to be only slightly less confidence than 100% confidence, such a procedure typically results in a narrow, informative, interval.

For simplicity, let us assume normality, homoscedasticity, and independent groups. (The procedure is easily generalized to confidence levels other than the 95% level.) (In cross-cultural research, we typically have to accept violation of the assumption of random sampling.) Independent groups can be roughly defined for our purposes as groups within which no individual's score on the dependent variable is related to or predictable from the scores of any individual in another group. Groups are independent if the probability that an individual in a group will produce a certain score remains the same regardless of what score is produced by an individual in another group. (Research with dependent groups requires methods for construction of confidence intervals that are different from methods used for research with independent groups.) If the assumptions of normality, homoscedasticity, and independence have been satisfied, and the usual (central) *t* distribution is applicable, it can be shown that for constructing a confidence interval for $\mu_a - \mu_b$ the margin of error (*ME*) is given by

$$ME = t^* \left[s_p^2 \left(\frac{1}{n_a} + \frac{1}{n_b} \right) \right]^{1/2}. \tag{9.2}$$

When Formula 9.2 is used to construct a 95% confidence interval, t^* is the absolute value of *t* from a table of critical values of *t* that is required to attain statistical significance at the .05 two-tailed level (or .025 one-tailed level) in a *t* test. For the 95% or any other level of confidence, s_p^2 is the pooled estimate of the assumed common variance of the two populations, σ^2. Use for the degrees-of-freedom (*df*) row of the *t* table, $df = n_a + n_b - 2$. Because for now we are assuming homoscedasticity, the best estimate of σ^2 is obtained by pooling the data from the two samples to calculate the usual weighted average of the two samples' estimates of σ^2 to produce (weighting by sample sizes via the separate sample's *dfs*)

$$s_p^2 = \frac{(n_a - 1)s_a^2 + (n_b - 1)s_b^2}{n_a + n_b - 2}. \tag{9.3}$$

Because approximately 95% of the time when such confidence intervals are constructed, in the current case, the value of $\overline{Y}_a - \overline{Y}_b$ might be overestimating or underestimating $\mu_a - \mu_b$ by the $ME_{.95}$, one can say that approximately 95% of the time the following interval of values will contain the value of $\mu_a - \mu_b$:

$$(\overline{Y}_a - \overline{Y}_b) \pm ME_{.95}. \tag{9.4}$$

The value $(\overline{Y}_a - \overline{Y}_b) - ME_{.95}$ is called the lower limit of the 95% confidence interval, and the value $(\overline{Y}_a - \overline{Y}_b) + ME_{.95}$ is called the upper limit of the 95% confidence interval. A confidence interval is (for our present purpose) the interval of values between the lower limit and the upper limit.

To construct a confidence interval other than the .95 CI, in general the $(1 - \alpha)$ CI, the value of t^* that is used in Formula 9.2 is the absolute value of t that a t table indicates is required for two-tailed statistical significance at the alpha significance level (the same t as for $\alpha/2$, one-tailed). One would likely find, however, that a .99 CI results in a very wide, less informative, interval. For a given set of data, the lower the confidence level, the narrower the interval.

The 95% CI is also called the .95 CI. Such a confidence interval is often mistakenly interpreted to mean that there is a .95 probability that $\mu_a - \mu_b$ will be one of the values within the calculated interval, as if $\mu_a - \mu_b$ were a variable. However, $\mu_a - \mu_b$ is actually a constant in any specific pair of populations (an unknown constant), and it is each confidence limit that is actually a variable. Theoretically, because of sampling variability, repeating a specific example of research by repeatedly randomly sampling equal-sized samples from two populations will produce varying values of $\overline{Y}_a - \overline{Y}_b$, whereas the actual value of $\mu_a - \mu_b$ remains constant for the specific pair of populations that are being repeatedly compared via their sample means. In other words, although a researcher actually typically samples Populations a and b only once each, varying results are possible for $\overline{Y}_a$, $\overline{Y}_b$, and, thereby, $\overline{Y}_a - \overline{Y}_b$ in any one instance of research. Similarly, sample variances from a population would vary from instance to instance of research, and thus the margin of error is also a variable. Therefore, instead of saying that there is a .95 probability that $\mu_a - \mu_b$ is a value within the calculated interval, the more appropriate interpretation is that there is a .95 probability that the calculated interval will contain the value of $\mu_a - \mu_b$. Stated theoretically, if research were repeated an indefinitely large number of times approaching infinity, the percentage of times that the calculated .95 confidence intervals would contain the true difference between the populations would approach 95% (if assumptions are satisfied). It is in this sense that the reader should interpret any statement that is made about the results from construction of confidence intervals.

MEASURES OF CULTURAL EFFECT SIZE COMPARING TWO GROUPS

The Standardized Difference Between Two Sample Means

The first measure we consider is the well-known standardized difference between two population means (Formula 9.5), in the case of comparing two means from a two- or multi-group study. This estimate assumes homogeneity of variance because it pools variances to obtain s_p or $\sqrt{MS_w}$ (Hedges & Olkin, 1985) and normality when interpreted in terms of the percentile attained by the average-performing member of one culture with respect to the distribution of scores of the other. It allows researchers to estimate what percentage of people in a culture has higher scores than the average member of a statistically significantly lower scoring culture.

$$g = \frac{\overline{Y}_a - \overline{Y}_b}{s_p}, \text{ where } s_p = \sqrt{\frac{(n_a - 1)s_a^2 + (n_b - 1)s_b^2}{n_a - n_b - 2}}. \tag{9.5}$$

For example, if the mean of Culture A is statistically significantly higher than the mean of Culture B and $g = +1.00$, an average member of Culture A scores 1.00 standard deviation unit higher than an average member of Culture B. A standard score of $+1.00$ lies at the 84th percentile. Therefore, we can conclude that the average member of Culture A is outscoring 84% of the members of Culture B. A value of g that is only slightly above 0, however, indicates that average-scoring members of the "statistically significantly higher scoring culture" may be outscoring only slightly more than 50% of the lower scoring culture. Thus, the statistically significant difference may be associated with little or practically no appreciable difference on the level of the individuals. Cohen (1988) suggested that values of approximately .20, .50, and .80 reflect small, moderate, and large differences, respectively. (Cohen's d uses the assumed common population standard deviation, σ, in the denominator instead of s_p.)

The Counternull Effect Size

Recall that a typical null hypothesis about μ_a and μ_b is that $\mu_a - \mu_b = 0$. This H_0 implies another – namely, $H_0 : \Delta = 0$. In traditional significance testing, if the obtained t is not far enough away from 0, one decides not to reject H_0, and, by implication, one concludes that the t test result provides insufficient evidence that Δ is other than 0. However, such reasoning is incomplete. For example, suppose that the Sample g is above 0, but insufficiently so as to attain statistical significance. This result can be explained, as is traditional, by the Population Δ actually being 0 and the Sample g happened by chance (sampling variability) to overestimate Δ in this instance of research. However, an equally plausible explanation of the result is that Δ is actually above 0, and more above 0 than g is, so g happened by chance to underestimate Δ

in this instance of research. Therefore, according to this reasoning, a value of g that is beyond 0 (above or below 0) by a certain amount is providing just as much evidence that $\Delta = 2g$ as it is providing evidence that $\Delta = 0$ because g is no closer to 0 (1 g distance away from 0) than g is to 2Δ (1 g distance away from 2Δ). For example, if g is +0.60, this result is just as consistent with $\Delta = +1.20$ as with $\Delta = 0$ because +0.60 is just as close to +1.20 as it is to 0. The Sample g is just as likely to be underestimating Δ by a certain amount as it is to be overestimating Δ by that amount (except for some positive bias as is discussed next). In this example, assuming that a t test results in t and, by implication, g being statistically insignificantly different from 0, it would be as justifiable to conclude that g is insignificantly different from +1.20 as it would be to conclude that g is insignificantly different from 0. (We must note, however, that the reasoning in this section is only approximately true because of the bias that standardized-difference estimators have toward overestimating ES. The reasoning is more accurate the larger the *ns* or if a bias-adjusted estimator, as was previously discussed, is used.)

This reasoning leads to a measure of ES called the *counternull value of an ES* (Rosenthal, Rosnow, & Rubin, 2000; Rosenthal & Rubin, 1994). Here we will simply call this measure the counternull ES, ES_{cn}. In the case of standardized-difference ESs, and in the case of some (but not all) other kinds of ESs, if one is, by implication of t testing, testing $H_0 : ES_{pop} = 0$, then

$$ES_{cn} = 2ES. \tag{9.6}$$

When null-hypothesizing a value of ES_{pop} other than 0, the more general formula is

$$ES_{cn} = 2\text{ES} - ES_{null}, \tag{9.7}$$

where ES_{null} is the null-hypothesized value of ES_{pop}. In our example, in which the estimate of ES (i.e., g) = +0.60, application of Formula 9.6 yields the estimate $ES_{cn} = 2(+0.60) = +1.20$. Therefore, the *null–counternull interval* ranges from 0 to +1.20. In other words, the results are approximately as consistent with $\Delta = +1.20$ as they are with $\Delta = 0$.

For situations in which construction of a confidence interval for an ES would be informative but not practicable, a researcher might consider reporting instead the ES_{null} and ES_{cn} as limits of a null–counternull interval. In the present example, the lower limit of the null–counternull interval is

0, and the estimated upper limit is +1.20.[3] A null–counternull interval can provide information that is only somewhat conceptually similar to, and not likely numerically the same as, the information that is provided by a confidence interval. Both intervals bracket the obtained estimate of ES, but, unlike the lower limit of a confidence interval, when $ES_{\text{null}} = 0$, the lower limit of the null–counternull interval will always be 0. Confidence intervals and null–counternull intervals cannot be directly compared or combined.

The Point-Biserial Correlation

Another measure is the point-biserial correlation between culture groups, coded dichotomously into any two values for the two cultures (the sign of the correlation will depend on which culture has higher scores; the value, however, will be unaffected), and the dependent variable *Y*. This is simply the Pearson *r* when *Y* is continuous and *X* is a dichotomy. This measure is easy to interpret because it uses the familiar scale of *r*, 0 to 1. Values closer to 1 indicate substantial differences between cultures; values closer to 0 indicate minimal or even negligible differences, regardless of statistical significance.

Although the value of r_{pb} does not depend on homogeneity of variance, the result of a *t* test testing whether r_{pb} is significantly different from zero can be affected by heterogeneity of variance. When sum of square (*SS*) values are based on two equal-sized groups, $r_{\text{pb}} = \sqrt{SS_{\text{B}}/SS_{\text{T}}}$. Unequal sample sizes attenuate r_{pb}. The attenuation-corrected r_{pb}, denoted r_{c}, is given by $r_{\text{c}} = ar_{\text{pb}}/\sqrt{(a^2 - 1)r^2_{\text{pb}} + 1}$, where $a = \sqrt{.25/pq}$, and *p* and *q* are the proportions of the total subjects that are in each group (Hunter & Schmidt, 2004).

The point-biserial correlation is preferable to other correlational measures of ES that estimate the proportion of variance explained, such as eta-squared, because the squaring nature of the latter results in a directionless measure and creates an impression that ESs are smaller than they are (Rosenthal & Rubin, 1982). One might conclude from an r^2_{pb} of .10, for instance, that culture is not an important predictor of a dependent variable because culture "only explains" 10% of the variance in the dependent

[3] Note that Formulas 10.6 and 10.7 are applicable only to estimators that have a symmetrical sampling distribution, such as *g* (or *d*); for formulas for application to estimators that have asymmetrical distributions, such as the correlation coefficient *r*, refer to Rosenthal, Rosnow, and Rubin (2000), who also discuss a kind of confidence level for a null-counternull interval.

variable. In this example, however, $r_{pb} = (.10)^{1/2} = .32$ which, under a simplifying assumption, is roughly equivalent to $g = .68$, a moderately large culture ES by Cohen's (1988) criteria. As mentioned earlier, Cohen (1988) categorized standardized differences measures of ES of .20, .50, and $\geq .80$ as small, medium, and large effects, respectively.

ES measures using $r_{pb} \leq .10$, .243, and $\geq .371$ can be similarly classified (Cohen, 1988). Moreover, using Rosenthal and Rubin's (1982) binomial ES display (BESD), a technique that allows for the conversion of an ES into prediction of group membership, 10% of the variance explained by culture in a data set translates to 66% of the members of one sampled culture having the characteristic of the measured dependent variable, whereas 34% of the other culture was not so categorized. Thus, when we examine these data in terms of individual members of cultures, we find that the relatively small $r_{pb}{}^2 = .10$ translates to nearly twice as many members of one culture falling into a category than members of another culture.

GOING BEYOND COMPARING TWO CENTERS

Probability of Superiority Effect Size Measure

Researchers can generate information from their data that go beyond just comparing two means. One is the probability that a randomly sampled member of Population *a* will have a score that is higher than a randomly sampled member of Population *b*, $\Pr(X_a > X_b)$. If there is no difference between the two distributions, $\Pr(X_a > X_b) = .50$. The more superior that Distribution a is compared with Distribution b, the more $\Pr(X_a > X_b)$ moves away from .5 toward 1. (Computation of these statistics may result in values $<.50$ if Culture a is the lower scoring culture.)

The number of times that the scores from one specified sample are higher than the scores from the other sample with which they are paired (i.e., the numerator of the sample proportion that is used to estimate the probability of superiority [*PS*]) is called the *U* statistic (Mann & Whitney, 1947). The total number of possible comparisons (pairings) between two samples is $n_a n_b$, and using $\hat{p}_{a>b}$ to denote the sample proportion that estimates the *PS* we can now define:

$$\hat{p}_{a>b} = \frac{U}{n_a n_b}. \tag{9.8}$$

In other words, in Formula 9.8, the numerator is the number of "wins" for a specified sample, and the denominator is the number of opportunities to win in head-to-head comparisons of each of its members' scores with each of the scores of the other sample's members. The value of U can be calculated by hand, but it can be laborious to do so except for very small samples. Although currently major statistical software packages do not calculate $\hat{p}_{a>b}$, many do calculate the Mann–Whitney U statistic or the equivalent W_m statistic. If the value of U is obtained through the use of software, one then divides this outputted U by $n_a n_b$ to find the estimator $\hat{p}_{a>b}$. If software provides the equivalent Wilcoxon (1945) W_m rank–sum statistic instead of the U statistic, if there are no ties, find U by calculating $U = W_m - [\, n_s\,(n_s + 1)]/2$, where n_s is the smaller sample size or, if sample sizes are equal, the size of one sample.

For example, suppose that $n_a = n_b = 10$ (although sample sizes need not be equal) and that the score obtained by each member of sample n_a is compared to the score obtained by each member of sample n_b, resulting in $n_a n_b = 10 \times 10 = 100$ such comparisons. Suppose further that 70 comparisons resulted in the sample n_a member having a score superior to that of the sample n_b member. Then $U/(n_a n_b) = 70/100 = .70$, the proportion of times that a member of sample n_a has a score that is superior to that of a member of sample n_b. A proportion in a sample estimates a probability in a population. In the present case, the estimate of $\Pr(X_a > X_b) = .70$.

When raw data are not available, $\Pr(X_a > X_b)$ can be estimated by the common language (*CL*) ES statistic (McGraw & Wong, 1992) that assumes normality and homogeneity of variance. It is based on a z score, $z_{cl} = (\overline{X}_a - \overline{X}_b)/\sqrt{s_a^2 + s_b^2}$, and is the proportion of area under the standardized normal curve that is below the obtained value of z_{cl}. For example, if $z_{cl} = -1.00$ or $+1.00$, $\Pr(X_a > X_b)$ is estimated to be approximately .16 or .84, respectively. The latter would indicate that 84% of the time a randomly sampled member of Culture A will outscore a randomly sampled member of Culture B. The closer z_{cl} is to zero, however, the less different are the two distributions; that is, the chance that a randomly sampled member of Culture A will score higher than a randomly sampled member of Culture B approaches .50. The *PS* has the advantage over *CL* of not assuming normality or homogeneity of variance.[4]

[4] For more information on the *PS*, see Grissom, 1994; for constructing confidence intervals for $\Pr(X_a > X_b)$, see Wilcox, 1996, 1997. Also, $\Pr(X_a > X_b)$ can be estimated from values of g using a table in Grissom (1994); g is denoted "delta" in Grissom (1994), assuming homogeneity of variance.

Cohen's *U1*

Another measure is Cohen's (1988) *U1*, the percent *non*overlap of two distributions. Assuming normality, homogeneity of variance, and populations of equal size, *U1* can be estimated from values of d (or Hedge's g) using a table in Cohen (1988). For example, if $d = 0$, the estimate is $U1 = 0\%$; there is 0% nonoverlap, 100% overlap, between the two cultures' scores. If $d = +1.00$ there is an estimated 55.4% nonoverlap and 44.6% overlap. Although Cohen's *U1* assumes equal population sizes, one can use these values to compare theoretical equal-sized versions of the two cultures' populations.

EFFECT SIZES FROM ONE-WAY DESIGNS

Eta-Squared (η^2)

A parameter that measures the proportion of the variance in the population that is accounted for by variation in the independent variable is η^2 (η is the lower case Greek letter "eta"). A traditional but sometimes problematic estimator of the strength-of-association parameter, η^2, is $\hat{\eta}^2$;

$$\hat{\eta}^2 = \frac{SS_b}{SS_{tot}}. \tag{9.9}$$

The original name for η itself was the *correlation ratio*, but this name has since come to be used by some also for η^2. When the independent variable is quantitative, η represents the correlation between the independent variable and the dependent variable, but, unlike r_{pop}, η reflects curvilinear as well as linear relationship in that case. When there are two groups, η has the same absolute size as r_{pop}.

A major flaw of $\hat{\eta}^2$ as an estimator of strength of association is that it is positively biased; that is, it tends to overestimate η^2. This estimator tends to overestimate because its numerator, SS_b, is inflated by some error variability. Bias is less for larger sample sizes and for larger values of η^2.

Epsilon Squared (ε^2) and Omega Squared (ω^2)

A somewhat less biased alternative estimator of η^2 is $\hat{\varepsilon}^2$ (lowercase Greek letter "epsilon"), and a more nearly unbiased estimator is $\hat{\omega}^2$ (lowercase

Greek letter "omega"); cf. Keselman (1975). The formulas are (Ezekiel, 1930)

$$\hat{\varepsilon}^2 = \frac{SS_b - (k-1)MS_w}{SS_{tot}} \tag{9.10}$$

and Hays's (1994)

$$\hat{\omega}^2 = \frac{SS_b - (k-1)MS_w}{SS_{tot} + MS_w}. \tag{9.11}$$

These assume equal sample sizes and homoscedasticity. Software output for the analysis of variance F test might include $\hat{\varepsilon}^2$, $\hat{\omega}^2$, or both. However, hand calculation is easy because the SS and MS_w values are available from output even if these estimators are not.

Observe that Formulas 9.10 and 9.11 attempt to compensate for the fact that $\hat{\eta}^2$ tends to overestimate η^2 by reducing the numerator of the estimators by $(k-1)\,MS_w$. Formula 9.11 goes even further in attempting to reduce the overestimation by also adding MS_w to the denominator. The $\hat{\omega}^2$ estimator is now more widely used than is $\hat{\varepsilon}^2$.

A statistically significant overall F can be taken as evidence that $\hat{\omega}^2$ is significantly greater than 0. However, confidence intervals are especially important here because of the high sampling variability of the estimators (Maxwell, Camp, & Arvey, 1981).[5] For rough purposes, approximate confidence limits for η^2 based on $\hat{\omega}^2$ can be obtained using graphs (called monographs) that can be found in Abu Libdeh (1984). Assuming normality and, especially, homoscedasticity, the use of noncentral distributions is appropriate for constructing such confidence intervals.

Note that as a measure of a proportion (of total variance of the dependent variable that is associated with variation of the independent variable), the value of η^2 cannot be below 0, but inspection of Formulas 9.10 and 9.11 reveals that the values of the estimators $\hat{\varepsilon}^2$ and $\hat{\omega}^2$ can themselves be below 0. Hays (1994), who had earlier introduced $\hat{\omega}^2$, recommended that when the value of this estimator is below 0, the value should be reported as 0. However, some meta-analysts are concerned that replacing negative estimates with zeros might cause an additional positive bias in an estimate that is based on averaging estimates in a meta-analysis. Similarly, Fidler and Thompson

[5] For example, Carroll and Nordholm (1975) found great sampling variability even when $N = 90$ and $k = 3$. Of course, high sampling variability results in estimates often being much above or much below the ES that is being estimated.

(2001) argued that any obtained negative value should be reported as such instead of converting it to 0 so that the full width of a confidence interval can be reported. Of course, when a negative value is reported, a reader of a research report has an opportunity to interpret it as 0 if he or she so chooses.

EFFECT SIZES FROM FACTORIAL DESIGNS

Strength of Association: Proportion of Variance Explained

Estimation of η_{pop^2}, the proportion of variance of the scores on the dependent variable that is related to variation of the independent variable, is more complicated with regard to factorial designs than is the case with the one-way design. This is true even in the simplest case, which we assume here, in which all sample sizes are equal. In general, for the effect of some factor, or the effect of interaction, when the peripheral factors are intrinsic, one can estimate proportion of variance using

$$\hat{\omega}^2 = \frac{SS_{\text{effect}} - (df_{\text{effect}} MS_{\text{w}})}{SS_{\text{tot}} + MS_{\text{w}}}. \tag{9.12}$$

All *MS*, *SS*, and *df* values are available or can be calculated from the ANOVA *F* test software output. With regard to the main effect of Factor A, $SS_{\text{effect}} = SS_{\text{A}}$ and $df_{\text{effect}} = a - 1$, in which a is the number of levels of Factor A. With regard to the main effect of Factor B, substitute B and b (i.e., the number of levels of Factor B) for A and a in the previous sentence, and so forth for the main effect of any other factor in the design. With regard to the interaction effect in a two-way design $SS_{\text{effect}} = SS_{\text{AB}}$ and $df_{\text{effect}} = (a - 1)(b - 1)$.

Formula 9.12 provides an estimate of the proportion of the total variance of the measure of the dependent variable that is accounted for by an independent variable (or by interaction as another example in the factorial case), as does Formula 9.11 for the one-way design. However, in the present case of factorial designs, there can be more sources of variance than in the one-way case because of the contributions made to total variance by one or more additional factors and interactions. An effect of, say, Factor A might yield a different value of $\hat{\omega}^2$ if it is researched in the context of a one-way design instead of a factorial design, in which there will be more sources of variance that account for the total variance. As was stated previously, estimates of ES must be interpreted in the context of the design results that produced the estimate.

Partial $\hat{\omega}^2$

An alternative conceptualization of estimation of proportion of variance (POV) from factorial designs modifies Formula 9.12 to attempt to eliminate the contribution that any extrinsic peripheral factor may make to total variance. The resulting measure is called a *partial* proportion of variance. Whereas a proportion of variance measures the strength of an effect relative to the total variability from error and from all effects, a partial proportion of variance measures the strength of an effect relative to variability that is not attributable to other effects. The excluded effects are those that would not be present if the levels of the targeted factor had been researched in a one-way design. For this purpose, partial eta-squared and partial omega-squared, the latter being less biased, have been traditionally used. Partial omega-squared, $\hat{\omega}^2_{\text{partial}}$, for any effect is given by

$$\hat{\omega}^2_{\text{partial}} = \frac{SS_{\text{effect}} - (df_{\text{effect}} MS_{\text{w}})}{SS_{\text{effect}} + (N - df_{\text{effect}})\, MS_{\text{w}}}, \qquad (9.13)$$

where N is the total sample size and calculation is again a matter of simple arithmetic because all of the needed values are available from the output from the ANOVA F test.

A research report must make clear whether a reported estimate of proportion of variance is based on the overall $\hat{\omega}^2$ or $\hat{\omega}^2_{\text{partial}}$. Unfortunately, because values of estimates of overall and of partial proportion of variance can be different – the more so, the more complex a design – some textbooks and some software may be unclear or incorrect about which of the two estimators it is discussing or outputting (Levine & Hullett, 2002). One serious consequence of such confusion would be misleading meta-analyses in which the meta-analysts are unknowingly integrating sets of two kinds of estimates. If a report of primary research provides a formula for the estimate of proportion of variance, readers should examine the denominator to observe whether Formula 9.12 or 9.13 is being used.

One should be cautious about deciding on the relative importance of two factors by inspecting the ratio of their estimates of ES. The ratio of values of $\hat{\omega}^2$ for two factors can be very different from the ratio of two estimates of standardized-difference ES for these two factors. Therefore, these two kinds of estimators can provide different perspectives on the relative ESs of the two factors. Maxwell, Camp, and Arvey (1981) provided an example in which the ratio of the two $\hat{\omega}^2$ values is approximately 4 to 1, which might lead some to conclude that one factor is roughly 4 times "more important" than the other factor. Such an interpretation would fail to take into account the relative strengths of manipulation of the two factors or the likely great sampling variabilities of the estimates. Moreover, in this current example, those authors found that the ratio of two standardized-difference estimates for those same two factors is not approximately 4 to 1 but instead 2 to 1, providing a quantitatively, if not qualitatively, somewhat different perspective on the relative importance of the two factors.

Summary

Several sources (e.g., Cohen, 1988; Dunlap, 1999; Grissom, 1994; Grissom & Kim, 2005) have described the relationships among the measures recommended here. The measures g and r_{pb} show the direction of cultural difference by their sign and by which culture's mean is coded 1 or produces the first mean in the calculation. The *PS* and *CL* reflect direction of difference by whether they are below or above .50, and by which culture is designated Culture *a*. The *U1* measure shows the direction of difference according to the value of *U1* and which culture has the higher mean. Finally, all ESs from one-way and factorial designs estimate the proportion of variance in the dependent variable attributed to the independent variable(s).

Although the transition from group- to individual-level interpretations is important in cross-cultural work, there is no universally accepted, objective standard of how large an effect must be to be considered "meaningful." Cohen's (1988) criteria for small, medium, and large effects in terms of values of g (and d) provide some rough benchmarks. Because the measures of ES presented here can readily be translated to d, r_{pb}, *CL*, or *PS*, any author or reader of a cross-cultural study can translate any of our recommended measures into one of the categories of small, medium, or large effect or estimates involving proportions of individuals, if desired.

Our position, however, is that how authors characterize their effects as small, medium, or large (or meaningful or not meaningful) is irrelevant, provided that they report the appropriate ES statistics that allow readers to make their own interpretations of meaningfulness. F, t, or p do not provide readers the information to determine whether their own standard of a meaningful difference between cultures has been attained; reporting measures of ES permits readers to evaluate the effect in terms of one's own sense of meaningfulness. In the example given previously, $r_{pb} = .32$ can translate to a binomial ES display showing that 66% of one culture is collectivistic and 34% of another culture is so. One reader may interpret this result as meaningful, another as not. We prefer not to provide such guidelines for interpretation. Instead, our thrust is to suggest solely that measures such as those recommended here be estimated and reported so that readers can make their own evaluations. In a sense, reporting ESs "democratizes" the evaluation of meaningfulness.[6]

AN EXAMPLE

Recently, Matsumoto and colleagues (Matsumoto et al., 2008) conducted a large-scale survey of cultural display rules involving approximately 6,000 participants in 33 countries. Cultural display rules are rules that dictate the management and modification of one's emotional expressive behavior depending on social circumstance (Ekman & Friesen, 1969). They are presumably learned early in life; studies have documented children as young as preschool children masking their emotions (Cole, 1986; Cole, Bruschi, & Tamang, 2002), and shortly thereafter, school-age children have verbal knowledge of display rules (Saarni, 1979, 1988).

In Matsumoto et al.'s (2006) study, respondents completed a modified version of the Display Rule Assessment Inventory (DRAI; Matsumoto, Takeuchi, Andayani, Kouznetsova, & Krupp, 1998; Matsumoto, Yoo, Hirayama, & Petrova, 2005), which asked respondents to select the behavioral response they believe they *should* do if they felt each of seven emotions in different contexts. The contexts comprised combinations of 21 interactants in two settings – public and private – and the seven emotions were those for which there is evidence of universal emotional expressions in the face – anger, contempt, disgust, fear, happiness, sadness, and surprise. The response categories provided were the six behavioral responses Ekman and Friesen (1969) originally considered as part of the repertoire of display rule responses: amplification (expressing the emotion more than one feels it), expression (expressing the emotion as one feels it), deamplification (expressing the emotion less than one feels it), neutralization (expressing nothing), qualification (expressing the emotions together with others), and masking (neutralizing the original emotion and showing another instead). The nominal data were transformed into scalar values on the basis of a multidimensional scaling (MDS) of the overall counts of each response category. The MDS generated a universal, two-dimensional solution, one of

[6] Authors may be inclined more than readers to interpret their findings as meaningful. Differences in interpretations of meaningfulness based on effect sizes as we argue here may be a consequence of the democratization of these evaluations, which generally does not occur with NHST because of the accepted standard of statistical significance among researchers.

which was labeled *expression*. The original nominal data were then recoded according to the values of each response category along this dimension.

To exemplify most of the ES statistics we discussed in this chapter, we selected four countries that would probably generate a range of differences in display rules – the United States, Australia, South Korea, and Japan. To demonstrate the utility of the ES for two group comparisons, we compared the United States with all three other countries, and Japan with South Korea, on the overall expressivity score, computed by averaging all ratings across all emotions and contexts. For each comparison, we computed a one-way ANOVA, the confidence interval of the difference between the means, Hedge's g, the counternull ES, the point-biserial correlation (both normally and corrected for unequal sample sizes), and the *PS* (Table 9.1).

The comparison between the United States and Australia was not statistically significant. The difference between their means was .009. With a margin of error of .034, this means that the 95% confidence interval of the difference between the means ranged from $-.025$ to .043. Because this range included zero, we are fairly confident that there was no difference between the population means. Hedge's g was .049, indicating a very small difference. The counternull ES, however, was .097, suggesting that there was equal evidence for some small difference (approximately $g = .10$) between the United States and Australia. Both estimates of the point-biserial correlation were negligible, and the *PS* indicated that the average American would have a higher score than the average Australian only 51.6% of the time, a negligible effect.

The other three comparisons were all statistically significant. The 95% confidence interval for the difference between the means for Japan and South Korea was $.035 \pm .033$; for the United States and Japan, it was $.088 \pm .022$; and for the United States and South Korea, it was $.123 \pm .032$. Each of these ranges did not include zero, and thus we can be fairly confident that there are real differences between their population means. Hedge's g was .200, .492, and .678 for these three comparisons, respectively, indicating small, medium, and large effects. The point-biserial correlations also mirrored these findings; note especially that the point-biserial for the United States–South Korea comparison, although not striking in absolute value, was associated with a very large Hedge's g. The *PS* indicated that the average Japanese would have a higher score than the average South Korean 55% of the time; the average American would have a higher score than the average Japanese 63.4% of the time; and the average American would have a higher score than the average South Korean 67.8% of the time.

Table 9.1. *Summary of two-country comparisons from Matsumoto et al.'s (2006) study of cultural display rules*

Comparison	Mean Country 1	SD Country 1	*n* Country 1	Mean Country 2	SD Country 2	*n* Country 2	*F*	*ME*[a]	*g*	ES_{cn}	r_{pb}	rc	PS
US–AUS	.042	.180	691	.033	.178	128	$F(1, 817) = .25$, *ns*	.034	.049	.097	.018	.024	.516
JPN–KOR	–.046	.173	377	–.081	.185	152	$F(1,527) = 4.35$, $p = .037$	.033	.200	.401	.091	.100	.550
US–JPN	.042	.180	691	–.046	.173	377	$F(1,1066) = 59.07$, $p < .001$	.022	.492	.984	.235	.246	.634
US–KOR	.042	.180	691	–.081	.185	152	$F(1,842) = 57.29$, $p < .001$	.032	.678	1.356	.261	.332	.678

Note: AUS = Australia; ES_{cn} = counternull effect size; JPN = Japan; KOR = Korea; ME = margin of error of the difference between the means; *PS* = probability of superiority; r_c = attenuation-corrected point-biserial correlation; r_{pb} = point-biserial correlation; US = United States.

Not surprisingly, a one-way ANOVA on the overall expressivity scores using all four countries as levels of an independent variable produced a statistically significant result, $F(3, 1344) = 32.65$, $p < .001$. η^2, computed by dividing the sum of squares for the country effect by the total sum of squares, was .068. $\hat{\varepsilon}^2$ and $\hat{\omega}^2$ provided slightly smaller estimates of the country ES, .066 and .066, respectively. In this example, therefore, whereas $\hat{\varepsilon}^2$ and $\hat{\omega}^2$ produced smaller ESs as expected, the differences may have been negligible.

For illustrative purposes, we also computed a full, five-factor mixed design ANOVA, using country (4) and gender (2) as between-subject variables, and interactant (21), setting (2, public vs. private), and emotion (7) as within-subject variables. The country main effect from this ANOVA was significant, $F(3, 1213) = 39.39$, $p < .001$ (there was a difference in sample size because of missing data). $\hat{\omega}^2$ was .086; partial η^2, provided by SPSS, was .089; and partial $\hat{\omega}^2$ was .086. The setting main effect was also significant, $F(1, 1213) = 1152.91$, $p < .001$, and $\hat{\omega}^2$, partial $\hat{\omega}^2$, and partial η^2 were .479, .485, and .487, respectively. The country-by-setting interaction was also significant, $F(1, 1213) = 6.42$, $p < .001$; $\hat{\omega}^2$, partial $\hat{\omega}^2$, and partial η^2 were .008, .015, and .016, respectively.

One of the first things to note is the radically different ESs associated with each of the three ANOVA effects just described. Each was statistically significant at the same *p* values to the third decimal place; yet each was very different. The country main effect indicated that approximately 9% of the total variability in the dependent variable, overall expressivity, was uniquely accounted for by between-country differences among the four countries. (The difference in the findings from the one-way ANOVA involving country reported immediately before that and the country main effect from the full-factorial model can be the result of several factors, including the missing data, the better estimates of error through the specification of a full factorial model, or the better specification of ES through partial η^2 and partial $\hat{\omega}^2$.) The setting main effect indicated that approximately 48% of the total variance in expressivity was accounted for by the difference between being in public or private; this was a sizable effect. Finally, although the effects of setting were moderated by country, this interaction accounted for only approximately 1% of the total variance in the dependent variable, a rather negligible effect.

CONCLUSION

Statistics such as *t*s and *F*s have dominated data analysis in cross-cultural research, and other areas of psychology as well. To be sure, they have their place and have led to many important findings. Research using them to document cultural differences is a cornerstone of cross-cultural psychology. Problems occur, however, when we interpret statistical significance to reflect meaningful differences among individuals. As we have argued, *t*s and *F*s cannot tell us about meaningful differences on the level of people, and their sole, continued use in this fashion will only foster stereotypes in research, theory, and practice, because group differences are used to infer differences among people.

Fortunately, alternative methods for analyzing data exist, some of which we discussed here. They provide us with valuable information about the magnitude of cultural differences that is unavailable from *t*s and *F*s. They allow us to make finer estimations of the degree to which observed group differences are represented on the level of individuals. They allow theorists to think more constructively and realistically about conceptual issues, forcing them to go beyond mere global, stereotypic notions that are assumed to be true for all members of a culture. Finally, they provide important guidelines concerning applications of cultural differences.

Just pause to consider the wealth of knowledge concerning cultural differences in any area of cross-cultural comparison that some may assume to be important or large on the level of individuals because previous research has documented statistically significant differences between culture means. How many of these are actually reflective of meaningful differences on the level of individuals? Unfortunately, the answer is unknown, unless tests of group differences in means are accompanied by measures of cultural ES such as those presented here. If theories, research, and practical work that are supposedly applicable to individuals are based on such limited group difference comparisons, theories, research, and applied programs based on these cultural differences may be based on a house of cards. Future theories in cross-cultural psychology, and all areas of psychology, should be built on a better foundation.

Of course, this foundation starts with better research methodology, and the points we raise are not intended to suggest that statistical methods can compensate for limitations of design in cross-cultural research, particularly when preexisting cultural groups are used as the independent variable (see also Wilkinson et al., 1999). Clearly, one of the biggest challenges facing cross-cultural research concerns the need to replace culture with specific, measurable psychological variables that are hypothesized to account for cultural differences. Incorporation of such "context" variables is an important improvement in method that transcends methods of data analysis in any cross-cultural study (Bond & Tedeschi, 2001; Poortinga, van de Vijver, Joe, & van de Koppel, 1987; van de Vijver & Leung, 1997).

Still, data analysis and statistical inference are important parts of methods, and it is these issues that this chapter addresses. The ability to explain, understand, and predict behavior on the individual level is one of the founding pillars of psychology. Although it is important for researchers to examine the influence of many social categories on human behavior – gender, culture, socioeconomic status, and the like – ultimately our goal is to understand individual differences on psychological phenomena and the influence of social structures on those individual differences. Thus, we urge researchers to consider using these and other measures in their future empirical work, and we encourage journal editors to require their authors to report such statistics. Only the continued development and refinement of methods in cross-cultural research can help it to enhance its contributions to psychology throughout the world.

REFERENCES

Abelson, R. P. (1997). On the surprising longevity of flogged horses: Why there is a case for the significance test. *Psychological Science, 8*, 12–15.

Abu Libdeh, O. (1984). *Strength of association in the simple general linear model: A comparative study of Hays' omega-squared.* Unpublished doctoral dissertation, University of Chicago, Chicago.

Bond, M. H., & Tedeschi, J. T. (2001). Polishing the jade: A modest proposal for improving the study of social psychology across cultures. In D. Matsumoto (Ed.), *Handbook of culture and psychology* (pp. 309–324). New York: Oxford University Press.

Brant, R. (1990). Comparing classical and resistant outlier rules. *Journal of the American Statistical Association, 85*, 1083–1090.

Carroll, R. M., & Nordholm, L. A. (1975). Sampling characteristics of Kelley's ε^2 and Hays' $\hat{\omega}^2$. *Educational and Psychological Measurement, 35*, 541–554.

Cohen, J. (1962). The statistical power of abnormal–social psychological research. *Journal of Abnormal and Social Psychology, 65*, 145–153.

Cohen, J. (1988). *Statistical power analysis for the behavioral sciences* (2nd ed.). New York: Academic Press.

Cole, P. M. (1986). Children's spontaneous control of facial expression. *Child Development, 57*, 1309–1321.

Cole, P. M., Bruschi, C. J., & Tamang, B. L. (2002). Cultural differences in children's emotional reactions to difficult situations. *Child Development, 73*, 983–996.

Dunlap, W. P. (1999). A program to compute McGraw and Wong's common language effect size indicator. *Behavior Research Methods, Instruments, and Computers, 31*, 706–709.

Ekman, P., & Friesen, W. (1969). The repertoire of nonverbal behavior: Categories, origins, usage, and coding. *Semiotica, 1*, 49–98.
Ezekiel, M. (1930). *Methods of correlational analysis.* New York: Wiley.
Feingold, A. (1992). Sex differences in variability in intellectual abilities: A new look at an old controversy. *Review of Educational Research, 62*, 61–84.
Feingold, A. (1995). The additive effects of differences in central tendency and variability are important in comparisons between groups. *American Psychologist, 50*, 5–13.
Feingold, A., & Mazzella, R. (1998). Gender differences in body image are increasing. *Psychological Science, 9*, 190–195.
Fidler, F., .& Thompson, B. (2001). Computing correct confidence intervals for ANOVA fixed- and random-effects effect sizes. *Educational and Psychological Measurement, 61*, 575–604.
Fisher, R. A. (1925). *Statistical methods for research workers.* London: Oliver & Boyd.
Grissom, R. J. (1994). Probability of the superior outcome of one treatment over another. *Journal of Applied Psychology, 79*, 314–316.
Grissom, R. J. (2000). Heterogeneity of variance in clinical data. *Journal of Consulting and Clinical Psychology, 68*, 155–165.
Grissom, R., & Kim, J. J. (2005). *Effect sizes for research: A broad practical approach.* Mahwah, NJ: Erlbaum.
Harris, R. J. (1997). Significance tests have their place. *Psychological Science, 8*, 8–11.
Hays, W. L. (1994). *Statistics for psychologists* (5th ed.). Fort Worth, TX: Hartcourt Brace.
Hedges, L. V., & Olkin, L. (1985). *Statistical methods for meta-analysis.* San Diego, CA: Academic Press.
Hunter, J. E. (1997). Needed: A ban on the significance test. *Psychological Science, 8*, 3–7.
Hunter, J. E., & Schmidt, F. L. (2004). *Methods and meta-analysis* (2nd ed.). Thousand Oaks, CA: Sage.
Keselman, H. (1975). A Monte Carlo investigation of three estimates of treatment magnitude: Epsilon squared, eta squared, and omega squared. *Canadian Psychological Review, 16*, 44–48.
Levine, T. R., & Hullett, C. R. (2002). Eta squared, partial eta squared, and misreporting of effect size in communication research. *Human Communication Research, 28*, 612–625.
Loftus, G. R. (1996). Psychology will be a much better science when we change the way we analyze data. *Current Directions in Psychological Science, 5*, 161–170.
Mann, H. B., & Whitney, D. R. (1947). On a test of whether one of two random variables is stochastically larger than the other. *Annals of Mathematical Statistics, 18*, 50–60.
Matsumoto, D., Grissom, R., & Dinnel, D. (2001). Do between-culture differences really mean that people are different? A look at some measures of cultural effect size. *Journal of Cross-Cultural Psychology, 32*, 478–490.
Matsumoto, D., Takeuchi, S., Andayani, S., Kouznetsova, N., & Krupp, D. (1998). The contribution of individualism–collectivism to cross-national differences in display rules. *Asian Journal of Social Psychology, 1*, 147–165.

Matsumoto, D., Yoo, S. H., Fontaine, J., Anguas-Wong, A. M., Arriola, M., Ataca, B., Bond, M. H., Boratav, H. B., Breugelmans, S. M., Cabecinhas, R., Chae, J., Chin, W. H., Comunian, A. L., DeGere, D. N., Djunaidi, A., Fok, H. K., Friedlmeier, W., Ghosh, A., Glamcevski, M., Granskaya, J. V., Groenvynck, H., Harb, C., Haron, F., Joshi, R., Kakai, H., Kashima, E., Khan, W., Kurman, J., Kwantes, C. T., Mahmud, S. H., Mandaric, M., Nizharadze, G., Odusanya, J. O. T., Ostrosky-Solis, F., Palaniappan, A. K., Papastylianou, D., Safdar, S., Setiono, K., Shigemasu, E., Singelis, T. M., Iva, P. S., Spieb, E., Sterkowicz, S., Sunar, D., Szarota, P., Vishnivetz, B., Vohra, N., Ward, C., Wong, S., Wu, R., Zebian, S., Zengeya, A. (2008). Mapping expressive differences around the world: The relationship between emotional display rules and Individualism v. Collectivism. *Journal of Cross-Cultural Psychology, 39*, 55–74.

Matsumoto, D., Yoo, S. H., Hirayama, S., & Petrova, G. (2005). Validation of an individual-level measure of display rules: The Display Rule Assessment Inventory (DRAI). *Emotion, 5*, 23–40.

Maxwell, S. E., Camp, C. C., & Arvey, R. D. (1981). Measures of strength of association: A comparative examination. *Journal of Applied Psychology, 66*, 525–534.

McGraw, K. O., & Wong, S. P. (1992). A common language effect size statistic. *Psychological Bulletin, 111*, 361–365.

Poortinga, Y. H., Van de Vijver, F. J. R., Joe, R. C., & Van de Koppel, J. M. H. (1987). Peeling the onion called culture: A synopsis. In C. Kagitcibasi (Ed.), *Growth and progress in cross-cultural psychology* (pp. 22–34). Berwyn, PA: Swets North America.

Rosenthal, R. (1991). *Meta-analytic procedures for social research.* Newbury Park, CA: Sage.

Rosenthal, R., Rosnow, R. L., & Rubin, D. B. (2000). *Contrasts and effect sizes in behavioral research: A correlational approach.* Cambridge: Cambridge University Press.

Rosenthal, R., & Rubin, D. B. (1982). A simple, general purpose display of magnitude of experimental effect. *Journal of Educational Psychology, 74*, 166–169.

Rosenthal, R., & Rubin, D. B. (1994). The counternull value of an effect size: A new statistic. *Psychological Science, 5*, 329–334.

Saarni, C. (1979). Children's understanding of display rules for expressive behavior. *Developmental Psychology, 15*, 424–429.

Saarni, C. (1988). Children's understanding of the interpersonal consequences of nonverbal emotional-expressive behavior. *Journal of Nonverbal Behavior, 3–4*, 275–295.

Shrout, P. E. (1997). Should significance tests be banned? Introduction to a special section exploring the pros and cons. *Psychological Science, 8*, 1–2.

Staudte, R. G., & Sheather, S. J. (1990). *Robust estimation and testing.* New York: Wiley.

Van de Vijver, F. J. R., & Leung, K. (1997). *Methods and data analysis for cross-cultural research.* Newbury Park, CA: Sage.

Wilcox, R. R. (1997). *Introduction to robust estimation and hypothesis testing.* San Diego, CA: Academic Press.

Wilcox, R. R. (1998). How many discoveries have been lost by ignoring modern statistical methods? *American Psychologist, 53*, 300–314.

Wilcox, R. R. (2001). *Fundamentals of modern statistical methods: Substantially improving power and accuracy.* New York: Springer-Verlag.

Wilcox, R. R. (2003). *Applying contemporary statistical techniques.* San Diego, CA: Academic Press.

Wilcoxon, F. (1945). Individual comparisons by ranking methods. *Biometrics, 1,* 80–83.

Wilkinson, L., and the Task Force on Statistical Inference, APA Board of Scientific Affairs. (1999). Statistical methods in psychology journals: Guidelines and explanations. *American Psychologist, 54,* 594–604.

10

Data Analytic Approaches for Investigating Isomorphism Between the Individual-Level and the Cultural-Level Internal Structure

JOHNNY R. J. FONTAINE AND RONALD FISCHER

It is standard practice in cross-cultural psychological research to apply a psychological instrument in different cultural groups and quantitatively compare them on the scale(s) of that instrument. Such cross-cultural comparisons can be misleading for three reasons: because of the cultural specificity of the construct, the distorting effects of methodological biases, and the lack of generalizability of individual-level constructs to the cultural level.

According to cultural relativists, psychological characteristics and processes are constructed by and derive their meaning from the cultural system in which they emerge (e.g., Miller, 1997). This implies that it is meaningless to compare cultural groups quantitatively, because it would amount to comparing apples and oranges. For instance, it has been claimed that *amae* is not only an untranslatable Japanese emotion term but also refers to a typical Japanese emotion process (e.g., Doi, 1971). Because the process is intimately tied to the Japanese culture, it makes no sense to compare cultural groups with respect to their salience of *amae*.

Methodological biases affecting specific items (e.g., due to translation errors) or possibly the whole instrument (e.g., due to culturally different response styles) form a second and well-acknowledged reason for why cross-cultural comparisons can be misleading. These biases have been extensively treated in the by-now classical bias and equivalence framework (e.g., Fontaine, 2005; Poortinga, 1989; van de Vijver & Leung, 1997a, 1997b). They entail for instance, underrepresentation of the construct domain by the content of the test, translation errors, response styles, lack of familiarity with the testing procedure, and so on. These methodological biases lead to a violation of the conditions for structural, metric, and full score equivalence. They distort the meaning of quantitative comparisons between cultural groups (see also Chapter 2).

There is still a third reason, however – namely that the psychological construct that is used to describe individuals does not form a meaningful characteristic of cultural groups. When making cross-cultural comparisons based on psychological scales, a conceptual shift takes place from the individual to the cultural level. Within cultural groups, a psychological instrument assesses characteristics of individuals. When average scores on a psychological scale are compared between cultural groups, these average scores become properties of those cultural groups. For instance, when a Big Five personality instrument is applied within a cultural group, the scores refer to characteristics of individuals. When cultural groups are compared with respect to their average scores on the Big Five personality traits, these traits are treated as characteristics of cultural groups. Cultural groups are then assumed to differ in extraversion, neuroticism, conscientiousness, agreeableness, and openness (e.g., McCrae & Terracciano, 2008).

The problem is that the attribution of individual-level characteristics to cultural groups can be fallacious. The meaning of a psychological assessment can shift dramatically when going from the individual to the cultural level. The cross-cultural value research of Schwartz (e.g., 1992, 1994, 2006) forms a point in case. He has studied values both at the individual and cultural level. At the individual level, he demonstrated that the value domain can be represented by 10 value types that are (quasi-)circularly ordered into a two-dimensional geometric representation. The opposition of self-transcendent (benevolence, universalism) to self-enhancement (power, achievement) values and of openness to change (self-direction and stimulation) to conservation (security, conformity, tradition) values represent the two major value conflicts at the individual level. When averaging the values scores per country and then looking at the cultural-level value structure, he observed a different structure. At the cultural level, he identified seven cultural-level value types organized around three cultural-level conflicts: mastery versus harmony, autonomy versus embeddedness, and hierarchy versus egalitarianism. The most striking difference between the individual and the cultural level was observed for the value items "humble" and "social power." At the individual level, these two value items are not, or even negatively, correlated. Individuals who strive for social power typically do not value humbleness, and vice versa. At the individual level, these two value items are thus indicators of two value types: power and tradition, respectively. At the cultural level, however, Schwartz observed that the average scores on "social power" and the average scores on "humble" are positively correlated. Moreover, they are represented in the same region of the cultural-level value structure. According to Schwartz (1994), these two items at the cultural level indicate the extent to which hierarchy is valued by the cultural system. In hierarchical cultures, both the importance of an uneven hierarchical distribution of power (social power) and the importance of respecting these hierarchical structures (humble) are instilled into their members. Because Schwartz observed that the value domain is differently structured at the individual compared with the cultural level, it cannot be justified to compare cultural groups on the basis of individual-level value scales. Vice versa, it cannot be justified to compare individuals within cultural groups on the basis of cultural-level value scales. Because the value domain is differently structured at both levels, such comparisons are misleading.

In general, a necessary source for justifying the construction and interpretation of psychological scales is the investigation of the internal structure of those scales[1] (e.g., Messick, 1989). When an instrument is applied to a sample of persons, associations between the items of that instrument can be computed. The question is whether and to what extent the observed associations can be represented or accounted for by the intended underlying dimensions. The internal structure of an instrument consists of these underlying dimensions and their relationships with the items of the instrument. For an instrument to be valid, the items have to be nontrivially related to the dimensions they are intended to measure and may not be related to other dimensions they are not supposed to measure. For instance, all personality questions that probe extraversion should be mutually positively correlated and should load on the extraversion factor. Moreover, they should not load on the other four personality factors. The better the expected internal structure represents the observed associations between the items, the more evidence there is for the validity of the instrument.

This chapter deals with the investigation of the comparability or noncomparability of the internal structure between the individual and the cultural levels of analysis. First, the research design is presented that is required for investigating the internal structure at both levels. Then, the terminology that is used to refer to comparability between the individual and the cultural levels of analysis is discussed. Subsequently, three prototypical scenarios are proposed for the comparability of internal structures in cross-cultural psychology. A stepwise data analytic approach is then presented

[1] Other important sources are the demonstration of the relevance and the representativeness of the content of the instrument for the construct domain (which has to be demonstrated in each cultural group in which the instrument is used) and the demonstration of a predicted network of antecedent, concurrent, and consequent relationships with other constructs and applied criteria (e.g., Messick, 1989).

to justify comparability. Finally, the stepwise approach is demonstrated by means of three examples from the literature.

THE MULTILEVEL RESEARCH DESIGN

Despite Hofstede's (1980) position in his seminal work *Culture's Consequences* that the individual and cultural levels of analysis should be distinguished and are organized according to different principles, scant attention has been paid to the possible shift in meaning between these levels of analysis in the methodology of cross-cultural psychology (however, see Leung & Bond, 1989, for an exception). The most important reason is probably the commonly used research designs in cross-cultural psychology. Culture is mostly treated as a fixed design factor. This means that only two or a few purposefully chosen cultural groups are studied and compared with one another. In such a design, it is impossible to investigate the internal structure at the cultural level. There are too few cultural groups (often just two), and the cultural groups have not been randomly selected. This means that it is unlikely that the sources of variation that differentiate the specific cultural groups can be generalized to the population of cultural groups. As it is not possible to detect the structure of personality traits by studying two or a few specific individuals, the cultural-level structure cannot be identified by studying two or a few specific cultural groups.

The cultural-level structure can only be identified and compared with the individual-level structure within a multilevel research design. Such a design has at least four fundamental characteristics (e.g., Goldstein, 2003; Hox, 2002, Raudenbush & Bryk, 2002). First, different levels of analyses are a priori distinguished, such as classrooms and pupils, individuals and emotional episodes, and cultural groups and individuals. Second, these different levels of analyses are hierarchically ordered; for example, pupils are nested in classrooms, emotional episodes are nested in persons, and individuals are nested in cultural groups. Third, a multistage sampling procedure is applied in which at each stage, a random sample is drawn for each unit that was selected in the previous stage. For instance, first, a random sample of classes is drawn, and then a random sample of pupils within those classes; or a random sample of individuals is drawn, and then a random sample of emotional episodes experienced by those individuals; or a random sample of cultural groups is sampled, and then a random sample of individuals within the selected cultural groups. Finally, each of the levels is analyzed in its own respect. For instance, relationships are investigated at the classroom and pupil levels, or at the person and episode levels, or at the cultural and individual levels. This last characteristic follows from a particular consequence of the multistage sampling procedure. The associations among variables are statistically independent between the hierarchically ordered levels of analyses. The total variance–covariance matrix can be decomposed into an individual level (pooled-within culture) and cultural level (between culture) variance–covariance matrix (Muthén, 1994).[2] Statistically, the associations observed at one level of analysis do not constrain the associations that can be observed at another level of analysis. Thus, only in a multilevel research design can the internal structure at the cultural level be investigated independently from the internal structure at the individual level.

Before the advent of widely accessible information and communication technology, these multilevel designs were difficult to execute in cross-cultural psychology, and therefore exceptional. However, today they have come within reach, and the number of databases that approach a random sampling of cultural groups is increasing rapidly. It thus becomes more and more feasible to investigate empirically whether the internal structure at individual and the cultural levels are comparable.

INTERNAL STRUCTURE ISOMORPHISM

Different labels have been proposed to describe whether and to which extent individual- and cultural-level associations are similar, such as isomorphism (e.g., Bliese, Chan, & Ployhart, 2007), homology (e.g., Chen, Bliese, & Mathieu, 2005), and configural, metric, and scalar similarity (e.g., Widaman, 2000). This chapter builds on the terminology proposed by van de Vijver, van Hemert, and Poortinga (2008) in the introductory chapter of their edited book on multilevel analysis for cross-cultural psychology. They proposed the notion of isomorphism to indicate that phenomena share the same monotonic relationships at both the individual and cultural levels. This means that the constructs have the same meaning at the two levels of analysis. Nonisomorphism then means that the phenomena at both levels do not share the same monotonic relationships. Other constructs are necessary to account for the phenomena at the cultural compared with the individual level of analysis.

[2] This holds both for the population variance–covariance matrix as for the sample variance–covariance matrix. The sample pooled-within culture variance–covariance matrix is an unbiased estimator of the population pooled-within culture variance–covariance matrix. The sample between culture variance–covariance matrix, however, is an estimator of a linear combination of both the population individual-level (pooled-within culture) and the population cultural-level (between culture) variance–covariance matrix.

In this chapter, the focus is only on one type of multilevel phenomena: the associations that are observed between indicators of the same construct. The question here is whether the same monotonic associations between those indicators can be observed at cultural and individual levels. More specifically, the question is whether a comparable internal structure can represent these associations at both levels of analysis. Therefore, the label *internal structure isomorphism* is used to indicate that the same nontrivial relationships exist between the variables (or indicators) and the underlying dimensions (or factors) at both levels of analysis. This is, for instance, the case if the same Big Five personality factors emerge at both the individual and the cultural levels with the same facets loading on the respective factors (McCrae & Terracciano, 2005).

It might be noted that the notion of internal structure isomorphism is comparable to the notion of internal structure equivalence. Both notions imply comparability of internal structures, meaning that comparable non-trivial associations are observed between the variables and the underlying dimensions (in confirmatory factor analysis (CFA) terminology, *configural invariance*). They differ, however, with respect to what is compared. In the case of internal structure equivalence, individual-level internal structures are compared between cultural groups. For instance, a Big Five personality instrument is applied in different cultural groups, and whether within each cultural group the same five factorial structure accounts for the response patterns on the personality items is investigated (McCrae, Zonderman, Costa, Bond, & Paunonen, 1996). If the same five factors emerge in each cultural group, there is a case for internal structure equivalence. With internal structure equivalence, the unit of analysis is always the individual. In the case of internal structure isomorphism, the "average" individual-level internal structure is compared with the cultural-level internal structure. With internal structure isomorphism, the unit of analysis shifts from individuals to cultural groups.

It is important to note that questions about internal structure equivalence and internal structure isomorphism are hierarchically related. Internal structure equivalence is a necessary, but insufficient condition for comparing cultural groups. The equivalence of the internal structure means that the same underlying dimensions account for the observed associations within each of the cultural groups (structural equivalence, as discussed in Chapter 7). Lack of internal structure equivalence could point to both methodological biases (e.g., differential impact of social desirable responding) or to cultural specificity of the psychological construct (what is expected from a relativistic stance). Whatever the explanation, if the internal structure is not equivalent between each of the cultural groups, no further direct comparisons of cultural groups can be justified. This would amount to the proverbial comparison of apples and oranges. However, if internal structure equivalence has been demonstrated, it does not necessarily imply that cultural groups can be directly compared. To compare cultural groups, it must be additionally demonstrated that the same internal structure applies to the cultural and to the individual levels. For instance, only if the same Big Five personality dimensions account for the associations between personality items in each of the cultural groups where they are investigated, is it justified to investigate quantitative cultural differences on personality items.

THREE PROTOTYPICAL SCENARIOS FOR THE INTERNAL STRUCTURE IN CROSS-CULTURAL PERSPECTIVE

Because the issues of internal structure equivalence and of internal structure isomorphism are hierarchically ordered, three prototypical scenarios for the internal structure in cross-cultural perspective can be identified (Fontaine, 2008): namely (a) no internal structure equivalence and no internal structure isomorphism, (b) internal structure equivalence and no internal structure isomorphism, and (c) internal structure equivalence and internal structure isomorphism.

Scenario 1: No internal structure equivalence and no isomorphism. As already indicated, this scenario is to be expected from a relativistic stance. It means that the individual-level internal structure of a psychological instrument is not comparable between cultural groups. Thus, the instrument is not measuring the same psychological construct within each of the cultural groups. It is not meaningful to compare cultural groups directly with one another. The instrument then must be further studied within each of the cultural groups separately. In can be investigated how it is molded by the specific cultural context in which it emerges and possibly which method factors bias the internal structure of the instrument.

Scenario 2: Internal structure equivalence and internal structure nonisomorphism. Internal structure equivalence is observed at the individual level, which forms a key condition for the valid use of the instrument in each of the different cultural groups involved. However, the average individual-level structure and cultural-level structure are different. At the cultural level, the domain is organized according to different principles compared to the individual level. In this scenario, the assessment instrument can be validly used *within* each of the cultural groups. However, because there is no internal structure isomorphism, the individual-level psychological constructs cannot be used to describe cultural differences (and vice versa). At the cultural level, different constructs and scales are needed. The different value scales proposed by Schwartz for the individual level (e.g., Schwartz, 1992) and cultural level (Schwartz, 1994) form a point in case.

It should be noted here that the internal structure equivalence and internal structure nonisomorphism scenario has implications for the investigation of full score equivalence. Internal structure nonisomorphism logically excludes full score equivalence because it implies that the cultural variation cannot be accounted for by the individual-level underlying dimensions. Thus, items will be scored higher or lower, independently of the standing of the individuals on the individual-level dimensions.

Scenario 3. Internal structure equivalence and internal structure isomorphism. In the last scenario, the same constructs are measured by the instrument at both the individual and cultural levels. Within each of the cultural groups, the same construct is measured, and the cultural-level variation is also structured according to the same constructs.

Here it is important to note that isomorphism does not necessarily imply full score equivalence of the instrument. It is possible that there are random fluctuations in the meaning of items that cause uniform or nonuniform bias (or both). If, however, these fluctuations are random, they will not necessarily affect the patterns of associations between the items at the cultural level. When a measurement model is used to analyze internal structure equivalence and internal structure isomorphism, these random fluctuations will enter into the cultural-level error terms. Thus, the observation of full score equivalence is a special case of the internal structure equivalence and internal structure isomorphism scenario.

A STEP-BY-STEP APPROACH FOR INVESTIGATING INTERNAL STRUCTURE EQUIVALENCE AND INTERNAL STRUCTURE ISOMORPHISM

On the basis of the conceptual framework that differentiates three prototypical scenarios for the internal structure of an instrument, a stepwise data analytic approach is presented for data that have been collected by a multilevel design. Thus, it is a design in which a random sample of cultural groups is first drawn, and within each cultural group a random sample of participants is selected. As was discussed in Chapter 7 on internal structure equivalence, there are four data analytic methods that are frequently used in the literature to investigate the internal structure – namely, multidimensional scaling (MDS), principal component analysis (PCA), exploratory factor analysis (EFA), and confirmatory factor analysis (CFA). In Chapter 7 on internal structure equivalence, how these methods could be applied to investigate the equivalence of the individual-level internal structure between two or a few cultural groups was presented. The present chapter builds further on the previous chapter. For an introduction into the differences and similarities between these methods, and how they can be applied to investigate comparability of internal structures, the reader is referred to that chapter. Here, how these methods can be used to investigate both internal structure equivalence at the individual level and internal structure isomorphism between the individual and cultural levels within a multilevel research design is presented.

On the basis of the conceptual model presented here and of the work of Muthén (1994) and van de Vijver and Poortinga (2002), a stepwise approach is proposed that can be applied to each of the four data analytic methods. This does not mean that the stepwise approach must be applied in a rigid way. Depending on the data analytic method, there are alternative approaches that can also be informative and adequate. The stepwise approach is structured around two fundamental steps, first the investigation of internal structure equivalence, and second, the investigation of internal structure isomorphism.[3] These two steps are presented in detail.

Step 1. Investigating Internal Structure Equivalence

Conceptually, the investigation of internal structure equivalence in a fixed-effect design in which two or a few cultural groups are purposefully selected

[3] Before starting with the analysis of the internal structure equivalence, it has been suggested in the literature to analyze the total association matrix across all individuals and cultural groups in an explorative way (Cheung & Au, 2005; Muthén, 1994; van de Vijver & Poortinga, 2002). We advise against this practice, however. On one hand, if there is internal structure isomorphism, confirmatory power of the process is lost. Because the individual and the cultural level are statistically independent, the average individual-level structure can be used as an independent point of reference for the cultural-level structure. This means that the investigation of internal structure isomorphism can be seen as a confirmatory process. However, if the total structure is first investigated, the comparison of the individual-level and the cultural-level structure is statistically dependent on the results from the first analyses on the total association matrix. On the other hand, if the two levels do not demonstrate isomorphism, the total structure could be difficult to interpret. Then the analysis of the total structure hampers, rather than contributes to, the interpretation of the different dynamics at both levels.

(see Chapter 7), is comparable to the investigation of internal structure equivalence in a multilevel design with a random sampling of cultural groups. The major difference consists in selecting the reference point. In a fixed effect design, it can be well justified to use one cultural group as a point of reference. Cross-cultural research is often initiated in one cultural group, and specific hypotheses are made about differences with other cultural groups. In a random effects design, there is no reference group because the cultural groups are selected randomly. Moreover, arbitrarily selecting a reference group could lead to an underestimation of the internal structure equivalence. It is quite possible that the arbitrarily selected reference group forms a deviant case. A possible solution could be to treat each cultural group as a point of reference and investigate the structural equivalence pairwise. However, with a large number of cultural groups, this leads to chance capitalization because of the large number of pairwise comparisons.[4] This approach is thus likely to identify nonexistent differences. The problems linked with selecting one reference culture or looking at all pairwise comparisons can be avoided by computing one internal structure across all cultural groups on the basis of the average associations between the items. This structure can then be used as a point of reference for all comparisons.

Practically, the first step boils down to three substeps: computing the average association matrix, identifying the average internal structure, and comparing the internal structure per cultural group with the average internal structure (see Figure 10.1 for a graphical presentation of the process).

Step 1.1. Computation of the Average Individual-Level Association Matrix
If the data consist of ratings of persons on a set of items that can be treated as interval-level data, the "average" association matrix can be best computed as the pooled-within correlation or covariance matrix. The pooled-within correlation or covariance matrix takes into account the sample sizes of the different cultural groups. Moreover, it forms an unbiased estimator of the population individual-level correlation and variance–covariance matrix, respectively (e.g., Muthén, 1994; Hox, 2002). The pooled-within variance–covariance matrix can be easily computed with the major statistical packages

[4] For instance, with 20 cultural groups, this approach would amount to 190 internal structure comparisons, and with 40 cultural groups, to 780 comparisons.

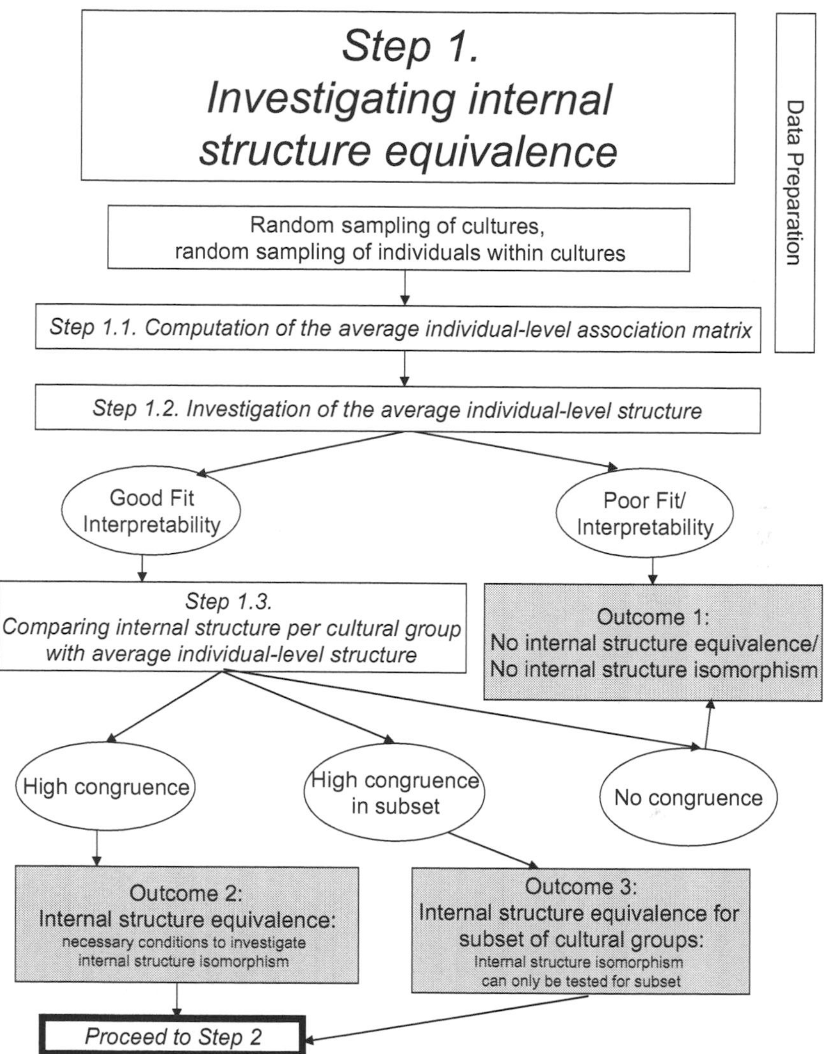

Figure 10.1. Step 1. Investigating the internal structure equivalence.

such as SAS and SPSS (e.g., see Box 10.1 for the computation of the pooled-within correlation or covariance matrix with the discriminant function in SPSS).

For MDS, the pooled-within correlation matrix must be transformed into a dissimilarity matrix. The correlations can, for instance, be transformed into average Euclidean distances between the standardized variables

Box 10.1. *Computing the individual-level (pooled-within) correlation and covariance matrix*

To obtain the pooled-within correlation and covariance matrix with SPSS, Discriminant Analysis under the Classify option (found under "Analyze") can be used. The group membership (including range of possible values) must be specified, and all variables of interest must be transferred into the independent box. Under "Statistics" the matrices function gives a number of options. The within-groups correlation or within-group covariance matrix can be requested. The resulting pooled-within correlation or covariance matrix will be printed in the output and can be used as an input in factor analysis syntax statements.

($d_{ij} = \sqrt{2 - 2r_{ij}}$). If the data cannot be treated at the interval level, there exist a range of other dissimilarity measures (see Borg & Groenen, 2005) that can be computed per cultural group and averaged. PCA and EFA are executed on the pooled-within correlation matrix. CFA is computed on the pooled-within variance–covariance matrix, with the number of observations equaling N – G (total number of observations minus the number of cultural groups).

Step 1.2. Investigation of the Average Individual-Level Structure

To be able to differentiate between a lack of validity of the presumed internal structure from a lack of internal structure equivalence, it is important to investigate the average internal structure. Often clear hypotheses exist about the "average" internal structure, because worldwide cross-cultural research builds on extensive research within one or a few cultural groups that have already supported theorizing and scale construction. Using MDS, congruence with the a priori expected structure can be investigated by applying generalized Procrustes analysis (GPA, see Chapter 7). With PCA and EFA, an orthogonal Procrustes rotation toward the a priori expected structure can be executed. The core feature of CFA is its confirmatory nature. The a priori expected structure must be specified to run the analysis. This means that it will often be investigated how well the "average" structure confirms the a priori theoretical expectations and previous findings (e.g., Leung & Bond, 2004). It is also possible to investigate the average internal structure in an exploratory fashion. Whichever approach is taken, the average internal structure should fit well and be well interpretable. Only then can the internal structure be used as a point for reference to investigate both the internal structure equivalence during the first step and the internal structure isomorphism during the second step. If no well-fitting and well-interpretable internal structure can be identified, the process stops. Then a central part of evidence for the 'average' validity of the instrument at the individual level is lacking. It means that the internal structure has to be analyzed and further explored in its own right within each cultural group.

Step 1.3. Comparing Internal Structure per Cultural Group With the Average Individual-Level Structure

If the average structure fits well and can be meaningfully interpreted, internal structure equivalence can be investigated between the individual-level structure of each specific cultural group and the average individual-level structure.

For MDS, a GPA can be applied for each cultural group with the average internal structure being the target (Barrett, 2005). An alternative approach in MDS is to apply the GPA program of Commandeur (1991). This program first computes a centroid structure across all samples involved, and the sample specific configurations are then rotated, flipped, shrunken or dilated, and transposed to be maximally congruent with the centroid structure. In this approach Steps 1.1 and 1.2 are redundant. The centroid structure functions as a point of reference.[5]

A PCA or EFA is executed on the correlation matrix of each cultural sample with the same number of factors as is found for the average factor structure. These sample-specific internal structures can then be orthogonally Procrustes rotated to the average internal structure. This is conceptually similar and follows the same steps as the pairwise comparisons outlined in Chapter 7.

With CFA, the situation is somewhat more complicated. In a typical multilevel design, there are too many cultural groups[6] to investigate the internal structures at the individual level using multigroup CFA. One possibility is to test the model that fitted the average individual-level association matrix for each cultural group separately. Another strategy is to split the

[5] Still another approach is to apply replicated MDS (RMDS). With RMDS a consensus configuration is directly computed that maximally fits with the observed dissimilarities of each group (e.g., Fontaine, 2003).

[6] Selig, Card, and Little (2008) advise using multilevel CFA if 20 or more cultural groups are involved. The number of cultural groups required for applying a multilevel approach is still a matter of debate. There are simulation studies that would indicate that at least 100 units would be needed at the highest level (Hox & Maas, 2001).

total sample into different subsamples and test with multigroup CFA the internal structure equivalence on each subsample (Selig, Card, & Little, 2008). Still another strategy within a CFA framework is to test the homogeneity of the correlation matrices across the cultural groups (Cheung & Au, 2005). If there is homogeneity across cultural groups, it also means that the same constructs can account for the observed interrelationships with the indicators.

At the end of Step 1, there are three possible outcomes. The first is that the average structure is not well interpretable or that many structural differences exist between the cultural groups (or both). There can be both methodological (e.g., instrument bias) and substantive causes (e.g., cultural construction) for this finding. In any case, further quantitative cross-cultural comparisons are precluded. By default, there is no internal structure isomorphism. This corresponds to the first outcome scenario discussed earlier: no internal structure equivalence and no internal structure isomorphism. The second possible outcome is that internal structure equivalence is observed for all cultural groups involved; then the necessary conditions are met to investigate internal structure isomorphism. In case of nonequivalence of internal structures, Welkenhuysen-Gybels, Van de Vijver, and Cambre (2007) and Cheung and Chan (2005) suggested strategies to find subsets of cultural groups that share equivalent internal structures. An intermediate result is that internal structure equivalence is only observed for a subset of cultural groups or for a subset of items.

As discussed before, internal structure isomorphism does not necessarily imply full score equivalence. If the aim is to compare specific cultural groups, or individuals from specific cultural groups, metric and full score equivalence have to be further investigated for those groups.

Step 2. Investigation of the Internal Structure Isomorphism

The second step is focused on the comparability of the internal structure between the individual and the cultural level. This second step falls apart into three concrete substeps: (a) estimating the size of the cultural variation, (b) computing the cultural-level association matrix, and (c) computing and comparing the cultural-level structure with the individual-level structure (see Figure 10.2 for an overview of these steps).

Step 2.1. Estimation of the Cultural-Level Variability

A necessary condition for discovering a cultural-level structure is that the indicators differ substantially between cultural groups. Only if there is

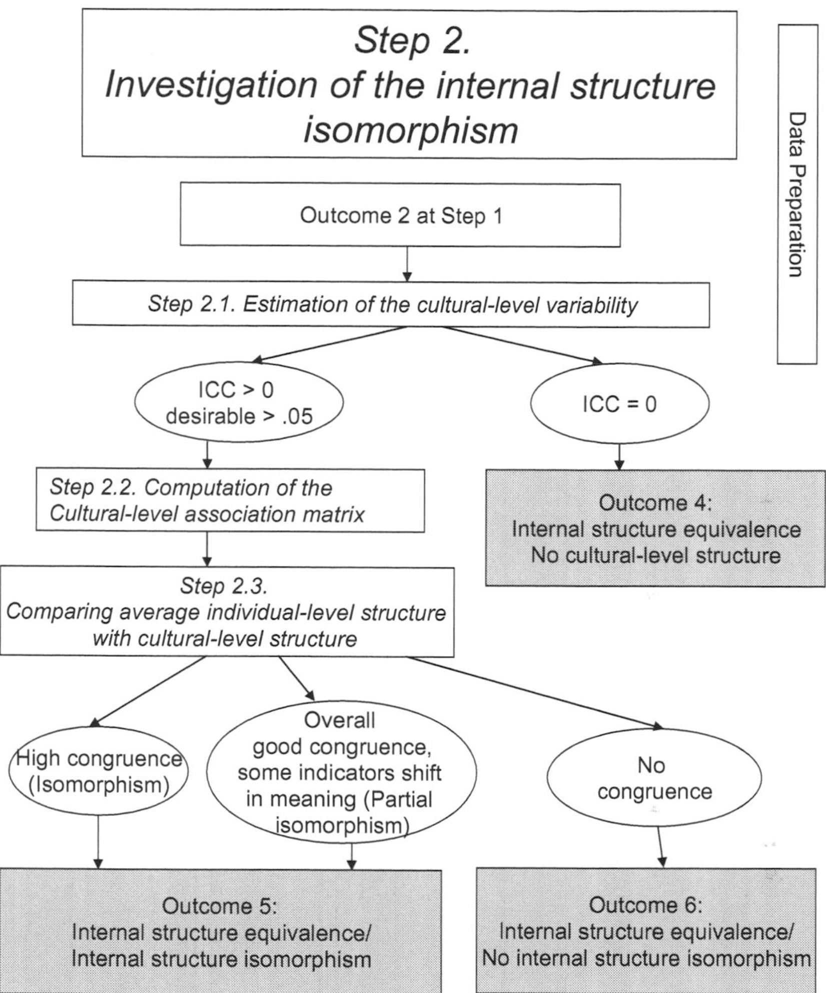

Figure 10.2. Step 2. Investigating the internal structure isomorphism.

sufficient cross-cultural variation does it make sense to investigate how this variation is structured. The size of the between-culture variation can be computed by intraclass correlations (ICC[1]) – for instance, by applying a one-way analysis of variance (ANOVA) with cultural group as a random variable (e.g.,, van de Vijver & Poortinga, 2002) or by computing a random coefficient model in HLM or Mplus.[7] As a rule of thumb, it has been

[7] There may be slight differences in the estimated variance component. The random coefficient model employed in HLM and Mplus sets negative within-group variance to zero,

proposed that culture should at least account for 5% of the variance of an indicator (e.g., Muthen, 1994; van de Vijver & Poortinga, 2002). If the intra-class correlation is 0 or close to 0, it means that a higher level does not exist and that all data can be analyzed as coming from the same population. Thus, if there are no cultural differences on the indicators, the issue of internal structure isomorphism becomes irrelevant.

Step 2.2. Computation of the Cultural Level Association Matrix

It is common practice to compute the cultural-level association matrix on the basis of the average item scores per cultural group (e.g., Bond et al. 2004; Schwartz 1994). This practice can be problematic for two reasons. First, the average item scores are based on a sample from each cultural group. They contain information not only about the cultural group but also about the specific individuals who have been included in the sample. They thus contain information about both the cultural and the individual level. However, the larger the sample size per cultural group, the more limited the impact of the individual-level variation on the mean item scores. Because sample sizes of 100 and more participants per cultural group are common in cross-cultural psychological research, the bias due to individual-level variation is limited. Second, by using average item scores, each cultural group is weighted equally. This is only adequate in a balanced design, with the same sample size per cultural group. In the case of unbalanced designs, the cultural-level association matrix can be computed on the basis of the disaggregated means[8] (Hox, 2002).

For MDS, the dissimilarity matrix can be computed as the Euclidian distances between the standardized mean scores at a cultural level (or by any other dissimilarity measure that contains ordinal information about the associations between items). For EFA or PCA, the correlation matrix can be computed on the average item scores per cultural group (in case of a balanced design) or on the basis of the disaggregated means (in the case of an unbalanced design). For CFA, a *scaled* variance–covariance matrix[9] at

whereas such values are permissible in random-effects ANOVA computations. Therefore, the range of ICC(1) ranges between −1 and 1 for ANOVA models but between 0 and 1 for random coefficient models. On the basis of the authors' experience, the differences are minor in most cross-cultural data sets. For example, the correlation between ICC values obtained through ANOVA and HLM across the 57 values included in the Schwartz Value Survey in student and teacher samples in more than 70 countries was .98. See Bliese (2000) for more details and interpretation of negative ICC(1) coefficients.

[8] This means that each score of each individual is replaced by its sample-specific mean.

[9] The scaled variance–covariance matrix is a weighted variance–covariance matrix based on the sample size(s) of the cultural groups.

the cultural level has to be computed. In the case of a balanced design, this scaled variance–covariance matrix can be computed by the major statistical packages on the basis of the disaggregated means. First, the correlations are computed. Then the standard deviations are computed. These standard deviations have to be corrected by multiplying them by $\sqrt{(N-1/G-1)}$ with N the total sample size and G the number of cultural groups. Another possibility is to have it computed by a freeware program, such as SPLIT2 (Hox, 1994). Also the major programs for structural equation modeling, such as LISREL, EQS, and Mplus, can generate the scaled variance–covariance matrix.

Step 2.3. Comparing Average Individual-Level Structure With Cultural-Level Structure

In the last step, the internal structure is computed on the basis of the cultural-level association matrix and compared with the average individual-level internal structure. Similarity of structure can be determined using similar procedures as discussed in Chapter 7.

In MDS, a geometrical representation is computed with the same dimensionality as the individual-level structure. By means of GPA, the congruence between the individual- and the cultural-level structure is investigated.

With EFA or PCA, a factor structure is computed with the same number of factors as at the individual level. The cultural-level factor structure is then orthogonally Procrustes rotated toward the individual-level structure.

With CFA, a multigroup CFA is computed with the individual level being treated as one group and the cultural level as another group. In the multigroup CFA, it is then tested whether the same factor model (configural invariance) holds for both levels of analysis.

Both within the domains of PCA or EFA and of CFA mathematical models and statistical software have been developed that allow joint investigation of the structure at the individual and cultural level. With these methods, it is not needed to compute separately the individual- and cultural-level association matrices. Multilevel principal component (MLCA) models that compute both the individual-level structure and the cultural-level structure within one model are developed (Timmerman, 2006). With this new model, no separate individual- and cultural-level correlation matrices have to be computed. Kuppens, Ceulemans, Timmerman, Diener, and Kim-Prieto (2006) demonstrated with MLCA that the two dimensions of positive and negative affect can be identified both at the individual and cultural levels. Moreover, with the recent versions of the major SEM programs such as LISREL, EQS, and Mplus, it is no longer necessary to compute separately an individual-level (pooled-within) and a scaled cultural-level (between) variance–covariance matrix and then run a multigroup CFA. They can jointly test the individual-level and the cultural-level models. These software developments offer other strategies to construct multilevel models than the one proposed here (see Selig, Card, & Little, 2008).

There are three possible outcomes of the research process: nonisomorphism, isomorphism, and partial isomorphism. If the structures are different (estimates of internal structure similarity between levels do not meet the a priori specified congruence or fit criteria), there is nonisomorphism. Nonisomorphism has far-reaching consequences for cross-cultural research. It implies that it is meaningless to compare the cultural groups on the individual-level constructs. It also implies that it makes no sense to test differences between specific cultural groups by statistically testing the average differences between individuals of those cultural groups. It implies that both levels must be studied in their own respect. If the structures are congruent, there is isomorphism: The psychological constructs apply to both the individual and cultural levels. It is also possible that some of the indicators that work well at the individual level do not work well at the cultural level (or vice versa), and then there is a case for partial isomorphism. It means that the underlying dimensions are the same at both levels but that there are individual indicators that shift in meaning. Once there is partial isomorphism, the same constructs and (possibly reduced) scales can be used both at the individual and cultural level.

Internal structure isomorphism, however, does not justify the comparability of specific cultural groups on the individual-level factors. The equivalence of the cultural-level structure does not exclude the presence of random measurement errors at the cultural level. These random measurement errors at the cultural level (for instance, due to small shifts of the intensity the translated words are referring to), will systematically bias the scores of individuals within cultural groups and bias the comparison between specific cultural groups. Thus, even if high congruence between the cultural- and individual-level structures is observed, checking for metric and full score equivalence at the individual level remains necessary to compare specific cultural groups.

Three Examples From the Research Literature

To illustrate the issues and data analytic steps that have been proposed in the present chapter, we briefly present three recent studies from the cross-cultural literature that focused on internal structure isomorphism. The first study revisited the claim of Schwartz (1994) that the value structure is different between the individual and cultural levels of analysis using multidimensional scaling techniques (Fischer, Vauclair, Fontaine, & Schwartz, 2010). The second study investigates with exploratory factor analysis whether subjective well-being can be differentiated from positive and negative affect at the cultural level in the same way as has been found at the individual level (Lucas & Diener, 2008). The third study tests with CFA whether the internal structure of social axioms indeed differs between the individual and cultural levels as was observed using exploratory factor analysis (Cheung, Leung, & Au, 2006).

Internal Structure Equivalence and Internal Structure Isomorphism of Values With Multidimensional Scaling

As we have already discussed, according to Schwartz's theorizing, the value domain is organized differently at the individual and cultural levels of analysis (Schwartz, 1992, 1994). In the past, however, the lack of internal structure isomorphism was never quantitatively investigated. Moreover, it was not investigated whether the differences in structure could be attributed to a few items that shift in meaning between both levels of analysis.

Fischer et al. (2010) first started with computing the pooled-within culture correlation matrix, which was transformed into Euclidean distances (Step 1.1). Subsequently, they computed a two-dimensional geometrical representation of the individual-level value domain (Step 1.2). The resulting structure confirmed the theoretical expectations with respect to the individual level – namely, 10 quasi-circularly ordered regions could be identified, which represented the 10 value types. The congruence between the culture-specific value structures and the average individual-level value structure (Step 1.3) was investigated in a previous study (Fontaine, Poortinga, Delbeke, & Schwartz, 2008). On one hand, Fontaine et al. (2008) observed that random sampling fluctuation formed a major cause for the observed differences in the internal structure between cultural groups. On the other hand, they discovered the systematic tendency that the opposition of security and power values (protection values) with universalism and self-direction values (growth values) was more pronounced in more societally developed countries (e.g., higher in gross domestic product, more industrialization). Fontaine et al. (2008) also demonstrated by means of split half procedures that the average individual-level value structure was highly robust and could be used as a point of reference for comparisons of internal structures.

Subsequently, the value items demonstrated sufficient cross-cultural variability to justify the investigation of internal structure isomorphism

(Step 2.1). On average, the intraclass correlation coefficient was .12 in the teacher samples and .11 in the student samples. The cultural-level dissimilarities were computed as Euclidian distances between the average standardized value scores (Step 2.2). A two-dimensional configuration was then computed at the cultural level, and a GPA (Commandeur, 1991) was applied to both the average individual-level and cultural-level structures (Step 2.3). After GPA, the coordinates on the first dimension of the individual- and cultural-level structures correlated at .79 and .65 for student and teacher samples, respectively. The coordinates on the second dimension of the individual- and cultural-level structures correlated at .76, and .68 for student and teacher samples, respectively. These congruence measures clearly fell below the criterion of .85, which indicated differences in structure.

Finally, Fischer et al. (2010) investigated to what extent the differences between the individual and the cultural levels could be attributed to a few value items that shift in meaning between both levels. Removing items did not lead to acceptable levels of congruence for either the teacher and the student samples. The results from Fischer et al. (2010) thus further supported the idea that there are structural differences in the value domain between the individual and the cultural level.

Internal Structure Equivalence and Internal Structure Isomorphism of Well-Being With Exploratory Factor Analysis or Principal Component Analysis

In the literature, it has been suggested that subjective well-being, as, for instance, measured with the Satisfaction With Life Scale (SWLS), has a different meaning between the individual and the cultural level. Kahneman and Riis (2005) have claimed that although it measures happiness at an individual level, it measures general culturally determined positivity at the cultural level. This thus implies a shift in meaning from the individual to the cultural level. Lucas and Diener (2008) investigated this hypothesis with a large-scale data set on life satisfaction, negative affect, and positive affect from 40 nations. It was found in earlier research that these three constructs are clearly differentiated at the individual level. However, if culturally determined positivity would account for the scores at the cultural level, not three but one dimensions should be found at the cultural level.

A pooled-within culture correlation matrix was computed across the 40 countries (Step 1.1). Then an exploratory factor analysis with varimax rotation was applied (Step 1.2.) At an individual level, the expected three-factorial structure of life satisfaction, positive affect, and negative affect clearly emerged. Subsequently, the factor structure from each sample was orthogonally Procrustes rotated toward the average individual-level structure (Step 1.3). For most countries, the congruence measures exceeded .90 or even .95. This finding supports the internal structure equivalence.

The individual items to measure life satisfaction, negative affect, and positive affect varied sufficiently between cultural groups (Step 2.1). The intraclass correlation coefficient ranged from .06 to .13. The between-culture correlation matrix was computed by means of Mplus (Muthén & Muthén, 2007; (Step 2.2). Exploratory factor analysis on the between-culture correlation matrix again revealed three factors that were highly congruent between the individual and the cultural levels (congruence measures exceeding .90; Step 2.3). Thus, no evidence was found for a general positivity factor at the cultural level. On the contrary, strong evidence was found for internal structure isomorphism.

Internal Structure Equivalence and Internal Structure Isomorphism of Social Axioms With Confirmatory Factor Analysis

Social axioms have been defined as general beliefs that help people make sense of their environment and guide the course of their actions (Leung & Bond, 2008). In a first study, Leung et al. (2002) developed a social axiom instrument on the basis of extensive literature study and qualitative research in Hong Kong and Venezuela. Subsequently, they applied the instrument in five countries, and identified a five-factorial structure, consisting of social cynicism, social complexity, reward for application, religiosity, and fate control. The research was then extended to 40 cultural groups. Leung and Bond (2004) first investigated and identified internal structural equivalence by investigating the average individual-level internal structure and then rotating the culture-specific individual-level structures toward the average individual-level structure. Bond et al. (2004) investigated separately the cultural-level internal structure on the basis of the average scores per cultural group. At the cultural level, they could only identify two factors, which they labeled *societal cynicism* and *dynamic externality*. The items that loaded on the social cynicism factor at the individual level also loaded on the societal cynicism factor at the cultural level. Dynamic externality, however, is characterized by items from the other four individual-level factors – namely social complexity, reward for application, religiosity, and fate control.

Cheung et al. (2006) revisited these data and applied a CFA approach to investigate in a more rigorous way whether the structures indeed differ from one another between the two levels of analyses. Rather than investigating internal structure equivalence, these authors statistically tested the homogeneity of the correlation matrices. If the correlation matrices were homogeneous, the same internal structure could be applied to all correlation matrices of these groups (alternative for Step 1).

With an average intraclass correlation of .12, social axioms demonstrated sufficient cultural differences to justify also an investigation of the cultural-level structure. Rather than separately computing the individual- and the cultural-level structures and apply CFA on each variance–covariance matrix separately, they jointly analyzed the individual- and cultural-level social axioms with Mplus (alternative for Step 2). The authors a priori specified three models, one model with five factors at both the individual and the cultural level, one model with five factors at the individual and two at the cultural level, and one model with five factors at the individual and five first-order and two higher order factors at the cultural level. The results confirmed by and large the results from the previous analyses: The first model did not fit the data well, and the second and the third model fit the data about equally well. The analyses confirmed that five factors can represent the individual-level structure and that the same model is not adequate for representing the cultural-level structure. The investigation of the nomological network was used to elucidate the meaning of the differences in factor structure between the two levels. According to Leung and Bond (2008), a psycho-logic applies at the individual level and an eco-logic at the cultural level. At the individual level, social axioms would be functional for the development of competence in social interaction and problem solving and guide persons in their choices. At a cultural level, they would be functionally related to societal poverty (dynamic externality), and economical, political, and social turmoil (societal cynicism).

CONCLUSIONS

The issues raised by internal structure isomorphism are at the heart of the cross-cultural enterprise. As indicated at the beginning of this chapter, quantitative comparisons of cultural groups on the basis of psychological assessment instruments are common practice in cross-cultural psychology.

The application of a multilevel approach has elucidated that such practice implies the ascription of psychological characteristics to cultural groups. As has been demonstrated by statistical multilevel modeling, however, the individual and the cultural level are statistically independent. Thus, the ascription of individual characteristics to culture, or the ascription of cultural characteristics to individuals, cannot be merely assumed. They are key hypotheses of the cross-cultural enterprise that must be substantiated empirically. Both the increasing opportunities to investigate a random sample of cultural groups across the world and the developments in statistical and methodological multilevel theorizing make it feasible to test these key assumptions empirically. Therefore, the investigation of internal structural isomorphism will contribute substantially to future developments in the field of cross-cultural psychology.

REFERENCES

Barrett, P. (2005). Orthosim 2 [statistical software]. Retrieved September 9, 2009, from http://www.pbarrett.net/orthosim2.htm.

Bliese, P. D. (2000). Within-group agreement, non-independence and reliability: Implications for data aggregation and analyses. In J. K. Klein & S. W. J. Kozlowski (Eds.), *Multilevel theory, research and methods in organizations. Foundations, extensions, and new directions* (pp. 349–381). San Francisco: Josey Bass.

Bliese, P. D., Chan, D., & Ployhart, R. E. (2007). Multilevel methods: Future directions in measurement, longitudinal analyses and nonnormal outcomes. *Organizational Research Methods, 10*, 551–563.

Bond, M. H., Leung, K., Au, A., Tong, K. K., Reimel de Carrasquel, S., Murakami, F., et al. (2004). Culture-level dimensions of social axioms and their societal correlates across 41 cultures. *Journal of Cross-Cultural Psychology, 35*, 548–570.

Borg, I., & Groenen, P. (2005). *Modern multidimensional scaling: Theory and applications* (2nd ed.). New York: Springer.

Chen, G., Bliese, P. D., & Mathieu, J. E. (2005). Conceptual framework and statistical procedures for delineating and testing multilevel theories of homology. *Organizational Research Methods, 8*, 375–409.

Cheung, M. W. L., & Au, K. (2005). Applications of multilevel structural equation modeling to cross-cultural research. *Structural Equation Modeling, 12*, 589–619.

Cheung, M. W.-L., & Chan, W. (2005). Classifying correlation matrices into relatively homogeneous subgroups: A cluster analytic approach. *Educational and Psychological Measurement, 65*, 954–979.

Cheung, M. W. L., Leung, K., & Au, K. (2006). Evaluating multilevel models in cross-cultural research: An illustration with social axioms. *Journal of Cross-Cultural Psychology, 37*, 522–541.

Commandeur, J. J. F. (1991). *Matching configurations.* Leiden, the Netherlands: DSWO Press. Retrieved on May 20, 2010, from http://three-mode.leidenuniv.nl/bibliogr/commandeurjjf_thesis/front.pdf.

Doi, T. (1971). *Amae no kozo [The anatomy of dependence]*. Tokyo: Kobundo.

Fischer, R., Vauclair, C-M., Fontaine, J. R. J., & Schwartz, S. H. (2010). Are individual-level and country-level value structures different? Testing Hofstede's legacy with the Schwartz Value Survey. *Journal of Cross-Cultural Psychology, 41*, 135–151.

Fontaine, J. R. J. (2003). Multidimensional scaling. In J. Harkness, F. J. R. Van de Vijver, & P. Ph. Mohler (Eds.), *Cross-cultural survey methods* (pp. 235–246). Hoboken, NJ: Wiley.

Fontaine, J. R. J. (2005). *Equivalence.* In K. Kempf-Leonard (Ed.), *Encyclopedia of social measurement* (Vol. 1, pp. 803–813). New York: Academic Press.

Fontaine, J. R. J. (2008). Traditional and multilevel approaches in cross-cultural research: An integration of methodological frameworks. In F. R. J. Van de Vijver, D. A. Van Hemert, & Y. H. Poortinga (Eds.), *Multilevel analysis of individuals and cultures* (pp. 65–92). New York: Erlbaum.

Fontaine, J. R. J., Poortinga, Y. H., Delbeke, L., & Schwartz, S. H. (2008). Structural equivalence of the values domain across cultures: Distinguishing sampling fluctuations from meaningful variation. *Journal of Cross-Cultural Psychology, 39,* 345–365.

Goldstein, H. (2003). *Multilevel statistical models* (3rd ed.). London: Arnold.

Hofstede, G. (1980). *Culture's consequences: International differences in work-related values.* Beverly Hills, CA: Sage.

Hox, J. J. (2002). *Multilevel analysis: Techniques and applications.* Mahwah, NJ: Erlbaum.

Hox, J. J. (1994, revised 2000). *Split2* [computer software]. Retrieved on May 20, 2010, from http://www.geocities.com/joophox/papers/papers.htm.

Hox, J. J., & Maas, C. J. M. (2001). The accuracy of multilevel structural equitation modeling with pseudobalanced groups and small samples. *Structural Equation Modeling, 8,* 157–174.

Kahneman, D., & Riis, J. (2005). Living and thinking about it: Two perspectives on life. In F. A. Huppert, N. Baylis, & B. Keverne (Eds.), *The science of well-being* (pp. 285–304). New York: Oxford University Press.

Kuppens, P., Ceulemans, E., Timmerman, M. E., Diener, E., & Kim-Prieto, C. (2006). Universal intracultural and intercultural dimensions of the recalled frequency of emotional experience. *Journal of Cross-Cultural Psychology, 37,* 491–515.

Leung, K., & Bond, M. H. (1989). On the empirical identification of dimensions for cross-cultural comparisons. *Journal of Cross-Cultural Psychology, 20,* 133–151.

Leung, K., & Bond, M. H. (2004). Social axioms: A model for social beliefs in multi-cultural perspective. *Advances in Experimental Social Psychology, 36,* 119–197.

Leung, K., & Bond, M. H. (2008). Psycho-logic and eco-logic: Insights from social axiom dimensions. In F. R. J. Van de Vijver, D. A. Van Hemert, & Y. H. Poortinga (Eds.), *Multilevel analysis of individuals and cultures* (pp. 199–221). New York: Erlbaum.

Leung, K., Bond, M. H., Reimel de Carrasquel, S., Munoz, C., Hernandez, M., Murakami, F., et al. (2002). Social axioms: The search for universal dimensions of general beliefs about how the world functions. *Journal of Cross-Cultural Psychology, 33,* 286–302.

Lucas, R. E., & Diener, E. (2008). Can we learn about national differences in happiness from individual responses? A multilevel approach. In F. R. J. Van de Vijver, D. A. Van Hemert, & Y. H. Poortinga (Eds.), *Multilevel analysis of individuals and cultures* (pp. 65–92). New York: Erlbaum.

McCrae, R. R., & Terracciano, A. (2008). The five-factor model and its correlates in individuals and cultures. In F. R. J. Van de Vijver, D. A. Van Hemert, & Y. H. Poortinga (Eds.), *Multilevel analysis of individuals and cultures* (pp. 249–283). New York: Erlbaum.

McCrae, R. R., Terracciano, A., & 78 Members of the Personality Profiles of Cultures Project. (2005). Universal features of personality traits from the observer's perspective: Data from 50 cultures. *Journal of Personality and Social Psychology, 88*, 3, 547–561.

McCrae, R. R., Zonderman, A. B., Costa, P. T., Jr., Bond, M. H., & Paunonen, S. V. (1996). Evaluating replicability of factors in the Revised NEO Personality Inventory: Confirmatory factor analysis versus Procrustes rotation. *Journal of Personality and Social Psychology, 70*, 552–566.

Messick, S. (1989). Validity. In R. L. Linn (Ed.), *Educational measurement* (3rd ed., pp. 13–103). New York: Macmillan.

Miller, J. G. (1997). Theoretical issues in cultural psychology. In J. W. Berry, Y. H. Poortinga, & J. Pandey (Eds.), *Handbook of cross-cultural psychology: Vol. I. Theory and method* (2nd ed., pp. 85–128). Boston: Allyn & Bacon.

Muthén, B. O. (1994). Multilevel covariance structure analysis. *Sociological Methods and Research, 22*, 376–398.

Muthén, L. K., & Muthén, B. O. (1998–2007). *Mplus statistical software.* Los Angeles: Muthén & Muthén.

Poortinga, Y. H. (1989). Equivalence in cross-cultural data: An overview of basic issues. *International Journal of Psychology, 24*, 737–756.

Raudenbuch, S. W., & Bryk, A. S. (2002). *Hierarchical linear models: Applications and data analysis methods* (2nd ed.). Thousand Oaks, CA: Sage.

Schwartz, S. H. (1992). Universals in the content and structure of values: Theoretical advances and empirical tests in 20 countries. *Advances in Experimental Social Psychology, 25*, 1–65.

Schwartz, S. H. (1994). Beyond individualism–collectivism: New cultural dimensions of values. In U. Kim, H. C. Triandis, C. Kagitcibasi, S. C. Choi, & G. Yoon (Eds.), *Individualism and collectivism: Theory, method and applications* (pp. 85–119). Thousand Oaks, CA: Sage.

Schwartz, S. H. (2006). A theory of cultural value orientations: Explication and applications. *Comparative Sociology, 5*, 136–182.

Selig, J. P., Card, N. A., & Little, T. D. (2008). Latent variable structural equation modeling in cross-cultural research: Multigroup and multilevel approaches. In F. J. R. Van de Vijver, D. A. Van Hemert, & Y. H. Poortinga (Eds.), *Individuals and cultures in multilevel analysis* (pp. 93–120). New York: Erlbaum.

Timmerman, M. E. (2006). Multilevel component analysis. *British Journal of Mathematical and Statistical Psychology, 59*, 301–320.

Van de Vijver, F. J. R., & Leung, K. (1997a). *Methods and data analysis for cross-cultural research.* London: Sage.

Van de Vijver, F. J. R., & Leung, K. (1997b). Methods and data analysis of comparative research. In J. W. Berry, Y. H. Poortinga, & J. Pandey (Eds.), *Handbook of cross-cultural psychology: Theory and method* (Vol. 1, pp. 85–128). Needham Heights, MA: Allyn & Bacon.

Van de Vijver, F. J. R., & Poortinga, Y. H. (2002). Internal structure equivalence in multilevel research. *Journal of Cross-Cultural Psychology, 33*, 141–156.

Van de Vijver, F. J. R., Van Hemert, D. A., & Poortinga, Y. H. (2008). Conceptual issues in multilevel models. In F. R. J. Van de Vijver, D. A. Van Hemert, & Y. H. Poortinga (Eds.), *Multilevel analysis of individuals and cultures* (pp. 3–26). New York: Erlbaum.

Welkenhuysen-Gybels, J., Van de Vijver, F. J. R., & Cambre, B. (2007). A comparison of method for the evaluation of construct equivalence in a multigroup setting. In G. Loosveldt, M. Swyngedouw, & B. Cambre (Eds.), *Measuring meaningful data in social research* (pp. 357–371). Leuven/Voorburg: Acco.

Widaman, K. F. (2000). Testing cross-group and cross-time constraints on parameters using the general linear model. In T. D. Little, K. U. Schnabel, & J. Baumert (Eds.), *Modeling longitudinal and multilevel data: Practical issues, applied approaches and specific examples* (pp. 163–186). Mahwah, NJ: Erlbaum.

11

Multilevel Modeling and Cross-Cultural Research

JOHN B. NEZLEK

Cross-cultural psychologists, and other scholars who are interested in the joint effects of cultural and individual-level constructs, often collect data and are interested in hypotheses that involve multiple levels of analysis simultaneously. For example, in cross-cultural research, it is not uncommon to collect data from numerous individuals in numerous countries (or cultures).[1] Such data structures are frequently referred to as *multilevel* or *hierarchically nested*, or simply *nested* data structures because observations at one level of analysis (e.g., individuals) are nested within observations at another (e.g., culture). Within a multilevel framework, questions of interest could be couched in terms of cultural differences in means of individual-level measures such as *Life Satisfaction*, within-culture relationships between individual-level measures such as *Life Satisfaction* and *Individualism*, and between-cultural differences in such within-culture relationships.

When analyzing such nested data structures, the possibility that relationships among constructs can vary across levels of analysis must be taken into account. That is, relationships between two variables at the between-country level (e.g., relationships among country-level aggregates, sometimes referred to as *ecological correlations*) may or may not be the same as the relationships between these two variables within countries (e.g., individual-level correlations). In fact, relationships at the two levels of analysis are mathematically independent (e.g., Nezlek, 2001), and it is inappropriate to draw conclusions about within-culture relationships from between-culture analyses. This inappropriateness is highlighted by the possibility that within-country (i.e., individual-level) relationships may vary across countries, undermining the validity of any estimate of "the"

[1] In this chapter, the terms *country* and *culture* are used interchangeably to denote a meaningful unit of analysis. For modeling purposes, the distinctions between country and culture are unimportant, although such distinctions can be critical substantively.

individual-level relationship, simply because there may not be a single, uniform individual-level relationship.

Some of these possibilities are illustrated in Tables 11.1 through 11.4. Each of these examples assumes a study in which *Life Satisfaction* and *Individualism* were measured for five people in each of three countries. For the data in Table 11.1, the relationship between *Satisfaction* and *Individualism* is positive in each of the three countries. As one goes up, the other goes up. In contrast, the relationship between country-level means is negative. The higher the mean score on *Satisfaction*, the lower the mean score on *Individualism*. In response to the question, "What is the relationship between *Satisfaction* and *Individualism*?" the answer should be: "It depends on the level of analysis in which you are interested." Either positive or negative could be correct.

The other tables demonstrate other possibilities. In Table 11.2, there is a negative relationship between *Satisfaction* and *Individualism* in each of the three countries, whereas at the country level, the relationship is positive. In Table 11.3, there is no relationship in any of the countries because there is no variance for *Individualism* within each country, but the relationship among country-level aggregates is positive. Finally, in Table 11.4, the relationship between *Satisfaction* and *Individualism* is different for all three countries (one positive, one no relationship, and one negative), although the relationship among country-level aggregates is positive.

Obviously, these examples do not exhaust the possible combinations of within- and between-country relationships. The point in presenting them is to illustrate that relationships at different levels of analysis are independent – any type of relationship can exist at one level of analysis simultaneously with any type of relationship at another. Moreover, as shown in Table 11.4, it is possible that within-country relationships vary across countries.

A consensus has emerged that such multilevel, nested data structures should be analyzed with what are referred to as *multilevel random coefficient models* (MRCM), sometimes referred to as MLM (multilevel modeling). In this chapter, I provide a brief review of analytic strategies for multilevel analyses, including a rationale for using MRCM and a brief discussion of the shortcomings of other approaches, typically some type of ordinary least squares analysis (OLS). I also provide guidelines for conducting and interpreting MRCM analyses, for reporting results, and for designing studies, as well as a discussion of the limitations of MRCM. That is, there may be occasions when it is conceptually desirable to use MRCM, but it is not practical or appropriate given the data at hand. General introductions to MRCM can be found in Kreft and de Leeuw (1998), Raudenbush and Bryk (2002), and Snijders and Bosker (1999).

Table 11.1. *Relationships: Positive at within-country level and negative at between-country level*

	Country 1		Country 2		Country 3	
	Satisfaction	Individual	Satisfaction	Individual	Satisfaction	Individual
	6	11	9	9	11	6
	7	12	10	10	12	7
	8	13	11	11	13	8
	9	14	12	12	14	9
	10	15	13	13	15	10
Mean	8	13	11	11	13	8

Table 11.2. *Relationships: Negative at within-country level and positive at between-country level*

	Country 1		Country 2		Country 3	
	Satisfaction	Individual	Satisfaction	Individual	Satisfaction	Individual
	1	8	9	9	9	18
	2	7	10	10	10	17
	3	6	11	11	11	16
	4	5	12	12	12	15
	5	4	13	13	13	14
Mean	3	6	11	11	11	16

Table 11.3. *Relationships: None at within-country level and positive at between-country level*

	Country 1		Country 2		Country 3	
	Satisfaction	Individual	Satisfaction	Individual	Satisfaction	Individual
	1	8	4	10	9	15
	2	8	5	10	10	15
	3	8	6	10	11	15
	4	8	7	10	12	15
	5	8	8	10	13	15
Mean	3	8	6	10	11	15

Table 11.4. *Relationships: Varying at within-country level and positive at between-country level*

	Country 1		Country 2		Country 3	
	Satisfaction	Individual	Satisfaction	Individual	Satisfaction	Individual
	1	10	4	10	9	13
	2	9	5	10	10	14
	3	8	6	10	11	15
	4	7	7	10	12	16
	5	6	8	10	13	17
Mean	3	8	6	10	11	15

ORDINARY LEAST SQUARES ANALYSES OF MULTILEVEL DATA STRUCTURES

Multilevel data structures have been analyzed with various types of analyses other than MRCM, and before describing MRCM, it will be useful to discuss these analyses and their shortcomings. Such analyses generally fall into one of two categories, *aggregation* and *disaggregation* procedures, and they generally rely on some type of OLS analysis.

Aggregation analyses were described briefly in the previous section. In aggregation analyses of a cross-cultural data set, country-level summary statistics are calculated and then analyzed. For example, mean *Life Satisfaction* and mean *Individualism* are calculated for each country and then correlated (ecological correlations). Conceptually, as discussed earlier, relationships between such aggregates cannot be assumed to describe relationships at the person level. Relationships between such aggregates are mathematically independent of relationships at the person level, and person-level relationships may vary across countries.

Moreover, unless adjustments are made to reflect differences across samples in terms of size and consistency, means based on aggregates may vary in terms of their reliability. For example, means based on larger samples will tend to be more accurate (representative) than means based on smaller samples. Similarly, the representativeness of a mean can vary as a function of the variance of a set of observations. For example, assume two sets of five observations each: 1, 1, 5, 9, 9 and 4, 4, 5, 6, 6. For both sets of observations, the mean is 5, but clearly 5 represents the second set of observations better than it does the first set. As explained subsequently, such factors are taken into account in MRCM analyses.[2]

In disaggregation analyses, analyses are performed at the level of the individual person, usually with some type of OLS regression. In such analyses, country-level variables are often included in individual-level analyses. For example, to examine relationships between a country-level variable (e.g., *Modernization* perhaps defined in terms of the state of a country's infrastructure) and an individual-level variable (e.g., *Life Satisfaction*), the individuals in each country are assigned the modernization score for their country, and a correlation between *Life Satisfaction* and *Modernization* is

[2] It is important to keep in mind that for constructs that exist primarily or solely at the country level, such as form of government and geographic characteristics, analyses at the country level are perfectly appropriate. There are observations at only one level of analysis – the country – and so multilevel analyses are not appropriate.

calculated. Such analyses are fundamentally flawed because there can be no purely individual-level relationship between *Modernization* and *Life Satisfaction.* By definition, *Modernization* exists at only the country level, and any analysis that estimates a relationship between *Modernization* and *Life Satisfaction* that does not take this into account confounds the two levels of analysis – for example, estimates of individual-level relationships – are confounded by country-level differences. An apparent solution to this problem is to calculate a mean *Life Satisfaction* score for each country and then correlate these means with *Modernization.* As noted earlier, however, such analyses cannot be used to estimate individual-level relationships.

Relationships between two variables that truly exist at the individual level (e.g., *Life Satisfaction* and *Individualism*) have also been analyzed with disaggregation analyses. In such analyses, persons are the units of analysis, and country-level differences in scores are partialled out through the use of $n - 1$ dummy-coded independent variables where n represents the number of countries, and relationships between *Life Satisfaction* and *Individualism* are examined. Such analyses are sometimes referred to as least squares dummy variable (LSDV) analyses. One of the major shortcomings of such analyses is that they assume that the relationship between variables at one level of analysis (e.g., between *Life Satisfaction* and *Individualism*) is identical across units at the other level of analysis (e.g., countries). The similarity of these relationships is something that needs to be tested, not assumed.

Advocates of the LSDV approach claim that differences in relationships can be examined by including interaction terms between predictors and the dummy variables; however, such analyses pose both practical and technical (statistical) problems. Practically speaking, the analyses are cumbersome. For example, a study across 25 countries with two predictors would require regression analyses with 72 independent variables, and determining which countries have similar relationships can be difficult, if not impossible. Technically, and more important, such analyses do not conceptualize error properly. In a study such as the hypothetical example I have been discussing, there are two sources of error – the error associated with sampling individuals in each country and the error associated with sampling countries. A LSDV analysis estimates only one error term, and this error term represents an inappropriate combination of the errors from both levels of analysis. The ability to estimate two error terms simultaneously is an important advantage of MRCM over comparable OLS techniques. Moreover, as explained in the section on fixed and random effects, MRCM analyses separate true and random variability, leading to more accurate significance tests.

Despite the shortcomings of these analyses, there are OLS analyses that can take into account the multilevel nature of a cross-cultural data set in which persons are nested within countries. For example, a researcher could calculate the correlation between two variables within each of the countries in a study and then use this correlation as a dependent measure in an analysis such as an analysis of variance (ANOVA) or regression at the country level. More formally, there is a technique known as *regression by groups* in which a separate regression equation is calculated for each group (i.e., country) in an analysis. The similarity of these equations is then compared with a *F* ratio, much like the *F* ratio that tests the similarity of means in an ANOVA. Nevertheless, these analyses are not as good as a MRCM (i.e., they do not produce estimates of relationships that are as accurate based on Monte Carlo studies). This is because they do not take into account simultaneously the error associated with sampling people within each country and the error associated with sampling countries from the population of countries.

Most researchers are familiar with the error associated with selecting a sample of people. In most studies, aside from questions about the extent to which a sample is similar in important ways (e.g., sex, age, ethnicity) to the population, little importance is placed on the specific people from whom data have been collected. Samples are assumed to be random and representative of the populations from which they were sampled. Moreover, as most researchers know, statistics based on different samples drawn from the same population will be similar, but not identical. For example, the standard error of the mean describes the variance of sample means.

Most researchers are probably not as familiar with issues that arise when a sample of countries is selected and, within each of these countries, the samples of individuals are selected. In most studies, little importance is placed on the specific countries in which data have been collected (aside, perhaps, from questions of representativeness of certain cultures such as the Third World). The assumption is that countries have been sampled from the universe of possible countries. Parameters estimated from one set of countries should be similar to parameters based on another set of countries, although it is not likely that the two sets of coefficients will be identical. That is, there is some error associated with the sampling of countries. For technical reasons that are beyond the scope of this chapter, accounting for both types of sampling errors (the error associated with sampling countries and the error associated with sampling individuals) cannot be done with OLS analyses (i.e., variations of ANOVA and regression); however, this can be done with maximum likelihood procedures, which are the basis of MRCM.

MULTILEVEL RANDOM COEFFICIENT MODELING

The principles underlying MRCM are discussed in this section in terms of the types of two-level data sets that have been discussed so far: persons nested within countries and cultures. It is possible to have more than two levels, but for an introduction and illustrative purposes, two levels will suffice. The present description of MRCM is organized in terms of the three types of research questions in which many cross-cultural psychologists are likely to be interested.

1. How can cultural-level variables explain cross-cultural differences in means of individual-level variables?
2. Controlling for cultural-level differences in means of individual-level variables, what are the within-culture (or individual-level) relationships between individual-level variables?
3. Controlling for cultural-level differences in means, how can cultural-level variables explain differences across cultures in relationships between individual-level variables?

One way to think of MRCM analyses is to consider them as a series of hierarchically nested regression equations in which the coefficients from one level of analysis become the dependent measures at the next level of analysis. In essence, a regression equation is estimated for each unit of analysis (country), and the coefficients from these equations become the dependent variables in regression equations at the next level of analysis. Note that although "two-stage" OLS regression analyses may be conceptually similar in some ways to MRCM, two-stage OLS regression is not the same as MRCM, and the differences in the relationships estimated by the two techniques can be meaningful.

Such differences in estimates of relationships reflect differences in the ways in which parameters are estimated, and the more "irregular" the data are, the more accurate MRCM analyses are compared with OLS analyses. Irregular in this instance refers to the similarity across units of analysis (countries in our case) in terms of the number of observations (i.e., individuals), similarity across countries in the variances of the measures, and most important, similarity across countries of the covariances among measures (i.e., the similarity of individual-level relationships). The greater accuracy of MRCM over OLS analyses has been demonstrated in numerous Monte Carlo studies in which random samples have been taken from populations with known parameters. In such cases, the parameter estimates provided by the MRCM techniques discussed in this chapter are meaningfully closer to the population parameters than the estimates provided by comparable OLS analyses.

Various aspects of conducting MRCM analyses are illustrated through the analyses of a hypothetical data set, presented in the Appendix. Conceptualized as a cross-cultural study, there are 10 countries (Level 2 units) and between 8 and 13 persons in each country (Level 1 units). For each country, *GDP per capita* was measured (values ranging from 8 to 16), and for each person, three measures were taken, *Life Satisfaction* (10–20), *Individualism* (1–10), and *Union Membership*, which was represented in different ways that are discussed later. There are additional variables that are discussed in other sections.

The analytic techniques described in this article are all available in the program HLM (Version 6; Raudenbush, Byrk, Cheong, and Congdon, 2004), and the analyses described in this chapter were conducted using this program. These analyses could have been conducted using other multilevel programs such as MLwiN (Rabash et al., 2000), a multilevel module in LISREL, SAS PROC MIXED (e.g., Singer, 1998), and others. Some of the terms and symbols may vary from program to program, but the terms used here should provide readers with a good introduction. Finally, many of the analytic conventions used by HLM are also used by other programs. That is, when the same models are specified, different programs should give identical results. This article describes results from HLM analyses because HLM is a popular multilevel program. HLM 6 produces two sets of results, one for robust estimates and one for nonrobust estimates. The discussion relies on nonrobust estimates because robust estimates require more Level 2 units than contained in the test data set. In HLM, the results of each analysis indicate whether robust estimates are appropriate.

It is important to keep in mind that in MRCM analyses, two parameters are (or can be) estimated for each coefficient. The first, referred to as a fixed effect, is an estimate of the central tendency (mean) of a coefficient. The questions posed by most cross-cultural psychologists concern tests of fixed effects. For example, on average, is a coefficient, such as the relationship between *Life Satisfaction* and *Individualism*, significantly different from 0? (Note that this does not examine the hypothesis that all coefficients are different from 0 or that all are less or greater than 0.) The second estimated parameter is the random error term associated with a coefficient, and it is also tested. Is the random error for a coefficient significantly different from 0? It is common in the modeling literature to discuss coefficients as random or fixed on the basis of whether the random error term is significant (a random effect) or not significant (a fixed effect). Random error terms are discussed subsequently.

In this chapter, MRCM models and analyses are described using the nomenclature that is fairly standard for multilevel analysis. This includes specific terms (e.g., Level 1 not "lower level") and specific letters (e.g., β not b or B). Although potentially cumbersome at first, the use of these conventions facilitates communication. Multilevel analyses are inherently more complex than many single-level analyses, and the use of different terms and symbols by different authors to refer to the same entities is likely to increase readers' confusion. In standard MRCM nomenclature, for two-level models, Level 1 coefficients are represented with βs (subscripted 0 for the intercept, 1 for the first predictor, 2 for the second, etc.), and Level 2 coefficients are represented with γs. As discussed later, there is a separate Level 2 equation for each Level 1 coefficient.

For pedagogical purposes, in this chapter I follow the lead of Bryk and Raudenbush (1992) and present the equations for each level separately. In fact, in MRCM analyses, all parameters in all equations (including error terms) are estimated simultaneously. Moreover, it is this simultaneity that is part of what distinguishes MRCM from comparable OLS techniques such as two-stage least squares. OLS analyses cannot estimate more than one error term at a time for a single equation.

The first step in any MRCM analysis should be running what is called a null or totally unconditional model. These terms are used because there are no predictors at either level of analysis. Such a model is as follows:

$$\text{Individual, Level 1:}\quad y_{ij} = \beta_{0j} + r_{ij}$$
$$\text{Country, Level 2:}\quad \beta_{0j} = \gamma_{00} + u_{0j}$$

In the Level 1 (individual-level) model, there are i persons for j countries on a variable y. These observations are modeled as a function of the intercept for each country (β_{0j}, the mean of y) and deviations of each person in a country from the country mean (r_{ij}). The variance of r_{ij} is the Level 1 (or person-level or within-country) variance. There are no constraints on the similarity of the sample sizes across the countries. In the Level 2 (country-level) model, the mean of y for each of j countries (β_{0j}) is modeled as a function of the grand mean (γ_{00} – the mean of means) and deviations of each country from the grand mean (u_{0j}). The variance of u_{0j} is the Level 2 (or country-level or between-country) variance. Such models are referred to as unconditional because y is not modeled as a function of another variable at Level 1 or at Level 2.

Although unconditional models typically do not test hypotheses, they can provide useful information. For example, they describe how much of the total variance of y is at each level of analysis. In a two-level model, the total variance is the sum of the variances of r_{ij} and of u_{0j}, and the distribution of the total variance of y suggests the levels at which further analyses might be productive. For example, if all the variance for a measure is at the person level (Level 1), it may be difficult to examine country-level differences (Level 2) in these means. The variance estimates provided by unconditional models also provide baselines that can be used to estimate effect sizes, which are discussed subsequently. The unconditional model of *Life Satisfaction* produced the following results (rounded to two decimals): $\gamma_{00} = 15.04$, Level 1 variance $= 3.05$, Level 2 variance $= 0.65$.

Analyzing Country-Level Differences in Means

A simple extension of the basic unconditional model is adding a predictor at Level 2. For example, a researcher might be interested in the relationship between mean *Life Satisfaction* (y) in a country and a country's per capita gross domestic product (*GDP*). Basically, are people living in more prosperous countries more satisfied with their lives? The equations for such a model are as follows:

$$\text{Level 1:} \quad y_{ij} = \beta_{0j} + r_{ij}$$
$$\text{Level 2:} \quad \beta_{0j} = \gamma_{00} + \gamma_{01}\,(GDP) + u_{0j}$$

In this model, a country-level mean for *Life Satisfaction* is estimated for each country (β_{0j}), and the relationship between these means and each country's *GDP* is represented by the γ_{01} coefficient in the Level 2 equation. If the γ_{01} coefficient is significantly different from 0, then the relationship between *Life Satisfaction* and *GDP* is statistically significant. The analyses of the sample data set produced the following estimates: $\gamma_{01} = 0.027$, $t = .30$, *ns*. These results suggest that the average *Life Satisfaction* in a country is not related to a country's *GDP*. In the test data set, approximately 15% (.65/3.70) of the total variance of *Life Satisfaction* was between countries, which is probably a greater percent at the country level than is the case in many actual cross-cultural studies. In this regard, keep in mind that although small amounts of variance at a level of analysis suggest that relationships may not exist there – they do not preclude entirely the possibility that such relationships exist.

Note that all coefficients in MRCM analyses are unstandardized. That is, the γ_{01} coefficient for *GDP* represents the expected change in *Life Satisfaction* for a 1 unit change in *GDP*. The exact meaning of the γ_{00} and γ_{01} coefficients also depends on how *GDP* is centered. In this analysis, *GDP* was grand-mean centered. Interpreting coefficients, including centering options and standardization, is discussed later in the chapter.[3]

Although conceptually similar, the multilevel analysis that was just described is different from using an OLS analysis such as regression with countries as the unit of analysis to examine the relationship between *GDP* and aggregated *Life Satisfaction*. The essential difference is that the MRCM analyses take into account differences across countries in the reliability of the intercepts (means) for *Life Satisfaction*. Such differences will primarily be a function of the number of observations (people) in each country and the consistency of their responses. In MRCM, variance estimates reflect what is called *Bayes shrinkage* – a process in which unreliable coefficients (e.g., those based on a small number of inconsistent responses) are "shrunken" towards the mean coefficient. See Raudenbush and Bryk (2002) for more detail about this topic.

ESTIMATING WITHIN-COUNTRY RELATIONSHIPS

Predictors can also be added to the Level 1, within-country model. For example, within-country relationships between *Life Satisfaction* and *Individualism* could be examined with the following model:

$$\text{Level 1:} \quad y_{ij} = \beta_{0j} + \beta_{1j}\,(\textit{Individualism}) + r_{ij}$$

$$\text{Level 2:} \quad \beta_{0j} = \gamma_{00} + u_{0j}$$

$$\beta_{1j} = \gamma_{10} + u_{1j}$$

In the Level 1 (within-country or person-level) model, β_{1j} is a coefficient, called a slope to distinguish it from an intercept, representing the relationship between *Individualism* and *Life Satisfaction*, and a slope is estimated for each country. The hypothesis that the mean relationship (the mean slope) is different from 0 is represented at Level 2 by the γ_{10} coefficient. If this

[3] Technically, any type of measure can be included at Level 2, country-level aggregates, categorical variables, and so forth. Researchers will need to make informed decisions about measures that make sense given their questions of interest.

coefficient is significantly different from 0, then the mean slope is different from 0.

The test data set contains a measure, *Individualism* (*Individ*), and *Individualism* was entered group-mean centered (centering is described subsequently). The analyses of the test data set produced the following results: for the intercept, $\gamma_{00} = 15.02$, Level 1 variance = .30, Level 2 variance = 0.94, and for the slope, $\gamma_{10} = 0.85$, $t = 5.13$, $p < .001$. On average, *Life Satisfaction* and *Individualism* were significantly related. Similar to the previous example, these coefficients are unstandardized. This means that the γ_{10} coefficient represents the change in *Life Satisfaction* associated with a 1.0 unit increase in *Individualism.* In the present example, this means that for every 1.0 *Individualism* increased, *Life Satisfaction* increased .85, *on average.* Note that the Level 1 variance is substantially lower in this analysis than it was in the unconditional model (.30 vs. 3.05). The differences in these variance estimates can be used to estimate effect sizes (and by extension, average within-country correlations), a topic discussed later. Finally, a more detailed interpretation of this slope and the intercept depends on how *Individualism* is centered.

EXAMINING DIFFERENCES BETWEEN COUNTRIES IN WITHIN-COUNTRY RELATIONSHIPS

In the analysis presented in the previous section, the hypothesis being tested concerns the average, or mean, relationship between *Life Satisfaction* and *Individualism.* It is entirely possible that the relationship between *Life Satisfaction* and *Individualism* may vary across countries. Differences between countries in the relationship between *Life Satisfaction* and *Individualism* could be examined with the following models. As in the first example, the country-level variable of interest is *GDP.*

$$\text{Level 1:} \quad y_{ij} = \beta_{0j} + \beta_{1j}\,(\textit{Individualism}) + r_{ij}$$
$$\text{Level 2:} \quad \beta_{0j} = \gamma_{00} + \gamma_{11}\,(\textit{GDP}) + u_{0j}$$
$$\beta_{1j} = \gamma_{10} + \gamma_{21}\,(\textit{GDP}) + u_{1j}$$

Note that *GDP* is in both equations. There is broad agreement among multilevel modelers that the same predictors should be included, at least initially, in all Level 2 equations. The primary reason for this is that MRCM analyses rely on covariance matrices. If a variable is not included in one equation, the tacit assumption is that it is not significant and that there is not any meaningful covariation between the coefficients across the equations.

Nevertheless, analysts will need to make their own decisions about the coefficients retained in final models.

The analyses of the test data set produced the following results: $\gamma_{21} = -0.15$, $t = -2.83$, $p < .05$. The significant γ_{21} coefficient indicated that the relationship between *Life Satisfaction* and *Individualism* varied as a function of *GDP*. Such a situation is sometimes referred to as a *cross-level interaction* or a moderating relationship because a relationship at one level of analysis varies, or is moderated by, a variable at another level of analysis.

Interpreting such a relationship is aided considerably by the calculation of estimated values. In the present example, the mean slope (the average coefficient between *Life Satisfaction* and *Individualism*) was .85. The coefficient representing the strength of the moderating relationship of *GDP* was $-.15$. Thus, for a country that was $+1.0$ above the mean on *GDP*, the estimated slope would be $.85 + 1 * (-.15) = .70$. In contrast, for a country that was –1.0 below the mean on *GDP*, the estimated slope would be $.85 - 1 * (-.15) = .90$. Note that for these analyses, *GDP* was grand-mean centered.

CENTERING

Centering refers to the reference value from which deviations of predictors are taken, and analysts need to choose centering methods carefully. Centering changes the meaning of coefficients and can change estimates and significance tests of both fixed and random effects. For analysts whose primary experience is OLS regression, it may be difficult at first to understand and appreciate the importance of centering in multilevel modeling. OLS regression analyses are almost invariably mean centered – the intercept represents the expected score for an observation at the mean of a predictor or set of predictors. Other options exist in MRCM. At Level 2 (the country level for our purposes), there are two options: uncentered (also called zero mean centering) and grand-mean centered. At Level 1 (the within-country level), there are three options: uncentered (or zero mean centered), group-mean centered, and grand-mean centered. Regardless of the level or the type of centering, analysts are strongly encouraged to generate predicted values to interpret the coefficients estimated in their analyses.[4]

[4] The way in which variables are centered varies considerably across software packages. For example, in HLM, the program centers variables automatically – analysts do not need to create any transformed variables. In contrast, when using SAS PROC MIXED, in some cases, analysts need to create centered variables before analysis. Analysts are encouraged to consult manuals for the software they intend to use to determine how variables are centered in the software they will be using.

Grand-mean centering at Level 2 is conceptually similar to the centering that is done in OLS regression. The intercept represents the expected value for the dependent measure (which could be an intercept or a slope) for a Level 2 unit (country in our case) that is at the mean of the predictor or predictors, just as it is in OLS regression.

When Level 2 predictors are uncentered, the intercept represents the expected value for the dependent measure when a predictor is 0. For example, assume that countries are classified in terms of the nature of their governments, with 0 = dual-party system and 1 = multiparty system. If this variable, which we will call *MParty*, is included uncentered, then the intercept will represent the expected value for countries for which *MParty* = 0, and the coefficient for *MParty* will represent the difference between the two types of countries. If the coefficient for *MParty* is significantly different from 0, then there is a difference in *Life Satisfaction* between countries with the two types of political systems. An analysis of *Life Satisfaction* with *MParty* as an uncentered Level 2 predictor is represented as follows.

$$\text{Level 1:} \quad y_{ij} = \beta_{0j} + r_{ij}$$
$$\text{Level 2:} \quad \beta_{0j} = \gamma_{00} + \gamma_{01}\,(\mathit{MParty}) + u_{0j}$$

This analysis of the test data set provided the following estimates: γ_{00} = 14.69, γ_{01} = 0.71, t = 1.32, *ns*. The γ_{00} coefficient represents the mean for countries that have a dual-party system, that is, when *MParty* = 0. These results suggest that the average *Life Satisfaction* in a country does not vary as a function of a country's *MParty* system. If the coefficient for *MParty* was significant, then the difference between the estimated mean *Life Satisfaction* for dual-party countries (estimated value: $14.69 + 0 * .71 = 14.69$) and the estimated mean *Life Satisfaction* for multiparty countries (estimated value: $14.69 + 1 * .71 = 15.40$) would be significant.

Centering at Level 1 follows the same logic as centering at Level 2, but it is important to keep in mind the implications that centering at Level 1 has for what is analyzed at Level 2. This is because the coefficients that are estimated at Level 1 are "carried up" (at least conceptually) to Level 2, and exactly what is estimated at Level 1 will vary as a function of how predictors are centered. Similar to Level 2, when Level 1 predictors are uncentered, relationships between the dependent measure and deviations of the predictors from 0 are modeled. The intercept represents the expected score when a predictor is 0, and it is this score that is then analyzed at Level 2.

It makes little sense to model predictors as uncentered when 0 is not a valid value for a predictor, for example, when a predictor is measured using a 1–10 point Likert scale that has no 0 point. In contrast, modeling predictors as uncentered may be sensible if predictors are coded variables for which 0 is a valid value (e.g., categorical variables) or for continuous variables for which 0 is a valid value. Moreover, by subtracting a constant, 0 can become a valid value for continuous variables that may not have a natural zero point. For example, if age is a predictor, an analyst can subtract a certain number of years so that a certain age is represented by 0. If such a variable is then entered uncentered, the intercept will represent the expected score for a person at that age. This is a common procedure in longitudinal studies in which a specific age is of primary importance.

Another option at Level 1 is group-mean centering. When predictors are group-mean centered, relationships between the dependent measure and deviations of the predictors from the mean of each group (Level 2 unit or country for many cross-cultural studies) are modeled. In this case, the intercept represents the expected score when a predictor is at the mean for each group. Aside from rounding error, when predictors are group-mean centered, intercepts are the same as they are when there are no predictors. In the example presented earlier, when *Life Satisfaction* was predicted by *Individualism*, which was group-mean centered, the mean intercept was 15.02, and it was 15.04 in the unconditional analysis. Group-mean centering is the option that is conceptually the closest to conducting a regression analysis for each group (for each country in the present case) and then using the coefficients from these analyses as dependent measures in another analysis, what is sometimes called two-stage regression. As noted previously, although group-mean centered MRCM and two stage-regression analyses are conceptually similar, they are not the same because of the differences between the two techniques in how parameters (including error) are estimated.

Substantively, group-mean centering Level 1 (individual-level) predictors may help alleviate concerns about cultural differences in mean responses. For example, if a researcher is concerned that there are country-level differences in acquiescence and wants to eliminate the influence of such differences on the results, group-mean centering predictors would eliminate such influences. Between-country differences in mean acquiescence would not influence the estimation of intercepts or coefficients representing within-country relationships. Note that this is not the same as standardizing the measures within each country (a topic discussed later) – it is simply a way to control for Level 2 (country-level) differences in the means of predictors.

The final centering option for Level 1 predictors is grand-mean centering. When predictors are grand-mean centered, relationships between the dependent measure and deviations of the predictors from the grand mean of all observations are modeled. In this case, the intercept represents the expected score when a predictor is at the grand mean. Substantively, when predictors are grand-mean centered, the intercept for each group is functionally equivalent to an adjusted mean. In this case, adjusted refers to adjusted for between-country differences in means of predictors.

There may be times when an analyst wants to make such adjustments. For example, in research on what is known as the Big Fish in a Little Pond Effect (e.g., Marsh & Hau, 2003) the negative classroom-level relationship between self-concept and mean classroom level ability occurs only when ability (an individual-level predictor) is entered grand-mean centered. There may be other occasions when analysts want to make such adjustments. Regardless, analysts need to be mindful of the implications of how they center predictors.

The similarity of the intercepts from analyses in which predictors are group- and grand-mean centered will depend upon how much group-level means for predictors (countries in our example) vary. Using the test data set, predicting *Life Satisfaction* from *Individualism*, with *Individualism* grand-mean centered, produced the following results: for the intercept, $\gamma_{00} = 15.37$, Level 1 variance = .30, Level 2 variance = 4.20, and for the slope, $\gamma_{10} = 0.85$, $t = 5.18$, $p < .001$. Notice the large difference in the Level 2 (country-level) variance of the intercept between this analysis and the group-mean centered analysis (.94 vs. 4.20). This difference is due to the fact that Level 2 (country-level) variance in *Individualism* has been introduced into the model, and there is meaningful country-level variance in *Individualism*, 2.01, estimated from an unconditional analysis of *Individualism*. The country-level variance in *Individualism* can also be seen from the Level 2 data provided in Appendix A.

The fact that group-mean centering controls for Level 2 differences in Level 1 predictors can be illustrated by making Level 2 differences in Level 1 predictors larger. For these analyses, a new variable, *Individ2*, was created. For countries a, b, c, and d, *Individ2* was the same as *Individualism* (*Individ*) from the original analyses. For countries e, f, g, h, and i, 100 was added to the original variable to create *Individ2*. When *Life Satisfaction* was predicted by *Individ2*, and *Individ2* was group-mean centered, the results were *identical* to those from the original analyses. The country-level differences in *Individ2* did not contribute to the analyses.

In contrast, when *Life Satisfaction* was predicted by *Individ2*, and *Individ2* was grand-mean centered, the following estimates were produced: intercept of the intercept, $\gamma_{00} = 1.69$; intercept of the slope, $\gamma_{10} = .38$; Level 1 variance, 1.54; Level 2 variance of the intercept, 272.29; Level 2 variance of the slope, .14. Given that this model estimates an intercept that is very different from the intercept from the unconditional model, an analyst would have to question the appropriateness of grand-mean centering in this case. Rarely are Level 2 differences in predictors as pronounced as the differences in this example; however, this example makes the point that such differences contribute to parameter estimates.

Nevertheless, some analysts argue that it is inappropriate to group-mean center predictors because the Level 2 variance in Level 1 predictors is not part of the model and it should be. Some suggest that when using group-mean centering, such variance can be included by including group means (i.e., country-level means in our case) as predictors at Level 2. At this point in time, it is difficult to provide a hard and fast recommendation regarding this specific issue. Some well-respected multi-level modelers (e.g., Raudenbush and Bryk) discuss group-mean centering without any mention of including group means as predictors at level 2. Moreover, there are scores of published articles that have reported analyses in which level 1 predictors have been entered group-mean centered and the group means of these predictors have not been included at level 2.

Given all this, I recommend group-mean centering continuous Level 1 predictors. Such a procedure makes the analyses similar (conceptually) to conducting individual regression equations for each country and using the within-country coefficients from such analyses in between-country analyses. Regarding the inclusion of group (i.e., country-level) means at level 2 to compensate for the fact that the country-level variance of these predictors is not modeled when level 1 predictors are group-mean centered, I will note that I do not include such means in my analyses. Nevertheless, individual analysts may read the literature and reach a different conclusion. Regardless, as the previous examples illustrate, different centering options (particularly at Level 1) can lead to very different results. Analysts may want to conduct group- and grand-mean centered analyses (and perhaps uncentered if appropriate) and compare the results, trying to understand whatever differences exist between or among the results. Nevertheless, as Bryk and Raudenbush (1992, p. 27) noted, "No single rule covers all cases," and analysts will need to make decisions about centering based on their questions of interest and the available data.

CODING AND CATEGORICAL VARIABLES AS PREDICTORS

Questions about centering naturally lead to questions about the nature of predictors. The previous discussion has concerned continuous variables as predictors, and although many analysts may be interested in continuous measures, categorical measures such as gender at the person-level and country characteristics at the country level may also be of interest. In this section, I describe the use of categorical variables as predictors. Analyzing categorical variables as dependent measures is described in a separate, subsequent section.

First, it is important to note that multilevel programs do not distinguish categorical and continuous predictors. Predictors are predictors. Analysts need to anticipate the analyses they want to conduct, the groups they want to represent in their analyses, and the comparisons they want to make, by creating categorical variables before analyses. Moreover, the same centering options are available for categorical predictors as for continuous predictors, and the judicious combination of coding schemes and centering options provides a flexible means of estimating coefficients and testing specific hypotheses. In this section, I describe some of these combinations, although this description is not exhaustive.

To review quickly, dummy codes are variables that are coded 0 and 1, usually with 1 representing the presence of a condition. Contrast codes (and effect codes) represent contrasts, and typically, the coefficients need to sum to 1. For a dichotomous system, one category would be represented by 1, and the other by –1. If there are three categories, the first could be compared with the second two by coding the first category 2, and the second and third categories –1 and –1, and so forth. As noted in the previous section, centering changes what the intercept represents. To ease interpretation, it is often convenient to enter categorical variables uncentered.

These principles are illustrated with the test data set. *Union* is a dummy-coded variable representing whether a person is a member of a labor union. For the test data set, the initial analysis in which *Life Satisfaction* was the dependent measure and *Union* was the independent measure (entered uncentered) produced a nonsignificant random error term for *Union* ($p > .50$). Modeling random error terms is discussed later. The model was rerun with *Union* as a fixed effect, which produced the following parameter estimates: intercept mean, $\gamma_{00} = 14.68$, variance = .69; intercept of the slope, $\gamma_{10} = .70$.

Interpreting these coefficients is aided by estimating predicted values. When the variable *Union* is entered uncentered, the estimated score for nonmembers (*Union* = 0) is $14.68 + (0 * .70) = 14.68$, that is, the intercept. The estimated score for members (*Union* = 1) is $14.68 + (1 * .70) =$

15.38. The slope for *Union* is significantly different from 0 ($t = 2.41$, $p = .02$), and this means that, on average, people who are members of labor unions are more satisfied with their lives (15.38) than those who are not members (14.68). This model estimates an intercept for each country, which represents the score for nonmembers, and a slope for each country, which represents the difference between members and nonmembers.

Another way to model the difference would be to use a contrast coded variable representing the difference, such as the variable *Ucnt* in the example data set (1 = member, −1 = nonmember). A model with *Ucnt* (uncentered, as a fixed effect – no random error term) as a Level 1 predictor produced the following parameter estimates: intercept mean, $\gamma_{00} = 15.03$, variance = .69; intercept of the slope, $\gamma_{10} = .35$. Interpreting these coefficients is aided by estimating predicted values. When the variable *Ucnt* is 1 (for members), the estimated score is $15.03 + (1 * .35) = 15.38$. When the variable *Ucnt* is −1 (for nonmembers), the estimated score is $15.30 + (-1 * .35) = 14.68$. The difference between members and nonmembers, .70, is the same as the difference found in the previous analysis. The difference between the two analyses is what the intercept and slope for union membership represent, something that matters when differences in the intercept are modeled at Level 2.

The importance of this difference can be illustrated when *Life Satisfaction* is modeled as a function of *Union* at Level 1, and both of these coefficients are then modeled as a function of *GDP* at Level 2.

$$\begin{aligned}
\text{Level 1:}\quad & y_{ij} = \beta_{0j} + \beta_{1j}\,(\textit{Union}) + r_{ij} \\
\text{Level 2:}\quad & \beta_{0j} = \gamma_{00} + \gamma_{01}\,(\textit{GDP}) + u_{0j} \\
& \beta_{1j} = \gamma_{10} + \gamma_{11}\,(\textit{GDP}) + u_{1j}
\end{aligned}$$

This analysis produced the following estimates: mean intercept, $\gamma_{00} = 14.56$, a significant relationship (slope) between *Union* and the intercept, $\gamma_{01} = .24$ ($t = 2.46$, $p > .05$), a significant mean slope (*Union* effect), $\gamma_{10} = .80$ ($t = 3.35$, $p > .01$), and a significant relationship between the *Union* effect (slope) and GDP, $\gamma_{11} = -.29$ ($t = 2.93$, $p > .01$). What is important about these results is that the intercept represents the *Life Satisfaction* for people who are not members of a union (i.e., when *Union* = 0). Therefore, the significant relationship between *GDP* and the intercept ($\gamma_{01} = .24$) represents a significant relationship between *GDP* and *Life Satisfaction* for nonmembers, not for all the members of a country.

If *Life Satisfaction* is modeled as a function of *Ucnt* (the contrast variable) at Level 1 and both of these coefficients are then modeled as a function of *GDP* at Level 2, slightly different results occur.

$$\begin{aligned} \text{Level 1:} \quad & y_{ij} = \beta_{0j} + \beta_{1j}\,(Ucnt) + r_{ij} \\ \text{Level 2:} \quad & \beta_{0j} = \gamma_{00} + \gamma_{01}\,(GDP) + u_{0j} \\ & \beta_{1j} = \gamma_{10} + \gamma_{11}\,(GDP) + u_{1j} \end{aligned}$$

This analysis produced the following estimates: mean intercept, $\gamma_{00} = 14.95$, a nonsignificant relationship (slope) between *Ucnt* and the intercept, $\gamma_{11} = .09$ ($t = 1.03$), a significant mean slope (*Ucnt* effect), $\gamma_{10} = .40$ ($t = 3.35$, $p > .01$), and a significant relationship between the *Ucnt* effect (slope) and GDP, $\gamma_{11} = -.145$ ($t = 2.93$, $p > .01$). What is important about these results is that the intercept represents the mean *Life Satisfaction* for people who are neither members nor nonmembers of a union (i.e., when *Unct* = 0), a sort of "average" person.

Comparing the two results reveals that analyses of the two slopes are identical when the fact that *Ucnt* is a contrast variable is taken into account – after all, the contrast variable is simply the dummy variable with 1 subtracted from the 0s for nonmembers. The two codes are correlated 1.0 and are mathematically equivalent, so the results should be the same. The difference is in the analyses of the intercepts, and the difference in the relationships between *GDP* and the intercepts in the two analyses suggests that *GDP* may be related differently to *Life Satisfaction* for members and nonmembers.

Such a possibility can be examined directly by conducting an analysis in which *Life Satisfaction* is modeled as a function of two dummy codes, one representing union members and the other representing nonmembers. In the test data set, the dummy coded variable for nonmembers is variable *NUn*. Note that in this model, the intercept is deleted, and such models are sometimes referred to as "zero or no intercept models." In such analyses, the coefficients represent the means for Level 1 categories, and in the present example, the coefficient *Union* represents the mean for members, and *NUn* represents the mean for nonmembers.

$$\begin{aligned} \text{Level 1:} \quad & y_{ij} = \beta_{1j}\,(Union) + \beta_{1j}\,(NUn) + r_{ij} \\ \text{Level 2:} \quad & \beta_{1j} = \gamma_{10} + \gamma_{11}\,(GDP) + u_{1j} \\ & \beta_{2j} = \gamma_{20} + \gamma_{21}\,(GDP) + u_{2j} \end{aligned}$$

This analysis produced the following estimates: mean intercept for *Union*, $\gamma_{10} = 15.36$, and a nonsignificant relationship (slope) between *GDP* and the *Union* coefficient, $\gamma_{11} = -.05$ ($t < 1$), mean intercept for *NUn*,

$\gamma_{20} = 14.55$, and a significant relationship between *GDP* and this coefficient, $\gamma_{11} = .24$ ($t = 2.53$, $p < .05$). In other words, *GDP* was related to *Life Satisfaction* for nonmembers, but was not related to *Life Satisfaction* for union members.

Using such dummy codes, means (e.g., γ_{10} and γ_{20}) can be compared using tests of fixed effects as described subsequently. Although the results of such comparisons of Level 1 coefficients representing means will typically be similar to the results of significance tests of Level 1 coefficients representing differences between categories, the results may not be exactly the same. This is because when differences are modeled at Level 1 with a contrast variable or a single dummy code, the model estimates a difference score between (or among) categories for each country and then estimates mean difference scores. When dummy codes are used with a no intercept model, means for each category are estimated for each country, and then differences among these means are tested. Note that this type of dummy-coded analysis is possible only when observations can be classified using a mutually exclusive system, that is, an observation falls into one and only one category. The number of categories that can be represented is not limited technically, but each Level 1 observation must be classified as belonging to one and only one category.

There is also an important caveat regarding relationships between Level 2 variables and Level 1 slopes (which in this instance represent means). The coefficients estimating means for each category are stable even when some Level 2 units do not have observations in all categories. For example, assume a three-category system in which 50% of participants do not have observations in the third of these categories. The coefficient (mean) for Category 3 estimated using all participants will be the same as a mean estimated from an analysis that includes only those who have some observations in Category 3; however, estimates of relationships between Level 2 variables and means for this category will not be the same. When a substantial number of Level 2 units (perhaps 10% or more) are missing observations in a category, analysts should conduct separate analyses on subsets of countries that have observations in all categories and those that do not to determine whether the subsamples differ meaningfully in other ways.

Analysts may also be interested in nonexclusive, overlapping categories at Level 1, for example, union membership and gender. One way to deal with such categories is to combine them into mutually exclusive categories (e.g., male members, female members, male nonmembers, and female nonmembers) and then use dummy codes for each of the resultant categories and proceed as described earlier. This may not always be practical or desirable, and categorical predictors can be represented with contrast (or effect) codes, as in the sample data set variable *Ucnt*.

An important advantage of contrast coding is that it allows level 2 (country-level in our case) differences in difference scores to be modeled. Moreover, multiple contrasts can be included simultaneously, including contrasts when there are more than two categories. When using multiple contrast codes, analysts need to be mindful of the fact that the coefficients are adjusted for each other, meaning that the estimate of a specific contrast may vary as a function of the other contrasts in a model. A disadvantage of contrast coding is that it does not allow for examination of differences in relationships between Level 2 variables and Level 1 category means.

Categorical codes can also be used to adjust for country-level differences in the distribution of within-country groups. If a categorical variable (dummy or contrast code) is entered "grand-mean centered," then the intercept represents the country-level mean adjusted for country-level differences in the relative frequency of the categorical variable. For example, in the test data set, when *Union* is entered grand-mean centered as a predictor of *Life Satisfaction*, the intercept for *Life Satisfaction* is 15.05, the same (within rounding) as it was from the unconditional model. By grand-mean centering *Union*, country-level differences in this variable were eliminated from the analysis.

I recommend that analysts prepare both dummy and contrast codes for categorical variables and model dependent measures in different ways. If contrast- and dummy-coded analyses provide dramatically different conclusions about mean differences, this should be investigated because they should not. The two types of coding provide different advantages, and analysts will need to understand when to use one type or the other. For example, at Level 1, contrast-coding groups allow analysts to examine between-country differences in within-country differences. Continuing the previous example, do differences between union members and nonmembers in work attitudes vary as a function of a country-level characteristic such as GDP? Dummy-coding groups allows analysts to determine whether relationships between country-level measures and within-country means vary across groups within each country. For example, do relationships between work attitudes and GDP differ between union members and nonmembers?

I think the use of the types of categorical codes I have described is one of the most underutilized and potentially powerful aspects of multilevel modeling. Through the creative and judicious use of different types of coding combined with different types of centering, analysts can estimate precise (in terms of the relationships they represent) parameters. Such estimates can then be compared using the test of fixed parameters discussed elsewhere in this chapter. The critical step in this process is to anticipate the exact analyses that are to be done and prepare variables that represent the parameters of interest. This topic is discussed in more detail in Nezlek (2001, 2003).

FIXED AND RANDOM EFFECTS

One of the advantages of the maximum-likelihood procedures used in MRCM is the separation of true and error (or random) variance, a separation similar to what is done in structural equation modeling. In contrast, in OLS analyses, there is only one variance estimate – true and random variance are not separated. In the results of a MRCM analysis, this separation is indicated by the fact that, as mentioned earlier, for each variable in a Level 1 equation, two terms are estimated, usually called a fixed effect and a random effect. The fixed effect, which is used to test whether a coefficient is significantly different from 0, has a variance (usually labeled a standard error), and there is a separate estimate of the random variance, usually called a random effect. The separation of true and random variance improves the accuracy of the significance tests of effects, part of what makes MRCM a better way to analyze multilevel data sets than comparable OLS analyses.

For most purposes, researchers will be interested in the fixed effects of the predictor variables included in their models. For example, the significance test of the slope between *Life Satisfaction* and *Individualism* (was it different from 0?) in the previous example was a test of the fixed effect. Like fixed effects, random effects are tested for significance. Is a random effect significantly different from 0? Unfortunately, some researchers interpret the significance of a random error term as a test of whether units of analysis vary. They assume that if the random variance associated with a slope is not significant, then all units of analysis have the same slope. For the example data set, this would mean that if the random variance associated with the slope between *Life Satisfaction* and *Individualism* was not significant, then it could be assumed that all countries had the same slope, the same relationship between *Life Satisfaction* and *Individualism.*

Although intuitively appealing, this is not quite true. Technically speaking, the significance test of the random effect associated with a coefficient indicates if true and random variance can be reliably separated. It does not formally test whether Level 2 units vary in some way, for example, do all countries have the same slope? Admittedly, the lack of a significant random error term suggests that there may not be a lot of variance in a coefficient.

The absence or presence of a random error term needs to be understood within the context of random and nonrandom variation. Coefficients that have a random error term are described as "randomly varying" or as random coefficients. Coefficients that do not have a random error term can be what is described as *nonrandomly varying*. In the previous example, the *Satisfaction–Individualism* slope was modeled as randomly varying, that is, there was a significant random error term estimated for the slope. If the random error term is deleted, the slope is "fixed" (and is called a fixed coefficient), although one can still model variability in the slope at Level 2, and such a slope would be termed *nonrandomly varying*.

Repeating the analyses of the *Satisfaction–Individualism* slope with the slope fixed (i.e., the random error term was deleted) and *Individualism* entered group-mean centered, produces the following results. The intercept of the slope (γ_{10}) with no Level 2 predictors was .68, different from the slope when the random error term was included (.85 from the previous analyses). It is not unusual for the fixed part of a coefficient to change when a random term is eliminated. Moreover and more important, the nature of this change cannot be predicted. Slopes that were significant when modeled as random can be nonsignificant when modeled as fixed, and vice versa.

When *GDP* was included at Level 2, the γ_{11} coefficient representing the moderating relationship was $-.08$, $p = .09$. That is, fixing the slope did not prevent modeling variability in the slope. The ability to model the variability in this slope without modeling it as a random coefficient was not a function of the fact that there was a significant random error term when the slope was modeled as random. Variability in slopes can be modeled even when they do not have a significant random error term.

The meaning of fixing a coefficient can also be understood by looking at estimated values for coefficients. In HLM, these are in residual files, and for the test data set, the Level 2 residual file contains the country-level estimates of the intercepts and slopes (and other statistics that are not relevant at this point). For the analysis in which slope for *Individualism* was fixed and *GDP* was not included as a predictor, the "fitted value" for the slope was .68 for all the Level 2 units (i.e., all countries). Some argue that this means that all countries had the same slope; however, this is not exactly true. When *GDP* was included as a predictor, the fitted values for the *Individualism* slope varied across countries. They varied nonrandomly as a function of *GDP*. When the slope was fixed and *GDP* was not included, the variability among the slopes was not being modeled. Not modeling the variability is not the same as saying that the slopes did not vary in some way.

It is inappropriate to conclude on the basis of a nonsignificant random error term that a Level 1 coefficient (usually a slope) does not (or can not) vary. To prove that a slope does not vary at all would require modeling the coefficient with an infinite number of Level 2 predictors. Short of this, a nonsignificant random error terms means that a coefficient does not vary randomly. A significant random error term means that a coefficient varies randomly, which formally means that there is enough information to separate true and random variability for that coefficient. For researchers interested in variability per se, the presence of a significant random error term means that Level 2 units (usually countries for a cross-cultural researcher) vary; however, the absence of a significant random error term does not mean that they do not vary.

Although random error terms typically do not test hypotheses per se (at least for many cross-cultural researchers), they must be properly specified before examining significance tests of fixed effects. The *error structure* (as the covariance matrix of random terms is called) must be specified properly because an improper error structure creates a "misspecified" model, which in turn, can lead to inaccurate significance tests of the fixed effects. Moreover, the direction of this inaccuracy cannot be predicted. That is, fixing an effect that should be modeled as random (deleting a random term that should be included) can make the fixed part of a coefficient significant when it should not be, or vice versa, just as including a random effect that should not be included. Practically speaking, the manner in which random error terms are specified varies dramatically across software packages, so much so that describing the various options is well beyond the scope of this chapter. It is worth noting that in HLM, by default, predictors are entered as fixed: Analysts need to "make them random" explicitly.

Conceptually, most coefficients in cross-cultural studies should probably be modeled as random – the countries have been randomly sampled from a population of countries, and this sampling needs to be represented. Nevertheless, the data may not be able to estimate reliably all the random error terms in a model and the covariances among these random error terms. Most multilevel modelers argue that nonreliable error terms should be eliminated, although a minority argue that some estimate of the random error should be made based on information from other sources, for example, previous studies. At this point, most researchers will be on solid ground if they eliminate unreliable random error terms from their models, keeping in mind that fixed coefficients can vary nonrandomly.

Also, the norm among multilevel modelers is to use a more generous probability level than .05 when making decisions about random error terms.

In my own work, I allow error terms that are significant at .10 to remain in a model and delete those that are above .15. When *p* values are between .10 and .15, I run models with and without the error term to see the impact of including or excluding the error term. Decisions about random error terms in this "gray area" can also be informed by comparing error covariance matrices from different models using goodness of fit indices.

A discussion of guidelines for making decisions about random error terms is provided in Nezlek (2001). In that article, I discussed three bases for making decisions about modeling coefficients as fixed or random: theoretical, statistical, and practical. Theoretically (or conceptually), it is possible (although not typical) that some coefficients should be fixed because they have a narrow *breadth of inference* or *inference space*, that is, they are meant to describe a very specific population. As already discussed, coefficients can be fixed if the random error term is not significant (statistical). Finally, coefficients may be fixed if estimating them (and their covariances with other error terms) prevents a model from converging, a practical issue. In this regard, many multilevel modelers look for models to converge in less than 500 iterations.

To me, modeling and interpreting error structures within the multilevel framework are perhaps the most puzzling aspects of planning and interpreting task multilevel analyses. What does a nonsignificant random error term mean? What do correlations between random error terms represent? Articles and books can provide seemingly (or actually) conflicting advice and interpretations regarding such topics. Even within the community of scholars who study such techniques per se, there is far from a consensus regarding how to interpret error within the multilevel framework. In this chapter, I have provided what I think is sound advice regarding the interpretation of error variances; this advice is based on my reading of the literature and, more important, on my experience analyzing multilevel data structures of all sorts. Other scholars may provide different advice, and at this point, analysts may need to consult various sources and make decisions for themselves.

INTERACTIONS

Within MRCM, understanding statistical interactions is a bit more complex than it is within single-level analyses because interactions can be either within or between levels or can blend the two. One of the simpler forms is the between-level interaction, often referred to as a cross-level interaction, which represents a type of moderated relationship. A cross-level interaction occurs when a Level 1 relationship (a slope) varies as a function of a Level 2 variable. The example from the test data set showing how the relationship between *Life Satisfaction* and *Individualism* varied as a function of *GDP* represents a cross-level interaction.

Within-level interactions at Level 2 are fairly straightforward. Setting up and interpreting within-level interactions at Level 2 (the country level for our purposes) are similar to setting up and conducting interactions in OLS regression (see Aiken & West, 1991). Continuous measures are mean-centered and then cross-multiplied with other continuous measures or categorical measures, and interactions are interpreted by estimating predicted values – typically for observations ± 1 *SD* from the mean for continuous measures and for observations in each group for categorical measures.

Within-level interactions at Level 1 are somewhat more complex, although the logic is the same. Most important, before creating the products representing the interaction terms, continuous variables should be centered within each group (i.e., within each country). For example, in the sample data set, to create an interaction involving *Individ*, the country mean for *Individ* would need to be subtracted from the raw *Individ* score within each country, and this centered score would be multiplied by the other variable involved. For Country A, this would be 2.75, for Country B, it would be 3.67, and so forth. The resulting interaction terms should be entered *uncentered* into the model because the terms used to create them were centered when they were created. Other terms would be entered group-mean centered. This makes generating predicted values easier.

Analysts who are interested in generating predicted scores ± 1 *SD* (the standard) need to exercise care when using predicted scores to understand Level 1 interactions. When doing so, it must be kept in mind that within-country *SD*s must be used, and these must be generated using variance estimates from unconditional models. Moreover, Level 1 interactions may also vary as a function of Level 2 variables. In such cases, different sets of Level 1 coefficients need to be generated representing countries at Level 2. This could entail different groups of countries at Level 2 or countries that are ± 1 *SD* on a Level 2 variable. Analyses of interactions within Level 1 and modeling of Level 2 differences in such interactions can be found in Nezlek and Plesko (2003). Resources for evaluating interactions within the multilevel context can also be found in Preacher, Curran, and Bauer (2006).

MODERATION AND MEDIATION

As with understanding interactions, understanding moderation and mediation within the multilevel framework is conceptually similar to understanding moderation and mediation within the single-level framework. Between levels, moderation can take the form of a cross-level interaction and can be examined through significance tests of Level 2 predictors of Level 1 slopes. In fact, cross-level interactions are sometimes referred to as moderating relationships because a Level 1 relationship varies as a function of, or is moderated by, a Level 2 variable. This was illustrated in the previous example in which cultural differences in individual-level relationships between *Life Satisfaction* and *Individualism* were modeled as a function of *GDP*.

Within levels, moderation can be examined by representing interactions of predictors much like what is done in OLS regression. For example, an interaction term between the country-level variables *MParty* and *GDP* could be created to determine if relationships between mean *Life Satisfaction* and *GDP* varied as a function of the political system in a country. Within Level 2, interpreting the results of such analyses is much like interpreting the results of OLS analyses: Significant interaction terms indicate moderation.

Evaluating moderation within Level 1 is similar, but somewhat more complex. Similar to Level 2, you need to create interaction terms representing the combined effects of the two variables in question. For example, union membership and individualism could be combined to determine if the relationship between *Life Satisfaction* and *Individualism* was similar for members and nonmembers. In this example, it would probably be best first to center *Individualism* around the mean for each country, then multiply these centered values by the union membership variable, and then enter the membership variable and interaction terms uncentered. If the interaction term is significant, one can conclude that the relationship between *Life Satisfaction* and *Individualism* for union members is different than it is for nonmembers. The exact nature of this difference could be determined by generating predicted values representing relationships for members and for nonmembers.

The tricky part of such an analysis is the possibility that coefficients representing moderating effects will vary across Level 2 units. The significance tests of the fixed effect of interaction terms representing a moderation effect test if the mean Level 1 moderation effect is significantly different from

0. It is possible that moderation may be stronger or weaker for different Level 2 units (countries for our purposes). For example, the difference between union members and nonmembers in relationships between *Life Satisfaction* and *Individualism* may be larger in some countries than it is in others. Moreover, the likelihood of such a possibility is not indicated by the significance test of the random error term of the Level 1 moderating effect. For example, Nezlek and Plesko (2003) found that Level 2 variables moderated Level 1 moderating effects even when the coefficient representing a Level 1 moderating effect had no significant random error term.

Evaluating mediation within multilevel models is not that well understood, and thus the following discussion should be treated as somewhat tentative. I think a good starting point is the traditional OLS rule as discussed by Baron and Kenny (1986). Mediation occurs when the relationship between an outcome and a predictor is rendered insignificant by including a second predictor that is itself related to the outcome and to the first predictor. Informed (albeit technically focused) discussions of mediation and suggestions for ways to evaluate mediation within the multilevel context can be found in Bauer, Preacher, and Gill (2006) and Krull and MacKinnon (2001).

At Level 2, it seems that the OLS rule discussed by Baron and Kenny can be applied relatively straightforwardly. In terms of the example I have been discussing, the relationship between *GDP* and *Life Satisfaction* might be mediated by another country-level measure such as the ease with which people in a society can change social statues (*Ease*). Assume that *Ease* is also related to *Life Satisfaction*, and at the country level, *Ease* is related to *GDP*, and when *Ease* is included in the Level 2 equation predicting *Life Satisfaction*, *Ease* is significant and *GDP* is not. Such a result suggests that *Ease* mediates the relationship between *Life Satisfaction* and *GDP*.

Within Level 1, the situation is much more complex, in part because Level 1 mediation may vary across Level 2 units of analysis. For example, let us assume that we measure an additional individual-level variable, *Self-esteem*, and we find that *Self-esteem* is related to both *Individualism* and *Life Satisfaction*. Furthermore, when *Life Satisfaction* is predicted by both *Self-esteem* and *Individualism*, the coefficient for *Self-esteem* is significant, whereas the coefficient for *Individualism* is not. This is a prima facie case for mediation.

Nonetheless, it is entirely possible that such mediation does not occur in all countries. As discussed previously, tests of fixed effects of Level 1 coefficients concern the average or mean coefficient. This leaves open the possibility that countries may have a pattern of relationships that differs from the mean, a situation that is sometimes referred to as *moderated mediation*. A small caveat is in order at this time. Some explanations of Level 1 mediation (e.g., Kenny, Korchmaros, & Bolger, 2003) rely on significance tests of the random error terms associated with slopes to determine if coefficients representing mediational relationships vary across Level 2 units. Such explanations do not consider the possibility that slopes representing medational effects may vary nonrandomly. Such problems are particularly salient for cross-cultural researchers who often have a limited number of Level 2 units (countries) available. Small numbers of Level 2 units make it difficult to estimate random error terms. If researchers rely solely on the presence of significance of random error terms to make judgments about whether Level 1 coefficients vary across countries, they may be drawing inaccurate conclusions. Moreover, as noted later, there is some confusion regarding the meaning of changes in Level 1 residual variances as a means of evaluating effect sizes. To the extent that explanations of mediation rely on changes in Level 1 variances, such explanations need to be evaluated cautiously.

At present, it is difficult to provide unambiguous guidelines regarding lower level mediation in multilevel models. The traditional OLS rule (e.g., Baron & Kenny, 1986) seems like a good place to start because it relies on significance tests of fixed effects rather than on variance estimates. Regardless, analysts need to be aware of the possibility that all of the relationships needed to establish mediation may vary across Level 2 units. That is mediation may exist in some countries but not in others.

COMPARING COEFFICIENTS: TESTS OF FIXED EFFECTS

Although the primary emphasis in much published research is on significance tests of individual coefficients, in MRCM coefficients can be compared. Such comparisons can involve slopes or intercepts, and depending on the sophistication of the analyst, these tests can be powerful. These tests (called tests of fixed effects in HLM) rely on the impact of constraints on a model. The procedure is the same as testing constraints within structural equation modeling. An analyst specifies a constraint, for example, the difference between two slopes is 0, and the impact of the fit of this constraint on a model is evaluated. If the constraint leads to a poorer fit, the hypothesis underlying the constraint is rejected, for example, the difference between the slopes is not 0 – the slopes are different.

For example, as represented in the following model, assume we are interested in the individual-level relationships between *Life Satisfaction* and *Individualism* and *Self-esteem.*

$$\begin{aligned} \text{Level 1:}\quad & y_{ij} = \beta_{0j} + \beta_{1j}\,(\mathit{Individualism}) + \beta_{2j}\,(\mathit{Self\text{-}esteem}) + r_{ij} \\ \text{Level 2:}\quad & \beta_{0j} = \gamma_{00} + u_{0j} \\ & \beta_{1j} = \gamma_{10} + u_{1j} \\ & \beta_{2j} = \gamma_{20} + u_{2j} \end{aligned}$$

The relative strength of the relationships between *Life Satisfaction* and *Individualism* and *Self-esteem* can be examined by comparing the γ_{10} and γ_{20} coefficients, representing the mean slope for *Individualism* and *Self-esteem*, respectively. This is done by imposing a constraint on the model – in this instance, constraining the difference between γ_{20} and γ_{30} to be 0. If the constraint leads to a significant decrease in the fit of the model, then one can conclude that the coefficients (the mean slopes) are not the same. The significance test is a chi-squared with 1 degree of freedom. Note that such a procedure can be used to compare the means for *Union* and *Non-Union* in the examples using dummy coded predictors.

These procedures are flexible and can be used to compare various types of relationships. For example, assume that a Level 2 predictor of the slopes is added to the previous model. *GDP* is a Level 2 predictor that is being used to model country-level differences in the *Individualism* and *Self-esteem* slopes.

$$\begin{aligned} \text{Level 2:}\quad & \beta_{0j} = \gamma_{00} + \gamma_{10}\,(\mathit{GDP}) + u_{0j} \\ & \beta_{1j} = \gamma_{10} + \gamma_{11}\,(\mathit{GDP}) + u_{1j} \\ & \beta_{2j} = \gamma_{20} + \gamma_{21}\,(\mathit{GDP}) + u_{2j} \end{aligned}$$

The strength of the moderating relationship of *GDP* on *Individualism* and *Self-esteem* can be compared by comparing the γ_{10} and γ_{20} coefficients. These two coefficients represent the moderating relationships of *GDP* for *Individualism* and *Self-esteem*, respectively.

These examples have focused on comparisons of only two coefficients, but constraints can involve more than two coefficients. For example, assume there are three Level 1 predictors in a model. This would generate four fixed effects at Level 2, one for the intercept (γ_{00}) and one for each of the three slopes (γ_{10}, γ_{20}, and γ_{30}). A constraint could compare the average of the first two slopes with the third (γ_{10}, γ_{20}, vs. γ_{30}), which could be coded -1, -1, 2. Similarly, the moderating relationship of the Level 2 variable on each of these slopes could be compared.

Constraints can also have more than 1 degree of freedom. Assume the broad hypothesis is that three slopes, X1, X2, and X3, are different, much like the null hypothesis of an ANOVA with more than two groups. This hypothesis could be tested with a 2 degree of freedom constraint, perhaps coded as 1; −1, 0; and 1, 0, −1 for γ_{10}, γ_{20}, and γ_{30} respectively. Keep in mind that just like the *F* test from an ANOVA, if such a constraint were significant, an analyst would not know exactly which slopes were different from each other.

These examples represent only a small sample of the possible applications of this technique. I believe tests of fixed effects are underutilized in research using MRCM. With appropriate coding schemes and constraints, analysts can use MRCM to conduct ANOVA-like analyses for categorical variables, they can compare the strength of relationships without having to rely on variance estimates of questionable meaning, and so forth. One reason I have emphasized the careful understanding of exactly what each coefficient in a model represents is to encourage analysts to create models in anticipation of using these tests.

STANDARDIZATION OF MEASURES

Contrary to the experience of analysts who have worked primarily with OLS regression, MRCM estimates only *unstandardized* coefficients. MRCM analyses estimate unstandardized coefficients because the algorithms rely on covariance, rather than correlation, matrices to estimate parameters. Although this is desirable from a modeling perspective (covariance matrices have more information than correlation matrices), it is not necessarily desirable from a substantive perspective. That is, frequently, researchers are interested in examining relationships in which the influence of differences in the variances of measures are controlled or eliminated, rather than maintained.

Although standardization per se is not possible, standardized coefficients can be indirectly estimated in some cases. This is easiest at Level 2. If Level 2 measures are standardized before analysis, coefficients representing relationships between Level 2 variables and Level 1 coefficients will represent the change in a Level 1 coefficient associated with a standard unit increase in the Level 2 predictor. Technically, the analysis will still estimate unstandardized coefficients – the change in a Level 1 coefficient associated with a 1-point change in a Level 2 measure; however, because the Level 2 measure is now standardized, a 1-point change represents a standard unit.

At Level 1, the situation is not so straightforward. First, it is best to avoid such problems by designing studies so that measures have similar variances, for example, use the same scale for different measures. This is not always possible, however (e.g., the data may have been collected), and so measures can be transformed to reduce or eliminate differences in variances (e.g., divided by a constant). Analysts should avoid (or consider carefully) standardizing *within* countries, that is, calculate a standard deviation for each country and represent observations in terms of standard deviations from each country's mean. Such standardization artificially sets the mean for all countries to 0 and, in the process, eliminates mean differences in intercepts by eliminating any variance in the intercept.

Although changing the variance of an individual measure using a linear transformation will not change the significance tests of individual coefficients, variance differences do contribute to the significance tests of comparisons of coefficients. For example, assume a model in which there are two Level 2 predictors of a Level 1 intercept. Changing the variance of these predictors will change the results of the comparison of the Level 2 coefficients. Tests of the individual effects will not change, but chi-squared tests of constraints will. Similarly, the variances of Level 1 predictors contribute to tests of constraints of their means at Level 2.

ESTIMATING EFFECT SIZES

Within the multilevel framework, the strength of the relationships between two variables can be evaluated in two ways. The first, and least controversial, is simply to interpret the size of the coefficient. This can be illustrated using analyses of the example data set, keeping in mind that MRCM estimates unstandardized coefficients. For example, the estimated mean slope between *Life Satisfaction* and *Individualism* in the original analysis was .86. This means that *Life Satisfaction* increases .86 for every 1-point increase in *Individualism*. To estimate the increase or decrease associated with a 1*SD* requires an estimate of the within-country *SD*. This is not done, however, using simple single-level descriptive statistics that ignore grouping.

The estimated within-country standard deviation can, and should, be derived from an unconditional analysis of the predictor. The within-country standard deviation is the Level 1 standard deviation, or the square root of the Level 1 variance if the standard deviation is not provided directly. For the sample data set, the Level 1 *SD* of *Individualism* is 2.16. By the way, simply taking the *SD* of all the Level 1 observations produces an estimate of 2.54. Estimated *Life Satisfaction* when *Individualism* is +1 *SD* would be 15.03 + (.86 ∗ 2.16) = 16.89. Estimated *Life Satisfaction* when *Individualism* is −1 *SD* would be 15.03 − (.86 ∗ 2.16) = 13.17.

The strength of the slope can also be evaluated by estimating the percent of variance in the dependent measure accounted for by the predictor. This is done by comparing the residual Level 1 variance from the totally unconditional model of the dependent measure (3.05 for *Life Satisfaction*) to the Level 1 variance with the predictor included (.30 when *Individualism* is included). In this analysis, the two variables share just over 90% of the variance, which translates into an average within-country correlation of approximately .95. Also, reversing the process (predicting *Individualism* from *Life Satisfaction*) produces approximately the same numbers, a similarity that is not always the case.

Using residual variances to estimate the strength of relationships is a somewhat controversial procedure among multilevel modelers. For example, although Kreft and de Leeuw (1998) discussed R^2, they advised caution when interpreting such estimates of effect sizes: "In general, we suggest not setting too much store by the calculation of R^2_B [Level-2 variance] or R^2_W [Level-1 variance] (p. 119)." In part this is because adding significant Level 1 predictors does not necessarily lead to a reduction in residual variances.

Unlike OLS analyses, in which significance tests of effects are based on reductions in error variance, in MRCM analyses, significance tests of the fixed effect of a coefficient and random error terms are estimated separately. In some rare cases, adding predictors to a Level 1 model may lead to an increase in residual variance, a mathematical impossibility in OLS. There are also questions about how centering affects such estimates (Raudenbush & Bryk, 2002), with the general agreement that predictors should be group-mean centered. My advice in this regard is to follow Kreft and deLeeuw (1998) and be cautious. For the moment, it suffices to note that it appears that models with single predictors at Level 1 with no Level 2 variables provide a reasonably stable estimate of the variance shared by two Level 1 variables and that using reductions in residual variances associated with additional Level 2 predictors seems less problematic.

NONLINEAR OUTCOMES

Thus far, the discussion has assumed that dependent measures are continuous and more or less normally distributed; however, cross-cultural researchers may be interested in outcomes that are not continuous or not normally distributed, for example, categorical measures, highly skewed count data, and so forth. Analyses of such measures rely on the same logic as analyses of measures that are normally distributed, but they use different algorithms. Different algorithms are necessary because for measures that are not normally distributed, means and variances are not independent, and this lack of independence violates a critical assumption. For example, the variance of a binomial is npq, where $n =$ number of observations, $p =$ the probability of the more common outcome, and $q = 1 - p$. As the mean changes (the expected value, p), the variance changes.

Analyses of nonlinear outcomes are structurally similar to the analyses of linear outcomes. A Level 1 model is estimated, and then the coefficients from Level 1 are then analyzed at Level 2. In the sample data set, there is a variable *Union*, which indicates whether a person belongs to a labor organization, and the percent of people who belong can be examined using a Bernoulli model with $n = 1$. The model is as follows:

$$\text{Prob}(\text{y} = 1|\beta_{0\text{j}}) = \phi.$$

The transformation represented in this equation normalizes Bernoulli ($N = 1$) outcomes. The null hypothesis, a mean of 0, represents 50%. The coefficient from this analysis, the log-odds of belonging, is .08 (unit-specific, nonrobust estimate) and corresponds to 52%, which is this case was not significantly different from 0. Although the null hypothesis is always that a coefficient is different from 0, what 0 represents will vary as a function of the transformation being used (i.e., the type of nonlinear outcome).

When analyzing nonlinear outcomes, predictors can be added at Levels 1 and 2 just as they are added to analyses of linear outcomes, and the results of the analyses are interpreted similarly. For example, when *GDP* is included in the Level 2 model (grand-mean centered), the resulting coefficient is $-.15$, which is not significant ($p = .17$). Assuming that it was, the relationship could be interpreted by generating predicted values for countries $\pm$ 1 *SD* on *GDP*. The *SD* of *GDP* is 2.63, so a country +1 *SD* would have a predicted log odds of $-.31 = .08 + (2.63 * (-.15))$, corresponding to 42%. A country -1 *SD* would have a predicted log odds of $.47 = .08 - (2.63 * (-.13))$, corresponding to 62%. Note that although *GDP* was grand-mean centered, the intercept in this analysis is slightly different from the intercept in the unconditional model.

When analyzing nonlinear outcomes, analysts should be aware of the following:

1. Interpreting the results of nonlinear analyses needs to be done carefully, particularly for analysts who are not familiar with logistical

regression and related techniques. Although transformations may be clearly described, producing predicted values, which are needed to understand the coefficients, can be quite complex. To generate predicted values, I use a spreadsheet with cells containing each step of the equation that is needed to generate point estimates from log odds.
2. In analyses of nonlinear outcomes, Level 1 variances are not estimated. This is because of the nature of the algorithms used in these analyses.
3. For analyses of nonlinear outcomes, HLM produces two sets of coefficients, unit-specific and population-average, and such coefficients can be meaningfully different. Estimating coefficients for nonlinear outcomes requires a "link function," and different link functions are available. A detailed discussion of link functions is well beyond the scope of this chapter. Nevertheless, it may be helpful to note that unit-specific coefficients refer to relationships such as a slope (e.g., the change due to a one-unit change in a predictor) at the discrete unit (e.g., country), whereas population-average coefficients refer to relationships as they exist in the population. Blanket recommendations regarding which of these is appropriate are not possible, and interested readers are encouraged to consult Raudenbush and Bryk (2002) for more detail.

INTERPRETING RESULTS

For analysts whose experience is primarily with single-level OLS analyses that produce standardized coefficients, developing a sense of how to interpret the results of MRCM analyses will take some time. Following are some important considerations.

1. MRCM analyses produce two (or more) sets of coefficients, and in the case of cross-level interactions (described subsequently), coefficients at lower levels of analysis may need to be interpreted in light of coefficients at higher levels of analysis. More levels create a more thorough understanding, but they also create more complexity.
2. Second, most coefficients in most analyses will be unstandardized. See the previous section on standardization. Although analysts can still rely on significance tests to determine whether relationships are significantly different from 0 or different from each other, the fact that coefficients are unstandardized needs to be kept in mind.
3. Significance tests of the fixed effect of a coefficient can vary as a function of the inclusion or exclusion of a random error term for that

coefficient. Before evaluating the results of significance tests of fixed effects (the tests that are most relevant for most researchers) error terms need to be specified properly. For most analyses, this will mean that error terms that are reliable should be retained, whereas those that are not reliable should be eliminated from the model, that is, the effects should be "fixed."

4. The meaning of coefficients depends on how variables are centered, and different centering options can produce different (sometimes dramatically different) significance tests. Unlike the specification of error structures, which often has a post hoc component (i.e., eliminating error terms that cannot be estimated reliably), centering is something that should be done in advance. Analysts should know in advance what they want each coefficient to represent and should select the centering options that represent these quantities.

With these considerations in mind, the key to understanding the results of MRCM analyses is to generate predicted or expected values as I have done with the analyses of the sample data set. In the case of categorical measures, this would mean expected values for each category, whereas for continuous measures, one might chose to estimate values for observations ± 1 *SD* on predictors. Given the potential complexity of the results, the importance of generating predicted values cannot be overstated. Such an emphasis contrasts sharply with the emphasis in many single-level OLS analyses on significance tests of standardized coefficients.

REPORTING RESULTS

As a guiding principle, authors need to recognize that, at least for the next few years, the majority of readers will probably not be that familiar with MRCM. Although scholarly articles are meant to educate, to expose readers to new approaches and new techniques, scholarly articles are also meant to inform, to provide readers with a better understanding of substantive issues. For most articles, this means that detailed presentations of results and aspects of the analyses that are not central to the substantive questions of the study may confuse more than they inform. Certainly, authors need to provide sufficient detail so that readers (and reviewers!) can understand what was done, but in most instances, answers to substantive questions are "the dog," whereas the analyses that provide the bases for these answers are "the tail."

When presenting the models themselves, most readers will probably be able to understand the analyses more readily if the models are presented using the "Raudenbush and Bryk" or "HLM" style (the style used in this chapter) compared with the mixed effect (or mixed model) style in which all coefficients are included in a single equation. In the HLM style, each Level 1 coefficient has a separate equation, and different letters are used for Level 1 and Level 2 coefficients. Note that I am not suggesting the analyses need to be conducted using HLM. I am simply suggesting to use the HLM style to present the models. In my experience, more people understand more readily the structure of models when they are presented using the HLM style.

The following recommendations about reporting the results of MRCM analyses assume that the primary focus of a paper is the fixed effects, that is, the results of the significance tests of the relationships between variables. Although random error terms can be of interest, the hypotheses of most researchers will probably concern fixed effects such as those that were presented in the previous sections. Were two individual variables related (e.g., the slope representing the relationship between *Life Satisfaction* and *Individualism*), did this relationship vary across countries in some predictable way (e.g., the moderating relationship of *GDP*), and so forth.

This emphasis reflects, in part, the fact that although a significant random error term for a coefficient indicates that a coefficient varies (randomly), as discussed previously, the lack of a significant random error term does not mean that a coefficient does not vary in any way. Even without a significant random error term, it is still possible for a coefficient to vary nonrandomly, for example, when a country-level characteristic is found to be related to a within-country slope. Given this possibility, I tend to deemphasize the importance of random error terms. For most purposes, it should suffice to describe which effects were modeled as random and which effects were fixed, and if they were fixed, why. Nevertheless, this issue is far from resolved among multilevel scholars, and researchers will need to make their own decisions about the results they report.

When reporting results, it will usually suffice to describe the fixed coefficients (usually γs of some kind), the significance level associated with the test of the hypothesis that the coefficients are 0, and the t values. There is no need to report the coefficient, the t value, and the standard error because the t value is simply the coefficient divided by the standard error. Analysts may want to report degrees of freedom, which will indicate whether an effect was modeled as fixed or random, although the probabilities associated with t values do not vary as a function of degrees of freedom as they would in an OLS analyses because in MRCM *t* values are approximations. Some other tests, such as multiparameter tests, produce chi-squares indicating differences in model fits, and for such tests, reporting the chi-squared and its associated degrees of freedom and *p* value is appropriate. Finally, in many, if not most, instances, it is probably inappropriate to report the results of the significance test of whether the intercept is significantly different from 0. Such results should be reported only when 0 is a meaningful value for the dependent measure, which, for example, would not be the case for a dependent measure that used a 1 to 7 scale.

Some authors present comparisons of models, similar to what is done when presenting SEM analyses. Although there can be good reasons to do this, for many if not most purposes, it is probably not necessary. Descriptions of MRCM analyses tend to focus on individual parameters more than the overall fit of a model, whereas in SEM, the overall fit of a model is typically the focus of the analyses. The overall fit of two MRCM models can be compared to make decisions about the inclusion of random error terms, although such procedures are probably not necessary for evaluating the inclusion or exclusion of individual error terms. The relative fits of sets of predictors can also be compared, although analysts should be certain to use the full maximum likelihood estimator when doing so (e.g., Raudenbush et al., 2004).

Finally, and most important, authors are strongly encouraged to include predicted values in the interpretation of their results. For continuous variables, a commonly accepted standard is $\pm$ 1 *SD* above and below the mean. When groups are involved (at either level of analysis) it is typically helpful to generate predicted values for each group. Such predicted values can be particularly useful when explaining complex findings such as cross-level interactions.

MODEL BUILDING

Broadly speaking, there seem to be two traditions in OLS regression: one in which predetermined sets of predictors are included and retained regardless of their statistical significance, and another, more exploratory approach, in which many predictors are included and only those that are significant are retained. Certainly, other possibilities exist and are used. Nevertheless, neither of these approaches may be appropriate for MRCM, particularly at Level 1 and particularly when the number of predictors is large.

This difference in strategies reflects one of the critical differences between the OLS regression and MRCM. In OLS regression, for each predictor only a fixed effect is estimated, and only one error term is estimated for the whole model. In contrast, in MRCM, for each Level 1 predictor, a fixed effect and a random effect are estimated, and the covariances among the random error terms are also estimated. This means that in a MRCM analysis, the number of parameters being estimated increases nonlinearly as predictors are added. For example, with a Level 1 model with no predictors, two parameters are estimated: fixed and random effects for the intercept. With one Level 1 predictor, five parameters are estimated: fixed and random effects for the intercept and the slope and the covariances between the error terms for the intercept and the slope. With three predictors, nine parameters are estimated: fixed and random effects for the intercept and the two slopes, and the covariances between the three error terms. And so on.

When thinking of building a model, statisticians will sometimes refer to the *carrying capacity* of the data. How many parameters can a data set estimate reliably? For these purposes, it may be helpful to think of a data structure as an information array and to think in terms of the amount of information that is available to estimate the parameters in a model. Assuming the same data structure, models that estimate more parameters will have less information for each parameter. At some point, a model requires too many parameters, and there is not enough information to estimate all or any of the parameters.

Given this, multilevel modelers tend to favor forward-stepping algorithms, that is, adding predictors one at a time and deleting those that are not significant or testing smaller models first and adding to them. This procedure is meaningfully different from backward-stepping algorithms in which many predictors are simultaneously included at the outset, and those that are not significant are deleted. Forward-stepping approaches tend to build smaller models with fewer, but more stable, parameter estimates than backward-stepping approaches. Of course, individual analysts will have to be guided by the specific situation they face and the norms in their disciplines. Regardless, analysts who are accustomed to including simultaneously many predictors in models may have to confront the possibility that they cannot include as many (perhaps not nearly as many) predictors in their Level 1 models as they may want to include, or have been accustomed to including, in OLS regression.

USING ESTIMATED COEFFICIENTS IN OTHER ANALYSES

The coefficients estimated in a MRCM analysis can be saved and used in other analyses; however, analysts are urged to be very cautious when doing this. First, as is the case with any technique involving multiple predictors, the estimates from any specific analysis will reflect the covariances among the variables that are included in the analysis, and with MRCM, such estimates will also reflect whatever error structure was in the model. Moreover, if a random error term is not estimated for a coefficient and no Level 2 predictor is in a model, some programs, such as HLM, will provide the same estimate for a coefficient for all Level 2 units (countries). This is a result of the algorithm that is used to estimate coefficients.

Analysts need to keep in mind that although it may be useful to think of MRCM models as a series of nested equations, in fact MRCM analyses rely on a single equation that simultaneously includes predictors at all levels. Second, if shrunken estimates are used (based on a Bayesian analysis, something commonly used in MRCM programs), they are typically highly correlated with OLS estimates. They differ from OLS estimates in terms of their variances, and so for pure correlational analyses, there may not be much of a difference in results using the two. Third, unless the coefficients are used in an analysis in which random error can be modeled, the analysis will not reflect this aspect of the multilevel analysis, undermining the value of using MRCM to estimate the coefficients.

With this in mind, analysts are encouraged to think creatively about how they can examine questions of interest within the multilevel context. For example, within-country differences such as changes across time can be examined using various coding schemes that reflect the trends of interest. Groups of countries can be compared by creating variables at Level 2. Analysts should think carefully before using the coefficients estimated by MRCM in some other type of analysis.

WEIGHTS

Decisions about weights in analyses are not unique to multilevel modeling. For various reasons, researchers may want to assign more importance (more weight) to some observations than to others. Such decisions frequently reflect desires to correct samples for the under- or overrepresentation of different types of respondents. For example, if 75% of the respondents in a sample are men and it is known that the population has the same number of men and women, each man might be weighted 2 and each women 3 (or .67 and 1, or some ratio reflecting the desired adjustment). There are no hard-and-fast rules for weighting observations, and such adjustments can reflect various considerations. See Haedler and Gabler (2003) for a broad discussion of weighting, and see the European Social Survey (ESS, 2009) for an excellent discussion of the use of weights within a multilevel, cross-cultural study.

The aspect of weighting that is unique to multilevel modeling is the fact that weights can be assigned to units at each level of analysis (country and person for present purposes). At the person level, such weights are sometimes referred to as *design weights* because they reflect the distribution of cases obtained from a certain sampling design. Design weights can be used to adjust for the lack of representativeness in a sample. Such nonrepresentativeness may be intentional. For example, certain groups may be oversampled (data are collected from proportionately more people than exist in the population) to ensure that researchers have adequate samples for groups with few members (e.g., immigrants). Nonrepresentativeness may also be unintentional. For example, attempts to create representative samples may fall short for various reasons. Regardless of the reasons, if samples are not representative, estimates of country-level statistics (within a multilevel framework or not) may be inaccurate because the sample on which they are based does not represent the population the statistics are meant to describe. Such problems can be addressed with appropriate weights for analyses.

At the country level, weights will usually reflect differences in the population of countries in a sample. For example, assume a study has 100 observations from both Finland and China. Between 5 and 6 million people live in Finland, whereas over 1 billion people live in China. When making inferences about humankind, it does not make much sense to treat these two groups of 100 observations similarly. Exactly how to take into account such disparities may not be fixed. A researcher may weigh countries (Level 2 observations) using population per se, log or other transforms of population, and so forth.

DESIGN CONSIDERATIONS AND ALTERNATIVE ANALYTIC STRATEGIES

Similar to the consideration of single-level data structures, researchers frequently have questions about the power of multilevel data design. How well can a sample of such-and-such detect a difference of such-and-such? Unfortunately, estimating the power of multilevel models is not well understood, and the following discussion should be interpreted as a discussion of guidelines rather than a description of hard and fast rules. Various rules, usually described in terms of the number of Level 2 and Level 1 observations, have been proposed such as, 30/30 (Kreft, 1996), 50/20, or 100/10 (Hox, 1998). It should be noted that these rules reflect research designs in which obtaining more Level 2 units is probably much easier than it is for cross-cultural researchers to obtain more countries. See Richter (2006) for an informed and accessible discussion of power analyses in multilevel models.

As is the case with single-level analyses, the axiom "more is better" certainly applies. More observations (at either level of analysis) will provide more stable parameter estimates. Unfortunately, particularly for cross-cultural research, it may be difficult, if not impossible, to obtain more observations, particularly at the country or culture level. Moreover, given the difficulty of obtaining data from multiple countries, researchers are often faced with am empirical fait accompli – country-level data have been collected, and the essential question is "Are there enough countries to justify a multilevel analysis?"

Answering this broader question requires answering other questions, the most important of which is probably this: Do the primary hypotheses concern intercepts or slopes from Level 1? Intercepts are invariably more reliable than slopes, and so it is easier (i.e., the data provide more power) to examine country-level differences in intercept than in slopes. More reliable coefficients are more efficient, meaning that fewer countries will be needed to model country-level differences in intercepts compared with slopes. Nevertheless, many hypotheses concern country-level differences in slopes, for example, how does the relationship between individual-level variables X and Y vary as a function of country-level variable Z?

Given that many cross-cultural researchers will be interested in country-level differences in within-country coefficients (intercepts and slopes), this discussion focuses on the number of countries that are needed. First, it is informative to think of the countries in an analysis as being sampled from the population of countries. Within such a context, analysts can think of the minimum number of observations they would need in a traditional, single-level design. Certainly, few researchers would consider a study in which there were only 4, 5, or 6 observations. Similarly, within the multilevel context, a small number of countries will not provide a good basis for estimating parameters, and such shortcomings will be particularly important for estimating random error terms. Coefficients that theoretically should be random will not be able to be modeled as such because there will not be enough information to estimate the random error component.

All this is well and good but begs the question, What can or should an analyst do if there are simply not enough countries to perform a multilevel analysis, for example, there are only two or three countries? Various options are available in such cases. If the research questions primarily concern differences in means, then some type of analysis of variance may be appropriate in which countries are treated as a between-groups factor. If the research questions primarily concern within-country relationships, the most appropriate option is probably a technique known as *regression by groups*. As mentioned in the introduction to this chapter, in such analyses, separate regression equations are estimated for each group (country), and then the coefficients for each group can be compared. Although this technique does not model the random variability in coefficients, it does not assume that coefficients (slopes) are equal across groups. Finally, I urge analysts to be cautious regarding the use of LSDV analyses. As explained in the introduction, unless such analyses explicitly include terms that test the similarity of slopes across groups (countries), the analyses assume that the slopes are similar.

It is important to keep in mind however, that such analyses do not provide the opportunity to model (to explain statistically) between-country differences in coefficients (either means or slopes). Although they may be able to establish the fact that coefficients vary across countries, they do not provide a statistical basis for drawing conclusions about why such differences exist. There are simply not enough countries to provide a basis for statistical inference. In such cases, analysts will need to rely on other bases for drawing conclusions about why countries differ.

SOFTWARE OPTIONS

In response to the growing interest in multilevel modeling, the number of programs that can perform such analyses has increased meaningfully since 1995. There are too many programs to discuss specific comparisons here, so I offer only broad guidelines. First, it is important to note that the major programs (i.e., programs offered by reputable software firms) will give the same results, *provided the same models are specified.* I have emphasized *the same models* because multilevel models require analysts to make numerous decisions about error structures, centering, and so forth, and different programs will implement different options in different ways.

For analysts who are familiar with the subtleties of MRCM, the selection of software can be guided by familiarity and accessibility. The situation is different for analysts who are not familiar with MRCM. For such analysts, I recommend programs such as HLM and MlwiN that have been specifically designed to do MRCM analyses, with HLM probably being the easiest to use. This recommendation is based on the ease with which models can be specified (error terms, centering, etc.), the ease with which the output can be interpreted, and my experience giving workshops. For analysts who are not familiar with MRCM, the array of options in many multipurpose programs can be confusing and can lead them to specify (unwittingly) inappropriate or incorrect models because such programs were designed to conduct more than just MRCM.

Finally, the availability of different software options highlights the importance of referring to the analyses discussed in this chapter as multilevel random coefficient models or sometimes simply as multilevel models (MLM) instead of using the term hierarchical linear models . In the multilevel world, HLM is a specific program that conducts MRCM, and authors should be careful to distinguish the statistical technique they used (MLM) from the program they used to conduct the analyses (e.g., HLM, SAS, etc.).

CONCLUDING REMARKS

The fit between multilevel modeling and cross-cultural research is a natural one, particularly for cross-cultural psychologists who are invariably interested in the joint effects of individual and cultural differences on the attitudes, beliefs, and behaviors of individuals. Such interests typically rely on analyses of data sets in which observations from multiple individuals within multiple cultures are collected, and multilevel modeling provides a comprehensive framework within which various types of relationships can be examined within such data structures.

My sense is that because of this fit, the use of multilevel modeling in cross-cultural research will grow over the next few years and beyond. Such growth will not be without its growing pains, however. Particularly for researchers whose primary training has concerned single-level OLS techniques, the considerations involved in conducting multilevel analyses can be daunting. Coefficients at multiple levels must be interpreted simultaneously, and relationships at different levels of analysis influence each other. Moreover, there are the complexities of modeling error structures.

One of the obstacles to the widespread use of multilevel modeling is the relative lack of university courses on the topic. Although this is changing, by no means is multilevel modeling currently part of the accepted canon for graduate education in statistics in the social sciences. Nevertheless, there are excellent resources available, in terms of books and articles, and professional training (e.g., workshops), and interested researchers can develop an understanding of multilevel modeling well after they have finished their formal training. One of my goals in writing this chapter was to provide enough information to allow researchers who are unfamiliar with the technique to consider using MRCM, or at the least provide them with enough information to understand the results of studies using MRCM. The longest journey begins with a single step.

REFERENCES

Aiken, L. S., & West, S. G. (1991). *Multiple regression: Testing and interpreting interactions.* Newbury Park, CA: Sage.

Baron, R. M., & Kenny. D. A. (1986). The moderator–mediator distinction in social psychological research: Conceptual, strategic, and statistical considerations. *Journal of Personality and Social Psychology, 51,* 1173–1182.

Bauer, D. J., Preacher, K. J., & Gil, K. M. (2006). Conceptualizing and testing random indirect effects and moderated mediation in multilevel models: New procedures and recommendations. *Psychological Methods, 11,* 142–163.

Bryk, A. S., & Raudenbush, S. W. (1992). *Hierarchical linear models.* Newbury Park, CA: Sage.

European Social Survey. (2009). *Weighting European social survey data.* London: Centre for Comparative Social Surveys, City University, London.

Haedler, S., & Gabler, S. (2003). Sampling and estimation. In J. A., Harkness, F. J. R. Van de Vijver, & P. Ph. Mohler (Eds.), *Cross-cultural survey methods* (pp. 117–134). New York: Wiley.

Hox, J. J. (1998). Multilevel modeling: When and why? In I. Balderjahn, R. Mather, & M. Schader (Eds.), *Classification, data analysis and data highways* (pp. 147–154). New York: Springer.

Kenny, D. A., Korchmaros, J. D., & Bolger, N. (2003). Lower level mediation in multilevel models. *Psychological Methods, 8,* 115–128.

Kreft, I. G. G. (1996). *Are multilevel techniques necessary? An overview, including simulation studies.* Retrieved March 31, 2006, from http://www.calstatela.edu/faculty/ikreft/quarterly/quarterly.html.

Kreft, I. G. G., & de Leeuw, J. (1998). *Introducing multilevel modeling.* Newbury Park, CA: Sage.

Krull, J. L., & MacKinnon, D. P. (2001). Multilevel modeling of individual and group level mediated effects. *Multivariate Behavioral Research, 36,* 249–277.

Marsh, H. W., & Hau, K. (2003). Big-fish-little-pond-effect on academic self-concept. A cross-cultural (26 country) test of the negative effects of academically selective schools. *American Psychologist, 58,* 364–376.

Nezlek, J. B. (2001). Multilevel random coefficient analyses of event and interval contingent data in social and personality psychology research. *Personality and Social Psychology Bulletin, 27,* 771–785.

Nezlek, J. B. (2003). Using multilevel random coefficient modeling to analyze social interaction diary data. *Journal of Social and Personal Relationships, 20,* 437–469.

Nezlek, J. B., & Plesko, R. M. (2003). Affect- and self-based models of relationships between daily events and daily well-being. *Personality and Social Psychology Bulletin, 29,* 584–596.

Preacher, K. J., Curran, P. J., & Bauer, D. J. (2006). Computational tools for probing interaction effects in multiple linear regression, multilevel modeling, and latent curve analysis. *Journal of Educational and Behavioral Statistics, 31,* 437–448.

Rabash, J., Browne, W., Goldstein, H., Yang, M., Plewis, I., Healy, M., et al. (2000). *MLn: Command reference guide.* London: Institute of Education.

Raudenbush, S. W., & Bryk, A. S. (2002). *Hierarchical linear models* (2nd ed.). Newbury Park, CA: Sage.

Raudenbush, S., Bryk, A., Cheong, Y. F., & Congdon, R. (2004). *HLM 6: Hierarchical linear and nonlinear modeling*. Lincolnwood, IL: Scientific Software International.

Richter, T. (2006). What is wrong with ANOVA and multiple regression? Analyzing sentence reading times with hierarchical linear models. *Discourse Processes, 41*, 221–250.

Singer, J. D. (1998). Using SAS PROC MIXED to fit multilevel models, hierarchical models, and individual growth models. *Journal of Educational and Behavioral Statistics, 23*, 323–355.

Snijders, T., & Bosker, R. (1999). *Multilevel analysis*. London: Sage.

APPENDIX

Sample Data Sets

Sample data set Level 1 data

Coun.	Life	Ind.	Ind2.	Union	NUn.	Ucnt.	Coun	Life	Ind.	Ind2.	Union	NUn.	Ucnt.
A	1	1	1	0	1	−1	D	5	5	5	1	0	1
A	2	2	2	1	0	1	D	6	6	6	1	0	1
A	3	2	2	1	0	1	D	6	7	7	1	0	1
A	4	3	3	1	0	1	D	7	8	8	1	0	1
A	5	3	3	0	1	−1	D	8	9	9	1	0	1
A	6	3	3	1	0	1	D	9	10	10	1	0	1
A	7	4	4	1	0	1	E	1	4	104	0	1	−1
A	8	4	4	1	0	1	E	2	5	105	1	0	1
B	2	2	2	0	1	−1	E	3	6	106	0	1	−1
B	2	2	2	0	1	−1	E	4	6	106	0	1	−1
B	3	2	2	0	1	−1	E	5	6	106	1	0	1
B	3	4	4	0	1	−1	E	6	7	107	0	1	−1
B	4	4	4	1	0	1	E	7	8	108	1	0	1
B	4	4	4	1	0	1	E	8	9	109	1	0	1
B	5	5	5	1	0	1	E	9	10	110	0	1	−1
B	6	5	5	0	1	−1	E	9	10	110	0	1	−1
B	6	5	5	0	1	−1	F	1	1	101	0	1	−1
C	3	3	3	0	1	−1	F	1	2	102	0	1	−1
C	3	3	3	1	0	1	F	4	5	105	0	1	−1
C	3	3	3	0	1	−1	F	5	7	107	1	0	1
C	4	6	6	1	0	1	F	5	8	108	1	0	1
C	4	6	6	1	0	1	F	6	10	110	0	1	−1
C	4	6	6	1	0	1	G	5	2	102	0	1	−1
C	5	8	8	1	0	1	G	5	2	102	0	1	−1
C	5	8	8	0	1	−1	G	5	2	102	0	1	−1
C	5	9	9	1	0	1	G	6	3	103	0	1	−1
C	6	9	9	1	0	1	G	6	3	103	1	0	1
D	2	1	1	0	1	−1	G	6	3	103	1	0	1
D	3	2	2	1	0	1	G	7	4	104	1	0	1
D	4	3	3	1	0	1	G	7	4	104	1	0	1
D	4	4	4	0	1	−1	G	7	5	105	0	1	−1
G	8	6	106	0	1	−1	I	6	6	106	0	1	−1

Coun.	Life	Ind.	Ind2.	Union	NUn.	Ucnt.	Coun	Life	Ind.	Ind2.	Union	NUn.	Ucnt.
H	4	1	101	0	1	−1	I	7	7	107	1	0	1
H	4	1	101	0	1	−1	I	7	7	107	1	0	1
H	4	2	102	1	0	1	I	7	8	108	1	0	1
H	5	2	102	1	0	1	I	7	9	109	1	0	1
H	5	3	103	1	0	1	I	8	10	110	0	1	−1
H	5	4	104	0	1	−1	I	8	10	110	0	1	−1
H	6	5	105	1	0	1	J	3	4	104	0	1	−1
H	6	5	105	1	0	1	J	3	4	104	0	1	−1
H	6	6	106	1	0	1	J	3	5	105	1	0	1
H	6	7	107	0	1	−1	J	4	5	105	1	0	1
H	7	5	105	1	0	1	J	4	5	105	1	0	1
H	7	5	105	1	0	1	J	5	8	108	0	1	−1
I	6	4	104	0	1	−1	J	5	8	108	0	1	−1
I	6	4	104	0	1	−1	J	7	8	108	0	1	−1
I	6	5	105	0	1	−1	J	7	8	108	0	1	−1

Coun. – Country identifier
Life – Life satisfaction
Ind. – Individualism
Ind2. – Individualism with 100 added to observations for some countries
Union – Dummy-coded variable representing membership in a union, member = 1, non-member = 0.
NUn. – Dummy-coded variable representing non-membership in a union, nonmember = 1, member = 0.
Ucnt. – Contrast-coded variable representing membership in a union, member = 1, non-member = −1.

Sample data set Level 2 data

	Means of Level 1			
Country	GDP	Individ	Individ2	Party
A	8	2.75	2.75	0
B	12	3.67	3.67	0
C	14	6.10	6.10	0
D	9	5.50	5.50	0
E	12	7.10	107.10	0
F	14	6.00	106.00	1
G	12	3.40	103.40	1
H	15	3.83	103.83	1
I	15	7.00	107.00	1
J	16	6.11	106.11	1

Country – Country identifier
GDP – Gross Domestic Product
Individ. – Country level mean of level 1 variable Ind
Individ2. – Country level mean of level 1 variable Ind2
Party – Dummy-coded variable representing multiparty political system in a country, 0 = dual-party system and 1 = multiparty system

12

Cross-Cultural Meta-Analysis

DIANNE A. VAN HEMERT

INTRODUCTION

The impact of culture on psychological functioning has received increasing attention over the past decades. Scrutiny of the PsycInfo database (May 2006) shows that the percentage of studies addressing culture, ethnicity, or race has been steadily increasing from 4.6% of all published psychological studies between 1960 and 1970 to 9.3% between 1990 and 2000. There is a clear need for accumulating and systematizing knowledge from this vast amount of cross-cultural studies and for developing models that deal with cross-cultural differences in psychology. Approaches to explaining cross-cultural differences and similarities seem to be dependent on research domain; for example, studies involving cross-cultural cognitive research generally regard cultural differences as evidence for a cultural bias in their measurement (Faucheux, 1976).

Cross-cultural psychology would benefit from a valid representation of magnitude and sources of cross-cultural variation across all research domains. Meta-analysis can provide such representation by summarizing a great range of results from many single-culture and cross-cultural studies and estimating the actual size of cross-cultural differences using effect sizes that are corrected for artifacts. A meta-analysis reanalyzes results from studies that report on a specific relationship to reach an overall conclusion on this research question, thereby accumulating research and fostering theory building (Hunter & Schmidt, 1990). In addition, meta-analysis can address questions not originally considered in the primary studies by taking into account characteristics of studies that can explain variance in the effect size. Meta-analytic techniques help reviewers avoid problems common to traditional reviews such as subjectivity of study selection, inability to quantify the effect size, and difficulties in accounting for methodological differences between studies. Further, meta-analysis can examine models of explanatory factors in cross-cultural differences using moderator variables. This asset of meta-analysis is particularly useful in view of the peculiarities of different research domains in psychology with respect to the preferred type of explanation for cross-cultural differences and similarities. Therefore, meta-analysis is a powerful tool for advancing cross-cultural theorizing and an exceptionally valuable contribution to cross-cultural research methods.

This chapter discusses the use of meta-analysis in cross-cultural psychological research. The goals of this chapter are threefold. First, I show how culture can be dealt with in meta-analytic techniques and outline two different types of cross-cultural meta-analysis. Second, guidelines are provided for performing a cross-cultural meta-analysis throughout all phases of conducting a meta-analysis. Third, I present an illustration of cross-cultural meta-analytic data from different cross-cultural research domains.

BRINGING CULTURE INTO META-ANALYSIS

Regular Meta-Analysis

Meta-analysis statistically combines independent empirical studies that report quantitative findings into a conceptually and methodologically meaningful analysis, using well-defined procedures for data collection, coding, and analysis (see, e.g., Hedges & Olkin, 1985; Hunter & Schmidt, 1990; Rosenthal, 1991). Basically, meta-analysis has two purposes: Differences in findings across studies are first described; if these differences are not just random fluctuations, they are then explained. Meta-analysis summarizes across a set of studies the *effect sizes* that quantify the relationship between an independent and a dependent variable and examines the strength of the overall effect size. Between-study differences in effect size are explained in terms of *moderator variables*, which are study characteristics that account for variability in the relationship between the independent and the dependent variable. For example, Eagly, Karau, and Makhijani (1995) conducted a meta-analysis on the relation between gender (independent variable) and effectiveness of leaders and managers (dependent variable) by comparing male and female scores on effectiveness as rated by subordinates or manifested in objective outcome measures. The authors were interested in the size and direction of gender differences in leadership effectiveness and in explanations of these differences by moderator variables. Their effect size was the mean difference between male and female scores, and moderator variables such as the type of role and type of organization were examined to explain differences in the effect sizes across the studies. Results showed equal effectiveness of women and men (i.e., a small, nonsignificant effect size) across all of the studies, but the type of role (more masculine or feminine), gender of the subordinates, the type of organization, and other variables moderated this overall effect.

Meta-Analysis and Culture

Applying meta-analytic techniques to culture-comparative research questions and using cross-cultural data as input for the analysis have consequences for different aspects of the meta-analysis, as I outline in the following sections. In general, bringing culture into meta-analysis introduces an extra level of analysis beyond the sample level and study level, that is, the culture level (van Hemert, 2003). The introduction of culture as a separate level results in an additional source of variance, which requires a new category of explanatory variables. Therefore, cross-cultural meta-analyses should always include moderators referring to characteristics of included samples and studies as well as culture-level moderators that explicate culture or country characteristics. If more moderators are used, more studies must be included to have sufficient sample sizes for stable estimates and to explain at least part of the variance in the effect sizes.

The process of explaining parts of the cross-cultural variance has been described as "peeling the onion called culture" (Poortinga, van de Vijver, Joe, & van de Koppel, 1987). A cross-cultural study should explain all cultural differences in terms of measurable variables that each peel away another layer of cross-cultural variance. For cross-cultural meta-analyses, this process implies that the influence of statistical artifacts and method-related factors that are not related to the research question should be ruled out before interpreting cross-cultural differences. De Leeuw and Hox (2002) mentioned three subsequent steps in the analysis of culture-comparative meta-analytic data: (a) The size and significance of cross-cultural differences should be estimated; (b) it should be investigated whether differences between cultures are attributable to methodological differences in the included studies; and (c) substantive explanatory variables should be examined. Consequently, cross-cultural variance is made up of (a) sampling variance (a nonsystematic artifact in meta-analyses that depends mainly on sample sizes in the studies), (b) variance due to methodological artifacts, and (c) systematic and substantive variance.[1] Lipsey (1997) added a fourth

[1] It should be noted that substantive variance in a cross-cultural meta-analysis can also be rooted in sample-level variables (such as gender or age) and study-level variables (such as different aspects of the dependent variable), depending on the research question.

category, residual variance, which is variance that cannot be accounted for by any of the three previous sources. In his meta-analysis combining about 300 meta-analyses of psychological, behavioral, and educational interventions, each of the four sources of variance, that is, sampling error variance, method variance, substantive variance (related to the target variable), and residual variance, explained about one fourth of the total variance. Thus, a cross-cultural meta-analysis should aim at maximizing the percentage of explained variance, peeling as many layers of the onion as possible, until nothing is left to be explained.

TWO TYPES OF CROSS-CULTURAL META-ANALYSIS

Bringing culture into meta-analysis can lead to two types of research questions: (a) Does the relationship between Variables A and B vary across cultures? and (b) How large are cross-cultural differences on Variable A and how can they be explained? These questions lead to two types of cross-cultural meta-analysis.

Culture-Moderated Meta-Analysis

The first type of research question concerns whether the relationship between two variables differs across cultures and therefore treats culture as a moderator variable. Examples are "Is the relationship between extraversion and happiness similar for ethnic groups across the United States?" and "Do men and women differ in aggressive behavior, and how is nationality related to this effect?" Many meta-analytic studies addressing this type of research question have been published, and their number is rapidly increasing. These studies do not necessarily focus on cultural differences; culture may be one of many moderators tested in the analyses. Different definitions of culture can be used; meta-analyses have been published distinguishing ethnic groups; geographic, religious, and cultural regions; language groups; or countries as their level of analysis.

An example of a meta-analysis using ethnic groups is Twenge and Campbell's (2002) review of studies examining the relation between self-esteem and socioeconomic status across four U.S. ethnic groups. The effect size was derived from correlations (for any of the ethnic groups) between any measure of general self-esteem and socioeconomic status. Ethnicity was a significant moderator: Effect sizes were positive for all groups, but considerably larger for Asians than for Blacks, Whites, and Hispanics, indicating that socioeconomic status is more salient to self-esteem in Asian culture. Another meta-analysis using ethnic group as a moderator was performed by LaFrance, Hecht, and Paluck (2003). They compared effect sizes for the gender differences in smiling for different ethnic groups: Females were found to smile more than males (the target effect), and this effect is significantly larger among White Americans than among other ethnic groups (moderator effect).

Many researchers who include culture in their meta-analysis distinguish only Western countries on one hand and Eastern or non-Western countries on the other hand, possibly because of a limited number of countries in the data. Watkins (2001) conducted a meta-analysis on the relationship of approaches to learning (such as learning styles) with variables such as self-concept, locus of control, learning environment, and academic grades, comparing correlations across 15 Western and non-Western countries. Correlations seemed to be fairly consistent across cultures. In the same line, Karau and Williams (1993) found social loafing effect sizes, defined as the difference between individual effort in individual and in collective conditions, to be more prevalent in participants from Western countries ($n_{\text{studies}} = 148$) than in participants from Eastern countries ($n_{\text{studies}} = 17$).

A less rudimentary division was used by Born, Bleichrodt, and van der Flier (1987); they compared gender differences on various intelligence measures for five clusters of cultures: White samples from Western countries, White samples that were used as reference groups for non-Western samples in cross-cultural studies, ethnic minorities in Western countries, African countries, and Asian countries. In total, 189 studies on intelligence measures were included. Across samples, similar patterns of gender differences were found. Khaleque and Rohner (2002) used reliability coefficients for measures of perceived parental acceptance–rejection and psychological adjustment as their effect size. They divided 10 countries into 4 regions and compared effect sizes for these regions, resulting in satisfactory reliabilities within regions; however, reliabilities were higher for American and Asian samples than for African samples.

Culture was conceptualized as language in a meta-analysis of neuroimaging results of word reading; effect sizes indicating the difference in cortical regions used during visual word recognition and a baseline situation were compared for different writing systems, that is, Western European alphabetic languages, Chinese characters, and Japanese syllabic and morpho-syllabic reading (Bolger, Perfetti, & Schneider, 2005). Findings suggested that different writing systems use the same brain regions for word processing, but localization within those regions might differ.

A few meta-analyses explicitly reported data from different countries. For example, Saroglou, Delpierre, and Dernelle (2004) compared correlation effect sizes between religiosity and Schwartz's values across 15 countries, grouped into Western European and Mediterranean-European countries and Jewish, Catholic, and Muslim religions, finding a moderating effect of economic development of countries on effect size. Mezulis, Abramson, Hyde, and Hankin's (2004) data allowed them to make a more specific distinction in their meta-analysis in which self-serving attributional bias was the effect size. They found significant differences in positivity bias, defined as a stronger internal attribution for positive events than negative events, across five broad cultural groups: United States, other Western countries, Asian countries, Eastern Europe and Russia, and Africa. The United States and Western countries scored significantly higher than the Asian samples. However, the effect sizes for the 16 separate national groups in their meta-analysis were far from homogeneous. In fact, the Chinese and Korean samples showed larger effect sizes (i.e., more self-serving bias) than the Western European samples.

It should be clear from this brief overview that many cross-cultural meta-analyses are troubled by the nonrepresentative sampling at the level of countries. This problem reflects the biased distribution of research across world regions. Most psychological studies are performed in the United States, followed by other English-speaking Western countries and European countries, rendering it impossible to arrive at a representative sample of countries for a cross-cultural meta-analysis. Authors can choose to use either very broad distinctions, such as Western versus non-Western countries, or work with the available countries, which are not representative of world nations. A rare example of a cross-cultural meta-analysis using separate countries as the level of analysis is Bond and Smith's (1996) analysis of 133 conformity studies using Asch's line judgment task across 17 countries. The impact of a number of study-related and country-related moderators on conformity was assessed. It was found that culture-level variables such as individualism scores and Schwartz's values were significantly related to conformity effect sizes.

The type of meta-analysis just described could be coined *culture-moderated meta-analysis*, in the sense that culture moderates variance in the effect size. As mentioned before, it is hard to collect relevant studies administered in a sufficient number of countries to allow for adequate cross-cultural comparisons. Since *culture* is a broad and diffuse concept, encompassing many aspects that may be relevant for the topic studied, one needs data from several countries to be able to explain cross-cultural differences adequately. Therefore, a second approach to cross-cultural meta-analysis might be valuable when one wants to describe patterns of differences and similarities in culture–behavior relationships across different areas of behavior.

Culture-Inclusive Meta-Analysis

The second type of research question, "How large are cross-cultural differences on Variable A, and how can they be explained?" implies that culture is an independent variable and therefore part of the target effect. Examples of this type of research question would be: "Which explanatory factors can account for cross-cultural differences in helping behavior?" and "What is the rank order of ethnic groups in the United States with respect to spatial abilities, and which group characteristics can explain these differences?" In other words, the meta-analysis focuses on the difference between Culture A and Culture B on a dependent variable. A meta-analysis addressing this type of research question could be called a *culture-inclusive meta-analysis*, because it specifically includes culture in the effect size. Consequently, culture-inclusive meta-analyses can use only culture-comparative studies as input.

Culture-inclusive meta-analyses have usually been based on comparisons of ethnic groups, typically within the United States. For example, Whites, Blacks, Hispanics, and American Indians were compared in a study by Twenge and Crocker (2002) on racial differences in self-esteem. Effect sizes were pairwise comparisons of self-esteem scores between two ethnic groups; Blacks were found to score higher than all other groups. Moderating variables included gender, socioeconomic status, and time period of the study. Ford, Kraiger, and Schechtman (1986) used a point-biserial r to indicate the relationship between race and either objective cognitive performance scores or subjective ratings. Across all conditions a positive effect size was found, meaning that Whites showed higher performance scores than Blacks. The number of culture-inclusive cross-cultural meta-analyses comparing ethnic groups has been increasing since 2000; recent examples of such projects are reviews by Gray-Little and Hafdahl (2000), Oyserman, Coon, and Kemmelmeier (2002), and Roth, Huffcutt, and Bobko (2003).

Culture-inclusive meta-analyses using countries are still rare. Heine and Hamamura (2005) contrasted East Asian countries and Western countries on a number of self-enhancement and self-esteem scales, using effect sizes of the difference between Asian and Western scores. They found much higher self-enhancement among Westerners than among Easterners. This finding was later debated by Sedikides, Gaertner, and Vevea (2007), who demonstrated that inclusion of two crucial moderator variables would lead to the conclusion that Westerners enhance more strongly on individualist dimensions and Easterners enhance more strongly on collectivistic dimensions. Oyserman et al. (2002) did a series of meta-analyses on cultural differences in individualism and collectivism, using the United States and Canada as comparison groups for the country analyses, and European Americans within the United States as comparison groups for the within-country analyses. Thus, their effect sizes indicated the mean difference in individualism and the mean difference in collectivism between the United States or Canada and other countries, and between European Americans and other ethnic groups within the United States. Americans were found to be more individualistic and less collectivistic than almost all other countries; European Americans showed lower individualism than African Americans and higher individualism than Asian Americans, and lower collectivism than both African Americans and Latino Americans.

In a culture-inclusive meta-analysis of intranational and cross-national comparisons, van de Vijver (1997) combined 197 cross-cultural studies reporting a variety of cognitive measures. The target effect was the difference in cognitive scores between two countries or cultural groups. Sample characteristics (such as age), aspects of the study (such as Western vs. non-Western tasks and complexity of the task), and country-level indicators (such as affluence and individualism) were found to explain cross-cultural differences.

Elfenbein and Ambady (2002) meta-analyzed cross-cultural studies on recognition of facial expressions of emotions, contrasting two groups in each effect size. Information on contact between the nations (geographic distance and the level of telephone contact) was included in the analyses. Results suggested an in-group advantage for emotion recognition, which was smaller when groups were living together in the same country or having more contact. In another publication (Elfenbein & Ambady, 2003), they used cultural distance variables based on Hofstede's measures to explain variation in recognition accuracy.

Most culture-inclusive meta-analyses that were described in this section compare countries in a fixed way, that is, the order of the countries in the effect sizes is the same for all effect sizes in the meta-analysis. For example, in a comparison of Western and Eastern countries, the Western country is always the first country in the effect size. However, when many cross-cultural studies including many countries are used in the meta-analysis, it is complicated to select a single reference country. In this case, a random order of countries in the effect sizes is necessary, introducing some specific complications in terms of analyses (see the Analyses section). The final section of this chapter discusses a series of random-order culture-inclusive meta-analyses that I have been conducting with colleagues (van Hemert, van de Vijver, & Poortinga, 2006).

Table 12.1. *Characteristics of culture-moderated and culture-inclusive meta-analyses*

Culture-moderated meta-analyses	Culture-inclusive meta-analyses
Orientation	
• Examines a single relationship	• Examines a single measure or thematic domain
• Focus on size of cultural difference	• Focus on interpretation of cultural difference in terms of culture-level moderators
• Allows for specific testing of hypotheses	• Allows for generalizations of culture-behavior relationships
Role of culture	
• Culture is moderator variable	• Culture is independent variable
• Effect sizes for different cultures compared	• Cultural comparison is embedded in effect size
• Both single-culture studies and culture-comparative studies can be included	• Only culture-comparative studies are included
• Moderators do not specifically address aspects of the cross-cultural comparison	• Moderators can address aspects of the cross-cultural comparison
Analysis	
• Effect size involves the relation between independent and dependent variable in one culture	• Effect size involves difference in dependent measure in two cultures (pairwise comparisons)
• Country-level moderator variables are straightforwardly linked to the country effect sizes	• Country-level moderator variables are difference scores congruent with the countries in the effect size

Characteristics of Culture-Moderated and Culture-Inclusive Meta-Analysis

In the previous sections, two ways to include culture in meta-analysis were described: (a) Culture-moderated meta-analysis treats culture as a moderator variable of the relationship between the independent and dependent variable; culture has the same status as other moderator variables; and (b) culture-inclusive meta-analysis treats culture as an independent variable, directly influencing the dependent variable; this method uses comparisons of two countries or cultural groups on a variable as the effect size. Table 12.1 shows an overview of characteristics of both types of cross-cultural meta-analysis.

The defining characteristic of culture-inclusive meta-analysis is the focus on a single variable such as self-esteem or a single thematic domain such as emotions rather than on a relationship between specific variables, resulting in a larger diversity of studies that are potentially included in a culture-inclusive meta-analysis. This larger variety of studies and the inclusion of entire thematic domains make it possible to outline broader patterns of cross-cultural similarities and differences. In addition, the nature of the effect size allows for the interpretation of cultural difference in terms of culture-level moderators, whereas culture-moderated meta-analysis merely focuses on the size of the cultural difference between effect sizes.

As mentioned earlier, culture-inclusive meta-analyses depend on the availability of studies that explicitly compare cultures on a dependent variable, whereas culture-moderated meta-analyses can use data from both single-culture studies and comparative studies. A consequence of the constraint in type of included studies is that culture-inclusive meta-analyses can address moderator variables on topics that are typically encountered in cross-cultural studies, such as potential cultural bias in instrument and administration, sample differences between cultural groups, and cross-cultural theoretical issues (see van de Vijver and Leung (1997) for an extensive overview of methodological aspects of cross-cultural research). Studies included in a culture-inclusive meta-analysis are all cross-cultural studies, and as such the sample of studies in the meta-analysis can provide useful information about typical cross-cultural issues and methods. In other words, culture-inclusive meta-analysis not only summarizes cross-cultural findings but also cross-cultural studies.

Culture-moderated and culture-inclusive approaches are also related to different ways of analyzing country-level moderator effects. In culture-inclusive meta-analyses, effect size differences between countries can be explained in terms of country characteristics simply by aggregating all effect sizes by country and assigning values of relevant country indicators to the countries. In culture-moderated meta-analyses, each comparison will need country-level variables of both countries compared. Consequently, country-level variables will be difference scores of country characteristics congruent with the two countries in the effect sizes (see the Analyses section).

To conclude, both culture-inclusive and culture-moderated meta-analyses can be useful in the study of culture and psychological functioning. Depending on the goal of the analysis, that is, assessing cultural variability in a relationship between two variables or assessing cultural variability in a single variable, culture-moderated or culture-inclusive methodology is more appropriate.

STAGES IN CROSS-CULTURAL META-ANALYSIS

This section deals with four stages of performing cross-cultural meta-analyses, both culture-moderated and culture-inclusive types: formulating a research question, searching the literature and selecting studies, coding, and analyzing. I mainly focus on aspects that are specific to cross-cultural meta-analysis; for complete instructions, readers are directed to more general texts (Cooper & Hedges, 1994; Hunter & Schmidt, 1990; Johnson & Eagly, 2000; Lipsey & Wilson, 2001).

Research Question

The first stage of any meta-analysis entails the definition of a theoretical relationship of interest. This relationship is reflected in the research question. For example, the research question "How large are national differences in emotional expressiveness, and can differences be explained in terms of country values?" implies a culture-inclusive meta-analysis, with country as the independent variable, the mean score on emotional expressiveness as the dependent variable, the mean differences between two countries on emotional expressiveness as the target effect, and country-level values as moderator variables. A culture-moderated meta-analysis of the question "How are the experience and expression of angry feelings related, and are there differences between ethnic groups in the United States?" would define the correlation between anger experience and anger expression as the target effect, and ethnic group as a moderator variable. A culture-inclusive meta-analysis demands cross-cultural studies reporting quantitative data on the dependent variable of interest; a culture-moderated analysis includes all studies reporting quantitative data on the relationship in question, regardless of the country in which the data were collected. Clearly, the research question implies several aspects of the design, such as the type of studies to be included in the meta-analysis, the type of effect size to be used, and potential moderator variables.

A much-debated issue that also applies to cross-cultural meta-analyses is the breadth of the research question. A meta-analysis on the relation between culture and emotion (van Hemert, Poortinga, & van de Vijver, 2007) may encompass a study examining score differences between 9 year olds from Israel, the United States, France, and Japan on the Children's Manifest Anxiety Scale (Ziv & Shauber, 1969), as well as a study on observed emotional reactions to an insult in northern and southern participants within the United States (C. Cohen, Nisbett, Bowdle, & Schwarz, 1996). An obvious criticism would be that a meta-analysis including studies as diverse as these two compares apples and oranges (see, e.g., Wolf, 1986). This criticism applies to culture-inclusive meta-analyses even more than to culture-moderated meta-analyses, because the former generally include broader domains of studies. As other authors pointed out (e.g., Rosenthal, 1991), combining apples and oranges is appropriate if the meta-analyst wants to make statements about fruit. Nonetheless, in broad meta-analyses containing diverse studies the so-called signal-to-noise ratio becomes worse, reducing reliability and requiring larger sample sizes. Moderator variables can play a crucial role in these meta-analyses by specifying conditions under which the effect is present and thus circumventing the apples and oranges criticism.

Literature Search and Selection of Studies

On the basis of the research question, the meta-analyst should be able to outline which studies are appropriate for analysis. Apart from the issue of culture-comparative studies versus single-culture studies that was discussed earlier, decisions need to be made with regard to the inclusion of instruments (e.g., accepting only self-reports or only specific operationalizations of the dependent measure), methods (e.g., including only studies using more than a minimum number of participants or only studies using a specific design), type of publication (e.g., considering only articles that were published in a specific time period), and type of samples used in the original studies (e.g., excluding clinical samples or specific age groups). These participant samples serve as representatives of a culture as a whole, which is the domain of inference. Therefore, samples consisting of patients, prisoners, addicts, or other people who can be expected to deviate in their psychological functioning should be excluded from most cross-cultural meta-analyses.

After the sample of relevant studies has been defined, studies can be searched and selected that may provide relevant data. Databases such as PsycInfo are the prime sources for studies; a broad inclusion of databases on a global basis (i.e., other than North American databases) is essential for the sampling of studies from different countries. The search for culture-inclusive meta-analyses should include both culture-related terms and target terms (because only culture-comparative studies are needed), whereas culture-moderated meta-analyses can make use of each study addressing the relevant relationship. For additional cross-cultural studies, one could turn to relevant journals such as *Journal of Cross-Cultural Psychology* and *Cross-Cultural Research* and contact cross-cultural researchers (the International Association for Cross-Cultural Psychology, www.iaccp.org, provides a researcher database).

Coding and Calculation of Effect Size

Each study that is found to be suitable for the meta-analysis needs to be coded in a database. This involves a coding scheme that defines all study characteristics that are to be coded for each study; I describe suggestions for a coding scheme in the next section. Each study should get at least one entry in the database. In culture-moderated meta-analyses, all entries apply to one country or cultural group, whereas entries in culture-inclusive meta-analyses compare two countries or cultural groups. The order in which those two groups appear in the effect size may be arbitrary when many countries are involved; another option is to settle the order by assigning one country as the reference group (see, e.g., Oyserman et al., 2002).

There are various reasons for coding more than one entry. In general, it is advisable to use separate entries for any factor that may be important in the moderator analyses, such as scores for relevant subgroups (such as males and females or different age groups) and all dependent measures that are related to the research question; for example, in an analysis of cultural differences in personality measures, all personality traits that appear in a study should be included. Multiple countries are dealt with differently in the two types of cross-cultural meta-analysis: In culture-moderated meta-analyses, each country should have a new entry; in a culture-inclusive meta-analysis, more than two sampled countries call for additional entries. In this case, all possible combinations of countries should be coded as separate entries. Alternatively, countries may be (randomly) coded in such a way that each country appears once; in case of an odd number of countries, one country will not be coded.

Calculation of the Effect Size

Effect sizes are typically either a standardized mean difference between two groups or conditions (d) or a correlation coefficient, indicating the relationship between two variables (r). To calculate d, one typically needs means, standard deviations, and sample sizes for the two groups in each comparison or statistics that indicate the difference between the groups on the dependent variable (such as a *t* value). For *r*, one needs a correlation coefficient or statistics that indicate the relationship between the independent and dependent variable (such as a regression coefficient). Lipsey and Wilson (2001) provided an extensive overview of ways to calculate effect sizes.

Coding Scheme

Coding schemes of all meta-analyses should consist of (a) variables that need to be coded for administrative reasons (regarding the reference and coding process), and (b) internal moderator variables (as opposed to external moderators that are added at a later stage, see the Analyses section), which describe characteristics of the studies and are potential moderator variables. Categories of internal moderator variables may be *sample characteristics*, *theory-relevant variables*, *design-related variables*, and *instrument characteristics*. An additional distinction can be made between low-inference and high-inference moderators (Hall, Tickle-Degnen, Rosenthal, & Mosteller, 1994), where the former are study characteristics that can be directly taken from the publication, such as sample size, gender, and included measures, and the latter are study features that are added by the meta-analyst and as such require more inference. For example, high-inference moderators such as the quality of a study and the expectations of the authors are less objectively codable than low-inference moderators such as the age of respondents and their nationality. Therefore, high-inference moderators should preferably be coded by raters who are unaware of the purpose of the meta-analysis. Table 12.2 shows an example of a coding scheme for a culture-inclusive meta-analysis (based on van Hemert et al., 2007). Most moderator variables described in this section apply to culture-inclusive meta-analyses only, because they specifically address issues that are dealt with in cross-cultural studies.

Sample characteristics of specific interest to cross-cultural meta-analyses are nationality or ethnicity of the two samples and the type of cultural comparison, that is, between or within countries. Each country and ethnic group should be given a unique code to facilitate linking with specific country characteristics at a later stage.

Theory-relevant variables may include the way in which culture is incorporated in the design of a study; such a moderator variable on the role of culture could consist of categories in line with a distinction by Lonner and Adamopoulos (1997) between culture as an independent variable (directly influencing the dependent variable), culture as a moderator (culture influences the relationship between independent and dependent variable), culture as a mediator (culture explains the relation between independent and

Table 12.2. *Coded variables for each study or comparison*

Administrative variables	
• Reference • Type of publication (journal article, book, book chapter, dissertation, unpublished) • Coder	
Sample characteristics	
• Sample size • Nationality or ethnicity • Gender • Age	• Socioeconomic status • Level of education • Type of sample (general, elderly, adults, students, adolescents, children) • Nature of comparison (cross-national or intranational)
Study characteristics	
Theory-relevant	• Status of culture in the study (moderator, independent, mediator, context variable) • Whether cross-cultural differences were expected from the theory • How were cross-cultural similarities and differences explained (through genetic, ecological, or sociocultural factors, or by referring to bias or the design of the study) • Nationality (by institutional affiliation) of first author
Design-related	Subject-level • Sampling methods in both groups (such as random sampling, stratified sampling, quota sampling, and convenience sampling) Sample-level • Background variables (such as age, education, gender, socioeconomic status, income, literacy, urban versus rural, and religious affiliation) used in the studies to match samples • Whether relevance of these background variables was checked during the design (a priori) or during analysis (a posteriori) Population-level • Type of sampling of cultural populations (convenience sampling, systematic sampling, random sampling; van de Vijver & Leung, 1997) • Independent variables underlying the sampling (individualism vs. collectivism, economic development, socialization patterms, Western vs. non-Western, religion, etc.) • Type of study (generalizability study, theory-driven study, psychological differences study, external validation study; van de Vijver & Leung, 1997) • Cultural bias checks (translation check, comparability of samples, comparability of instruments, independent variables check, and alternative interpretations check)

Instrument-related	• Nature of the task (psychophysiological, reaction time, discrimination and matching, decision, experimental task, observation (by researcher), self-report, reports by others) • Instrument origin (common Western tasks, adapted Western tasks, assembly of Western tasks or made for this study, locally developed non-Western tasks) • Cultural loading of the instrument based on (a) importance of language for completing the task and (b) importance of general knowledge of the culture for completing the task • Type of translation (back-translation, committee approach, single translator) • Level of inference (Poortinga, 1989): the level of interpretation that is employed in the study • Setting of the administration of the task (standard, variable across groups)

dependent variable), and culture as a context variable (systems of variables, including culture, indirectly influence the dependent variable). Another moderator variable that is relevant in cross-cultural studies concerns prior expectations by researchers with regard to the results of their study, that is, whether they expect to find cross-cultural similarities or differences or both. Brouwers, van Hemert, Breugelmans, and van de Vijver (2004) showed that cross-cultural studies are generally "difference driven" when it comes to expectations, whereas most studies find evidence for both similarities and differences. Also, types of explanations employed by researchers to account for their cross-cultural findings may be coded: Cultural differences and similarities can be explained by referring to biological factors (genetic inheritance), ecological factors such as climate or means of subsistence (hunting, gathering, and so on), sociocultural factors such as political variables, economic variables, and social variables (socialization patterns, values), and aspects of the study design, such as sample composition or nature of the instrument. Finally, nationality of the author(s) can be an informative moderator variable, for example, to establish forms of ingroup bias in the results.

Relevant *design-related variables* concern both sample-level and population-level issues. At the sample level, it may be interesting to code the extent to which and the way in which samples in the two cultures were matched; samples in both cultures should preferably be similar with respect to sociodemographic characteristics. Quite a few population-level aspects of design can be thought of. For example, cultures can be sampled (a) on the basis of theoretical considerations (systematic sampling), (b) in large numbers so as to represent all world populations (random sampling), and (c) as the result of availability (convenience sampling; van de Vijver & Leung, 1997). In addition, different concepts may underlie the choice of cultures in the study, such as different socialization patterns, economic and political systems, religions, and values. Another moderator variable that seems to be relevant in cross-cultural meta-analyses could be based on van de Vijver and Leung's (2000) description of four types of studies in terms of (a) the focus on either hypothesis testing or exploring cultural differences and similarities, and (b) the use of contextual variables to explain cultural differences or similarities. They distinguished generalizability studies (hypothesis testing, no consideration of contextual variables), theory-driven studies (hypothesis testing, contextual variables included), psychological differences studies (exploratory, no consideration of contextual variables), and external validation studies (exploratory, contextual variables included). Also relevant for cross-cultural studies is the presence of cultural bias checks, that is, did the researchers examine translation problems, did they check comparability of samples and instruments across cultures, did they evaluate the appropriateness of concepts that underlie the choice of cultures, and did they test alternative interpretations.

Instrument-related moderator variables in cross-cultural meta-analyses may include the origin of the instruments. Categories can include frequently used questionnaires that were developed in the West and are literally translated, Western questionnaires that are adapted (items changed, added, or removed), locally developed instruments based on Western theory, and locally developed and non-Western tasks that are based on an indigenous construct (based on van de Vijver & Leung, 1997). Cultural loading of the instrument can be measured as a combination of two indicators, the share of language for completing the task (particularly relevant in cognitive, perceptual, and psychophysiological tasks), and the importance of general knowledge of the culture for completing the task (see also Helms-Lorenz, van de Vijver, & Poortinga, 2003). In cross-cultural research, the translation of a questionnaire is often necessary; Brislin (1986) suggested different ways to deal with translations that can be coded as a moderator variable, that is, back-translation, committee approach, and a single translator. Another instrument-related moderator variable can be derived from Poortinga's (1989) description of different levels of inference, which refer to the relation between the measurement and the central concept in terms of which the data are interpreted. For example, low-inference relations indicate identical concept and measurement (e.g., in the measurement of color blindness or reaction times), and high-inference relationships amount to a test being used as an index or hypothetical construct (e.g., personality trait). Finally, settings in which the instruments were administered may differ across cultural groups in different respects such as physical conditions, administration, instruction, interviewer, and so on; a variable may be coded to indicate to what extent this was the case.

Many of the previously mentioned moderator variables can be taken as indicators of study quality. For example, cross-cultural methodologists have argued that high-quality culture-comparative studies should sample cultures in a systematic way, control for cultural biases, and decompose culture into context variables (van de Vijver & Leung, 1997). Indicators of study quality may serve as criteria for excluding low-quality studies or be used in the moderator analyses to examine how they influence the effect size. Alternatively, weights could be assigned in line with relative study quality, allowing more influence of high-quality studies in the overall effect size (see also Wortman, 1994, for a discussion of two general systems for assessing study quality of primary studies from social and medical sciences).

The decision about which variables to code is dependent on a number of considerations. Meta-analysts can include variables either because they are theoretically or methodologically crucial for testing their research question or because they proved to be relevant in previous research (Hall et al., 1994). However, one may want to include variables merely for descriptive reasons (Lipsey, 1994). In reality, no study will provide data on all coded variables, and many of the previously mentioned variables will show too many missing data to be included in data analysis.

Coding Procedure

Coding procedures are identical to those in regular meta-analyses, so there are no specific procedures for cross-cultural meta-analyses. Coding of the studies should be done by at least two independent coders, who need to have a basic understanding of cross-cultural research and have to be trained. Many of the moderator variables suggested here can be categorized as high-inference variables, which all the more necessitates a thorough training. Intercoder reliability (calculated by Cohen's kappa) should be reported; variables that cannot be coded reliably may have to be removed from the meta-analysis.

Analyses

The basic outline of analyses in cross-cultural meta-analyses does not differ from other meta-analyses; analyses start with preparation of the database (calculation of effect sizes, etc.), followed by descriptive analyses of the sample of studies, examination of the effect size distribution (including the average effect size and confidence interval), and the moderator analyses. Interested readers are referred to textbooks on meta-analyses for more detailed, technical information (Cooper & Hedges, 1994; Hunter & Schmidt, 1990). Some aspects of each of these analytical stages deserve further attention.

Preparation of the Data Set

Preparing a cross-cultural database for analyses involves calculating the effect sizes, applying weights, and adding country-level variables for moderator analyses. Effect sizes in culture-inclusive meta-analyses are calculated by dividing the mean score difference of the two countries in the comparison by the pooled standard deviation. Thus, a comparison between the United States and Japan would result in an effect size of the United States mean minus the Japanese mean divided by the square root of the average of the two variances (corrected for sample size).

The application of weights is similar to practices in regular meta-analyses as far as the coding of multiple samples or measures from one study is concerned. The only specific issue in culture-inclusive meta-analyses is the problem of dependency arising from studies providing data for more than two countries. As mentioned earlier, all possible comparisons of countries from studies comparing more than two countries should be coded in separate entries in the database. Coding more entries from a single study with (partly) overlapping data violates the independency assumptions by statistics used in meta-analysis, because data points are included more than once. This problem can be solved either by randomly selecting specific country comparisons (e.g., out of three countries only Countries 1 and 3 are coded) or by assigning weights to all entries in such a way that each cultural sample has a weight of 1 (e.g., all three possible comparisons are coded and assigned a weight of .50 each).

Culture-inclusive meta-analyses differ from other meta-analyses in the inclusion of country-level moderator variables that are taken from other databases. These variables are either indicators measured at the country level or psychological measures that are aggregated to the country level (congruent with Bond and van de Vijver's (Chapter 4, this volume) distinction between "hard" and "soft" dimensions). Country indicators such as demographic, ecological, economic, and political characteristics are available from annual reports or Web sites from organizations such as the United Nations, World Bank, and Freedom House. Aggregated psychological variables may include value dimensions (Hofstede, 1980, 2001), social axioms

(Leung et al., 2002; Leung & Bond, 2004), well-being scores (Diener, Diener, & Diener, 1995), and personality traits (McCrae, 2002). Bond and van de Vijver (Chapter 4, this volume) provide an extensive overview of potential explanatory country-level variables. Meta-analyses based on ethnic groups only may also include culture-level moderators. Although less extensive than for country indicators, there are databases for different demographic and socioeconomic characteristics of ethnic groups in the United States, such as those by the U.S. Census Bureau for general demographic and economic data (http://www.census.gov) and the National Center for Health Statistics (http://www.cdc.gov/nchs). Theory could decide which variables to use for explaining cross-cultural differences. Alternatively, a large number of country-level variables could be used to establish a nomological network that helps to delineate the meaning of country-level differences.

As indicated earlier, these country-level indicators are used in a different way in culture-inclusive and culture-moderated meta-analyses. Because of the nature of effect sizes in culture-inclusive meta-analyses, that is, based on the difference between two countries on a single dependent variable, difference scores of country-level moderators are needed for the moderator analyses, corresponding to the two countries in the effect sizes. Thus, a comparison of the United States and Japan should either have an effect size of the United States minus Japan and a matched country-level variable score of the United States minus Japan (e.g., individualism scores for both countries), or a Japan minus the United States effect size with a similar individualism difference score. Culture-moderated meta-analyses do not require difference scores of country-level moderators; because each effect size relates to one country only, plain country scores can be used.

Descriptive Analyses and Effect Size Distribution

Initial analyses should be aimed at describing the sample of studies, the samples of respondents, the countries involved, and the instruments used. Further, the effect size should be averaged across studies or comparisons, to enable statements about the size and distribution of the effect and its confidence interval. Averaging effect sizes involves correcting for sampling error (and possibly some other artifacts, see Hunter & Schmidt, 1990). In addition, it is customary to report the 95% confidence interval and a file drawer statistic (fail safe N) to indicate the reliability of the mean effect size, as well as a homogeneity index (Q; χ^2 – distribution), which indicates whether all studies come from the same population. A significant Q means heterogeneity and serves as a prerequisite for searching for moderators.

Basically, these analyses are identical for regular and cross-cultural meta-analyses. The only exception is the use of absolute effect sizes in random-order culture-inclusive meta-analyses; when the order of the countries in the effect sizes is arbitrary, it makes no sense simply to report mean effect sizes (which would probably be around zero). Therefore, these descriptive analyses, including distribution of the effect size, should be based on absolute effect sizes.

Moderator Analyses

Moderator analyses are used to explain methodological as well substantive variance. The relevance of moderators can be checked by various types of analyses: Continuous moderators entail correlation or regression analyses similar to regular analyses, whereas categorical moderators such as gender can be evaluated using categorical models based on the partitioning of Q. Essentially, this entails calculating the between-group homogeneity (Q_B) as an indicator of how much variability can be explained by a moderator as opposed to the within-group homogeneity (Q_W) as a measure of how much variability the moderator fails to explain.

In random-order culture-inclusive meta-analyses, one should be cautious about whether to use regular or absolute differences in effect sizes. For some moderator analyses, the specific direction of the effect size is not relevant; in those analyses, one can use the absolute effect size, which merely indicates the size of the cultural difference. Thus, most analyses on internal moderators require absolute effect sizes. However, country-level moderator analyses can be performed with regular effect sizes, because the country-level moderators are country-specific and use the same order as the effect sizes.

ILLUSTRATION OF A RANDOM-ORDER CULTURE-INCLUSIVE META-ANALYSIS

As an illustration of the "peeling-the-onion" method in cross-cultural meta-analyses, I reanalyzed data sets from two random-order culture-inclusive meta-analyses on personality and social behavior (van Hemert, van de Vijver, & Poortinga, 2006). Results are discussed in terms of the distinction between different types of variance rather than in substantive (i.e., psychological) terms.

In both meta-analyses, the research question was formulated as follows: "How large are cross-cultural differences in personality / social behavior, and how can they be explained?" The databases were restricted to 50 studies

Table 12.3. *Descriptive statistics for the two data sets of cross-national studies*

	Personality	Social behavior
N comparisons	361	317
N studies	50	50
Median publication year	1993	1989
% of students	60.2	48.0
Most researched countries	US (25.1%)	US (31.1%)
	UK (8.1%)	Japan (10.6%)
	India (6.1%)	UK (7.0%)
Choice of countries based on		
• Individualism versus collectivism	13.0%	17.5%
• Western versus non-Western	10.7%	11.2%
Explanation of cross-cultural findings		
• Differences due to sociocultural factors	64.0%	70.8%
• Similarities due to sociocultural factors	2.2%	23.0%
Mean absolute Hedges' *d* (*SD*)	.45 (.49)	.38 (.35)

Note: All descriptive statistics are at comparison level.

each, which required a selection of all available studies. Coding schemes resembled the coding scheme as described in Table 12.2 (see the Coding and Calculation of Effect Size section).

To reduce statistical dependency in the data when more than one effect size was reported in a study (Hunter & Schmidt, 1990), weights were assigned to all comparisons in such a way that no data point was included more than once. The weights were applied in all analyses.

Table 12.3 shows descriptive statistics for the two data sets. Less than half of all included social psychological studies used student samples. A disproportionate percentage of cross-cultural studies included the United States, and closer scrutiny of the data revealed that comparisons of Western English-speaking countries, and Eastern countries (such as Japan and China) were fairly common across both data sets. Effect sizes were small to moderate according to J. Cohen's (1992) rules of thumb (effect sizes are small when around .20, moderate when around .50, and large when around .80). Personality effect sizes were clearly larger than social behavior effects. However, the goal of these meta-analyses was to explain cross-cultural variance rather than compare effect sizes. Because the chi-square tests for homogeneity (Q) indicated that both data sets were heterogeneous in terms of their effect sizes, moderator analyses were conducted.

To assess the question of the relative influence of method-related factors (statistical artifacts and method-related variables) and substantive factors (related to culture), a three-step analysis was performed on all data. First, the impact of the correction for sample fluctuations was examined. This correction was based on the question of what the expected effect size would be if all reported effect sizes would merely reflect sampling fluctuations. The expected value of the absolute Hedges' *d*, $E(|d|)$, can be defined as the absolute standardized difference between two samples from normal distributions. It is expressed by $E(|d|) = 2 / \sqrt{(\pi n)}$, in which π is 3.14 and n is the average sample size of the two groups. All effect sizes in the data sets were corrected for sampling fluctuation by subtracting $E(|d|)$ from the absolute observed Hedges' *d*. Second, in a regression analysis, method-related variables that proved to be important in preceding analyses were entered as a block with effect size (corrected for sample fluctuations) as the dependent variable. Third, in subsequent stepwise regression analyses, country-level variables were entered as separate blocks with the unstandardized residuals of the preceding analysis as the dependent variable. In this way, I was able to estimate the relative contribution of method-related factors (statistical artifacts and method-related variables) and substantive factors (country-level variables).

The order in which country-level variables were entered into the analyses was based on a model that links nation scores (i.e., ecological, economic, community-related, political, and socialization variables) to individual scores (psychological outcomes as well as practices) as proposed by Smith, Bond, and Kagitcibasi (2006, chap. 4) as well as the ecocultural framework (Berry, 1976; Berry, Poortinga, Segall, & Dasen, 2002). The ecocultural framework holds that individual variables are influenced by three kinds of antecedents: ecological indices, sociopolitical indices, and aggregated psychological characteristics, the last of which involve psychological variables that are aggregated at the country level, such as the average level of extraversion in a country. Additional antecedents were proposed by Ronen and Shenkar (1985); they combined the results of eight cluster studies on employees' attitudes and behavior and found four important dimensions along which countries could be grouped: geography, language, religion, and technological development. Georgas, van de Vijver, and Berry (2004) found two factors that predicted cross-national differences in values and subjective well-being: affluence and religious denomination. On the basis of these models and previous findings, five sets of country-level indicators were selected: ecological context, sociopolitical context, religion, values, and personality.

Table 12.4 shows percentages of cross-cultural variance in personality and social behavior attributable to statistical artifacts (sampling), method-related factors, and substantive factors (country-level indicators). The largest proportion of cultural variance in the personality data set could be explained by method-related factors such as the complexity and cultural loading of the task, theoretical approach, and the type of sample. Country-level variables explained a relatively small part of the overall variance. In contrast, aggregated personality variables explained a lot of variance in the social behavior data set, beyond a considerable impact of sociopolitical context and values.

These analyses show the usefulness of cross-cultural meta-analysis for accumulating knowledge of cultural influences on psychological functioning. Despite the focus of researchers in the field of social psychology on explaining cross-cultural differences in terms of values – in particular, individualism versus collectivism – the previous moderator analyses show that the validity of this paradigm is restricted, at least for social behavior, and foregoes more basic and comprehensive explanations, specifically sociopolitical context. Thus, meta-analysis can address questions not originally considered by the included studies by examining the impact of study characteristics on the effect size. As such, it can advance the cross-cultural field, go beyond domain peculiarities and biases, and test explanations for cross-cultural differences in psychological functioning.

CONCLUSION

Berry et al. (2002) distinguished three goals of cross-cultural research: to transport and test hypotheses and findings to other cultural settings, to explore other cultures to discover cultural and psychological variations, and to assemble and integrate findings into a more universal psychology. An increasing number of studies address the first two goals. Cross-cultural meta-analysis can accommodate the third goal, by combining psychological findings from different cultures and linking them to ecological and socio-cultural variables. As such, this technique can help to advance knowledge of patterns in cross-cultural differences and similarities and to explain these patterns.

Two approaches to addressing culture in meta-analysis, that is, culture-moderated and culture-inclusive meta-analysis, were discussed in terms of general orientation, the role of culture, and analyses. The choice of one or the other approach depends on the research question that the meta-analyst

Table 12.4. *Overview of percentages of explained variance in effect size accounted for by three categories of factors*

		Percentage of variance attributable to:								
				Country-level indicators						
Data set	*N*	Statistical artifacts	Method-related factors	Ecological context	Sociopolitical context	Religion	Values	Personality	Total	Unexplained
Personality	361	5.3	25.8	0.1	3.2	0.3	5.1	0.0	8.7	60.2
Social behavior	317	0.0	12.6	2.7	22.8	0.0	11.9	36.6	74.0	13.4

Note: Explained variance was calculated by hierarchical regression. In each column, the residuals of the previous regression were used as the dependent variable. Consequently, percentages in all columns except the *Statistical Artifacts* column were corrected by the percentage of variance explained by sample fluctuations. *Method-related factors* included complexity of task (3-point Likert scale), cultural loading of task (3-point Likert scale), bias control (yes vs. no), type of sample (students vs. adults), independent variable used to sample the countries (country, race, individualism vs. collectivism, Western vs. non-Western, education, socialization, and language; yes vs. no), nature of task (psychophysiological, discrimination and matching, decision, experimental task, and self-report), instrument origin (Western task vs. task especially made for study or assembly of tasks), and theoretical approach (similarities explained by genetic inheritance vs. differences explained by sociocultural factors). *Ecological context* variables included highest average temperature (Georgas & Berry, 1995) and the percentage of workers in service professions (Georgas & Berry, 1995). *Sociopolitical context* variables included gross national product per capita (Georgas & Berry, 1995), the level of democracy 1990 (Inglehart, 1997), the Gini index (World Bank, 1999), and the Human Rights Index (Humana, 1986). The indicator for *Religion* was the percentage of Christians (Georgas & Berry, 1995). Included *Values* were Individualism, Uncertainty Avoidance, Power Distance, Masculinity, and Long-Term Orientation (Hofstede, 1980, 2001), and Religiosity (based on six items taken from Inglehart's (1993) World Values Survey database; see van Hemert, van de Vijver, & Poortinga, 2002). *Personality* variables included subjective well-being (Diener, Diener, & Diener, 1995) and the Revised NEO Personality Inventory NEO-PI-R extraversion scale (McCrae, 2002). The percentage of *Unexplained Variance* was calculated by subtracting from 100 the sum of percentages in the *Statistical artifacts*, *Method-related factors*, and *Country-level indicators* columns.

wants to address. Both types of meta-analysis, as well as a combination of the two, can contribute to attaining a more universal psychology.

To gain knowledge about the size and patterning of cross-cultural differences, it is crucial to distinguish different sources of variance. Variance should be explained in terms of statistical artifacts, as well as methodological factors and substantive factors unrelated to culture, before turning to the explanation of variance in terms of cultural factors. The analysis of two cross-cultural data sets revealed that domains in psychology might differ with respect to the appropriateness of various explanatory factors. Meta-analysis provides a resourceful method to explore all layers of the onion called culture.

REFERENCES

Berry, J. W. (1976). *Human ecology and cognitive style: Comparative studies in cultural and psychological adaptation.* New York: Sage/Halsted.

Berry, J. W., Poortinga, Y. H., Segall, M. H., & Dasen, P. R. (2002). *Cross-cultural psychology: Research and applications* (2nd ed.). New York: Cambridge University Press.

Bolger, D. J., Perfetti, C. A., & Schneider, W. (2005). Cross-cultural effect on the brain revisited: Universal structures plus writing system variation. *Human Brain Mapping, 25,* 92–104.

Bond, M. H, & Van De Vijver, F. J. R.. (2007). Making scientific sense of cultural differences in psychological outcomes: Unpackaging the *magnum mysteriosum.* In D. Matsumoto & F. J. R. Van de Vijver (Eds.), *Cross-cultural research methods in psychology.* New York: Cambridge University Press.

Bond, R., & Smith, P. B. (1996). Culture and conformity: A meta-analysis of studies using Asch's (1952b, 1956) line judgment task. *Psychological Bulletin, 119,* 111–137.

Born, M. Ph., Bleichrodt, N., & Van Der Flier, H. (1987). Cross-cultural comparison of sex-related differences on intelligence tests: A meta-analysis. *Journal of Cross-Cultural Psychology, 18,* 283–314.

Brislin, R. W. (1986). The wording and translation of research instruments. In W. J. Lonner & J. W. Berry (Eds.), *Field methods in cross-cultural research* (pp. 137–164). Thousand Oaks, CA: Sage.

Brouwers, S. A., Van Hemert, D. A., Breugelmans, S. M., & Van de Vijver, F. J. R. (2004). A historical analysis of empirical studies published in the *Journal of Cross-Cultural Psychology. Journal of Cross-Cultural Psychology, 35,* 251–262.

Cohen, C., Nisbett, R. E., Bowdle, B. F., & Schwarz, N. (1996). Insult, aggression, and the southern culture of honor: An "experimental ethnography." *Journal of Personality and Social Psychology, 70,* 945–960.

Cohen, J. (1992). A power primer. *Psychological Bulletin, 112,* 155–159.

Cooper, H., & Hedges, L. V. (Eds.). (1994). *The handbook of research synthesis.* New York: Russell Sage Foundation.

De Leeuw, E. D., & Hox, J. J. (2002). The use of meta-analysis in cross-national studies. In J. A. Harkness, F. J. R. van de Vijver, & P. P. Mohler (Eds.), *Cross-cultural survey methods* (pp. 327–344). New York: Wiley.

Diener, E., Diener, M., & Diener, C. (1995). Factors predicting subjective well-being of nations. *Journal of Personality and Social Psychology, 69*, 851–864.

Eagly, A. H., Karau, S., & Makhijani, M. (1995). Gender and the effectiveness of leaders: A meta-analysis. *Psychological Bulletin, 117*, 125–145.

Elfenbein, H. A., & Ambady, N. (2002). On the universality and cultural specificity of emotion recognition: A meta-analysis. *Psychological Bulletin, 128*, 203–235.

Elfenbein, H. A., & Ambady, N. (2003). Cultural similarity's consequences: A distance perspective on cross-cultural differences in emotion recognition. *Journal of Cross Cultural Psychology, 34*, 92–109.

Eysenck, H. J., & Eysenck, S. B. G. (1975). *Manual of the Eysenck Personality Questionnaire.* London: Hodder and Stoughton.

Faucheux, C. (1976). Cross-cultural research in experimental social psychology. *European Journal of Social Psychology, 6*, 269–322.

Ford, J. K., Kraiger, K., & Schechtman, S. L. (1986). Study of race effects in objective indices and subjective evaluations of performance: A meta-analysis of performance criteria. *Psychological Bulletin, 99*, 330–337.

Georgas, J., & Berry, J. W. (1995). An ecocultural taxonomy for cross-cultural psychology. *Cross-Cultural Research, 29*, 121–157.

Georgas, J., Van de Vijver, F. J. R., & Berry, J. W. (2004). The ecocultural framework, ecosocial indices, and psychological variables in cross-cultural research. *Journal of Cross-Cultural Psychology, 35*, 74–96.

Gray-Little, B., & Hafdahl, A. R. (2000). Factors influencing racial comparisons of self-esteem: A quantitative review. *Psychological Bulletin, 126*, 26–54.

Hall, J. A., Tickle-Degnen, L., Rosenthal, R., & Mosteller, F. (1994). Hypotheses and problems in research synthesis. In H. Cooper & L. V. Hedges (Eds.), *The handbook of research synthesis* (pp. 17–28). New York: Russell Sage Foundation.

Hedges, L. V., & Olkin, I. (1985). *Statistical methods for meta-analysis.* Orlando, FL: Academic Press.

Heine, S. J., & Hamamura, T. (2007). In search of East Asian self-enhancement. *Personality and Social Psychology Review, 11*, 4–27.

Helms-Lorenz, M., Van de Vijver, F. J. R., & Poortinga, Y. H. (2003). Cross-cultural differences in cognitive performance and Spearman's hypothesis: *g* or *c*? *Intelligence, 31*, 9–29.

Hofstede, G. (1980). *Culture's consequences.* Beverly Hills, CA: Sage.

Hofstede, G. (2001). *Culture's consequences. Comparing values, behaviors, institutions, and organizations across nations* (2nd ed.). Thousand Oaks, CA: Sage.

Hunter, J. E., & Schmidt, F. L. (1990). *Methods of meta-analysis: Correcting error and bias in research findings.* Newbury Park, CA: Sage.

Inglehart, R. (1993). *World values survey 1990–1991. WVS Program.* J.D. Systems, S.L. ASEP S.A.

Inglehart, R. (1997). *Modernization and postmodernization. Cultural, economic, and political change in 43 countries.* Princeton, NJ: Princeton University Press.

Johnson, B. T., & Eagly, A. H. (2000). Quantitative synthesis of social psychological research. In H. T. Reis & C. M. Judd (Eds.), *Handbook of research methods in social and personality psychology* (pp. 496–528). New York: Cambridge University Press.

Karau, S. J., & Williams, K. D. (1993). Social loafing: A meta-analytic review and theoretical integration. *Journal of Personality and Social Psychology, 65*, 681–706.

Khaleque, A., & Rohner, R. P. (2002). Reliability of measures assessing the pancultural association between perceived parental acceptance-rejection and psychological adjustment: A meta-analysis of cross-cultural and intracultural studies. *Journal of Cross-Cultural Psychology, 33*, 87–99.

LaFrance, M., Hecht, M. A., & Paluck, E. L. (2003). The contingent smile: A meta-analysis of sex differences in smiling. *Psychological Bulletin, 129*, 305–334.

Leung, K., & Bond, M. H. (2004). Social axioms: A model of social beliefs in multi-cultural perspective. In M. P. Zanna (Ed.), *Advances in experimental social psychology* (Vol. 36, pp. 119–197). San Diego, CA: Elsevier Academic Press.

Leung, K., Bond, M. H., Reimel de Carrasquel, S., Muñoz, C., Hernández, M., Murakami, F., et al. (2002). Social axioms: The search for universal dimensions of general beliefs about how the world functions. *Journal of Cross-Cultural Psychology, 33*, 286–302.

Lipsey, M. W. (1994). Identifying potentially interesting variables and analysis opportunities. In H. Cooper & L. V. Hedges (Eds.), *The handbook of research synthesis* (pp. 111–123). New York: Russell Sage Foundation.

Lipsey, M. W. (1997). What can you build with thousands of bricks? Musings on the cumulation of knowledge in program evaluation. *New Directions for Evaluation, 76*, 7–23.

Lipsey, M. W., & Wilson, D. B. (2001). *Applied social research methods series: Vol. 49. Practical meta-analysis.* Thousand Oaks, CA: Sage.

Lonner, W. J., & Adamopoulos, J. (1997). Culture as antecedent behavior. In J. W. Berry, Y. H. Poortinga, & J. Pandey (Eds.), *Handbook of cross-cultural psychology: Volume 1. Theory and method* (pp. 43–83). Boston: Allyn & Bacon.

McCrae, R. R. (2002). NEO-PI-R data from 36 cultures. In A. J. Marsella (Series Ed.), R. R. McCrae, & J. Allik (Eds.), *The Five-Factor Model of personality across cultures*, (pp. 105–125). New York: Kluwer Academic.

Mezulis, A. H., Abramson, L.Y., Hyde, J. S., & Hankin, B. L. (2004). Is there a universal positivity bias in attributions? A meta-analytic review of individual, developmental, and cultural differences in the self-serving attributional bias. *Psychological Bulletin, 130*, 711–747.

Oyserman, D., Coon, H. M., & Kemmelmeier, M. (2002). Rethinking individualism and collectivism: Evaluation of theoretical assumptions and meta-analyses. *Psychological Bulletin, 128*, 3–72.

Poortinga, Y. H. (1989). Equivalence of cross-cultural data: An overview of basic issues. *International Journal of Psychology, 24*, 737–756.

Poortinga, Y. H., Van de Vijver, F. J. R., Joe, R. C., & Van de Koppel, J. M. H. (1987). Peeling the onion called culture: A synopsis. In Ç. Kağitçibaši (Ed.), *Growth and progress in cross-cultural psychology* (pp. 22–34). Lisse, The Netherlands: Swets & Zeitlinger.

Ronen, S., & Shenkar, O. (1985). Clustering countries on attitudinal dimensions: A review and synthesis. *Academy of Management Review*, 10, 435–454.

Rosenthal, R. (1991). *Meta-analytic procedures for social research.* Newbury Park, CA: Sage.

Roth, P. L., Huffcutt, A. I., & Bobko, P. (2003). Ethnic group differences in measures of job performance: A new meta-analysis. *Journal of Applied Psychology, 88,* 694–706.

Saroglou, V., Delpierre, V., & Dernelle, R. (2004). Values and religiosity: A meta-analysis of studies using Schwartz's model. *Personality and Individual Differences, 37,* 721–734.

Sedikides, C., Gaertner, L., & Vevea, J. L. (2007). Inclusion of theory-relevant moderators yield the same conclusions as Sedikides, Gaertner, and Vevea (2005): A meta-analytical reply to Heine, Kitayama, and Hamamura (2007). *Asian Journal of Social Psychology, 10,* 59–67.

Smith, P. B., Bond, M. H., & Kagitcibasi, C. (2006). *Understanding social psychology across cultures: Living and working in a changing world.* Thousand Oaks, CA: Sage.

Twenge, J. M., & Campbell, W. K. (2002). Self-esteem and socioeconomic status: A meta-analytic review. *Personality and Social Psychology Review, 6,* 59–71.

Twenge, J. M., & Crocker, J. (2002). Race and self-esteem: Meta-analyses comparing Whites, Blacks, Hispanics, Asians, and American Indians and comment on Gray-Little and Hafdahl (2000). *Psychological Bulletin, 128,* 371–408.

Van de Vijver, F. J. R. (1997). Meta-analysis of cross-cultural comparisons of cognitive test performance. *Journal of Cross-Cultural Psychology, 28,* 678–709.

Van de Vijver, F. J. R., & Leung, K. (1997). *Methods and data analysis for cross-cultural research.* Newbury Park, CA: Sage.

Van de Vijver, F. J. R., & Leung, K. (2000). Methodological issues in psychological research on culture. *Journal of Cross-Cultural Psychology, 31,* 33–51.

Van de Vijver, F. J. R., & Leung, K. (2007). Equivalence and bias. In D. Matsumoto & F. J. R. van de Vijver (Eds.), *Cross-cultural research methods in psychology.* New York: Cambridge University Press.

Van Hemert, D. A. (2003). Cross-cultural meta-analyses. In W. J. Lonner, D. L. Dinnel, S. A. Hayes, & D. N. Sattler (Eds.), *Online readings in psychology and culture* (Unit 2, Chapter 13). Bellingham: Center for Cross-Cultural Research, Western Washington University, Washington USA. Retrieved from http://www.wwu.edu/~culture on May 20, 2010.

Van Hemert, D. A., Poortinga, Y. H., & Van de Vijver, F. J. R. (2007). Emotion and culture: A meta-analysis. *Cognition and Emotion, 21,* 913–943.

Van Hemert, D. A., Van de Vijver, F. J. R., & Poortinga, Y. H. (2002). The Beck Depression Inventory as a measure of subjective well-being: A cross-national study. *Journal of Happiness Studies, 3,* 257–286.

Van Hemert, D. A., Van de Vijver, F. J. R., & Poortinga, Y. H. (2006). *Evaluating frameworks of cross-cultural differences and similarities: A meta-analysis.* Unpublished manuscript. Tilburg, Netherlands: Tilburg University.

Watkins, D. (2001). Correlates of approaches to learning: A cross-cultural meta-analysis. In R. Sternberg & L. Zhang (Eds.), *Perspectives on thinking, learning and cognitive styles* (pp. 165–195). Mahwah, NJ: Erlbaum.

Wolf, F. M. (1986). *Meta-analysis: Quantitative methods for research synthesis.* Beverly Hills, CA: Sage.

World Bank. (1999). *World development report 1998/1999.* New York: Oxford University Press.

Wortman, P. M. (1994). Judging research quality. In H. Cooper & L. V. Hedges (Eds.), *The handbook of research synthesis* (pp. 98–109). New York: Russell Sage Foundation.

Ziv, A., & Shauber, H. (1969). Contribution to a cross-cultural study of manifest anxiety in children. *Human Development, 12*, 178–191.

NAME INDEX

SUBJECT INDEX

Made in the USA
Lexington, KY
16 October 2014